DATE DUE

DEMCO 38-296

A History of the British Labour Party

British Studies Series

General Editor JEREMY BLACK

Published

John Charmley: *A History of Conservative Politics, 1900–1996*
David Childs: *Britain since 1939*
Brian Hill: *The Early Parties and Politics in Britain, 1688–1832*
T. A. Jenkins: *The Liberal Ascendancy, 1830–1886*
David Loades: *Power in Tudor England*
Andrew Thorpe: *A History of the British Labour Party*

Forthcoming

D. G. Boyce: *Britain and Decolonisation*
Glenn Burgess: *British Political Thought from Reformation to Revolution*
J. B. Christoph: *The Twentieth-Century British State*
Gary De Krey: *Restoration and Revolution in Britain*
David Eastwood: *Government and Community in the English Provinces, 1700–1870*
W. H. Fraser: *The Rise and Fall of British Trade Unionism*
Jeremy Gregory: *The Long Reformation: Religion and Society in England c. 1530–1870*
Jon Lawrence: *Britain and the First World War*
F. J. Levy: *Politics and Culture in Tudor England*
Diarmaid MacCulloch: *The Reformation in Britain, 1480–1680*
Allan Macinnes: *The British Revolution*
G. I. T. Machin: *The Rise of British Democracy*
Thomas Mayer: *Britain, 1450–1603*
Michael Mendle: *The English Civil War and Political Thought*
Alexander Murdoch: *British History, 1660–1832*
Murray G. H. Pittock: *Inventing and Resisting Britain: Cultural Identities in Britain and Ireland, 1685–1789*
W. Rubinstein: *History of Britain in the Twentieth Century*
Howard Temperley: *Britain and America*

A History of the British Labour Party

Andrew Thorpe

St. Martin's Press
New York

This book is printed on paper suitable for recycling and
made from fully managed and sustained forest sources.

Printed in Hong Kong

ISBN 0–312–16504–8

Library of Congress Cataloging-in-Publication Data
Thorpe, Andrew, 1962–
A history of the British Labour Party / Andrew Thorpe.
   p.   cm.
Includes bibliographical references (p.   ) and index.
ISBN 0–312–16504–8 (cloth)
1. Labour Party (Great Britain)—History.   I. Title.
JN1129.L32T47   1997
324.24107'09'04—dc20   96–31879
                                                     CIP

To my sisters
Catherine Laughton and Sally Spafford

Contents

Acknowledgements

Labour history is one of the most vibrant areas of historical study in Britain today, and my first debt must be to the hundreds of scholars who have done so much to enliven and enlighten the subject of this book. I would also like to thank my editors at Macmillan, Vanessa Graham and Simon Winder, as well as the series editor, Jeremy Black, for their enthusiasm for this project and their patience in seeing it through. To my colleagues at Exeter I owe a huge debt, but I would like to thank in particular Tim Rees, Jeremy Smith, Neil Riddell and Garry Tregidga, who were prepared to discuss many of the issues in the book at such length. In this context I must also mention Bruce Coleman, whose very different views have been a constant source of stimulus. My students, past and present, have also helped me to refine many of my ideas, and to them I owe a huge debt which cannot be repaid. Parts of this book were completed in less than ideal circumstances, and I would particularly like to thank, for their support over that time, Giles Bowen, Mandy Carter, Roger Fisk, Andrew Jay and Sara Wyn Roberts. The book is dedicated, with love and respect, to my sisters, Catherine Laughton and Sally Spafford.

Abbreviations

ASE	Amalgamated Society of Engineers
ASRS	Amalgamated Society of Railway Servants
AUEW	Amalgamated Union of Engineering Workers
BL	British Leyland
BSP	British Socialist Party
CBI	Confederation of British Industries
CLP	Constituency Labour Party
CLPD	Campaign for Labour Party Democracy
CPGB	Communist Party of Great Britain
DEA	Department of Economic Affairs
EAC	Economic Advisory Council
EC	European Community
EEC	European Economic Community
EU	European Union
GATT	General Agreement on Tariffs and Trade
GFTU	General Federation of Trade Unions
ILP	Independent Labour Party
IMF	International Monetary Fund
LPYS	Labour Party Young Socialists
LRC	Labour Representation Committee
MFGB	Miners' Federation of Great Britain
Mintech	Ministry of Technology
NATO	North Atlantic Treaty Organisation
NCL	National Council of Labour
NEB	National Enterprise Board
NEC	National Executive Committee
NHS	National Health Service
NJC	National Joint Council
NLWM	National Left Wing Movement
NTWF	National Transport Workers' Federation
NUM	National Union of Mineworkers
NUR	National Union of Railwaymen
PLP	Parliamentary Labour Party
PSBR	Public Sector Borrowing Requirement
R & D	Research and Development

SDF	Social Democratic Federation
SDP	Social Democratic Party
SLP	Socialist Labour Party
SNP	Scottish National Party
SSIP	Society for Socialist Information and Propaganda
TGWU	Transport and General Workers' Union
TUC	Trades Union Congress
UDC	Union of Democratic Control
WEC	War Emergency Workers' National Committee

Introduction

The British Labour party has not exactly been neglected by historians. However, while history is about the past, it is essentially a product of the time in which it is written. Accordingly, interpretations of the party's history have varied dramatically over the years, not just in the light of the evidence available and the personal and professional predilections of the historian involved, but also with reference to the state of the Labour party itself at the time in which the historian was writing. This book is no exception, and cannot claim, in that (or indeed any other) sense, to be any 'better' than what has gone before. What it attempts to do, however, is synthesize the current historiography, and to provide a view from the perspective of the mid-1990s on the history of the party as it approaches its centenary in the year 2000.

The Labour Representation committee was formed in 1900, and elected two MPs at that year's general election. There had been attempts to form independent labour organizations before: the difference was that this one survived. In 1906 it won 29 seats at the general election, and immediately renamed itself the Labour party. Although the party did develop somewhat in the years up to 1914, it was still very much the third party in British politics, indeed, only the fourth largest party in parliament, the Irish Nationalists having roughly twice as many seats. From 1915 it participated, as a junior partner, in wartime Coalition governments, and in 1918 it adopted a new constitution which made it more independent of the Liberals and, having withdrawn from the Coalition, won 57 seats at that year's general election. In 1922 it became the main Opposition party, with 142 seats, and Ramsay MacDonald was elected the party's first 'leader'. Under MacDonald, progress was rapid during the 1920s, with Labour forming its first minority government (although not the largest party) for nine months in 1924 and, in 1929, winning 287 seats to form its second administration. However, that government fell apart in 1931, and at that year's general election the party was reduced to just 46 MPs as the National government under

1

MacDonald won a massive victory. During the 1930s there was limited recovery, but a further election was lost in 1935 and, under its leader Clement Attlee, the party would almost certainly have been defeated at the next election as well had not the Second World War intervened. In 1940, the National government fell and was replaced by a Coalition under Winston Churchill, in which Labour had a more than fair share of positions. At the 1945 election Labour, with 393 seats, won an overall majority for the first time, and the Attlee governments proceeded to implement significant reforms. In 1951, though, Labour was defeated and, after further defeats in 1955 and 1959, was eventually out of office for thirteen years. It returned to power under Wilson in 1964, but despite a landslide re-election in 1966 it was perceived by many, by the end of its term, to have failed, and was defeated in 1970. Rather fortuitously, perhaps, Labour returned as a minority government in February 1974, and that October was re-elected with a tiny overall majority. Once again, by the end of its term in office this government, first under Wilson and then under Callaghan, was incapable of securing re-election. The victory of the Conservatives under Margaret Thatcher in 1979 ushered in, as it transpired, a long period of opposition for Labour, during which much of what it had previously achieved in office was undone and many vital bastions of the party came under fierce attack. Even by the mid-1990s, Labour was still in opposition, despite the radical changes carried through by leaders Kinnock (1983–92), Smith (1992–4) and Blair.

As the party's centenary drew close, then, it could point to only five periods in government totalling just under twenty years. Yet, paradoxically, there had been times when it seemed that Labour would carry all before it. Herbert Morrison claimed in the aftermath of the 1929 victory that Labour was 'the miracle of politics' and Labourites looked forward to rolling back remaining 'bastions of reaction', constituencies which had not yet realized that Labour was the party of the future. In April 1946, Sir Hartley Shawcross, a Labour minister, claimed that 'we are the masters at the moment – and not only for the moment, but for a very long time to come'. And Wilson claimed, more than once, that Labour had become 'a natural party of government'.[1]

These vicissitudes, personal political opinions and the fads of academic fashion have led different historians to very different conclusions about the Labour party and its history. The tone of

Labour historiography in the aftermath of Labour's landslide victory in 1945, for example, was triumphalist. Written, overwhelmingly, by official and semi-official party figures, this work was not without its merits; indeed, G. D. H. Cole's *History of the Labour Party from 1914* (1948) repays study even today. Yet the assumptions were all about a 'forward march' of Labour: from adversity and oppression, the party had evolved from a small start into the body which might govern Britain for a generation or more. According to this view, the rise of Labour had been inevitable, and would have come about earlier had the party not been tricked out of office in 1931 and bamboozled by devious, scheming opponents during the 1930s. This was truly a whiggish interpretation of history, if by that we mean the idea of history leading to the triumph of good over evil, or rationality over superstition.

It was hard to remain entirely triumphalist, though, in the 1950s, as Labour found itself confined to a long period in opposition. And, as Labour's leadership promised less and less in the way of radical social and economic change, so the history of the party began to be interpreted in a negative light. The classic Marxist critique of the party's history came from Ralph Miliband, whose trenchant *Parliamentary Socialism*, first published in 1961, condemned Labour for being more concerned about 'parliamentarism' than about socialism.[2] Once the Wilson governments had passed through their honeymoon period, this type of condemnation became widespread, with a series of works attacking the party and its record, and pointing to its 'repeated retreats from its socialist promise in the twentieth century'.[3] Such critiques were carried on alongside a vigorous academic debate as to whether the rise of the Labour party had been inevitable, or whether in fact the Liberals could have evolved into a (by implication much more successful) progressive party had it not been for the accident of the First World War. Whiggish triumphalism was off the agenda.

However, developments in British politics since 1979 have tended to change matters. It is no longer fashionable to attack Labour from a left standpoint. As the Thatcher government took hold, and challenged many of the institutions and ideas people of a leftish persuasion held dear, there was an increasing tendency to believe that *any* Labour administration must be better than this particular Conservative one. When this was allied to the opening of some archives and the publication of masses of diary and memoir material, there was a tendency to rehabilitate the 1964–70 government in particular. (It must also be remembered that most historians work in institutions of higher education, one area viciously attacked in the 1980s but which had fared quite well under Wilson.) In addition, wider developments in the world also tended to suggest that socialism was more problematic and less easily achieved than left critics of 'Labourism' had tended to imply.

Meanwhile, new directions in labour history also tended to offer a more nuanced picture. Local studies of the development of the Labour movement, and a new emphasis on the social and cultural history of the working class, helped to suggest that, far from betraying a solid and at times militant following, Labour's leaders had in fact done well to go as far towards socialism as they had, given the flawed (in a socialist sense) material with which they had had to work. In such studies 'the working class' became 'the working classes', deeply divided within themselves and fundamentally uninterested in most aspects of the socialist project. This revisionist view was once characterized to me by one sceptical historian as 'blaming the working class for the failings of the Labour leadership': while this is, perhaps, a little unfair, it does convey some of the basics of the approach.

What follows is an attempt to synthesize these approaches in a single-volume history of the party from its foundation in 1900 to its general election defeat of 1992. It can, by its nature, be no more than an introduction to the party's history. As such, it will have limited appeal to specialists in the field, but hopefully those relatively new to the subject will try to fill out its inadequacies by reference to the massive and rich literature that has been, and continues to be, produced.

1
Creation and Early Years, 1900–14

In 1899 the annual Trades Union Congress debated a resolution, proposed by the Amalgamated Society of Railway Servants (ASRS), calling on the parliamentary committee of the TUC to organize a joint conference with socialist and co-operative bodies to discuss Labour representation. The motion was passed by the narrow margin of 546 000 votes to 434 000. The conference met in London on 27 February 1900, and agreed to establish 'a distinct Labour group in Parliament, who shall have their own whips, and agree upon their policy'; to support it financially through affiliation fees; and to elect Ramsay MacDonald, a leading member of the Independent Labour party (ILP), as the secretary of the new organization, which was to be known as the Labour Representation Committee (LRC).[1] After winning 29 seats at the 1906 general election, it was renamed the Labour party. But by 1914 its successes had not been all that striking, and it faced a somewhat uncertain future.

The central cause of the formation of the LRC was not a massive upsurge in socialist sentiment among trade unionists, but fears about the unions' legal position. British trade unions had not, traditionally, wanted massive social change. True, towards the end of the nineteenth century some, such as the ASRS, had become more interested in aspects of state regulation and collectivism. But on the whole they wanted to be left alone to negotiate with employers on equal terms, the way to achieve 'a fair day's work for a fair day's pay' being through free collective bargaining with employers.

But there was a history of the state placing obstructions in the way of such free collective bargaining, as many trade unionists were only too well aware. Trade unionism had not enjoyed an easy legal existence in the nineteenth century. The Combination Acts of 1799 and 1800, however ineffectual in practice before their repeal in the 1820s, had entered popular memory as repressive legislation aiming to destroy trade unionism. Even after their repeal, the position of unions remained legally dubious. Thus the six Dorset labourers, the so-called Tolpuddle Martyrs, could be convicted of administering illegal oaths and transported in 1834. As economic conditions eased and transport and postage services improved around mid-century, it became easier to organize national unions, and their legal position appeared to be secure, with even a degree of picketing being legalized in 1859.

In reality, trade union law remained somewhat obscure: even if no longer considered criminal, the unions often found it difficult to obtain legal protection against, say, the embezzlement of funds. The formation of the Trades Union Congress in 1868 was, in many ways, a defensive measure, taken in anticipation of renewed assaults. Somewhat haltingly, though, the 1870s saw some improvements: in 1871 the Liberal government's Trade Union Act gave legal protection to union funds, while in 1875 and 1876 a Conservative government exempted trade disputes from the laws of conspiracy, made breach of contract a matter for civil rather than criminal action, and legalized peaceful picketing. This was, it seemed, a very satisfactory outcome. Unions could now go about their business unimpeded by legislation or outside interference. With many working-class men possessing the franchise after the 1867 Reform Act, the prospect of a further extension in the not too distant future, and two working-class trade unionists, Alexander Macdonald and Thomas Burt, elected to parliament in 1874, it seemed that the position of trade unionism was secure.

At this stage trade unionism was far from being all-pervasive. Even in 1874, a peak year, only about 1 200 000 members were represented at the TUC: by the end of the decade even that figure had halved, as economic recession cut into the membership of all unions and effectively destroyed many of the newer organizations which had sprung up to cater for less skilled workers in the early 1870s.[2] Even the newer unions which survived struggled, while the ASRS, formed in 1871, had the additional handicap that the railway companies refused to recognize it. However, the settlement of the legal position made up for a great deal; and expansion began again in the second half of the 1880s as trade began to pick up. Meanwhile, the 1884 Reform Act enfranchised new groups of working-class men in non-borough areas (hence large numbers of coal miners, among others, got the vote for the first time). From then until 1918, around 60 per cent of men had the right to vote at any one time.[3]

It was, paradoxically, the 'new unionism' of the later 1880s and the indirect results of the Reform Act which led to a new challenge to the unions. Historians have long debated what was new about the 'new unionism' and, on the whole, have argued that it was not a great deal. However, the scale of the expansion, and the spectacular victory of the London dockers in their strike of 1889, aroused many fears. The employers were determined not to be caught out again, and from 1890 onwards there was a concerted effort by bodies like the Shipping Federation to weaken the unions' position. The formation of the Engineering Employers' Federation, aiming to counter, not a 'new' union but the most respectable of the older ones, the Amalgamated Society of Engineers, suggested new threats ahead. At the same time, the Conservative party, under the leadership of Lord Salisbury, was seeking to end years of Liberal ascendancy by appealing to the middle and lower-middle classes, and one way of doing this was to play up the threat of a militant working class and 'socialism': many of the leaders, though few of the followers, of the 'new unions' were committed to this creed. Trade unionism, therefore, provided an admirable target. Lord Halsbury, Lord Chancellor in all the Conservative governments between 1885 and 1905, was an arch-reactionary who appointed anti-union judges with alacrity. During the 1890s, trade union law was increasingly made, not by parliament, but by the judges, in a series of high-profile and controversial rulings. *Inter alia*, these called into doubt unions' exemption from claims for damages arising out of industrial action, and the right to peaceful picketing.

These factors, then, made the legal position of trade unions look much more dubious than it had for a long time. Increasingly, they began to look at better methods of mutual support, a fact demonstrated when a minority of unions formed the General Federation of Trade Unions (GFTU) in 1899 as a means of pooling some financial resources. It is in this context, of a renewed and bitter threat to the legal position of trade unions to go about their business freely and without hindrance, that the reasons for the formation of the LRC in 1900 must be sought.

In previous periods there would have been a tendency to rely on the Liberal party for this kind of political support. In fact, most working-class voters continued to support the Liberal party up to the First World War. Yet, at the same time, there were doubts about its ability and/or willingness to stand up for trade union interests. The long Liberal ascendancy had now passed; at the 1895 general election the party was heavily defeated, and it looked unlikely to do well at the next election, either. In addition, the Liberals had become, in their programmes, more 'faddist': partly to avoid identification with 'class politics' they attempted to emphasize other questions, but this was bound to leave at least some trade unionists dissatisfied, especially at a time of increasing threats to the union movement.[4] This combination of unelectability and inattention was merely exacerbated by the fact that local Liberal associations, partly for social and partly for financial reasons, were very reluctant to adopt 'Labour' candidates, the only exceptions being in areas which were so dominated by a single industry that it would have been perverse to put up anyone else; overwhelmingly, these were mining districts. It would be ludicrous to say that the working class was turning its back on the Liberals by 1900, but a critical mass of trade unionists was more prepared than previously to turn away from, or at least use new means to increase the pressure on, the party if it meant a more secure future for trade unionism.

Other factors are more problematic. There has been much debate on how far the process of industrial change radicalized the working class, or forced it into new degrees of class consciousness which then made adherence to an independent working-class party inevitable. In many ways the assumptions behind this statement are shot through with errors. It is true that local examples of drastic change during the 1890s can be found: the Leicester footwear industry is one good example.[5] But, in general, there was no sudden creation of a factory-based proletariat.[6] Most workers 'did not join trade unions and most remained remarkably little affected either by structural changes in the economy, by new legislation, by decreasing regionalisation, by closer supervision or by the introduction of more advanced mechanisation'.[7] Even in the industries at the cutting edge of mechanization, progress was usually slow; for example, in engineering, where the employers won a lengthy lockout in 1897–8, and where there was perhaps greater change than anywhere else, the period up to the First World War did not see a radical transformation.[8] On the other hand, we are not trying to explain a massive breakthrough for working-class politics, just the formation of the LRC as it existed, feeble and with an uncertain future, in 1900. In that sense, it can be suggested that, while there was not change on such a scale as to *revolutionize* class and production relations, there was *enough* fear of change, and *enough* pressure at certain limited points of the production process, to convince some trade unionists that worse might follow, and that it might thus be sensible to demonstrate that labour had some political, as well as industrial, muscle. While not as important as the desire to protect the legal position of trade unions, therefore, this was a contributory factor to the creation of the LRC.

So far there has been no discussion of socialists. This has not been an accident. The socialist groups which existed in Britain in the 1880s and 1890s were not mere sects, but they were small and sometimes struggling. Their involvement in the formation of the LRC was not decisive, although it helped. It must also be remembered that some socialists had no enthusiasm for the new organization, and stayed outside or rapidly left it. Still, it is worth discussing the various socialist groups and socialism briefly, since they were, in time, to play an important role (although not always the role their supporters intended) in the new organization.

Britain had been one of the main centres of early socialism, but by mid-century little of this remained. It was not until the 1880s that socialism began to revive. The Democratic Federation, a radical group, came increasingly under the influence of socialists like the upper-middle class Henry Myers Hyndman, and was transformed into a Marxist group in 1884. The Social Democratic Federation (SDF) was in many ways a curious body. Hyndman's arrogance and autocratic tendencies made it difficult for many people to work with him. At the same time, his views were as much derived from passionate patriotism and imperialism as from Marxism: he saw socialist transformation as the best way of preserving Britain's world pre-eminence at a time when it was being challenged by the United States and Germany in particular. However, Hyndman was not the SDF: the party claimed a membership which peaked at 10 536 in 1895 (although dues-paying membership was much lower). At grassroots level, members of the SDF played a significant part in putting socialism on the agenda in many parts of the country, especially where it was strongest, in London and Lancashire. A number of younger trade union leaders, such as Tom Mann, Will Thorne and Ben Tillett, were members. And, despite the SDF's reputation for sectarianism,

many SDF members did co-operate with members of other socialist groups in campaigns in the 1880s and 1890s: ultimately it
affiliated to the LRC in 1900, albeit briefly.

The Socialist League was formed in 1884 as a breakaway from
the SDF. It was never more than a few hundred strong, and collapsed in the later 1880s. But it did include the artist and poet
William Morris, who wrote a series of utopian works describing
what a socialist society could be like. These showed a spiritual
side of socialism which was not really to be found with the SDF
or the Fabians. Morris offered a vision of a free and equal society, a return to a pre-industrial, pre-urban age. Such idealized
medievalism was hopelessly impractical, and its rejection of
modernity and conventional morality aroused hostility, among
working-class leaders as much as anyone, and gave socialists an
image they would long try to slough off. Yet at the same time,
Morris inspired many, particularly younger, people to work for
the movement, presenting a vision of socialism in quasi-religious
terms as a heaven on earth.

By contrast, the Fabian Society, formed in 1884, was intensely
concerned with the practical. While always a heterogeneous body,[9]
the Society was dominated by the later 1880s by people like Sidney
Webb and George Bernard Shaw, who aimed to influence the
existing parties in a 'socialistic' direction. While the Fabians were
not as influential as they liked to claim, they did help to stimu-
late interest in and debate about socialism, and many of their
leading figures, most notably the Webbs, were to have a significant role to play in Labour politics in the future.

Relations between these socialists and the trade unions were
far from straightforward. The Fabians and the Socialist League
had little contact with the unions at all, somewhat predictably
given their members' social backgrounds. But in the case of the
SDF, things were more complicated. Hyndman, in the early years
at least, saw unions as restrictive organizations of skilled workers which were only out for their own members, not the working class as a whole, and would have little to do with them. He
has been criticized for this: but trade unions were, after all, very
much a minority sport at this time. Even by 1900, only 2 022 000
out of a potential membership of just under 16 000 000 were
unionized, which meant that almost 87 per cent of potential
members were not in unions.[10] In such circumstances, the view
that unions were an obstruction to working-class unity, concerned

with narrow economic gains, and with a mostly elite membership, rather than representative of the interests of the workers
as a whole, was at least plausible. However, it is important not
to focus too exclusively on Hyndman and his acolytes: many
SDFers were keen advocates of trade unionism, as the participation of members like Mann and Thorne in the 'new unionism' of
the late 1880s made clear. The question of the correct line to
take towards the unions remained one of the most hotly debated
issues within the SDF for years to come.

The formation of the Independent Labour party (ILP) in 1893
was a stronger move in the direction of co-operation between
socialists and trade unionists. Its leading figure, Keir Hardie, was
himself a former miner. While the ILP always had a strong middle-
class element, it also included significant numbers of workers
and trade unionists. Hardie, elected to parliament in 1892 as MP
for West Ham South, was a keen advocate of the 'Labour Alliance' between trade unionists and socialists. But he did not get
very far at first, and the TUC effectively excluded him from its
proceedings in 1895. It will not do to see Hardie as the inspired
manipulator behind the formation of the LRC; and, for much of
the decade, events seemed to be moving against the ILP. At the
1895 election, Hardie lost his seat and all the other 27 ILP candidates were also defeated. However, the commitment of individual
ILPers helped push some unions towards the idea of the LRC,
and the ILP did play an important role in keeping the idea alive
in the 1890s.

Why did the appeal of socialism take root in the 1880s and
1890s? Socialism was essentially a reaction against the perceived
arbitrariness of the market.[11] At the least, it demanded sterner
regulations on market forces; at most, their abolition, and replacement by a 'better' form of economic and social system. The
idea had little appeal in the mid-nineteenth century, since the
market seemed at that stage to be working, by delivering steadily
increasing living standards and a degree of security which, though
tiny by later standards, was a considerable improvement on what
had gone before. However, by the mid-1870s there was a growing perception of economic difficulties, and some people began
to look for an alternative. One such was the proposal for a single
tax on land: it says a great deal that the chief work advocating
such a policy, Henry George's *Progress and Poverty* (1880), rapidly became a bestseller in Britain. The idea of greater regulation

of market forces, linked in some cases to specific socialist demands such as the eight-hour day, also began to have a wider appeal, not least among trade unionists.[12] At the same time, the idea of a larger role for public authorities also appealed to many middle-class people, particularly civil servants like the young Sidney Webb: their status in society would be greatly enhanced, at the expense of capitalists, in a society based on public service rather than the generation of profit. But socialism was not just about controlling markets and other apparently mundane issues. As the work of Morris showed, it also had a strong spiritual appeal, especially to those who, for one reason or another, had begun to reject orthodox religion but who still felt the need for something like it in their lives. Hence not just the utopian, 'heaven-on-earth' writings of Morris, but also the Labour Church movement, which became relatively strong in the 1890s, and the evangelical preaching style of socialist propagandists like the ILPer, Philip Snowden (author of a book published in 1903 entitled *The Christ That Is To Be*). Finally, the departure of Gladstone was probably important here, too. He had, in many ways, delivered less than he had seemed to promise in a radical direction, but radicals' faith in him seems to have remained high to the end. Few radicals can have expected as much from his successors at the head of the Liberal party; certainly none of the latter was ever able to tap into working-class radicalism as effectively. For all these reasons, then, socialism secured a small niche in late nineteenth-century Britain, and appealed to small sections of both the working and middle classes. Crucially, too, it developed potential points of contact with the established labour movement: while most trade unionists did not become socialists, they did, from time to time, hear socialists saying things that they liked. This helped to ensure the participation of socialists at the founding conference of the LRC in 1900.

But, on the whole, the formation of the LRC in 1900 was not the uprising of a class, or the ineluctable and inevitable result of changing production relations or the product of the work of socialists more 'realistic' than Hyndman. It was, primarily, a new chapter in the struggle of the trade union movement for the right to be left alone to negotiate on equal terms with employers and to apply sanctions, such as strike action, where this was deemed necessary. Socialism was not utterly insignificant, but it did not lead the process. The 1900 conference not only rejected a call from the SDF to base the party upon 'a recognition of the class war'; it did not commit itself to any other form of socialism, either.[13] However, the socialists were not as impotent as they might have been: as individuals, they were often valued, even by non-socialists, for their dedication and hard work, and it was partly for this reason that the composition of the LRC's executive committee was amended from 12 trade unionists and 6 socialists to 7 of the former and 5 of the latter.[14]

What must also be noted is the tiny size of the new organization. The overwhelming majority of the population (between three-quarters and four-fifths) could be described as working class. Yet only around 13 per cent of those who could have been members of unions were. And, even of those, only 17.4 per cent were affiliated to the LRC at its formation: just 41 unions with a total of 353 070 members, and about half of those were affiliated through just five unions.[15] Among others, the miners, who could already elect a significant number of MPs under the auspices of the Liberal party as 'Lib-Labs', stayed outside. And, although the conference elected Ramsay MacDonald, a socialist ILPer, as its secretary, this was not really because of his socialism, but because of his reputation as a hard worker and good organizer and, perhaps crucially, because since his marriage he had a solid income through his wife and so could afford to work for nothing.[16]

Thus the LRC was formed in 1900. But it was not very firmly based; there were no guarantees that it would grow, or even remain in existence. That it did so was largely due to the events of the next few years, particularly the continuing legal threats to the unions. But even by 1914 the new organization would still be facing a rather uncertain future, and would still be very much a minority taste.

The new organization lacked most of the features associated with a political party. It had no programme as such; its machinery was utterly rudimentary. It was not committed in any way to socialist policies. Even among affiliated unions there was often hostility towards co-operation with socialists. For their part, many socialists resented the unions and despaired of their moderation: the SDF voted in 1901 to withdraw from the LRC. Meanwhile, hopes that the Co-operative movement might become involved were dashed: it continued with a broadly Liberal orientation. If anything, therefore, trade union power within the LRC grew. By the end of 1901, the addition of a trades council representative,

and the withdrawal of the SDF, meant the unions had 10 of the
13 positions on the executive.

The new organization was faced with a general election almost straight away. The conditions were not promising: the Conservatives were taking advantage of apparent success in the Boer
War to give themselves another spell in office. Labour was able
to run just 15 candidates, who took a total of 62 698 votes. Two
were elected, both in double-member seats: at Merthyr, where
Hardie had to face two Liberal opponents, and at Derby, where
Richard Bell of the ASRS fought and won in tandem with a single
Liberal candidate. All things considered, this was not a bad performance, but it hardly augured massive short-term advances.

However, the LRC's affiliates were soon reminded of the original
reason for the formation of the committee. In September 1900
the High Court ruled that the ASRS could be held liable for damages arising out of its dispute with the Taff Vale Railway Company in south Wales. This decision was overturned on appeal,
but in July 1901 the House of Lords backed the initial judgement. Ultimately, in January 1903, the ASRS was forced to pay
damages of £23 000 to the company. Meanwhile, the 1901 case
of *Quinn v. Leathem* effectively outlawed boycotts of third parties
in a dispute. The Denaby Main and Cadeby Case, started against
the Yorkshire Miners' Association in 1903, although eventually
won by the union in 1906, tended to reinforce the view that the
unions were under serious threat.[17]

All this uncertainty helped to keep the LRC together and moving
forward. At the time of the February 1901 conference, the number of unions affiliating had fallen from 41 to 34, and the union-
affiliated membership by about 14 000 to just under 339 577.
However, the Lords' decision on Taff Vale led to a stream of
affiliations: by February 1902, 65 unions were affiliating 455 450
members. The damages case against the ASRS, culminating in
the adverse judgment of January 1903, led to a further surge in
affiliations, so that by the following month 127 unions and 861 150
members were affiliated. Thus 1902 had seen a rise of 25 per
cent over the previous year, and 1903 a staggering 84 per cent
increase.[18] This was followed by a rise of 13 per cent in the year
to February 1904. At that year's conference, a compulsory levy
of a penny per member per year was imposed in order to pay
Labour MPs and help with election expenses. This enabled the
party to pay its MPs a salary of £200 a year from 1904 onwards,

but did result in some disaffiliations of smaller unions and some underreporting of membership by others.[19] But the committee had come a very long way, thanks largely to the decisions of the courts. By 1906, the main unions outside the Labour party were in mining: the Miners' Federation of Great Britain (MFGB) and the separate Durham and Northumberland Miners' Associations. Even here, though, it seemed progress was being made, with the Lancashire and Cheshire Miners' Federation affiliating in 1903. Meanwhile, attempts to place the LRC under the direct control of the parliamentary committee of the TUC were thwarted in 1902/3.

At this stage, though, the future of the organization still looked rather hazy. It was not entirely clear how far it would co-operate with other parties, or even with the eleven Lib–Lab MPs. Bell moved steadily towards the Liberals, and effectively abandoned the LRC in 1904. During 1902, though, two by-elections showed a degree of Liberal goodwill towards the LRC. At Wakefield, Philip Snowden, a former civil servant who, following a crippling illness, had become a kind of itinerant preacher on behalf of the ILP, was defeated in a straight fight with a Conservative. Although the Liberals, who had withdrawn, made no recommendation as to how their supporters should vote, many of them were impressed with the line Snowden had taken against the Boer War, and backed him all the same.[20] That August, David Shackleton, a textile union official, was elected as MP for Clitheroe in Lancashire; the Liberals, who had held the seat, did not put up a candidate. This victory was a major factor in pushing the textile workers towards affiliation to the LRC, a step they took shortly afterwards.

Two events in 1903 defined the position of the LRC more clearly. The first was the decision of Joseph Chamberlain, the Colonial Secretary, to resign from the cabinet and campaign for protective tariffs. This was a development of great significance. Free trade was not, according to labour and radical traditions in Britain, merely one of a number of variations of fiscal policy. It had long been seen as a key radical demand, and during the nineteenth century had become 'the kernel of a new "moral economy" of working-class consumers, supported with great earnestness and an almost religious fervour'.[21] Free trade meant cheap food, but was also seen as the key to other classic tenets of British radicalism, notably international peace, clean government and fair play. Protection had its working-class supporters, of course, but it was an issue that united most socialists and trade unionists.

The other result of Chamberlain's venture was that it gave new point to ongoing efforts to achieve a *rapprochement* between Labour and the Liberals. The Liberals had been struggling politically for too long to want to stand on ceremony, and for his part MacDonald was prepared to explore the possibilities of some kind of electoral deal if it meant a bigger share of seats for Labour after the next election. Thus in 1903, MacDonald and the Liberal chief whip, Herbert Gladstone, agreed secretly that, in England and Wales, Liberals would be discouraged from opposing Labour candidates in a number of seats, and that, in return, Labour would restrict its number of candidates elsewhere. Although the agreement was not always easy to enforce, it was to prove a major help to Labour at the next general election.

The fact that such a deal could be struck, and that it was adhered to by both sides, tells us much about Labour in this period. It also helps to demonstrate the domination of a certain outlook at this time. First, there was the essentially limited outlook which has been characterized by some writers as 'labourism'. This point of view, identified especially with the unions, stated that Labour's essential aim was to safeguard workers' rights, by enabling unions to bargain on equal terms with employers, and achieve such – essentially limited – legislation as would improve workers' conditions at work, and, to some extent, away from the workplace. Such claims could be couched in quasi-Gladstonian terms as bringing labour 'into the pale of the constitution'. Labour, in this formulation, was not looking for a revolution, even a peaceful one, but merely a fair deal. While some Liberals felt that this was a dangerous road to go down, many, especially those on the 'progressive' wing of the party, could see little wrong with it, as witness the large number of Liberal candidates who were to pledge themselves at the 1906 election to the full repeal of Taff Vale.

Secondly, in so far as Labour did go beyond this 'labourism' to be socialist, its dominant strain was moderate and, in relation to progressive Liberalism, largely consensual, at least in all but the very long term. MacDonald is a good example of this outlook. In his speeches and writings, he stressed the view that Marx was out of date, with all his talk of class struggles, capitalist collapse, and revolution. Instead, strongly influenced by German 'Revisionists' like Eduard Bernstein, with whose work he was well acquainted, he argued the opposite. Society, far from becoming more straightforwardly divided between two main classes, was becoming infinitely more complex. Many workers were becoming increasingly self-reliant as they became more prosperous, and this was a tendency that other workers should be encouraged to emulate. For MacDonald, socialism would come about gradually, organically, from the existing social and economic structures: it would emerge from the growing success of capitalism. It was thus the job of socialists to promote this success, to use its fruits to pass 'useful' reforms, to point to continuing areas where action was needed, and to build upon the workers' developing sense of self-reliance. In concrete terms, this view meant that there would be ample scope for co-operation between progressive Liberals and moderate socialists like himself. Indeed, progressives were moving society towards socialism even if they did not realize or admit it. In this way, instrumentality combined with ideology to suggest that the best way forward was in collaboration with progressive Liberalism. It should come as no surprise, then, that MacDonald was, at this time, a leading figure in the progressive Rainbow Circle, a discussion group most of whose members owed some allegiance to the Liberal party.

This 'progressive alliance' approach was not without its critics, of course. There were those in Labour politics who took a different view, and who were more influenced by Marxism. People like George Lansbury and Fred Jowett argued for more radical changes in the short term, especially in the form of extensive social policy innovations financed from general taxation. They repeatedly lost the arguments, not least because such policies ran counter to the radical traditions of self-help to which MacDonald and, indeed, the bulk of the skilled working class were so wedded. Yet, as Tanner has shown, both aspects of Labour's appeal were important. MacDonald's approach attracted working-class Liberals; yet the less moralizing, more concrete approach of the dissenters was more appealing to working-class Conservatives, a group for whom the Liberals had little appeal, and so 'Labour's ability to tap into this [Conservative] tradition . . . helped create' the 1903 pact.[22]

Between the conclusion of the pact and the 1906 general election, Labour made two more by-election gains. The first came at Woolwich in March 1903, where Will Crooks, unhindered by

Liberal opposition, gained the seat from the Conservatives. The second came at Barnard Castle in County Durham in July of the same year. Here, the Labour candidate was Arthur Henderson, who had previously been a Liberal party agent. Henderson was reluctant to fight at first, particularly as he would face Liberal opposition. However, his union, the Ironfounders, pressed him to stand as an LRC candidate, and he was helped by the fact that the Liberal candidate appeared to come out in favour of protection. Ultimately, he won the seat by a narrow majority, with the Liberal trailing in third place.

Meanwhile, the Conservatives were in increasing difficulties. Finally, in December 1905, A. J. Balfour, the Prime Minister, resigned in the hope that the Liberal leader, Sir Henry Campbell-Bannerman, would be unable to form a government. However, the latter succeeded, and once the government was formed, he dissolved parliament. Polling took place between 11 January and 8 February 1906. The main issue was free trade: other issues, like education and Chinese labour in South Africa, were also of importance, although at a secondary level. This suited the MacDonald–Gladstone Pact very well, since Labour candidates were overwhelmingly in support of free trade. In so far as Labour had a distinct policy, it was the reversal of Taff Vale: but even here, many Liberal candidates, keen to court trade union votes and certainly not keen to defend the judge-made law that the Conservatives had been instrumental in creating, offered pledges of reform. Labour's manifesto was studiously moderate, stressing those aspects of the LRC which were of general appeal: there was no mention of socialism. This did not mean, though, that individual candidates did not mention it and campaign for it: we must beware of attributing too monolithic an outlook to what remained very much a federal organization. But, on the whole, it was a campaign in which points of contact with the Liberals were emphasized.

There were 50 LRC-endorsed candidates, with a further five being endorsed by the Scottish Workers' Representation Committee. Three-fifths of the Labour candidates stood in Lancashire, Yorkshire, and the North-East. As well as the five in Scotland, there were only four candidates in the whole of the London area, five in the Midlands and two in Wales. This shows clearly the northern English bias of LRC strength. It was clearly a party rooted in the most heavily unionized areas, the heartlands of the Industrial Revolution. Generally, the MacDonald–Gladstone Pact worked well enough. It enabled many Labour candidates to have a free run against the Conservatives. It was particularly successful in Lancashire, where the Liberals were weak, the Labour movement relatively strong, there were numerous double-member constituencies which allowed each party to run a candidate, and the threat of tariffs helped to mobilize an unexpectedly strong reaction against the Conservatives in what had been one of their stronger areas. The pact worked less well in places where these factors did not apply, notable examples being Yorkshire and, in particular, Scotland, where official Liberalism would accept no agreement at all. In other parts of the country, the fact that the MFGB was still outside the LRC meant Lib–Lab, rather than LRC, candidatures.[23]

The results were very encouraging for the LRC, although they paled somewhat at the side of the Liberals' achievement in winning almost 400 seats. There were 29 LRC MPs, which increased to 30 as soon as parliament met, as one of the Lib–Labbers took the Labour whip. Thirteen of these came from the Lancashire area, four from Yorkshire, and three from the north-east: in other words, two-thirds of the Labour MPs sat for northern English seats. There were only three MPs from the London area, two from Scotland and one from Wales. Only five seats had been won against Liberal opposition.

In some senses, therefore, this was hardly a great victory: Labour had made a breakthrough, but was heavily dependent on the pact with the Liberals and was very much a sectional party with scarcely any presence at all outside areas of heavy industry and relatively high levels of unionization. Yet, in the immediate aftermath of the 1906 election, a wave of euphoria went through Labour's ranks. Viewed from later standpoints of success, such as the 1920s or the 1940s, it could be seen as the first instalment of the party's inexorable push towards power.[24] Yet even by 1914 Labour's position was far from assured.

Immediately after the election, the LRC changed its name to the Labour party. The change to 'party' seemed to signify a new bid for status. But the retention of 'Labour', which was hardly disputed, was also significant. It lacked the foreign and sectarian connotations of 'social democracy'. It could also mean all things to all people, for its connotations with manual work suited the defensive class consciousness of the trade unions which dominated it, while at the same time, MacDonald and others who hoped ultimately to broaden its appeal could resort to the formulation that all employees, manual or not, were workers, and hence 'Labour'.

The parliamentary Labour party (PLP) elected in 1906 was firmly rooted in the working class. Twenty-three of the MPs were active trade unionists. Yet 18 described themselves also as socialists, showing the dangers of resorting to too rigid a typology of 'trade unionists' versus 'socialists' in the early Labour party. In policy terms, most were concerned especially with welfare issues and, particularly, unemployment. On the whole, they were middle-aged and 'respectable'. Most had been Liberals as young men or even, as in the case of Henderson, into early middle age. A significant number were active nonconformists. On the other hand, the fact that only one was a Roman Catholic was a sign of Labour's failure to break into that potentially rich vein of working-class support before the 1920s.[25]

The party did not have a 'leader' as such until 1922. The key position, therefore, was chairman of the PLP, and here, after a tied first ballot, Hardie defeated Shackleton by a single vote. This is usually seen as a poor choice, given that Hardie was clearly a less able organizer than Shackleton. But the former's appeal within the party was broader than that of his rival, and he was, at least, a useful figurehead, behind whom Shackleton (vice chairman), MacDonald (secretary) and Henderson (chief whip) could do business. Later, the chairmanship rotated in turn to Henderson (1908–10) and George Barnes (1910–11). It is perhaps significant that by 1911 Henderson had decided that the party was best led by a moderate socialist, rather than a leading trade unionist.[26]

The first couple of years of the new parliament saw Labour emerge with a by no means discreditable record. There had been fears, for example, that the legislation to sort out the mess created by Taff Vale might not restore the *status quo ante*. Campbell-Bannerman, buttressed by the recommendations of a Royal Commission, was keen for a new definition which would leave the unions with greater responsibilities than before. However, a number of Liberal MPs had pledged themselves to the Labour position during the election campaign, and Shackleton was able to use this fact to convince the premier of the need for the acceptance of Labour's demands. This could then be presented as a great victory for the party, and can hardly have harmed it with the trade unions, particularly the MFGB. While the miners stayed outside for the time being, the proportion of TUC members affiliated to the Labour party rose from 57.4 per cent in 1906 to 66.1 per cent two years later. Labour also played a part in the implementation of other reforms, such as the introduction of school meals, the extension of the scope of workmen's compensation, and a slight increase in expenditure on unemployment relief works.

But bigger projects made much less progress. In 1907 the party put forward its 'Right to Work' Bill, which called on the government to increase expenditure at times of slump in order to offset increased unemployment, but this got nowhere.[27] In the following year, the Minority Report of the Poor Law Commission, written largely by the Fabian Beatrice Webb and Labour MP George Lansbury, made suggestions for sweeping changes in social policy, including the abolition of the Poor Law and the prevention of poverty through comprehensive social reforms. But, apart from old age pensions, which were introduced in 1908, this too was largely ignored by the Liberal government. On the whole, the Liberals seem to have seen Labour MPs as a useful gauge of working-class opinion, but little more. They were certainly not being forced to enact legislation by the Labour party.

The result was that many Labourites became discontented with the PLP's performance, and this disenchantment manifested itself in a number of ways. First, there were efforts to get Labour MPs to act as delegates of the wider party. The MPs, not surprisingly, rejected this view. At the 1907 conference a compromise was reached: conference would lay down the broad lines of policy, but the PLP would retain discretion as to how to follow the policy so laid down. Another point of dispute was the leadership's reluctance to fight by-elections. Although the MacDonald–Gladstone Pact had applied to the 1906 election alone, the basic strategy of trying to avoid conflict with the Liberals remained. Thus Labour left many by-elections uncontested. This galled Labour activists, particularly in areas like west Yorkshire, where the Liberals were neither 'progressive' in their policies nor socially acceptable to Labourites. A spectacular manifestation of these discontents came in July 1907 in the by-election in the west Yorkshire constituency of Colne Valley. Against the strongly expressed hostility of the party leadership, Victor Grayson stood as an independent socialist candidate and won the seat in a three-cornered fight against Conservative and Liberal candidates.

Grayson's candidature, election and subsequent erratic behaviour as an MP were all worrying to a Labour leadership keen above all to maintain links with the Liberals and to stress their own party's moderation. A further sign of discontent came in 1908, with the publication of Ben Tillett's vitriolic pamphlet *Is the Parliamentary Labour Party a Failure?* Unemployment was rising rapidly and, for Tillett, it was here that the party should make its stand, on moral and political grounds. Yet with the failure of the Right to Work Bill Labour seemed to have little to say, and seemed instead to be increasingly obsessed with fringe issues like temperance and Welsh Church disestablishment. As MacDonald pointed out, Labour had still been campaigning about unemployment, but it could do only a limited amount given its small size.[28] The dispute did highlight, though, a number of themes which were to be present throughout Labour's history: the conflict between a concentration on parliament and attempts to urge an extra-parliamentary approach in times of crisis; questions of prioritization of policies; and the belief that full employment was the key objective of the party.

In any case, the party was becoming even more union-dominated in this period. TUC membership rose in the first decade of the twentieth century by 38.5 per cent to 1 662 133, and the percentage of members affiliated to the party also increased. Thus, although from mid-decade the membership of the socialist societies was rising, the unions formed 97.5 per cent of Labour party membership in 1910 as opposed to 93.9 per cent at the formation of the LRC in 1900.[29] While it would be wrong to read too much into this – many leading trade unionists were socialists – it shows that Tillett's fears of the party's increasing lack of radicalism had some basis in fact.

The single most important development in this field concerned the miners. The MFGB was the largest union in the country, with over half a million members by 1908. But hitherto it had remained committed to a Lib–Lab outlook.[30] However, things were changing. The federation's legal problems had suggested to some the need for a shift; this was facilitated by the death of some staunch Lib–Lab leaders like Ben Pickard in Yorkshire and the tireless propaganda work of ILPers in the coalfields.[31] There was a ballot on affiliation in the summer of 1906, but on a turnout of 57 per cent, the miners voted by 101 714 to 92 222 against. Majorities in favour in the four areas of greatest membership – south

Wales, Yorkshire, Scotland and Lancashire – were not enough to offset massive opposition in the Midlands and most of the smaller coalfields.[32] But so close a result was unlikely to be conclusive, and a further ballot in May 1908 saw a vote of 213 137 to 168 446 in favour of affiliation on a 69 per cent turnout. The coalfields of the Midlands and north Wales opposed affiliation, however; and given that 61 per cent of the membership overall had either not voted or opposed the move, it could hardly be claimed that there was a major sea-change in the miners' attitudes.[33] That would be reserved for the period after the First World War. But at least the MFGB was now ready to affiliate, which it duly did in 1909. This meant that Labour's trade union membership was now 88 per cent of that of the TUC. The move also meant that 13 Lib–Lab MPs now joined the PLP.[34] In many ways, their political attitudes were not very different from those of the Labour MPs they joined; but clearly the effect was to move the centre of gravity within the Labour party still further from socialism.

The anti-Labour strain within trade unions remained significant, however. One result of this caused Labour considerable problems from 1909 onwards. In that year, the House of Lords adjudged union contributions to political parties to be illegal. The railwayman who had brought the case, W. V. Osborne, was a staunch trade unionist, but opposed union involvement in party politics. The Osborne Judgment was clearly a threat to Labour's long-term development. In the short term, many local Labour parties collapsed and Labour candidates at the 1910 elections were often desperately short of money.[35] The party itself coped – it had few paid staff and headquarters were modest and inexpensive to run – but the Judgment was obviously a threat to its position and, more broadly, yet another example of legal interference in trade union affairs.

To make matters worse, Labour was soon faced with a general election. The 1906 parliament, with its massive Liberal majority, might have been expected to run until 1912 or 1913, but in 1909, David Lloyd George, who had succeeded as Chancellor of the Exchequer when Asquith had succeeded Campbell-Bannerman as premier the previous year, introduced a radical budget which so antagonized Conservative opinion that the Tory majority in the House of Lords took the unprecedented step of vetoing it. In order to re-establish his mandate, Asquith dissolved parliament. This was hardly a prospect to gladden the Labour heart. Of ten by-elections fought by official Labour candidates since 1906, eight had been three-cornered fights and Labour had come bottom of the poll in five. Its only gains had come in peculiar circumstances: at Jarrow in 1907 when an Irish Nationalist candidate took enough votes from the Liberal to let Labour in, and at Sheffield Attercliffe in 1909 when two rival Conservative candidates had caused enough confusion to allow Labour to steal the seat.

Labour's leaders, therefore, had little inclination to fight on a much broader front than in 1906, even before the Osborne Judgment clipped their wings still further. A new deal was done with the Liberals, allowing most Labour MPs a free run against the Conservatives. In a campaign dominated by the radical rhetoric of 'peers against people' and free trade versus protection, Labour had little to say that was distinctive from the Liberals. Forty of Labour's 78 candidates were victorious, more than in 1906, but a net loss of five seats on its pre-dissolution strength. Significantly, only one of Labour's successful candidates faced Liberal opposition. Overall, the Liberals lost heavily, emerging with 275 seats to the Conservatives' 272. But Labour did not really hold the parliamentary balance of power. There could be no question of them allying with the Conservatives, so they were forced, willy-nilly, to back the Liberals; and, still more significantly, the Liberals had the greater strength of the 82 Irish Nationalists to back them.

A second election soon followed. The budget was passed, but the government was eager to deal with the House of Lords as well, and could only do so with a fresh electoral mandate. At the December 1910 election, Labour, more strapped than ever by the Osborne Judgment, could field only 62 candidates; it emerged with 42 seats. The other parties' positions scarcely changed: the Liberals emerged with the same number of seats as the Conservatives, but were safe in power because of Irish and Labour support.

Labour's position in the period between the end of 1910 and the outbreak of the First World War just over three-and-a-half years later did not suggest that the party was about to make a major leap forward. Performance in by-elections was indifferent: indeed, Labour lost four seats. Three of these were north Midland mining seats where there had been no Liberal candidates in 1910 but where Lib–Labbism remained a potent force. The fact that Labour came third in all three contests was also a worrying sign. In eight other seats, Labour put up candidates where it had not done so in December 1910: all came last. True, Labour's candidates were picking up a fair number of votes. But Labour was clearly a third party, and not yet challenging the Liberals on anything like equal terms. Evidence from local government elections offers a somewhat less bleak picture. In some areas, at least, Labour was capable of gaining votes from the Liberals. In every year between 1909 and 1913 Labour made a net gain of seats, with especially strong performances in 1911 and 1913.[36] But still the image remains of a third party struggling with no great success to establish a greater presence in most parts of the country.

There were other, more encouraging, developments, however. The party's performance in parliament improved somewhat. The rotating chairmanship had not been a great success, and when Barnes fell ill in 1911 a deal was struck whereby MacDonald retired from the party secretaryship in favour of Henderson and took over the chairmanship from Barnes. This was a development of considerable significance. MacDonald was man of charisma and style, a fine (if often rather nebulous) orator, and had clear electoral appeal. These points are commonplace. What is sometimes forgotten is that he was also a master of organization and strategy and had (at least by contemporary Labour standards) a relatively coherent ideology. His aim, as stated above, was to stress the points of contact between an evolutionary, consensual form of socialism with, on the one hand, the trade unionists who made up the bulk of the party and, on the other, those 'progressives' who were still in the Liberal party but who, on many issues, were close to the Labour outlook. In the short-term, Labour continued to support the Liberals, but also became more professional in parliament.

The concomitant of this was the aim of improving Labour's organization in the country. Here, the period between 1910 and 1914 saw significant developments. The staff at head office was increased, with the appointment of two national organizers. It was agreed in principle to establish a separate Scottish organization. And in London, severe difficulties were overcome finally in May 1914 with the formation of the London Labour party. Across the country, local trades councils became increasingly Labour dominated.[37] While it would be rash to argue that these changes led inexorably towards the party's post-war progress, they did signify that Labour would be pushing the Liberals for a greater role in the not-too-distant future.

Labour's consolidation was assisted by two pieces of legislation passed in reaction to the Osborne Judgment. The first, in 1911, resulted in the payment to MPs of a salary of £400 a year, which removed a burden from sponsoring organizations (mainly unions) which had previously had to find the money for MPs' wages. In retrospect, this can be seen to have removed a potential obstacle to Labour's growth. The second was the Trade Union Act of 1913. Labour grumbled about this, first because it was a long time coming, and secondly because it did not restore the *status quo ante*, as the party had wanted. Indeed, it confirmed that unions should not make political donations from their general funds. However, it allowed unions to set up, subject to a membership ballot, a separate political fund, from which contributions could be made to the party. This would be financed by a special 'political levy' from which individuals like Osborne could 'contract out' if they so wished. Many Liberals hoped these complexities would stymie Labour, but, in fact, the Act was to prove a blessing in disguise: the legal position was now clarified in a way that satisfied natural justice; most of the ballots went in favour of establishing political funds, although in some cases by a very narrow margin; and, finally, there was little else that the political fund money could be spent on *except* the Labour party, giving the latter a firmer base of income and budgeting than ever before. However, union executives often remained reluctant to adopt a very expansive policy of funding, with many 'refusing to finance enough Labour parliamentary candidates to sustain a broad anti-Liberal campaign'.[38]

The clarification of the legal financial relationship between party and unions was especially important given the considerable expansion of trade unionism during this period. TUC-affiliated unions had had 1 200 000 members in 1900. This rose by 37.3 per cent in the next ten years, and then by a further 62.8 per cent between 1910 and 1914, when membership stood at almost 2 700 000.[39] This increased rate of expansion after 1910 was due to three main causes. First, it was a period of trade prosperity. Secondly, many members were recruited around the time of the major industrial disputes of the period. These included, among others, a short national railway strike in August 1911, which resulted – at last – in the recognition of the rail unions by the railway companies, and a national miners' strike early in 1912. The number of working days lost through disputes soared, peaking at over 40 000 000 in 1912. Many contemporaries suggested that the strikes were caused by revolutionary trade unionism, or syndicalism (see below). This was not the case, although a few strike leaders were influenced by such ideas. In fact, the reasons were much more prosaic, most notably resistance to changing industrial practices and the levelling off of real wages. Indeed, the third cause of the increase in union membership suggested that workers were still thinking in terms of the continuation of the existing social system. Under the National Insurance Act, friendly societies and unions which already ran benefit schemes of their own became 'approved societies' for the administration of the scheme on behalf of the state. This helped to consolidate, and even increase, union membership at the time.

This expansion benefited the Labour party. Its trade union affiliated membership rose by a third to 1 858 178 between 1910 and 1912. The immediate effect of the 1913 Trade Union Act, of course, was to reduce this figure somewhat, given the 'contracting out' clause. Even so, membership was still over 1.5 million in 1914. But trade unionists were still only a minority of workers, and any notion of a working class homogenizing rapidly and therefore about to turn, inevitably, to Labour is deeply flawed.

In particular, the proportion of women unionized was far lower than that of men. But this, and the fact that women were still barred from the parliamentary franchise, should not be taken to mean that the party totally ignored women. Although women were typically treated as second-class members in trade unions, they could not be ignored entirely, as the leaders of the textile and footwear workers' unions found to their cost.[40] Women also played a significant role in the socialist societies. Alongside women prominent at the national level, like Katharine Bruce Glasier, were women at the grassroots, who could, and often did, play a significant role. For many, socialism was the appeal; for others, Labour seemed the most likely party to push for women's suffrage.[41] As pressure grew from women's groups for the vote and for greater rights in trade unions, so Labour came to take these issues more seriously. In 1911, when the government introduced a franchise reform bill which did not include women's suffrage, the Labour party conference declared that this, or any similar legislation, would be unacceptable. This led to greater co-operation between the Labour party and the moderate National Union of Women's Suffrage Societies (NUWSS), and many Liberal women began to see Labour as the better bet on this issue. Ultimately, the NUWSS set up a fund to support Labour candidates in by-elections where there was no pro-suffrage candidate.[42] While it would be clearly absurd to see Labour as a 'women's party', it was at least starting to make wider connections with women and the organized women's movement than would have been possible through a narrowly trade union-oriented approach. However, the fact that the Co-operative movement remained outside the sphere of Labour politics posed a continuing obstacle towards making those links still closer.

If there were still many workers outside trade unions, and trade unionists outside the Labour party, it must also be remembered that there were significant numbers of socialists who did not accept the Labour lead. During this period three basic challengers contested the claims of the 'Labour alliance' to be the sole representative of socialism in Britain: Marxism, syndicalism and guild socialism.

The Marxist left had fragmented somewhat after the SDF's disaffiliation from the LRC in 1901. In 1903, supporters of Daniel de Leon's ideas of industrial unionism had broken away to form the Socialist Labour party (SLP), a small but influential group whose main strength was on Clydeside. The following year, a group had broken off to form the Socialist party of Great Britain. The SDF (renamed the Social Democratic party in 1907) remained the most significant force, but made little progress. However, in 1911 left ILPers, including Grayson, led a secession to join the Social Democrats in a new British Socialist party (BSP). The BSP hoped to outflank Labour, but although it claimed 40 000 members at the outset, this figure had fallen by two-thirds by 1914. Its attempt to defeat Labour from without having failed, it applied for affiliation to the Labour party, and this was finally accepted in 1916. For its part, the SLP was also in decline by 1914, with a membership of around 300 in 15 branches.[43] In other words, the challenge of orthodox Marxism had, for the time being at least, been contained.

The second challenge was that of syndicalism. Syndicalists rejected the state, arguing that full unionization of the workforce and the amalgamation of unions would lead to a revolutionary general strike to overthrow capitalism and replace it with a new order of society based on workers' control. From 1910 onwards a number of trade unionists became influenced by the doctrine, and many of the leaders of the Rhondda coal strike in 1911 were avowed supporters. However, other causes account for the strike wave of 1910–14. Meanwhile, union amalgamations were more of an attempt by moderate leaders to increase their hold over the membership than the prelude to a revolutionary general strike. This was certainly true in the case of the merger of the ASRS with other unions to form the National Union of Railwaymen in 1912, while the formation in 1914 of the Triple Alliance, whereby the MFGB, NUR and National Transport Workers' Federation (NTWF) pledged to support each other in disputes, was essentially a defensive action.[44]

The third 'threat', guild socialism, originated in the first decade of the century. Despite its occasionally ludicrous medievalism, guild socialism was a serious attempt to marry the syndicalist critique of statism with the Labour critique of syndicalism. It argued that a future socialist society dominated by the state might well be just as undemocratic, even tyrannous, as capitalism; but that, on the other hand, syndicalism alone would not guarantee freedom from industrial tyranny. Accordingly, its leading advocate, the young academic G. D. H. Cole, put forward a model of society in which reformed trade unions, or guilds, would remain to run industry on the basis of democratic workers' control (representing the producers), while the state would remain to represent consumers and guarantee broader liberties. There were all kinds of problems with this concept, of course. In particular, there was the danger of frequent clashes between guilds and state, producers and consumers. Cole argued that in the new spirit of a socialist society such clashes either would not occur or else be easily dealt with, but this was not terribly convincing. Even so, guild socialism did address problems of power in society which MacDonald and his colleagues tended to ignore or to brush aside. It must be admitted, though, that before 1914 the influence of guild socialism outside intellectual circles was not very great.[45]

The development of syndicalism and guild socialism did demonstrate disquiet with two aspects of the 'socialism' of Labour's leaders. First, there was concern as to the uncritical conception of the state held by many Labour socialists, and in particular by leaders like MacDonald. At a time when members of all parties were questioning the unprecedented expansion of the state which was coming with social reform, administrative intervention in industrial disputes and war preparation measures (for example, the Official Secrets Act, 1911), it was at least a sign of health that some socialists were talking about these issues. That most Labour leaders were so keen simply to dismiss and, to a certain extent, suppress the debate was to be a foretaste of later developments in the party's history. Secondly, there were questions about the way in which Labour's leaders saw a socialist society emerging. The conflicts between MacDonald's mix of ethical socialism and revisionism, on the one hand, and the more interventionist socialists like Lansbury, on the other, remained significant. The former view continued to hold sway, but the fact that the left was looking, albeit rather unsuccessfully, for an alternative suggests that it sensed that there might be problems with the approach. This conflict, in turn, spilled over into electoral policy: if MacDonald was right, then continued co-operation would seem to have a certain logic, but, if a more radical policy was called for, then clearly it would make more sense to attack the Liberals. Indeed, the increasing pressure from grassroots Labourites to run candidates in these years, and the increasing difficulty that the leadership had in stopping such contests with the Liberals, is indicative of a broader debate about the right strategy for the party.

Not surprisingly, then, the question of how far the 'progressive alliance' would have been maintained in the next general election (due, probably, in 1915) has excited some historical debate. It is frequently argued that Labour would have fought that election as 'a truly independent party of the left and of the trade union movement', with anything up to 170 candidates.[46] There is evidence in favour of this argument. The Liberals were in trouble: the tactical advantages of some form of alliance were not, perhaps, as clear to Labour as they had been in 1903 or 1910. The Liberals' social reforming impulse, though not obliterated, had nonetheless been somewhat obscured by issues like Ireland, rearmament, strikes and women's suffrage: and this in turn meant that any alliance would have been harder for the Labour leadership to 'sell' to its increasingly restive followers. Labour's organization was much improved. On the whole, it does seem fair to say that even given disappointing by-election performances, the mere passage of time made it more assertive.

Yet there are also reasons to doubt whether, ultimately, MacDonald and Henderson would have stuck to their guns. Their bold talk of a broader front may well have been tactical: both to frighten the Liberals into conceding a better deal than last time, and also to appease their own more confrontational supporters. It was one thing to 'talk big' at a time when an election was still some way off. It might have been different if it had meant a real split threatening the imminent election of a protectionist, Unionist, rearming government under the perceivedly extreme Andrew Bonar Law and staffed by some of the very people who had cheered on every piece of anti-union judge-made law since the 1890s. We cannot know for sure, since, due to the First World War, the 1915 election never took place. But it does not seem wholly unlikely that, had matters taken their course, Labour and the Liberals would have renewed their pact for the next election, albeit with Labour being given, perhaps, a few more seats to fight.[47]

The period between 1900 and the outbreak of war in August 1914 saw Labour establish itself as a force in British politics. But it would be rash to claim that there was any very clear pattern to the movement of events. The idea that Labour was on the brink of second-party status seems untenable. The wilder hopes expressed in the aftermath of the 1906 election had not been borne out by events. Yet to argue that Labour was in some kind of decline also seems wide of the mark. It had developed its organization, forged deeper links with the expanding trade unions and new links with women, and acquired a more polished and effective leadership. However unsteadily, it had begun to establish a few real electoral strongholds. While it would be facile to claim that industrial, production and class relations had been revolutionized by 1914, it would be equally silly to claim that there had been no change, or that class divisions mattered less than they had eight years earlier. Labour was certainly not poised on the brink of displacing the Liberals as the main anti-Conservative party, but its strength had been consolidated and its position was unlikely to decline. In 1906 Labour had outperformed its potential, gaining position on the back of an anti-Conservative and pro-free trade reaction that took almost everyone by surprise in its magnitude. By 1914 it had not grown very far, but it now had a firmer base. It would not have expanded as far as it ultimately did in so short a space of time had it not been for the First World War, but at least developments to 1914 meant that it was in a position to take advantage of the opportunities which that war was to offer.

2

The Surge to Second-Party Status, 1914–22

The period between 1914 and 1922 saw massive changes on the world stage. In 1914 it had seemed to many that the established order would never change. Eight years later, millions had died in a bloody war, old empires were no more and regimes professing communism and fascism were installed in two of Europe's great states. No major nation had been left unscathed by the conflict. British politics had also been transformed, to the considerable benefit of the Labour party. In 1914 Labour was still the fourth party in parliament, with just over three dozen MPs and an uncertain future. By 1922 it was the main opposition party, with 142 MPs, a new constitution, and a much-improved organization. The war gave Labour leaders their first experience of ministerial office. This period saw not only tangible electoral and political advances, but also a shift from the loose federal structure of the Edwardian era to a much tighter party, closer in many ways to the continental social democratic parties. Many of these changes were directly attributable to the First World War.

Labour's ability to make so much of the opportunities offered by the war was due, first, to the party's basic underlying unity during the conflict. It is true that a number of issues did split the party during the war. The first was entry into the war itself. Labour, as a member of the Second International, was formally committed to opposing a war. On Sunday 2 August, the day the Germans launched a massive offensive in the west, Labour organized a big anti-war demonstration in London's Trafalgar Square. Henderson invited the main institutions in the Labour movement to a meeting on 5 August to discuss the next steps. However, this apparent anti-war unity then collapsed. In fact, some Labourites would have supported the war in any case; but the German violation of Belgian neutrality allowed many more to come over, couching their support for the war in conventional radical terms. When parliament debated the situation on 3 August, the PLP majority was in favour of a declaration of war on Germany. MacDonald spoke against entry but, realizing his minority position, resigned the same day as PLP chairman, and was replaced by Henderson. The declaration of war followed the next day. Before the end of the month, an electoral truce had been agreed, and the party was soon supporting the war effort, even to the extent of putting its organization at the disposal of the military recruiting campaign.

To a large extent, this was a division born of conviction: there was a patriotic surge, and most Labour leaders were unlikely to be immune from it. But it was not just that Labourites wrapped themselves in the flag. Many leaders who were sceptical about the war realized Labour might cause itself great damage by going against the tide of patriotism sweeping the country. The overwhelming view was that the war would be short-lived. For most leading Labourites, including Henderson, the fear was that a critical approach would isolate Labour and leave it vulnerable to charges of defeatism at the general election which would shortly follow. In addition, there was a more principled argument that Britain (and France) had parliamentary structures which offered at least some possibilities of 'progressive' advance, and that these were therefore worth preserving. The alternative, presented rather hesitatingly by MacDonald, was that Labour should stand on principle, launch a radical critique of pre-war 'secret diplomacy', and so draw in those discontented radical Liberals who were to form the basis of the Union of Democratic Control: in short, it should steal the radical thunder from the discredited Liberal party. At first, official party statements tried to paper over the cracks between the two positions, but, as attitudes hardened, Labour's stance became more overtly patriotic and anti-German.[1]

Even so, the party did not fall apart. One reason for this was the formation of the War Emergency Workers' National Committee (WEC), as a result, ironically, of the meeting called by Henderson for 5 August. Its original purpose was, typically, defensive: to protect working-class living standards against the economic distress and social dislocation which it was believed the war would bring. It included representatives of the Labour party, the TUC and the GFTU, plus further elected and co-opted members, meeting under the chairmanship of Henderson and with J. S. Middleton, assistant secretary of the party, as secretary. Members included MacDonald, Sidney Webb, Hyndman, the miners' president Robert Smillie, Mary Macarthur of the National Federation of Women Workers, and Marion Phillips, later to be chief woman officer of the Labour party. The WEC thus provided a point of contact for a very broad swathe of Labourites who might otherwise have drifted apart.[2]

The WEC could not, of course, totally prevent further disputes. One came over compulsory military service, which became an issue later in 1915 as the war dragged on. Conscription was suspect in itself, as a manifestation of the kind of militarism that Britain was supposed to be opposing, but it also raised the spectre of industrial compulsion and an end to the free market in labour which was so important to British unions. It was partly to head off pressure for conscription that Labour entered so keenly into the recruitment of volunteers. Once in the Asquith cabinet, Henderson was a keen opponent of compulsion. But the government moved towards conscription, and ultimately Henderson decided that it was better to remain in the cabinet and be in a position to resist industrial conscription. The wider party took the same view, although a minority of Labour MPs continued to work in close alliance with Liberal rebels in voting against extensions of military conscription to new groups of men.[3]

Further disputes surrounded Labour's entry into the Lloyd George Coalition in 1916. As Asquith came under increasing pressure, Labour stressed its support for him: on 1 December Henderson described the premier as 'the indispensable man'.[4] On 5 December, probably seeking to demonstrate that he was indeed 'indispensable', Asquith offered the King his resignation. The Conservative leaders decided to support Lloyd George, but the latter clearly needed Labour support, given that the bulk of the Liberal party would move into opposition if Asquith were ousted, and given the continuing importance of labour questions to the war effort. Ultimately, Labour did join the new government, with Henderson becoming a Minister without Portfolio in the five-man war cabinet. This seemed a startling volte-face. But while Henderson, as a loyal member of the cabinet, had had little choice but to back Asquith when the latter had been premier, once the change had taken place, it was another story. After all, Asquith had displayed poor judgement, even perversity, in offering his resignation. Labour had little to gain from leaving office, and perhaps much to lose if it did so. Thus on 7 December Henderson and his leading colleagues on the NEC and PLP met Lloyd George. As well as a place for Henderson in the war cabinet, he offered terms better than Asquith had ever conceded: new ministries of Labour and Pensions to be placed under Labour ministers, state control of the coal mines, and a pledge not to introduce industrial conscription. Thus the Labour leaders voted, by a majority, to join the new government.

A further source of dispute came in 1917 with the proposal for a meeting of European socialists at Stockholm. In March 1917 a revolution in Russia overthrew the Tsar, and on 22 April Camille Huysmans, secretary of the Second International, proposed a conference of socialists in the Swedish capital to discuss plans for the future. Peace terms would obviously be on the agenda. The Petrograd Soviet endorsed the appeal in May, but Labour's NEC rejected it because it did not wish to meet with 'enemy' socialists, and proposed a conference of Allied socialists instead. Henderson was then dispatched by Lloyd George to persuade the Russian socialists of the need to stay in the war and to boycott the Stockholm conference. On arriving in Russia, though, Henderson was appalled by the prospects for the Provisional government if steps were not made towards peace, and came to the view that Stockholm would at least show the impotence of the German socialists and the fact that there was no alternative to continuing the fight. On his return he talked the NEC into provisional support for the conference, but it was clear that there would be deep divisions within the movement as a result. However, the war cabinet's position had hardened, and it refused to issue passports to Labourites wishing to attend. Henderson was forced to resign from the war cabinet.[5] In this way, then, he was pushed back towards the party. Paradoxically, a threat to its unity served ultimately to reunite Labour.

In short, a series of crises at the top of the Labour movement were overcome without irreparable damage. This is not to say, though, that there were no divisions at all. 'Super patriots' like Hyndman and the secretary of the GFTU, W. C. Appleton, took the view that everything must be subordinated to the defeat of Germany; on the other hand, revolutionary defeatists like the Marxist John Maclean argued that the war should be turned into a European class war. On the whole, neither strain was strong: Hyndman was forced out of the BSP in 1916 for his views, while the defeatist strain was very weak indeed. Most Labourites took a line similar to that of Henderson and Webb, that the war was just but that the defence of working-class interests should not be forsaken. MacDonald, while critical of the war, 'was no more prepared to see Germany win ... than Henderson was'.[6] Other members of the Labour party, most notably those in the ILP, did take a stronger anti-war stance, sometimes verging on pacifism. But most of these divisions tended to mend as Henderson and others moved towards consideration of a 'just' peace and earlier battles over conscription faded.[7]

Politicians, in the public eye, had to maintain at least a semblance of consistency. But this applied less the further down the movement one went. Here, it was not unusual for the general swings in the public mood which accompanied Britain's fluctuating fortunes in the war to have a significant impact on attitudes. Thus in the period 1914–16, the patriotic mood was dominant. In 1917, this waned, as war-weariness grew with increasing casualties and no prospect of an end to the war. But the crises of early 1918, when it seemed that Britain stood on the verge of defeat in the face of renewed German offensives, led to a revival of patriotic sentiment, and as the tables were turned and victory approached in later 1918 this mood reached near fever pitch.[8] Clearly, in other words, many people were not consistent in their views, but responded to changing circumstances with a combination of patriotism and defensive class instinct. In this sense, the presence of apparently different tendencies at the top of the Labour movement enabled it to avoid brittleness and remain responsive to its followers, while the fact that the divisions were often more apparent than real helped to keep the party together.

Labour, then, was able to exploit many of the opportunities offered by the war because of its basic underlying unity. The same could not be said for the Liberals. The most spectacular symbol of Liberal problems, of course, was the split between Asquith and Lloyd George in December 1916. Lloyd George took with him only about a third of the party's MPs; the rest, including most leading Liberals, followed Asquith into opposition.[9] The two sides were to reunite only in 1923, and in the intervening period a series of disputes embittered relations still further. But Liberal decline was about more than leadership jealousies. It was difficult for the party to move forward on policy in wartime. This was less true of the Labour party, where, after a fashion, policies were made by the annual conference and implemented by the NEC and PLP. In the Liberal party, where the institutional framework was weaker, policy depended much more on the agency of individuals. Here, Lloyd George had been a crucial figure before the war, while the 'New Liberals' had also been significant in keeping the party leaning in a 'progressive' direction. But both Lloyd George and many of the New Liberals were weakened as agents of progressivism by the war, and power moved towards more traditional figures, opening up the gap on the left of British politics that Labour had found so elusive in the pre-war years.[10] The split of 1916 merely reinforced this. Thirdly, Liberal ideology was deeply questioned by the war. The traditional watchwords of most Liberals – 'peace, retrenchment and reform' – were mocked by a bloody and costly war, a massively expanded state (and, between 1914 and 1916, an eightfold increase in public expenditure), the introduction of protective tariffs on luxury imports in 1915, and the clear infringement of individual liberties involved in conscription. All this served massively to weaken the self-confidence and moral force which had been such crucial components of nineteenth-century Liberalism. At the same time, though, the resistance of the Liberals to measures like conscription meant that it was easier than ever for the Conservatives to portray themselves as the truly patriotic party.[11] A more prosaic, but still important, problem the war created for the Liberals was that of finance. Here again, Labour's structure, and the Liberals' lack of it, enabled the newer party to benefit. The Liberals depended heavily on rich men's gifts, many of them donated in the expectation of a mention in the Honours List. After 1916, such people often chose to fund Lloyd George, rather than the party, since he now had the patronage at his disposal. Contributions to Liberal headquarters simply dried up.[12] By contrast, the political levy assured Labour of a significant and growing income at all levels of the party organization.

The impact of franchise reform, which was hastened by the war, on the Liberal party is more problematic. Before 1914, only about 60 per cent of men, and no women, had had the parliamentary vote. The 1918 Representation of the People Act, however, enfranchised all men of twenty-one and over, and most women of thirty and over. It has been argued that Labour had suffered particularly under the old arrangements, because they discriminated against the working class: thus the post-1918 electorate was more prone to vote Labour, and, in so far as it did not, it voted for the Conservatives, whose simple patriotic appeals were easier to comprehend than those of the more cerebral Liberals.[13] However, this argument is not terribly convincing. First, the excluded voters were not all working class, by any means. Professionals who moved frequently and so lost out under the lengthy residence requirements of the pre-war franchise, commercial travellers, and, perhaps most significantly, young men who lived with their parents were all effectively excluded from the franchise. Even where they were not middle-class, they included groups – like domestic servants and soldiers living in barracks – who were hardly natural Labour voters.[14] Secondly, Liberal appeals to the electorate were not necessarily less populist than their opponents'. It scarcely took an Oxford don to understand such stock Liberal cries as 'the Big Loaf of Free Trade and the Little Loaf of Protection'. Thirdly, it is clear from the evidence of 1920s elections that the Liberals did gain some support, at least when united, from the new voters. And, finally, Labour had no 'prior call' on most of the new voters. The new voters were a heterogeneous bunch, and they were to be faced, at the end of the war, with an incredibly confusing political landscape. What was reasonably clear, at least by 1918, was that the Liberals were the party which had taken Britain into a bloody war that had left scarcely a family in Britain untouched by grief, and that they were divided and doubtful at a time when Labour and the Conservatives were united and self-confident. In that sense, the war becomes once again central to interpretations of Liberal decline.

The war strengthened Labour in other ways, too. Labour gained experience in office: Henderson served in cabinet as President of the Board of Education (1915–16) and later as Paymaster-General under Asquith, and as Minister without Portfolio (1916–17) in Lloyd George's small war cabinet. Essentially, he acted in all three posts as an adviser on labour matters. When he was forced out in August 1917 he was replaced by another Labour man, Barnes. The new ministries of Labour and Pensions went to Labourites, and others served in junior posts. In a sense, the gains were not as great as they might have been, for three of the eight Labourites to serve stayed in the Coalition after Labour withdrew in 1918. Still, the significance of having Labour MPs in ministerial office for the first time can hardly be exaggerated. Labour men had shown that they could fill office, in some cases with distinction.

Labour also benefited from the expansion of trade union membership during the war. The economy was soon at full stretch to fuel the war effort: thus employers were more willing to tolerate union membership, and indeed government sometimes actively encouraged it as a way of increasing labour discipline. The inflationary pressures of the war, and constantly changing workplace conditions (or fear thereof) in many industries, encouraged workers to join unions as a defence against state and/or employer incursions on real wage levels and established working practices. The result was a massive increase in membership, with TUC membership almost doubling to 5 283 676 in 1918, and peaking at over 6 500 000 the following year.[15]

The Labour party benefited directly from this. Its trade union membership increased rapidly, by 88.3 per cent during the war and more than doubling to 2 960 409 between 1910 and 1918.[16] With the membership of affiliated socialist societies also increasing, the party was boosted to new heights. The financial implications were very favourable, and so it is not surprising that Henderson was able to contemplate major reorganization in the latter part of the war.

Furthermore, the war brought to the fore the question of the role of the state in society, in a way which was profoundly helpful to the Labour party's prospects. The state 'as threat' raised its head in a number of ways. One area, industrial conscription, has already been discussed. This was, perhaps, something of a chimera, although it had no shortage of advocates in the Conservative party. More realistic was the perceived threat to established working practices and production relations. At first, Asquith had hoped that the war could be won by 'business as usual'. Soon, however, it became clear that labour was at a premium. This led in turn to a series of measures which sought to speed up production by extending the level of state intervention in production relations. Thus, by the Treasury Agreement of March 1915, most of the major unions agreed to concessions which included the suspension of certain established working practices and the dilution of labour, whereby skilled workers' jobs would be done by semi- or unskilled workers, often women. This was followed in May by the first of a number of Munitions of War Acts which made further incursions into what had been considered hitherto to be sacred territory. There was an understanding that the changes would be temporary, but it is worth noting that legislation for the restoration of pre-war practices did not in fact come until 1919. Until then, matters were, understandably, somewhat fraught. Some employers clearly saw an opportunity to remove 'restrictive practices' for good, with the state's help.[17] This led to severe tensions both at the workplace and within the unions – particularly in engineering – where the leaders were often seen as becoming too cosy with government and employers to be reliable. At the same time that unprecedented numbers were joining the unions, therefore, there were severe doubts as to the effectiveness of the established union leadership.

This led to an upsurge in rank-and-file militancy in many areas. It is worth noting that even in the worst year, 1918, far fewer working days were lost in disputes than in the calmest pre-war year, 1913. Nevertheless, the number and scale of disputes was far greater than it was to be in the Second World War. A leading role was played in engineering by the shop stewards – ordinary workers elected to act as *de facto* union officials at workshop level. The shop stewards' movement grew especially in major munitions centres like Clydeside, Sheffield and Manchester. How far this could have been the basis for something more significant is not clear: a national committee was set up but after a peak of activity in the winter of 1917–18 it fell apart, and it must be doubted whether it could have formed the basis of a serious revolutionary movement.[18] Much of the discontent stemmed from craft exclusiveness rather than class consciousness, and some of those who appeared to be potential revolutionaries in late 1917 were probably demanding the trial of the Kaiser within a few months. Still, it seems possible that the encroachments made by the state on production relations both fuelled union recruitment and aroused working-class fears of what the state might do if in the wrong hands. In that sense, they probably helped draw support to the Labour party.

The danger of the state being in the wrong hands also played a significant part in pushing the Co-operative movement towards independent political action. Membership of the Co-ops had been increasing steadily, from 1 793 770 in 1901 to 3 054 297 in 1914; by 1919 it was to stand at 4 131 477.[19] Labourite Co-operators had tried to align the movement with the Labour party before 1914 but without success: the Co-operative movement had not been on the verge of a shift to Labour by 1914. What changed, or at least greatly speeded, matters was the war's demonstration of the state as threat. By 1917, the movement had very real, war-induced grievances. The imposition of excess profits duty on the Co-ops' trading surpluses, the feeling that essential Co-op employees were discriminated against by military service tribunals, and discrimination by the Ministry of Food – both in allocation of foodstuffs and in the exclusion of Co-op representatives from local food control committees – all caused great anger. More generally, the 'businessmen in government' air of the Lloyd George Coalition, allied to the debility of the opposition Liberals, suggested that old loyalties must be reviewed. In May 1917 the Co-operative Congress voted by 1979 votes to 201 to set up a political wing, which became known as the Co-operative Representation Committee and later, in 1919, the Co-operative party. Although a national Labour–Co-operative agreement was not concluded until 1927, the two parties were to form effective alliances in many parts of the country long before then; and the Co-operative party was to prove a source of great strength to Labour. In addition, the fact that women had most day-to-day contact with the Co-op shops meant that, however tentatively and partially, a link was made between those women and the Labour movement. Labour would be able to pose, through actions and rhetoric, as the party which protected Co-operators, and this must have been a help in the party's relationship with the new women voters after 1918. It was crucial in extending Labour's appeal further beyond the workplace and trade unionists.[20]

While showing the threats that the state could pose, however, the war also demonstrated its positive potential, and made more credible and practicable the collectivist policies with which Labour was associated. This was demonstrated in three areas in particular: housing, 'fair shares', and industry. The housing issue made itself felt over the question of rents. At this time, 90 per cent of housing was rented from private landlords. Faced with rising wartime prices, and in some cases at least seeing a chance of profiteering, landlords sought to increase rents. This led in 1915 to a series of largely spontaneous protests which were then often co-ordinated by local Labour movements, as in Glasgow, where the ILP played a leading role.[21] Ultimately the government was forced to pass legislation fixing working-class rents at pre-war levels. This was significant in that it showed that Labour, more than its rivals, was the party which would defend working-class interests in housing: as with the Co-ops later, it helped move

Labour away from union-based issues and towards areas with some direct appeal to women, in particular. It also added credibility to the idea of state action to control market forces which disadvantaged the working class.

Labour also campaigned for 'fair shares', building up a powerful rhetoric which once again attacked unrestricted market forces and profiteering. Indeed, the main significance of this may have been symbolic: there were few better images for 'fair shares' in twentieth-century Britain than that of the profiteering capitalist growing fat while the people suffered both at home and on the battlefields. The gains were not only rhetorical, though, for some advances were made through pressure on government. Labour pushed hard for high taxation of war profits, rationing, and other controls. Price control from early 1917 led to the stabilization of food prices, while rationing, which came into effect at the start of 1918, ensured a degree of 'fair play'. In taxation, the excess profits duty was imposed in 1915 and reached 80 per cent by 1917. The WEC's 'Conscription of Riches' campaign, which began in 1916, further established Labour's credentials. Since 'fair play' was one of the great traditions of British radicalism, it was clearly to Labour's advantage to push in this direction, and the fact that such policies could be implemented greatly enhanced Labour's general credibility.[22]

Collectivism also gained credibility in industry. Rail and coal were taken under state control. Although there was no intention to nationalize them permanently, this showed the miners, in particular, the potential benefits of a shift from private ownership. By the end of the war, there was a widespread feeling that state intervention in industry was, at least in part, the reason for victory.[23]

Labour also gained from its stance on foreign policy. Prior to the outbreak of war this could not have been predicted. Labour had professed to be an internationalist party, but the unions had left foreign policy largely to the 'socialists' in the party leadership, continental socialists had seen Labour as hopelessly parochial, and some members of the movement had been positively jingoistic. However, men like Hardie, MacDonald and Snowden had toed a fairly consistent line over foreign affairs before the war, criticizing the increasing division of Europe into armed camps, favouring *rapprochement* with Germany, and advocating greater openness in the conduct of foreign policy.[24] Two weeks after war broke out, MacDonald became chairman of a new body, the Union of Democratic Control (UDC), which brought together ILPers and radical Liberals critical of Grey's foreign policy. It called for an end to 'secret diplomacy', a negotiated peace, defence of free trade and national self-determination; it later campaigned against conscription. Links between the Labour and Liberal dissidents also flourished in other pressure groups formed later in the war. These bodies were not supported by the Labour party as such. But they fostered links between people who had been, and might expect to be once more, prominent in the Labour party, on the one hand, and dissenting Liberals who were becoming semi-detached from their party on the other. Many of those involved, like E. D. Morel and C. P. Trevelyan, later drifted into the ILP and ended up as Labour MPs. The UDC and analogous bodies were, therefore, a crucial conduit of middle-class radicals into the Labour party.[25]

They were also important, ultimately, in setting the Labour party's foreign policy agenda. At first, Labour in wartime was more than ever parochial in its concerns.[26] But the party conference of January 1916 set up a committee, which included MacDonald, to look at post-war issues, and the party's new-found prominence in government after December 1916 also encouraged it to think in larger terms. The March 1917 revolution in Russia caused great excitement on the British left. That June, an unofficial Labour convention in Leeds, attended by over 1000 delegates, called for a peace without annexations or indemnities. During his stay in Russia that summer, meanwhile, Henderson saw the threat posed to the nascent regime by the far left Bolsheviks.[27]

All this had two main consequences. First, Labour was pushed towards a wide-ranging statement on foreign policy. When the Bolsheviks seized power that November and published the secret treaties between the Tsarist regime and Britain (among others), new urgency was added, and a special party conference in November adopted a 'Memorandum on War Aims', which essentially accepted UDC policy, including a League of Nations.[28] The result was that many UDCers now saw Labour as the party most likely to fulfil their aims.[29]

Secondly, further urgency was added to the recasting of the Labour party constitution. This would have happened in any case, given the extension of the franchise which was now planned and the fact that the party was better resourced than ever before.

But following his expulsion from the government, Henderson was able, with Webb, to devote more time to it than might otherwise have been the case. After some wrangling, it was adopted by a party conference in February 1918. The new constitution changed the structure of, and method of election to, the NEC; permitted the establishment of constituency Labour parties (CLPs) with individual membership; and committed Labour, by Clause Four, to a form of socialism for the first time.

While many observers have focused on Clause Four, it was in fact hardly mentioned at all in the debates of the time. Its insertion seems to have been the result of a number of factors: Webb's influence; a fear that otherwise Labour, like the Russian Provisional government, might be unable to compete with the far left in the anticipated leftward swing of working-class opinion; and a desire to mark a clear line of demarcation between Labour and the Liberals. It also served to sweeten the pill for committed socialists of a constitution which gave more power than ever to the unions.[30] Its uncontroversial passage was due also to the perceived 'success' of collectivism during the war and, perhaps, to a heightened sense of animosity towards capitalism as a result of wartime profiteering. But the fact that there was little debate about Clause Four does not mean that it was unimportant. It became a touchstone of what Labour stood for. In the 1950s, the party leader, Hugh Gaitskell, would be thwarted in his attempts to get rid of it; and only in the very changed atmosphere of the 1990s would a party leader dare to raise the issue again.

The decision to establish CLPs with individual membership also aroused little real opposition, although there was some union grumbling at the prospect of middle-class recruits taking over; Labour now saw itself appealing broadly, and to garner that appeal it needed both a nationwide organization and a means whereby people who were not members of affiliated organizations (especially unions) could join it. The biggest battles, in fact, came over the composition of the NEC.

Until 1917, the NEC had comprised 16 members: the treasurer, one individual representing the trades councils, local organizations and women's organizations together, three socialist societies' representatives, and 11 union representatives. Each group nominated and elected its own representatives. But at the 1917 conference, a group of large unions had pushed through a proposal that the party conference as a whole should elect the NEC. Given the overwhelming dominance of union votes at conference, this marked a clear shift towards greater union control. Under the first draft of the 1918 constitution, the same method of election would prevail, but the composition of the NEC would change, with an increase in size to 21 members, comprising 11 trade unionists, five nominees of the local Labour parties, four women, and the treasurer.[31] Union dominance was pretty well assured, given the fact that the whole conference would be the electorate throughout. But the first party conference of 1918 rejected the proposals, and it was not until the unions were given 13 representatives – that is, greater power still – that agreement could be reached. In addition, the PLP was given a role in policy-making at election times, and stricter disciplinary measures were imposed to ensure greater obedience by Labour MPs.[32] In the light of all this, it would be facile to see the 1918 constitution as a 'socialist victory'. The hegemony of the unions was now clearer than ever; the ILP, whose main functions had been to campaign for the adoption of socialism by Labour and to provide a conduit for individual membership, was faced with an uncertain future.

A further party conference, in June 1918, adopted a new programme, *Labour and the New Social Order*, drafted by Sidney Webb. This programme committed Labour to full employment at decent wages and, failing that, a comprehensive system of benefits; nationalization of land, railways, canals, coal and electricity; taxation based on ability to pay, plus a capital levy (wealth tax) to pay off the huge national debt that had been accumulated during the war; and the use of the fruits of prosperity which would follow from all this for social reforms in housing, education, health, and so on. In many ways this was a radical programme, and can be seen to have formed the basis of Labour policy for the next thirty years. Yet, at the same time, it must be noted that it was essentially a conservative programme, aiming to preserve the extended wartime state and the increased saliency of working-class demands that the war had brought. It was, in that sense, very much a product of its time; it would soon, in fact, be massively out of date.

It was also very much a product of Webb. It viewed socialism as an agent of national efficiency. It offered bureaucratic, 'top-down' socialism. What is a little surprising is that Webb's view was so readily accepted at a time when there was debate about the nature of socialism and, in particular, whether it could be brought about by state action alone. Contemporary pluralists like Harold Laski were contesting the view that the state was anything more than one agent of social change among many. From the Labour point of view, the main critique came from the guild socialists. They had increased their strength during the war, and by 1917 the movement had grounds for optimism. Revolution in Russia seemed to presage a move to the left across the world. In Britain, the expansion of trade unionism was proceeding apace: perhaps all workers would soon be unionized. Further, the rise of the shop stewards' movement suggested that the nature of unions was changing, and augured well for participatory democracy and workers' control. And the 'threat and promise' aspects of the state's performance in wartime seemed to fit hand-in-glove with guild socialist analysis. A National Building Guild was formed, and enjoyed early success. Indeed, Webb's inclusion in 'Labour and the New Social Order' of a section entitled 'democratic control of industry' can be seen as a concession to this rising strength.[33]

Yet, in effect, the debate was stymied.[34] A powerful, cogent and still surprisingly valid critique of statism was brushed under the carpet. Of course – as has been stressed – there was, in the event, no great debate over Clause Four, and it would be difficult to sustain the argument that guild socialism could have won the day in 1918. The point was, though, that the most far-reaching and perceptive analysis of the experience of war and its implications for the future of socialism was not allowed in any meaningful sense to inform party debate. At a time when Labour could have afforded to be radical it chose to be safe, conserving and consolidating the gains made in recent years. This was entirely understandable, given the realities of power within the party. But it was also a major step on the road towards the largely unthinking statism of post-1945 Labour governments.

The war ended on 11 November. At a Labour conference three days later it was decided by 2 117 000 votes to 810 000 to leave the Coalition and fight the anticipated general election as a separate party. The minority included a number of Labour ministers; while J. R. Clynes and others abided by the decision, some, like Barnes, chose to abandon Labour rather than the government. But few followed their lead. Meanwhile, it was announced that day that a general election would be held on Saturday 14 December.

At the election, the voters faced a very unfamiliar political landscape; so did the politicians, the electorate being three times as large as in 1910. Lloyd George and the Conservatives fought as the Coalition that had won the war. It was almost inevitable that the government would do well, given the prevalence of patriotism and relief. Labour put up 361 candidates, far more than ever before, but the result was a massive victory for the Coalition. It took 473 seats with 47.1 per cent of the poll; in addition, 50 'uncouponed' Tory MPs were returned. Labour took only 57 seats and 20.8 per cent of the votes. Given the Irish republican party Sinn Fein's refusal to sit at Westminster, however, it emerged as the largest party of opposition, since the Asquithians numbered less than two dozen.

The 1918 general election was the first time Labour put up enough candidates to be considered as a player for government, at least in theory. To take a fifth of the votes cast was clearly progress: at the same time, since the turnout was very low, not many more than one in ten of eligible voters cast their votes for Labour. And to emerge with only 57 seats was worse than anyone had predicted.[35] It doubled its Scottish representation, but only from three to six; in Wales, it was helped by redistribution which gave more seats to the industrial south, and rose from five seats to nine. The position in England was disappointing: it only won eight more seats (42) than it had in December 1910. '[O]nly in the midlands did Labour win seats in distinctly new areas', and this was due in part to the decline of Lib–Labbism.[36] Labour was still to a large extent concentrated in northern England: London, in particular, was a disappointment, only three seats being won. Other than these, and a solitary victory at Wellingborough in Northamptonshire, there was not a single Labour seat south of a line between the Severn and the Wash. Its performance in mining areas was weaker than might be expected given subsequent developments: of the 50 seats with the highest proportion of miners in the male working population, only 24 went to Labour. It also fared badly in most of the big cities, taking only six out of the 87 seats available in the 12 largest provincial centres. While the party often polled well where it did not win, and clearly had avenues of further advance, the 1918 result could not fail to be seen as a disappointment.

The PLP elected in 1918 was somewhat lacklustre.[37] All 57 MPs were men, the party's four women candidates all having been defeated. Of the 57, 49 had been sponsored by trade unions. No fewer than 25 were nominees of the MFGB, which, on the whole, tended to nominate as parliamentary candidates officials who were no longer deemed of much value to the union. The General and Municipal Workers and the Textile Workers had four MPs apiece. A single Co-operator, elected for Kettering, sat with Labour. In contrast, many of Labour's brightest leaders, including MacDonald, Snowden and Henderson, were defeated. This left the party's parliamentary leadership pretty nondescript. The ex-ministers who had remained with Labour were re-elected to parliament but, Clynes aside, they made little impact. J. H. Thomas, first elected in 1910, retained his seat, but was too busy as general secretary of the NUR to consider acting as chairman of the PLP. Henderson was re-elected to parliament at a by-election in August 1919, but, as party secretary, was mainly concerned with party organization, and played little part at Westminster. Almost by default, therefore, the job went to William Adamson, a right-wing Scottish miners' leader of almost legendary dourness. By contrast, Lloyd George's government sparkled with charismatic figures like Winston Churchill, Austen Chamberlain and Lord Birkenhead. These 'supermen', elected with a massive majority and promising social reconstruction at home and pacification abroad, did not make life easy for Labour's parliamentary leadership.

However, Labour's parliamentary strength was but a pale reflection of the strength of the Labour movement as a whole in the period up to mid-1920. During that period, full employment among men was preserved on the back of a rapid comb-out of women from industry and an inflationary boom fuelled by high public expenditure. Employers and government remained, on the whole, favourably disposed towards organized labour, in order to allow the boom to continue and in fear of provoking revolution. The result was that union membership continued to grow: by 1920, almost half of the male, and a quarter of the female, workforce was unionized, a doubling of 'union density' as compared with 1913. (These figures were not to be reached again until 1946.)[38] The movement suffered few reverses in industrial disputes. Workers were strong enough to force major reductions in working hours. In January 1919 the miners threatened to strike for a six-hour day, large wage increases, and nationalization. Hastily, Lloyd George conceded a Coal Commission under Justice John Sankey, which comprised three miners, three sympathetic intellectuals, three mine-owners, and three businessmen. The Commission offered a seven-hour day, and later recommended nationalization, though only on the casting vote of the chairman. However, the resolution of the hours issue had taken some of the steam out of the pressure for nationalization, and Lloyd George was able to sidestep it without any immediate industrial conflict. Still, it was a moral victory for the miners. That September, a national railway strike secured improved wages. And early in 1920 an inquiry into dockers' wages and conditions led to the award of better pay, a shorter working week and a national agreement, largely thanks to the advocacy of Ernest Bevin, assistant secretary of the dockers' union.

All this led to demands that union power be used for political ends. The potential of this course was demonstrated in 1920. That May, London dockers refused to allow a ship to sail to Poland until all war materials intended to help the Poles in their war against Soviet Russia were removed. When, in August, the British government seemed to be moving towards direct intervention, a joint meeting of the parliamentary committee of the TUC, the PLP and the NEC warned the government that 'the whole industrial power of the organized workers [would] be used' to prevent this, and set up a Council of Action to monitor the situation.[39] Local councils of action were formed across Britain to prepare for the threatened conflict.

Ultimately, Britain did not intervene in the Russo-Polish War. This suggested that the threat of 'direct action' (as it became known) had been successful. That September, Robert Williams, secretary of the NTWF and a member of the NEC, advocated the use of direct action to force the government to call an election which, he believed, Labour would win easily. Henderson rejected this view. He told the NEC that '"direct action" propaganda . . . ha[d] been definitely harmful' to the party, 'frightening away many voters who were inclined to support Labour'. An election fought on the issue of direct action would play straight into Lloyd George's hands.[40] Meanwhile, party headquarters tried to cool down the local councils of action, which, having been formed, were in many cases itching for a fight. There seems little doubt that Henderson assessed the situation more accurately than Williams. Lloyd George had been reluctant to help the Poles anyway; at most, Labour's stand had strengthened his hand against his more feverish colleagues, like Churchill.[41]

By this time, in any case, the economic tide had turned. The government had been deliberately slowing down the economy through tax and interest rate increases and spending cuts. Export orders declined. By August 1920 the economy was moving towards 'one of the worst recessions in history', and by May 1921, unemployment would be over 22 per cent, peaking at 2.4 million.[42] The corollary of this was a massive reduction in union bargaining power. Of course, it took some time for the true gravity of the situation to sink in. In October 1920, the miners struck briefly for better pay and a reduction in the price of coal. The strike ended in a draw. It was to be the last time a major conflict did not end in defeat for the unions for many years.

Indeed, it was in the coal industry that the first major battle came. The mines had been taken under public control during the war, with benefits to the miners which included national pay bargaining and wage rates. The government now wanted to be rid of the mines, and brought forward the date for decontrol from August to 31 March 1921. It was clear that this would mean wage cuts in many areas.[43] On the day the mines were decontrolled, therefore, a lockout began. The MFGB appealed to its partners in the Triple Alliance, the railwaymen and transport workers, for support, and it was agreed that they would commence sympathetic strike action on 16 April. However, the leaders of the NUR and NTWF were not over-eager for the fray: there was some feeling that the miners were keener to receive help than to offer it, and both Thomas and Williams realized that strike action in the current economic climate might well damage their own members' interests. When it emerged that the MFGB executive was split, the NUR and NTWF called off their proposed action. In so doing, Thomas earned the undying hatred of many miners, trade unionists and socialists, while Williams was expelled from the recently formed Communist party. In the annals of Labour history, 15 April 1921 went down as 'Black Friday'. It is difficult to see what else the railwaymen and transport workers could have done, but the result was a lengthy lockout which only ended when the miners were forced back to work on the owners' terms. Two direct results of the débâcle were the abolition of the old parliamentary committee of the TUC and its replacement by a larger and more powerful general council, and the establishment, in 1922, of the Transport and General Workers' Union (TGWU) under Bevin, which aimed to be better organized and disciplined than the old Federation. But there was no quick end to the setbacks: in 1922, a lengthy lockout in engineering resulted in the defeat of the engineers, one of the strongest and, in recent times, one of the most militant unions.

The collapse of industrial militancy, and the associated collapse of the guild socialist movement, meant that attention returned to parliamentary methods. Here, Labour's performances improved a little from February 1921 when Clynes took over as chairman from Adamson. Matters might have improved further had MacDonald been able to return to Westminster, but when he stood as Labour's candidate in Crooks's old seat of East Woolwich in March 1921, he faced a ferocious campaign from the Coalition candidate, who attacked his war record, and attacks from the Communists, and he was defeated by a narrow margin.

Meanwhile, the party organization had been developing steadily. Standing sub-committees on organization and elections, policy and programme, research and publicity, and finance and general purposes had been established. In January 1922 three joint party–TUC departments (research and information, international affairs, and press and publicity) came into being. The new national agent, Egerton Wake, proved more effective than his predecessor, and Labour had 133 full-time constituency agents by 1922. The number of CLPs increased impressively, from 400 in 1919 to 527 in 1922. By 1924, only 19 British territorial constituencies would lack a party.[44]

It was not all good news. Although some of the constituency women's sections, in particular, did recruit large numbers, individual membership as a whole was disappointing, and in some places probably non-existent.[45] Where there were no strong trade unions to pay the constituency party's way, parliamentary candidatures were often open to the highest bidder who could show at least a semblance of commitment to the party.[46] In rural areas, Labour was often pitifully weak: if anything it became weaker during the 1920s, following the collapse of agricultural trade unionism in the early part of the decade. Attempts to develop a powerful Labour press at national and local level met with, at best, mixed results, and would continue to do so until the spectacular success of the relaunched *Daily Herald* as a partnership between the TUC and a commercial publisher in 1930.[47] Furthermore, the recession meant that union-affiliated membership of the party fell by about a quarter between 1920 and 1922. While the potentially adverse results of this were offset by increases in affiliation fees, such increases could not go on indefinitely, and the optimism that had characterized the period since 1917 was qualified, at least.[48]

The increasingly illiberal record of the Coalition, on the other hand, was a godsend to Labour. While Clause Four had marked off a line of demarcation between Labour and the Liberals as parties, Labour's instinctive adherence to many of the precepts of liberal or radical politics meant that it was able to draw in the support of many more anti-Conservative voters than hitherto. In foreign policy, Labour emerged gradually as a critic of the perceivedly harsh peace imposed on Germany at Versailles. It also attacked the adventurism which seemed to threaten new conflicts and entanglements, like intervention in Russia and the support for Greece which almost brought Britain and Turkey into conflict at Chanak in 1922. While Labour could hardly be described as a consistently anti-imperialist party, its criticisms of incidents such as the 1919 Amritsar Massacre in India established it in the mainstream of British radicalism. Labour emerged as the major critic of the government's increasingly brutal attempts to suppress the Irish rebellion. And, as the government intruded on free trade with measures like 'safeguarding' and the continuation of the wartime tariffs, Labour established its credentials as a defender of one of the canons of the radical tradition. In addition, its attacks on the traffic in honours pursued by the government and its agents set it firmly on the side of 'clean government'. In all these ways, then, Labour was laying claim, with some success, to core Liberal issues, while its advocacy of social reform, increasingly abandoned by the Lloyd George government from 1920 onwards, meant that it was able to consolidate support among groups which felt the promises of 1918 were being betrayed. Although Clause Four had closed off most possibilities of institutional links with the Liberal party, therefore, the Labour party was continuing to employ a radical rhetoric with considerable resonance in the British political tradition at the same time that it was addressing newly salient issues like housing and unemployment. Increasingly, Labour was able to pose as the champion of public sector housing (construction of which had started in earnest in 1919) and of full employment. The issue of mines nationalization also gave Labour increased purchase among the miners, who were to be staunch Labour supporters from 1922 onwards. Finally, the government's decision in 1920 to extend unemployment insurance to virtually all manual workers meant that, for the first time, there were actual figures of the number of unemployed. This enabled Labour to speak with authority about the 'victims of capitalism' and, since the number of unemployed did not fall below one million for the rest of the decade and beyond, allowed it a key piece of rhetoric.

By-elections and local government polls were also encouraging. Most by-elections were fought, a significant development in itself; the party lost only one seat (East Woolwich) and gained 14. The 1919 local elections saw substantial gains: Labour took control of three counties (Durham, Glamorgan and Monmouthshire) and greatly increased its representation on borough councils nationwide. In London, it increased its representation on the county council from one to 15 in March 1919, and on the borough councils from 46 to 572 that November. A rather flat performance in 1920 was followed by further gains in 1921, when Labour took control of Falkirk, its first major authority in Scotland. The auguries for the next general election, then, seemed bright.

The general election came in November 1922, following the withdrawal of Conservative support from the Lloyd George Coalition. Andrew Bonar Law, who had retired as Conservative leader on health grounds the previous year, resumed his post and replaced Lloyd George as premier. Having dealt with the tricky question of protection by pledging that there would be no general interference with free trade prior to a further election, Law could be confident of victory, and in the event his party took 345 seats, and an overall majority of over 70, although with only 38.5 per cent of the votes cast. The Asquithians took 62 seats, and the followers of Lloyd George 53. The real sensation, though, was Labour's performance. Fielding 414 candidates, it took 29.3 per cent of the votes and emerged with 142 seats. MacDonald and Snowden both returned to parliament, and at the first meeting of the new PLP MacDonald challenged, and narrowly defeated, Clynes to be elected 'leader' of the party. For the first time it could be argued plausibly that Labour was clearly the second party in the state, with a leader who looked like a potential Prime Minister.

The true scale of the transformation could only be recognized when people looked back across the turmoil of 'peace' and the battlefields of war to the Labour party of 1914. Then, it had been little more than a trade-union pressure group with pretensions, not a serious candidate for power. Lurking in the shadow of the Liberals, it had been marginalized by the salient issues of politics, about which it had had little distinctive to say, and had been in considerable doubt about where its future lay. By 1922, it had asserted its independence, was clearly the opposition to the Conservatives, had asserted the primacy of parliamentary over other methods of achieving change, and felt comfortable with and had credibility on the salient political issues. It might very well be that, war or no war, the Liberals would eventually have been supplanted: Britain was by no means alone in enjoying a Liberal party in serious decline at this time. That the transformation had come about as it had, and at the pace that it had, and that it had benefited the particular type of party that Labour had become by 1918 (and still more, 1922), however, was largely due to the impact and legacy of the First World War.

3

Progress and Collapse, 1922–31

Labour now entered a period of considerable achievement but also one which ended, ultimately, in defeat and demoralization. The 1922 election result more than made up for the disappointment of 1918. MacDonald's return to the head of the party brought back to the fore the most charismatic leader the party has ever possessed. The collapse of industrial militancy seemed to leave the field clear for a moderate parliamentary socialism, meshed with a labourist conception of trade unionism, which seemed to augur well for the kind of party that the leadership wanted. The party still had a programme of sorts, and could still claim that if only it were given office it would be able to make a significant advance towards a better society.

For all its progress at the 1922 election, Labour was still a long way from a parliamentary majority. It had won only 142 seats, and polled 29.7 per cent of the votes cast. This vote, further, was concentrated heavily in certain regions and localities. The mining areas were now fairly solid for Labour: of the 50 seats with the heaviest concentration of miners, 44 were now held by the party. On the other hand, only eight of the 20 seats most dominated by textiles returned Labour MPs. The working-class areas of many major cities went to Labour: there were especially striking gains in Glasgow, where Labour took 10 of the 15 seats as opposed to only one in 1918. But elsewhere it failed to break through, winning no seats in Birmingham, Liverpool, Bristol, Hull, or Cardiff, and only nine of the 62 in London. Labour won virtually no seats with a substantial middle-class electorate, and in rural areas their performance was lamentable: of the 150 seats in Britain which had at least 15 per cent of their adult male population working in agriculture, Labour won only five. Labour was a party based on the votes of the urban working class in certain towns and cities, plus the miners and a handful of others.[1] While all this meant that Labour had a solid base, it was still a long

55

way from 'replacing' the old Liberal coalition as a credible anti-Conservative force. It was not even a 'class party': it was instead the party of a section of the working class, with a limited ability to appeal even to further members of the working class.

MacDonald and his colleagues recognized these problems, and sought to overcome them. Three main areas were targeted: the middle class; the remainder of the industrial working class which was so far impervious to Labour's appeal; and the agricultural community. Labour would need to gain significant sections of all three if it was to emulate the old Liberal coalition. To achieve this, organization would be improved, especially in the rural areas; emphasis would be laid on the party's 'national' as opposed to 'class' image; and Labour would proceed cautiously, trying to impress doubters – not least in the working class – of its respectability and fitness to rule.

In the immediate aftermath of the 1922 election there had seemed no reason to think that the Law government would not survive until the middle of the decade. However, the death of Law in May 1923 changed matters. He was succeeded as premier by the Chancellor of the Exchequer, Stanley Baldwin. Like the Labour leadership, Baldwin was keen to marginalize the Liberals and establish an uncomplicated, two-party fight between left and right. He was also keen to accommodate Labour within the constitution and, as a much less abrasive and partisan figure than Law, strengthened Labour moderates' position by discrediting ideas of a polarization of politics.[2]

Inadvertently, Baldwin soon helped Labour. In a speech at Plymouth in October 1923 he came out for protection as the solution to continuing high unemployment. Since Law had pledged in 1922 that tariffs would not be introduced, this meant a dissolution of parliament. For Labour, the move was a godsend. For one thing, it allowed the party to fight for the defence of free trade, which remained popular, at least in urban areas and in areas dependent on cheap imports, such as the Lancashire cotton belt, and international trade, such as port towns. The chance to fight a fairly negative campaign against tariffs also meant that Labour could·play down the more controversial elements of the 1918 programme, like the capital levy and nationalization.[3]

The result of the election was confusing. The Conservatives remained the largest party, but lost almost 100 seats, emerging with 258 MPs. The Liberals, who had reunited in defence of free trade, emerged with 159 members; Labour won 191 seats. Webb had spoken at that year's party conference of the 'inevitability of gradualness', and that prediction seemed to be borne out by this progress.[4] However, the respective poll shares of the parties had not changed massively. Labour edged up from 29.7 to 30.7 per cent; the Liberals rose from 28.8 to 29.7; and the Conservatives fell from 38.5 to 38.0 per cent. In other words, Labour had made little advance, in voting terms, on its performance in the previous year. It remained very much a party of the mining areas plus many – but not all – working-class urban areas. Though it made significant gains in London, winning 22 seats as opposed to nine in 1922, it still won no seats in Birmingham and only managed one in Liverpool. Only one in five eligible voters had voted for the party.

Baldwin did not resign immediately. Instead, he presented a protectionist King's Speech to the House in January 1924, was defeated, and advised the King to send for MacDonald. The latter had spent the time since the election planning strategy and deciding who should be in his cabinet. That it should be *his* cabinet, he was in no doubt. He was determined to act just like any other Prime Minister, to show that he – and his party – were 'fit to govern'. Hence, too, when he and his ministers arrived at Buckingham Palace to be sworn in, they wore court dress. This made them look ridiculous, and worse, to many Labourites and others on the left, but the main motive was to avoid empty gestures which would only alienate potential support, not least among working-class voters.[5]

MacDonald's 20-strong cabinet included seven trade unionists, three of them miners, plus one each from the textile workers, ironfounders, railwaymen and the General and Municipal Workers. Only two of the ILPers in the cabinet (John Wheatley and Fred Jowett) could be described as left-wingers. Webb and Lord Olivier represented Fabianism. Seven members of the cabinet had not been in the Labour party in 1914. Five had been Liberals, who had come to the Labour party via the UDC; two had been Conservatives, and one of those, Lord Chelmsford (who became First Lord of the Admiralty) still was. The cabinet was dominated by the 'Big Five': MacDonald, who doubled as Foreign Secretary; Snowden, seen as Labour's leading financial expert, who became Chancellor of the Exchequer; Henderson, who became Home Secretary despite MacDonald's efforts to keep him out on the grounds that, as party secretary, he would be of greater value preparing for the next general election;[6] Thomas, who became Secretary of State for the Colonies; and Clynes, the party's deputy leader, who was made Lord Privy Seal and appointed to lead the House of Commons in order to relieve some of the pressure from MacDonald. The cabinet did not represent all sections of the movement. Even from a cynically electoral viewpoint it was probably a mistake not to include a woman or a Co-operator. The left was clearly under-represented. And there was a skewing of trade union representation towards the old staple industries.

There was no attempt to form a coalition with the Liberals. Labour wanted to compromise, and so destroy, the Liberal party; in any case, the Liberals were so afraid of a further general election that they had no alternative, for the time being, but to give general support to the government.[7] Other possible strategies were also ruled out. Some Labourites wanted the government to announce a radical socialist programme, be defeated in the Commons, and then call another election at which, it was believed, the party would win a majority for 'socialism', or at least lay down a marker around which socialists could subsequently muster.[8] This was rejected out of hand by the party leadership, which believed, with reason, that it would simply alienate voters. In any case, it would have been a fight for an undefined vision of 'socialism': electors wanting to know what a nationalized industry would look like, for example, would have found that Labour had few concrete plans.

That the first Labour government did not achieve much in policy terms was not surprising, given its parliamentary position, whereby the Liberals only had to abstain to allow the Conservatives to defeat it. Benefits were liberalized somewhat, and expenditure on education increased. Wheatley, as Minister of Health, introduced a Housing Act which gave state subsidies to local authorities to build houses for rent, a major achievement which improved the lot of many working-class families over the next few years. Also significant in this field was legislation to protect tenants from eviction, a major issue since rents became 'decontrolled' once a change of tenancy took place. And, in foreign affairs, there was a general reduction of international tension, a revision of German reparations payments under the Dawes Plan, and progress towards giving the League of Nations some teeth in the negotiations for the Geneva Protocol (although the last fell with the government, and it was an open question whether, in the light of MacDonald's ambivalence towards the League, even a Labour government would have pushed it forward).

All these things earned some credit with the wider Labour movement. There was more criticism, though, in other areas. The government backed a private members' bill to nationalize the coal industry, but it made little progress and fell with the government. Other sectors of the economy identified specifically in *Labour and the New Social Order* did not even get that far. Legislation to improve agricultural labourers' wages remained something of a dead letter. No attempt was made to dismantle emergency powers apparatus for dealing with strikes, and indeed the government itself prepared to use this against threatened transport and docks strikes. Finally, there was no radical attempt to deal with continuing high levels of unemployment, which remained at over one million.

Instead, the government, believing that socialism would emerge from a vibrant, successful capitalism, aimed to restore capitalism to health. The way to do this, it was felt, was to return to the pre-war guarantors of prosperity: free trade, the gold standard and a balanced budget, while setting taxation at levels which would not impair industrial efficiency. Therefore, since budgets were now showing a good surplus, Snowden cut tariffs and taxation. He also continued previous governments' policies of aiming to return to the gold standard in 1925. All this undoubtedly suggests that he was somewhat backward-looking, but most people still believed in such a strategy, and Snowden believed sincerely that it would advance progress towards socialism. Finally, since British prosperity was believed to depend upon world prosperity and trade, Labour saw foreign policy as central to the restoration of Britain's economic fortunes.[9]

One aspect of this economic internationalism was the improvement of relations with Soviet Russia, but ultimately this was to be the government's undoing. Over the summer there were negotiations for a treaty and a trade agreement, which aroused widespread unease, even among some Labourites. In particular, Liberal qualms about continuing to support the government grew. At the same time, an article by J. R. Campbell in the Communist *Workers' Weekly*, calling on troops not to fire on strikers, led to a hasty decision to prosecute him under the Incitement to Disaffection Act. When, following wider consultations, the cabinet withdrew the prosecution, Labour's opponents claimed that the decision had been taken as a result of far-left pressure on the Labour leadership. In October, MacDonald treated a Liberal motion for the appointment of a committee of inquiry as a matter of confidence. When it was passed, the government resigned and called a general election. In fact, this was merely a pretext. The government had done all that it could. MacDonald himself was worn down by a heavy workload, and demoralized by the allegations of corruption that had surrounded the conferring of a baronetcy on Alexander Grant, his longtime friend and recent benefactor. This was as good a time as any to bow out.[10]

A bitter election campaign followed. Labour was attacked for being a Communist party in disguise, and Labourites had to try to deal with the accusation that they were conscious agents or unconscious dupes of the extreme left. Scandal and sensation, though, were reserved for the last few days of the campaign, after the *Daily Mail* published a document which was said to be from the Executive Committee of the Communist International, advising British Communists to prepare for revolution. Whether genuine or not, the so-called 'Zinoviev Letter' was not the cause of Labour's electoral defeat.[11] The party had been in no position, and had not seriously expected, to win the election even before the letter was published. In the event, Labour lost over 40 seats to emerge with 151 MPs, as against the Conservatives' 412. Even so, the result was, in some ways, a good one for Labour. First, the 1924 government had shown that Labour could run the country, and made a future bid for office more credible, since the party's leaders now had ministerial experience. Secondly, the Zinoviev Letter episode allowed Labour's leaders to deceive many of their followers into believing that the electoral reverse had been based, not on the shortcomings of Labour's performance in office or its unacceptably narrow electoral base, but on the tricks and deceit of the Conservatives and the 'Establishment'. In other words, a 'fair' fight would see 'the inevitability of gradualness' reassert itself. Thirdly, and most importantly, the Liberals had apparently collapsed, losing over 100 seats to emerge with only 40 MPs, their poll share falling from 29.7 to 17.8 per cent. Conversely, Labour's poll share actually increased from 30.7 to 33.3 per cent. In so far as the 'Red Scare' had any electoral impact, it seems it had forced Liberal voters to choose between Labour and Conservative; and while most had gone Conservative this time, there was no reason that they should not go Labour next.

But there were more worrying signs, too. Some leading ministers had performed indifferently. MacDonald's own record gave cause for concern: he had tired easily, shown poor judgement, and been rather aloof and difficult with colleagues.[12] Secondly, the party's weakness on policy had emerged. Such distinctive policies as it had, such as the capital levy or nationalization, had been virtually ignored, and there was no sign that even with a majority it would have been much bolder. Despite the stress on the belief that prospering capitalist industry would be the motor force of the transition to socialism, there was a virtual void in terms of industrial policy, while the failure to come up with any kind of policy on unemployment suggested something of a vacuum beneath the rhetoric about the iniquities of capitalism.[13]

Ever since the 1920s, the Labour party has entered a period of recriminations once it has lost office, but this only happened to a limited extent in the aftermath of 1924. There were attempts at the 1925 party conference, led by Bevin, to ensure that Labour never again took office without a majority, but these were beaten off.[14] There were also tentative moves, in which Bevin was once more involved, to replace MacDonald as party leader. But, given Henderson's continuing support for MacDonald, there was no viable alternative.[15]

Indeed, the main theme of the period after 1924 was the increasing stranglehold that the MacDonald–Henderson–Snowden regime had over the party. The process was not, however, a smooth one. At first, the unions were a source of concern. They had welcomed the first Labour government, but hoped-for legislation on hours and conditions had not been forthcoming, and the apparent readiness of the government to use anti-union emergency powers machinery to smash strikes had increased tensions. Then, in 1925, the question of 'direct action' re-emerged. That July, the coal owners, forced to charge higher prices for their exports as a result of Britain's return to the gold standard in April, proposed cuts in miners' wages. The TUC threatened an embargo on the transportation of coal, and on 31 July ('Red Friday') the Conservative government announced a nine-month subsidy to maintain wages at their present level. This simply led to over-confidence. When the subsidy ended in May 1926, and the owners locked out the miners until they agreed to work at lower wages, the unions miscalculated and called a general strike. They believed that Red Friday had shown that the government could be forced into supporting the level of miners' wages. In fact, the government was determined not to repeat the experiment, and had used the nine months to prepare for such a strike. Accordingly, when the strike began on 4 May, it was met with firm government resistance, and the TUC was forced into unconditional surrender after nine days.

The Labour party leadership looked on with growing, but largely silent, horror as the events of the General Strike unfolded. So far as it was concerned, the strike was an unmitigated disaster, threatening Labour's claim to be a constitutional party. The strike marked a low point in union–party communications – the misgivings of the party leadership were simply ignored.[16] This seemed to confirm a new distance in relations which had been suggested by the TUC's decision to withdraw from the joint departments with the Labour party in 1925.[17] A major result of the strike, the Trade Disputes Act of 1927, replaced 'contracting out' of the political levy (as established by the 1913 Act) with 'contracting in'. This was a significant threat to Labour, because whereas under the 1913 Act the apathetic worker had been deemed to wish to pay the levy and so paid it, under the 1927 legislation he or she was deemed *not* to wish to do so, and so did not. Labour tried to arouse nationwide opposition to the legislation, but its protest campaign flopped and the party had to face a significant fall in income.[18]

Ultimately, these events helped to accelerate Labour's rightward drift. They seemed finally to discredit the idea that direct action could have significant bonuses denied to patient electoral effort. They also pushed the unions, at least at the level of the TUC general council, towards a more compromising stance *vis-à-vis* employers: industrial gradualism came to complement political gradualism.

The organizational consolidation which characterized this period also represented a growth in the control the leadership exerted over the rest of the party. Constituency Labour parties were now a feature of almost all areas of Britain. However, with notable exceptions (like Woolwich and Derby), individual membership was usually low, and active membership lower still. In many places CLPs were dominated by single unions or cliques; some CLPs were so financially embarrassed that they were forced to select candidates who could finance their own election campaigns, which sat ill with Labour's democratic protestations.[19] The emphasis on organization emanating from headquarters meant that debate on policy was not encouraged. Even the annual party conference became more and more pliant as the decade progressed.

Closely linked to this was a continuing, and intensifying, marginalization of dissent. This was particularly the case with Communists and with women. The Communist party of Great Britain (CPGB) had been formed in 1920, and had applied for affiliation to the Labour party. That application, and another in 1921, had been rejected, but the Communists were difficult to shake off. A 1922 conference decision to bar Communists as delegates to party conference remained a dead letter, and 38 Communists attended the 1923 conference.[20] At the 1922 election a CPGB member, Shapurji Saklatvala, was elected as Labour MP for North Battersea. However, the screw tightened. Some CLPs began to expel Communists unilaterally, and such actions were endorsed by the NEC in October 1923. Following the Campbell Case, the 1924 conference decided that Communists were not eligible to be either candidates for or individual members of the Labour party. Relations deteriorated further during and after the General Strike, and in 1928 Communists were barred from attending Labour's party conference as trade union delegates. Meanwhile, Labour headquarters had begun to disband CLPs which refused to expel Communists or showed signs of Communist leanings, reconstituting them under keen anti-Communists. Between 1926 and 1928 this happened to no fewer than 26 constituency or borough Labour parties, 15 of them in London.[21] The Communists attempted to work through the disbanded parties via the National Left Wing Movement, set up in September 1926, but its successes, such as they were, were fleeting ones, and by 1928 it was in steep decline. Further attempts to promote the united front, most notably the involvement of some Communists in the Cook-Maxton campaign of 1928 (see below), failed. The move to 'class against class', whereby the Communists came out strongly against Labour, was, in some ways, the logical end of the dispute. It also meant that, for a time, the issue of Labour–Communist relations could be largely ignored by the Labour party.

The other section of the Labour movement to be consciously marginalized was the women's movement. Before 1914, radical feminism had played a part in Labour politics. The 1912 by-election agreement between Labour and the NUWSS has already been noted. In 1918, the party constitution had provided for separate women's representation on the NEC, the formation of women's sections in the CLPs, and an annual women's conference. All this had led to high expectations among women, but their hopes were soon disappointed. Attempts to achieve a higher status for the women's conference were repeatedly rejected by the NEC, and calls for the women members of the NEC to be elected by women, rather than by the party conference as a whole, were similarly unsuccessful. Issues like birth control were swept under the carpet, despite strong support from the women in the party, partly for fear of alienating voters, especially the Catholics who had begun to come over to Labour in large numbers after the collapse of the Liberal party and the resolution of the Irish question. Women continued to play an important role in the party, especially at the grassroots, but overall the party slid away from too overt a link with 'women's issues'.[22]

More broadly, the later 1920s saw a degree of ideological stagnation. The 1910s had been a decade of considerable debate about the future of socialism. Yet most of the alternatives to statism had lost steam by 1922, and Labour intellectuals, like Cole, Laski and R. H. Tawney, moved into a period of confusion and reassessment, trying to come to terms with the apparent failure of their pet schemes. Increasingly, such intellectuals could only play a significant role if they accepted and co-operated with the leadership's outlook. Thus they were drawn into mainstream Labour politics, but more for appearance's sake than for any distinctive contribution they could make. On the one hand, they felt that they could do more within the party than outside it, and preferred a little inside influence to crying in the wilderness; on the other, they seem to have been impressed with Labour's progress and came to believe (or convinced themselves) that MacDonald's strategy might be successful.

In policy, Labour moved away from specifics. *Labour and the New Social Order* was massively out of date by the mid-1920s. It had been the product of a confident party, issued in a context of relative prosperity, at a time when government was big and when it did not seem outlandish to prioritize working-class demands. What had happened since then, of course, had served to vitiate that programme. The agenda of government had been changed:

inflation was seen as a bigger threat than unemployment by governments from 1920 onwards. High levels of unemployment and disappointing industrial performance were held to rule out some of Labour's most radical and distinctive policies, such as the capital levy.[23] At the same time, some things had not changed enough for Labour to feel able to put forward a radical alternative. Thus it was still possible to argue that, if only international problems, like tariffs and war debts and reparations, could be solved, prosperity would return. Thus Labour moved towards a set of policies which sought minimal short-term change at home alongside 'pacification' abroad. The result was the 1928 programme, *Labour and the Nation*. This took almost a year to produce, and it was, in many ways, more comprehensive than *Labour and the New Social Order*. But its very comprehensiveness was its downfall. It was significant that at the 1928 conference Wheatley (who undoubtedly opposed it for other reasons) chose in his speech to attack the lack of prioritization and specificity of the proposals. As he said, what was needed was not a list of ideal policies to be implemented over fifty or a hundred years, but a hard-nosed choice of policies which would be implemented by a single Labour government in a five-year term.[24] This hit the nail on the head: as Tawney, its chief draughtsman, was later to write, it was 'a glittering forest of Christmas trees, with presents for everyone'.[25] Its vagueness was to be part of the reason why the second Labour government fared so badly.

So why was it adopted? A number of reasons can be identified. First, there was the need to appeal to the 'centre-ground' of British politics, since it was clear that Labour needed to pick up more votes than it had ever done before if it was to win a majority, or even be the largest party in parliament. Secondly, the Labour movement was too fractious to permit a more concrete appeal. A ruthless delineation of a plan for five years in office would, inevitably, have led to discontent and dissension. Thirdly, it seems possible that Labour's leaders did not expect, seriously, to win the next election.[26] The Conservatives did not fare well at by-elections throughout the 1924 parliament, but the swings were not so heavy as to presage electoral disaster: they needed, after all, to lose around 100 seats just to be deprived of a majority at the next election. The Liberals were also reviving from 1926 onwards with the help of Lloyd George's leadership and money, to the extent that some leading Labourites, including

Snowden, began to wonder whether some Lib–Lab pact might be necessary.[27] It is also worth bearing in mind that the really heavy tide of Conservative reverses only began in 1928, when the parameters for *Labour and the Nation* had already been set. Had it begun earlier, it is just possible that Labour might have adopted a clearer programme in the keener expectation of victory.

But while all these considerations bore some weight, it is clear that a vague programme suited the party leadership. MacDonald was by now firmly established as leader: but he was also much more than that. His was the prevailing voice in the Labour party by 1927, in a way that was emulated by no other leader before Kinnock. MacDonald was seen by one foreign observer at the time as 'the focus of the mute hopes of a whole class'.[28] His view of socialism had always been a consensual one, aiming to break down barriers, not to set them up; and part of this was convincing people that Labour, while envisaging, ultimately, a society that would be very different from the present one, would not make sudden radical changes.

Not everyone was prepared to bite his or her tongue, however. The ILP, long seen as the intellectual wing of the Labour party, had been somewhat uncertain of its role since 1918. But in the mid-1920s, a section of the party began to emerge as the most significant dissentient group within the Labour party. In 1926, the ILP elected the Glasgow left-winger James Maxton as its chairman and adopted the radical 'Living Wage' policy. Based on an under-consumptionist analysis, it called for a high-wage economy, in which firms failing to pay the state-set standard would be nationalized. Although there were many different views within the ILP as to what this would mean in practice, it was a useful contribution to a wider debate. However, the proposals were easily defeated at Labour's 1927 conference. The fact that the ILP refused to nominate MacDonald for the Labour treasurer-ship that year, and the increasingly radical rhetoric of Maxton, Wheatley and others, however, played into the Labour leadership's hands, and the brief and unsuccessful Cook–Maxton campaign of 1928 completed the process. Cook–Maxton was not an official ILP campaign. Its manifesto was drafted by a number of ILP leaders, most notably Maxton and Wheatley, the MFGB secretary, A. J. Cook, and a number of leading Communists. The manifesto called for an end to compromise and the launching of a new period of class struggle. But the campaign was a dismal failure.[29] Ultimately, it helped no one more than the Labour leadership, which has always found it difficult to deal with open debate on policy and ideology, and has been happiest when using the labourist ethos of loyalty to majority decisions and the leadership to slap down the 'disloyalty' of 'a party within a party'. Thus anathematized, the campaign had no chance of success in the Labour party as a whole. The ILP's doings could be condemned *en bloc* and the Labour leadership's prestige was concomitantly enhanced.

By the time of the next general election, therefore, the hold of the leadership over the Labour party was very tight indeed. By then, too, the government had been running out of steam for some time. In the spring of 1929 Baldwin called an election, basing his appeal on the record of his government: in a conscious attempt to play on fears about 'socialism' and the Liberals' radical programme, the Tories fought on the slogan 'Safety First'. However, when the results were declared, Labour had 287 seats to the Conservatives' 260, with the Liberals taking 59. Ostensibly, Labour had made significant gains, and seemed well on the way towards becoming a 'national' party in its appeal. Only in East Anglia did it gain fewer seats than in 1923, thanks to a Liberal revival based on a farming policy which seemed well suited to the area. In every other region of the country it had never done better in terms of seats gained, doubling its representation in London, the Midlands and Lancashire, for example. Even erstwhile deserts showed significant improvements, with Labour taking six of the 12 seats in Birmingham and four of the 11 in Liverpool. Baldwin, refusing to negotiate with Lloyd George for Liberal support, resigned immediately, and left MacDonald to form his second minority administration.

Understandably, many Labourites were ecstatic. However, the results were not as good as they looked at first sight. The Conservatives had actually gained more votes than Labour (38.1 to 37.1 per cent), but the latter's greater concentration of support in certain areas meant that it took more seats. In addition, 1929 was the first election, and the last until February 1974, at which all three parties put up over 500 candidates. The result of this was that 123 Labour MPs were elected with less than 50 per cent of the votes in their constituencies. This might not have mattered had it looked likely that the Liberals would again put up a large number of candidates, but this was not going to happen

– Lloyd George was soon to withdraw most of his financial subsidies to the party organization. A reduction in the number of
Liberal candidates – a certainty – and even a small swing of
support towards the Conservatives – always likely, and absolutely certain from early 1930 onwards – would be enough to
reduce Labour to around 200 seats at the next election.[30]

In forming his government, MacDonald experienced one major setback: he was unable to put Thomas into the Foreign Office once Henderson pushed his own claim, and Thomas became
Lord Privy Seal in charge of employment schemes.[31] Although
this was not a very promising start, the rest of the cabinet did
not pose such difficulties. Snowden, still a popular figure, returned to the Treasury. Clynes became a fairly undistinguished
Home Secretary. Seven other members of the 1924 cabinet returned, and there were seven new faces. The veteran George
Lansbury came in as First Commissioner of Works, as a sop to
the left and to represent London in an otherwise heavily non-
metropolitan team. Margaret Bondfield became the first woman
cabinet member, as Minister of Labour. Sankey, darling of the
miners on the strength of the 1919 coal commission, became Lord
Chancellor. Younger men included William Wedgwood Benn, a
former Liberal who had only joined Labour in 1927, Arthur Greenwood, A. V. Alexander (the Co-operative party's leading MP),
and William Graham (at 42 the youngest member of the cabinet)
who as President of the Board of Trade would be one of the few
people to emerge from the government with an enhanced reputation. This was by no means a bad team, and in so far as it
included a woman and a Co-operator it was rather more representative than the 1924 cabinet. But the average age of ministers
was higher than that of the outgoing cabinet (which itself had
been criticized for its ageing appearance); promising younger
people, like Morrison, Sir Oswald Mosley, and Hugh Dalton, were
not included; and it was even more right-wing than the cabinet
appointed in 1924.

There was no attempt to bring in the Liberals: given Baldwin's
refusal to negotiate with Lloyd George, and the Liberals' terror
of an early election, they were forced, willy-nilly, into giving
general support to the government. This meant that Labour's
parliamentary position was reasonably secure. Although there
were periodic crises, as over the Coal Mines Bill in late 1929 and
early 1930, even when Lloyd George threatened to withdraw

Liberal support, enough Liberal MPs were usually prepared to back the government to allow it to survive. Closer links were to be established following the resignation of Mosley from the government in May 1930, and during the 1930–1 parliamentary session there was a loose agreement that the Liberals would keep the government in office so long as it carried forward electoral reform legislation.[32]

The government enjoyed early minor successes, particularly in foreign policy, but it was soon overshadowed by economic crisis and rising unemployment. In October 1929 the Wall Street Crash compounded a downturn in American industrial production to produce a worldwide slump. In Britain, unemployment, which had stood at 1.1 million when Labour had taken office, passed 1.5 million in January 1930 and then rose every month that year, to reach 2.7 million by the year's end. After that it levelled off a little, but even so the figure of almost 2.8 million in July 1931 was disastrous. In the face of this, MacDonald and his colleagues had little to offer, since they had always believed that socialism would emerge from a capitalism which was vibrant and bound to expand.

The government did try to solve the problem, but to little effect. It attempted to secure international pacification. It promoted attempts to revise reparations payments (enjoying some success with the Young Plan of late 1929), and to sort out other intergovernmental debts (where less progress was made). It achieved a limited degree of naval disarmament in 1930. And, in May 1931, the League of Nations, encouraged assiduously by Henderson, finally agreed to convene a world disarmament conference for February 1932 (with Henderson as its president).[33] It also aimed to negotiate a tariff truce at Geneva, although this was less successful, the short-term agreement eventually secured by Graham in late 1930 covering only a few, generally minor, nations.

Labour also sought to encourage the rationalization of industry: that is, the reduction of excess capacity and the consolidation and unification of enterprises in the staple industrial sector. The government was keen not to intervene too far, however, and the bulk of the process was left to industry itself and to the Bankers' Industrial Development Corporation, set up by the Bank of England. Although some schemes were carried out, the results were not startling, and their main short-term effect was to increase unemployment by throwing out 'excess' labour. The government's room for manoeuvre was limited, not just by what it was then deemed permissible for governments to do in terms of intervention in industry, but also by the fact that trade unionism was especially concentrated in the staple industries and the government could not seriously go against the interests of the unions involved, especially at a time when the party was struggling for financial survival and so very dependent on union goodwill.[34]

Attempts were also made to improve the quality of information available to government. This was done both informally, through consultations with business people and, to a much lesser extent, trade unions, but also in a formal way through the Economic Advisory Council, set up in February 1930. It was hoped that the EAC, which included representatives of business, unions and academia, would advise ministers on solutions for Britain's economic ills. In fact, it was too unwieldy a body to be effective, and the lack of a firm lead from government meant its discussions were usually too diffuse to be of value. In reality, the time for such a generalized body had been when Labour was in opposition. But its existence then seems not to have been considered; besides, it might have forced the party to take up some definite positions on economic reorganization, and there had been no place for that in the party of the 1920s. An even more academic exercise was the Macmillan committee on finance and industry, which included Bevin and the Liberal economist John Maynard Keynes, among others, but whose proceedings and report proved to be of far more value to historians than to the politicians of the time.

Finally, the government invested limited sums of money in public works, but the jobs created were a drop in the ocean, and such schemes were viewed with extreme scepticism by 'informed' opinion. And this mattered because, above all else, the government did not want to damage business confidence. Crucially, the national budget had to be seen to be balanced; but, with the slump leading to rising expenditure and falling tax revenues, this was difficult to achieve. It is easy, in retrospect, to sneer at this, to argue that balanced budgets were, in fact, deflationary, or to say that confidence did not matter. But such arguments were not widely accepted at the time, even in the Labour party. Since gradualism was still the order of the day, anything which would impair the long-term prospects of economic recovery would be fatal. And, because the internationalist argument held that free trade and the gold standard were essential guarantors of co-operation and trade with other countries, Labour was caught in a very difficult position indeed.

The results of all this effort were unimpressive. By late 1930 most of the rationalization schemes were running into the sand, international efforts to promote recovery had produced negligible results, and few had any serious hopes for the EAC. Ministers were publicly rubbishing public works. The government seems to have decided that nothing within the power of human agency could do much good. Essentially, the cabinet sat tight and waited for a trade revival.[35]

Could more have been done? Some people thought so, especially Mosley, who had been appointed to minor office in 1929, with a brief to work with Thomas, Lansbury and another junior minister, Thomas Johnston, on schemes to reduce unemployment. Disillusioned with Thomas's apparent ineptitude at an early stage, his three lieutenants began to freelance. By January 1930 they had drawn up a radical set of proposals which became known as the 'Mosley Memorandum'. It argued that economic activity should be increased by the inauguration of a big scheme of loan-financed public works; that tariffs and imperial preference should be used to create a largely autarkic imperial trading bloc; and that the size of the labour market should be reduced through an increased school-leaving age and improved retirement pensions. The whole scheme would be implemented by a small emergency cabinet.[36]

In a sense, the scheme had no chance. There was even criticism of the fact that it was presented directly to MacDonald, rather than to Thomas. The decision to refer it to a cabinet committee under Snowden ensured its demise. When the committee duly reported against the proposals in May 1930, Mosley resigned, and was humiliated in a PLP meeting when he pressed for a vote on the issue. That October he was received warmly by the Labour party conference, but a motion asking the NEC to look again at his proposals was narrowly defeated. In December, he issued a radical 'Mosley Manifesto' which was signed by 17 Labour MPs and Cook, but it made little impact. In February 1931 Mosley, having abandoned Labour, formed the New party with the aid of three other Labour MPs and an Ulster Unionist.[37]

Could the Mosley proposals have been implemented, and, if so, could they have succeeded? The parliamentary position was one obstacle. Skidelsky has argued that this was just an excuse: the Liberals, having fought the 1929 election on a not dissimilar programme, would have followed a Labour lead.[38] But this is a dubious assumption. The two programmes were different in significant ways, especially tariffs: the Liberals had been elected on a free trade ticket, and could certainly not have been convinced to move *en bloc* towards protectionism. In addition, even if Lloyd George had been convinced, his party was so fissile that he would probably not have been able to deliver its votes in parliament. Many of the Liberal MPs elected in 1929 had not favoured Lloyd George's programme even in relatively calm times, and were not going to support anything like it now.[39] There were other objections too. Attempts by government to raise large loans would almost certainly have pushed up interest rates, at a time when these were already crippling industry. Raising the school-leaving age and improving pensions were both expensive, at a time when all the pressure was to restrict rather than to expand government spending. There were administrative difficulties: it was one thing to allocate money to public works schemes but another thing to spend it, since public inquiries were often necessary. The effects on business confidence were not likely to be positive.[40] Finally, it would be difficult to persuade the bulk of Labour MPs, let alone the wider movement, that the tariffs many had spent their political lives attacking were now necessary. In sum, then, the Mosley Memorandum was not a lost opportunity. Its chances had been minimal; and it might be argued that, had an attempt been made to implement it, the results would have been far more catastrophic than those which ensued from its rejection.

The final attempt to change the government's outlook significantly came in the late summer of 1930. Following Mosley's resignation, a minor reshuffle had sent Thomas to the Dominions Office and brought Addison, the former Coalition Liberal, into the cabinet as Minister of Agriculture. The effect of these changes was to strengthen MacDonald's hand in the crucial area of trade policy. For some time the premier had been convinced that tariffs should be tried. In August 1930, a thinly attended cabinet was persuaded by MacDonald and Thomas to defer ratification of Graham's rather feeble tariff truce. However, the likelihood of the government ever getting to the point of imposing tariffs was slim. Resistance would have come at all levels of the Labour movement. For most Labourites, free trade was not just a trade policy, but a guarantee of peace, cheap food, a thriving export industry and a corruption-free public life. The free traders within the cabinet soon regrouped, and a meeting in September agreed to push ahead with ratification after all.[41] Tariffs were ruled out for the winter; by the following spring, when the truce expired, the Conservatives had come all out for protection, and Labour was virtually forced to re-entrench itself as a party of free trade.

Labour saw itself as a party of full employment, so to have a Labour government presiding over constantly increasing levels of joblessness agonized Labourites. The only thing which made the situation at all bearable was the notion of 'work or maintenance': the fact that the government continued to pay unemployment benefit at relatively generous levels, and indeed extended entitlement to such benefits. By early 1931, however, it was clear that a budgetary crisis was looming. The unemployment insurance fund, which was supposed to balance, was in debt to the tune of around £70 million, and the figure was rising. A Royal Commission was set up by Bondfield with an implied brief to propose drastic economies. Most areas of public opinion outside the Labour movement were clamouring for 'economy', and the Conservatives and Liberals took up the theme. On 14 February 1931 a committee on national expenditure was set up following a Liberal motion in the House of Commons, under the chairmanship of Sir George May, head of an insurance company. Although there were two Labour representatives, it was not difficult to predict that substantial cuts in expenditure would be recommended.

In other areas, meanwhile, little in the way of constructive legislation had been achieved. The Coal Mines Act, when eventually passed, could only offer a seven and a half hour day to miners instead of the promised seven. More successful was Greenwood's Housing Act, which, in offering state subsidies for local authority slum clearance and replacement housing schemes, was to make a major contribution to improving working-class living conditions during the coming years. By early 1931, however, the government was experiencing severe difficulties in passing legislation. Trevelyan's attempt to increase the school-leaving age to fifteen was crushed by the House of Lords after being emasculated by Catholic Labour backbenchers who believed that the financial provisions of the measure would force denominational schools into the hands of the local authorities. The presence of leading nonconformists, like the Wesleyan Methodist Henderson, in the cabinet did little to allay Catholic suspicions here. The results were Trevelyan's resignation from the government and, much more importantly, the loss of much Catholic support at elections throughout the year.[42] (Many Jewish voters had already deserted Labour over the Passfield White Paper, which proposed stringent limitations on Jewish immigration to British-controlled Palestine.) And an attempt to repeal the 1927 Trade Disputes Act was destroyed by Liberal amendments.

By mid-1931 the government was in trouble. The cabinet was ageing, ailing and acrimonious. A reshuffle was required, but MacDonald havered. Some have suggested that he was on the verge of introducing some Liberals into the cabinet,[43] but there is little evidence for this, and neither the Liberal party nor the TUC would have stood for such a move. The TUC, and individual trade unions, had been alienated from the government, not just over the failure to do anything tangible about unemployment, but also by the failure to deliver reforms promised in 1929. Textile workers were particularly disaffected by the government-sponsored wage-cutting settlements to their industrial disputes. Radical groups within the PLP moved towards virtual independence, as the New party departed and a more substantial group of ILPers began to issue their own whips and refuse to accept Labour ones. Party finances were in turmoil, as the effects of the slump and the Trade Disputes Act took hold, and some antagonized unions were refusing to hand over their affiliation fees. In many parts of the country the party organization was crumbling as demoralization spread.[44] And the Conservative party, itself much divided in the period since 1929, was now reunited under Baldwin on a policy of economy, protection, imperial preference and help to agriculture which promised, if not to end the slump overnight, then at least to do something to protect jobs and expand employment.

It was on to this unpromising scene that the financial crises of 1931 burst.[45] The collapse of the main Austrian bank in May 1931 led to the freezing of assets across Europe, which in turn meant that London became subject to large withdrawals of gold. This threatened Britain's position on the gold standard, and very few people doubted that to leave the gold standard would lead to financial and economic disaster. The reason that this became a political problem was that the British budget was clearly out of balance, with the government doing little to solve the problem.

One of the few decisive steps it did take was to pass legislation to rectify 'anomalies' whereby married women, among others, could receive unemployment benefit. This saved £3 million, but also alienated working-class voters in areas like Lancashire where married women made up a substantial part of the workforce.

On 31 July the report of Sir George May's committee on national expenditure was published. It predicted a budget deficit of £120 million, to meet which it recommended tax increases bringing in £24 million and spending cuts amounting to £96 million, including a 20 per cent cut in unemployment benefit; cuts of up to the same level in public servants' salaries; and more stringent testing of the needs of unemployed persons who had exhausted their insurance benefit entitlement. At first, the cabinet was calm. No statement was issued on the May report, but it was decided that a committee of five – MacDonald, Snowden, Henderson, Thomas and Graham – would meet on 25 August to discuss the report and prepare a set of suggestions for the full cabinet. However, a run on sterling prompted a series of meetings of the committee in mid-August, and it finally came up with a package of suggestions which were put to the full cabinet on 19 August. Since Snowden had now been informed by the Treasury that the likely deficit was not £120 but £170 million, the economy committee suggested cuts of £78.5 million – less than May had recommended because the economy committee rejected the 20 per cent cut in benefits – and increased taxation to the tune of £88.5 million.

The economy committee's suggestions were, for the most part, accepted by a day-long cabinet meeting on 19 August, but the proposal to transfer responsibility for transitional benefit to local authorities was deleted, leaving a total economy package of £56 million. Most ministers seemed to hope that this would suffice, and that the crisis could be contained. However, when Snowden and MacDonald met opposition leaders – whose support, given the parliamentary position, was essential – they were told that even the £78.5 million package was inadequate. Then in the afternoon, MacDonald and Snowden addressed a joint meeting of the NEC and the TUC general council. The latter came out against all cuts. Despite this opposition, however, the cabinet agreed on the evening of Friday 21 August to go ahead with the £56 million package; and no one resigned.

The problem was, of course, that the £56 million package was not large enough to satisfy the opposition leaders and still less the bankers. MacDonald and Snowden were already aware of this, so next day they recalled their – doubtless somewhat be-mused – colleagues and tried to persuade them to increase the level of cuts, but to no avail. Henderson, in particular, now came to the view that Labour should resign rather than place itself in the hands of the Opposition. The most that the premier could attain was permission to put a hypothetical question to bankers in New York: would they grant the additional credits needed to preserve the gold standard if there was a 10 per cent cut in un-employment benefit? The answer, that Sunday evening, was that the loan would probably be forthcoming if such a cut were an-nounced. (Some ministers took this, wrongly, as a sign that the bankers were seeking to dictate to the government on the ques-tion of benefits, hence the subsequent myth of a 'Bankers' Ramp'.[46]) MacDonald asked his colleagues whether they were prepared to support the cut: of the 20 ministers present, nine (including Henderson, Graham and Clynes) refused to entertain the idea. This was a fatal split, so MacDonald set off to see the King to offer the administration's resignation. At this stage he was still probably thinking in terms of resigning the premiership, but the King, and then the Opposition leaders, realizing that the cuts might be less controversial if introduced by a 'socialist' Prime Minister, encouraged him to stay on. The result was that MacDonald next day (24 August) formed a National government. Its ten-strong cabinet included Snowden, Thomas and Sankey, plus four Conservatives and two Liberals.

Some Labourites welcomed this development, feeling that with the government dead and buried the party would be able to re-group under new leadership and with a clearer purpose. How-ever, the next six weeks in opposition were a dispiriting time. Defections to MacDonald were gratifyingly few – only about a dozen backbenchers joined what became the 'National Labour party', and no constituency parties or trade unions followed him, although there were odd local defections. This consolidation was undoubtedly helped by the fact that the party, prodded by the TUC general council, came out in firm opposition to the govern-ment and rapidly elected a reluctant Henderson to replace MacDonald. Labour's new stance against all cuts inevitably raised questions about the political honesty of the ex-ministers, since it rapidly became known that the cabinet as a whole had discussed and agreed to the £56 million package.

This was just a foretaste of things to come. Henderson proved a poor leader, unable to come to terms with the situation, unwilling to be too radical and opposed to too strenuous a line against MacDonald, who he still hoped would honour his pledge to return to the party. Labour speakers moved away from specifics, and argued that only 'socialism' could help, yet with little clear idea of what that meant. The National government passed the economy legislation and maintained a parliamentary majority. It soon became clear, in fact, that the government would not collapse, and, indeed, that it was preparing for a general election. By the time parliament was dissolved on 7 October, Labour headquarters was pessimistic, expecting the loss of a hundred seats.

Such pessimism was well founded, and the general election campaign was a bitter experience for Labourites. Labour's image was that of a party of depression and unemployment, whereas unemployment had fallen under the National government and the Conservatives' protectionism seemed to offer a chance of combating the worst ravages of the depression. Labour called for the defence of free trade, but it was a policy that had lost popularity sharply in the face of the slump. There was scepticism over Labour's commitment to reverse the benefit cut while balancing the budget, and its pledge to restore the wage cuts as resources allowed was little better than that of the government. The ex-ministers were taken to task for their disingenuous attitude towards the cuts. Catholic and Jewish voters were alienated by the late government's policies. It is true, of course, that all kinds of stunts and scares were used against Labour: but these were not in any sense decisive. Labour was beaten because of its recent record in office, because it lacked clear policies, because its leaders had forfeited their credibility, and because their opponents were more attractive to a country desperate for economic improvement.

The result was disastrous. Labour gained no new seats and held on to only 46 of those it already held, with unendorsed (mainly ILP) candidates winning six more. The leadership was swept away: old stagers like Henderson, Clynes and Adamson went along with the potential future leaders such as Graham, Greenwood, Morrison and Dalton. The only member of the former cabinet to survive was Lansbury; he was joined by Clement Attlee and Sir Stafford Cripps, who had been junior ministers. The new PLP, half of whose members were sponsored by the MFGB, was singularly short of distinction. Arrayed against it were 554 National MPs, 470 of them Conservatives.

Even in terms of votes Labour's performance was dismal. True, its poll share did not fall by nearly so large a proportion as its parliamentary representation, for it took 6.3 million votes (29.3 per cent) as against 8.4 million (37.1 per cent) in 1929. But it would have been complacent to draw much comfort from this fact. First, to lose 21 per cent of the poll share of 1929 was a heavy loss indeed: since the 1867 Reform Act it had been exceeded only by the Liberals, in 1918 and 1924 – hardly an encouraging precedent. To lose such a proportion of support in an election when Labour's socialist and trade union bases were so much to the fore was even more worrying. Secondly, the election had been fought on much more of a two-'party' basis than that of 1929: Labour candidates had been involved in 359 straight fights as against less than 100 in 1929, when extensive Liberal interventions had created almost 450 three-cornered contests.[47] And the large number of unopposed returns (67) meant Labour was relieved of a number of inevitable and heavy defeats which would have depressed its poll share below 28 per cent had they all been contested. It takes a peculiar form of optimism, then, to see anything to cheer about in Labour's performance.

The high hopes of 1922, when MacDonald had returned to parliament and assumed the leadership of the party, had been shattered. Three of Labour's dominant and most popular figures during the 1920s had now passed to the other side, replaced by a leadership which was considerably less distinguished. The party's central assumptions of the 1920s – that capitalism was essentially prosperous and that this prosperity could be used as the route towards socialism, and that internationalism could solve what problems remained – seemed to be in tatters. Labour's advance during the 1920s had been spectacular, and its formation of two minority governments had at least eclipsed the Liberals. But the record of the second government, in particular, showed that Labour had a lot of hard decisions to make. In 1923, Webb had spoken of the 'inevitability of gradualness', but during the 1930s it was to seem that the only thing inevitable about British politics was Labour's presence on the opposition benches.

4

Remaking the Party?
1931–9

In the aftermath of the 1931 election Labour faced a long haul if it was to return to power. By 1939, a further general election had been lost and it seemed highly unlikely that the next one would bring substantially better results. All in all, then, the 1930s was a decade of disappointment. However, developments during the period would help Labour's ultimate return to power.

The immediate position was dire. Labour's parliamentary representation had collapsed to 46, confined to parts of certain coalfields and assorted slum areas in a few cities. The National government had 554 MPs, and even if, as Labourites often predicted, it broke up early under the weight of its apparent internal contradictions, the Conservatives, with their 470 MPs, would still be in a strong position. The next election would need to produce a swing of 17.5 per cent merely for Labour to return to its 1929 representation of 287 MPs; only a 20 per cent swing would give it a bare overall majority.[1] It is difficult to imagine any set of circumstances in the 1930s which could have provided such a revolution in the party's fortunes.

The party's leadership had been smashed by 1931. Lansbury, by default, became chairman of the PLP, acting as leader in parliament (pending the expected return of Henderson), with Attlee and Cripps joining him in a leftish leadership troika. The gradualist ideology which had dominated Labour's thinking seemed to be in ruins. And, finally, the party's policy was confused, to say the least. The election manifesto had been a call for a return to fundamentals, but its promises had been vague aspirations rather than blueprints for action, and much hard thinking remained to be done.

There were some crumbs of comfort. The 46 seats could be seen as a bedrock. In particular, the mining areas, which as recently as 1918 had not been electing Labour MPs, were now much more solid than they had been then. There were discrepancies, to be sure – south Wales was more solid than the Yorks, Notts and Derby coalfield which, in turn, produced better returns than County Durham – but even in Durham two of the 11 seats won in 1929 had been retained, and only a mild swing would be needed at the next election to bring most of the others back. The change in leadership at least cleared out the gerontocracy of the 'Big Five', and offered hope of a new, younger leadership in the medium term, which cannot have failed to inspire those who had found preferment so difficult to gain under the MacDonald regime. The lack of policy was a problem, but also an opportunity. Perhaps it was the chance of fundamental change within the party that encouraged the growth of individual membership at this time. The collapse of the Labour government had also opened the wallets of the unions: after MacDonald's departure money flooded in, and the party conference agreed to increase affiliation fees, a move it had been resisting for some time.[2] The party's organization remained intact, too. MacDonald's 'National Labour' party was never a significant threat. Labour's base remained essentially firm.

But the question of how to build on that base was a matter of fierce dispute. Some people believed that capitalism was in its death throes, quoting the renewed increase in unemployment, which peaked at around three million late in 1932, to support their apocalyptic rhetoric. This view was found most notably – but not exclusively – within the ILP. Maxton and other leading figures argued that the Labour party had now become a hindrance to the progress of socialism.[3] A new movement of the left was needed to capture the growing radicalism of the masses. At a special conference in July 1932 the ILP voted by 241 votes to 142 to disaffiliate from Labour.[4] Although it is easy to understand why a section of the ILP believed that this was a sensible, even necessary, move, it was ultimately to prove disastrous. Many ILPers left that party rather than be forced to abandon Labour.[5] Then, the economic upturn from early 1933 onwards threw doubt on the ILP's apocalyptic rhetoric. And, through 'co-operation' with the CPGB in 1933 and 1934, the ILP found itself asset-stripped of members and property. By 1935, therefore, ILP membership was less than a third of its level at the time of disaffiliation.[6]

Those ILPers who remained with the Labour party in 1932 combined with the Society for Socialist Inquiry and Propaganda (SSIP) (established by Cole in June 1931) to form the Socialist League.

This aimed to replicate the role of the 'old' ILP within the Labour party, and be a force for radicalism but not for disloyalty. This was a fine line to tread, and ultimately the League fell foul of the party bureaucracy, just as the ILP had.

Paradoxically, the disaffiliation of the ILP strengthened the left within the Labour party. From the mid-1920s the Labour leadership had been able to deal with the ILP not on the level of ideas, but on that of party management, and at that level the left was always likely to lose. However, such a course could not be pursued with the Socialist League in 1932, for three reasons. First, the League was hardly formed by the time of the 1932 party conference, and so could hardly be portrayed as 'a party within a party'. Secondly, it had been formed by people who were palpably loyal to the Labour party: had they not been, they would have gone with the ILP. And, finally, the Labour bureaucracy, shaken by crisis and continuing uncertainty and serving a divided leadership itself lacking in self-confidence, was in no position to launch a counter-offensive. The result was that the left scored a number of successes at the 1932 conference, most notably in defeating the NEC to pass resolutions, against the NEC's advice, calling for the nationalization of commercial banks and opposing Labour's taking office again as a minority government.[7]

The ill-tempered delegates at the 1932 Leicester conference dealt a death-blow to the second strand of opinion which had emerged from the 1931 crisis. This strand argued that 1931 had been an aberration; that the 'pendulum' of electoral politics would 'swing back'; and that therefore the party should stick to the approach set out in *Labour and the Nation* and avoid 'false and ill-considered moves'.[8] The keenest exponent of this line was the party's leader, secretary and treasurer, Henderson. But it carried little weight. Henderson himself spent much of 1932 ill, or presiding over the world disarmament conference at Geneva. He had still not managed to find time or opportunity to fight a by-election to secure his return to parliament. He was so out of touch by the time of Leicester that when he spoke for the NEC against the resolution on minority governments, he was heckled severely.[9] A few days later he resigned the party leadership, to be succeeded by Lansbury. Although he did return to parliament in 1933, remained party secretary until 1934, and was treasurer until his death in 1935, Henderson was now a marginal figure. Surprisingly rapidly, he had become a throwback to a bygone age of Labour politics.[10]

The third clear strategy to emerge from the wreckage was that favoured by the central figures on the TUC general council, like Bevin and Walter Citrine (general secretary of the TUC), and also by leading moderates such as Dalton. They aimed to bind a future government more closely to the general council, and also to en-sure that it had more clearly defined policies to implement once elected. Moves along these lines had started in September 1931, when the general council had voted to revive the moribund national joint council (NJC), with an in-built trade union major-ity over the representatives of the NEC and the PLP. The small size of the post-election PLP helped these plans, as did the fact that it and the NEC were now much more union-dominated than before. The NJC was to become the leading arbiter within the party during the 1930s, a role symbolized by its adoption of the grander title, National Council of Labour (NCL) in 1934. This is not to argue that 'the unions' always got what they wanted; for one thing, 'the unions' were not homogeneous. Still, the NJC/ NCL was to be the forum via which leading trade unionists, in alliance with leading party figures, were able to steer the party gen-erally in directions they liked and away from those they did not.[11]

Moves on policy had started as early as 1929. Cole's *The Next Ten Years*, published that year, called for radical measures to re-structure the economy, with a shift away from staple export in-dustries and towards 'new' industries producing for the less volatile domestic market. On nationalization, Cole argued that ownership was less important than control.[12] Although this work was very largely ignored by MacDonald's government, Cole and others pushed matters forward with the formation of the New Fabian Research Bureau in early 1931 and SSIP some months later. In the immediate aftermath of the government's collapse, a number of policy committees were set up, and these formed the nucleus of similar committees formed after the election. Young economists like Evan Durbin and Hugh Gaitskell were drafted in by Cole and Dalton to work on policy; a quasi-conspiratorial group of City experts sympathetic to Labour, the XYZ Club, advised on financial policy. At first the results were rather piece-meal, but at least there was a recognition of the need for much greater policy planning than had ever been accepted in the 1920s.[13]

Of course, the three categories outlined above were neither watertight compartments nor the whole story. Many people from top to bottom of the party shifted from position to position, or accepted parts of one position and parts of another. Others, perhaps most, continued with the workaday tasks of fundraising, canvassing, voting, and attending meetings, without delineating clearly their view of the path the party should take. This confusion became clear during 1932–3 when the party flapped in the wind, first one way, then another. But if any pattern can be detected, it is that the PLP and conference tended to be (rather inchoately) leftish, while the NEC, NJC and policy bodies cleaved much more closely to the Bevin–Citrine–Dalton axis, particularly as it became increasingly clear, from 1933 onwards, that capitalism was not on the verge of collapse.

Even so, there was, even on the Labour left, no rejection of parliamentary methods. True, the 1933 conference passed a motion calling for the organization of a general strike to prevent British participation in a future war, and Labourites talked of the need for a future Labour government to use 'emergency powers' or an Enabling Act to cut through opposition to its policies. But the essential commitment to parliamentarism remained intact.[14] No serious attempts were made to work through rank-and-file movements or to mobilize the masses.[15] In contrast to the 1910s, no alternative means of transformation, such as syndicalism or guild socialism, emerged with any force. Even at the high point of the party's early 1930s swing to the left, therefore, the swing was piecemeal and qualified: and perhaps, as was to be the case in the early 1980s, the surprising aspect is less that there was a swing to the left, than the fact that it was so shallow, so partial in its effects, and so short-lived.

The containment of the swing to the left could be seen in the adoption of the new party programme, *For Socialism and Peace*, by the Southport party conference in October 1934. This replaced *Labour and the Nation*. It differed from the latter in giving a higher priority to nationalization – explicitly, of land, banking, coal, iron and steel, transport, power, and water supply. It also called for the setting up of a National Investment Board, to plan investments and industrial development. The changes were not as great as they might have been – there was no commitment, for example, to deficit financing. The Socialist League, which saw it as far too moderate, put forward 75 amendments, but all were defeated very heavily.[16]

The reasons for the defeat of the Socialist League in 1934 are not difficult to find. The League itself had not developed far at the grassroots. Its amendments were offered on something of a 'take-it-or-leave-it' basis. In addition, by 1934 the League had developed a degree of organization and, since the emergence of Cripps as its leading figure, a higher profile: and so it could be seen as 'a party within a party', which meant that it could be dealt with on a more managerial basis than hitherto.[17] The fact that the Communists were now moving back towards united front policies also damaged the League in this respect.

More general factors also limited the League's appeal. By late 1934, the next general election was starting to loom. This inevitably served to rally the party around its leaders. The success of Morrison in leading Labour to victory in the London County Council elections of 1934 suggested that moderation might have electoral benefits. The economic upturn apparent from the start of 1933 also affected the party, questioning, if not wholly invalidating, the left's apocalyptic rhetoric, while also, possibly, allowing union leaders to pay more attention to the party as their own organizations' problems began to ease.

In some ways, *For Socialism and Peace* marked a significant change from MacDonaldism. It was definite and full-blooded where *Labour and the Nation* had been vague and anaemic, and was much more strategic and less wishful than the earlier document. At the same time, there were continuities. This was particularly so in its rejection of any agency other than the state in the transformation to and administration of a socialist society. Indeed, in so far as the emphasis was now on planning from the centre, the state assumed a primacy in the party's doctrine which was virtually unchallenged.

Labour socialists had always placed a great burden on the state in their vision of how society would be transformed. Until the 1920s, however, there had always been an alternative, though less powerful, strain in Labour's thought which pointed to the importance and potential of other agencies. Even the Webbs had argued that local government should retain extensive powers and be a major player in the change.[18] Syndicalism and guild socialism had also stressed alternative visions, while thinkers like Tawney and, in particular, Laski had stressed the importance of pluralism in their writings until the mid-1920s. Even after his turn from guild socialism in the mid-1920s, Cole was still keen on some form of devolution of power to workplace councils in nationalized industries.[19]

Yet such calls were heard less frequently thereafter. It is true that the conference defeated the NEC on workers' control in 1932 and again in 1933. But these were the last glowings of a dying ember rather than the sparks to light a new flame. Over the decade, Labour moved towards Morrison's conception of the 'public corporation', whereby an industry would be nationalized but then run by a government-appointed board along essentially business lines. Even the idea that union representatives should sit on the boards – a very different thing from workers' control – was soon abandoned. The place of the worker, then, in his or her day-to-day working life would be no different from what it was under private ownership. Similarly, local government's possible role was downplayed: the old idea of a Local Authorities Enabling Bill, which would have allowed councils far greater powers to enter into trade and so on, was dropped in the early 1930s.[20] Labour was set fair to become the statist party of the post-war period.

Why? For one thing, the failure of the second Labour government and depression throughout the capitalist world jolted people into new ways of thinking, particularly as the one country which seemed to be prospering at the time was the USSR, whose first Five Year Plan (1928–32) seemed to prove the efficacy of centralized planning. These views were merely reinforced by the apparent success of later experiments by the Social Democrats in Sweden and by Labour in New Zealand.[21] 'Planning' became a vogue word and the idea found its way into party policy with, for example, the National Investment Board. Clearly implied in planning, though, was a strong central authority whose edicts would be fulfilled by a wider nation grateful for the wisdom of its socialist rulers. Obviously, then, emphasis had to be placed on the power of the state. In addition, there was greater emphasis than previously on the obstacles that Labour would have to overcome in implementing a socialist programme. MacDonaldite gradualism had assumed that progress could be piecemeal, incrementally gaining support and improving society – more and more people would come over to socialism as they saw its benefits in action. The 1930s offered little comfort for such a view. The fall of the second Labour government was attributed widely to the machinations of international capital, and especially financiers. Far from giving up their advantages voluntarily, it seemed, capitalists would fight tenaciously and ruthlessly in order to cling on to them.[22] The rise of Hitler in Germany in 1933 seemed merely to confirm this view. In such a context, socialists should not footle with minor agencies, but must take control of the most powerful – the state – and ensure that the others were in no position to challenge it.

In any case, the position of the other agencies seemed uncertain. Trade unionism now covered fewer than a quarter of all workers.[23] Similarly, what had once seemed an inexorable Labour advance in local government was severely interrupted, with heavy losses in 1930 and 1931 and only marginal gains in 1932. While the setbacks would probably only be temporary, they suggested that there was a ceiling to Labour's potential achievement at this level. Put crudely, Labour was likely to gain a majority at Westminster before it gained control of a great many local authorities. By the mid-1930s, earlier intellectual advocates of pluralism, like Laski, were increasingly statist in their outlook, while younger thinkers like Gaitskell, Durbin and Douglas Jay were expressing 'intellectual scorn' over 'naive and irrelevant' ideas like workers' control.[24] By the mid-1930s, then, Labour was putting its money on the nose of the state. There would be no each-way bets.

In the aftermath of the 1931 election many people might have been tempted to bet that the National government would soon fall apart. If so, they would have lost their stakes, for the government displayed considerable resilience. The resignation of Snowden and the free trade Liberals over protectionism in September 1932 caused little more than a ripple; otherwise, the government plodded along steadily.[25] There were periodic crises, for example over India and unemployment assistance, but these were overcome without too much difficulty.[26] By the late spring of 1935, the crises were largely past; Baldwin replaced MacDonald as premier and reshuffled the cabinet to give it a more appealing look; and it became clear that an election would not be far off.

Labour's electoral performance between 1931 and 1935 suggested that it could expect to make some advances. Ten seats were gained in by-elections, some on very large swings, and there were heavy local election gains in 1933 and 1934. But Labour, on the whole, were merely recovering ground lost in 1931 and 1932, and in other areas the party was making few inroads, not least because for most, though assuredly not all, people the government was presiding over generally rising living standards.

As if this was not bad enough, Labour lost its leader just before the dissolution of parliament in October 1935. That September, the TUC had voted in favour of economic sanctions against Italy should it proceed with its threatened invasion of Abyssinia (Ethiopia), and it was clear that the party would follow suit. However, some Labourites feared that sanctions would lead to war, and Cripps resigned from the NEC, and the pacifist Lord Ponsonby as leader in the Lords, in protest.[27] Lansbury, also a pacifist, was left in an impossible position. At the party conference, he made a well-received speech, but the vote went against him by a massive majority, and he was fiercely attacked by Bevin. Lansbury resigned; next day the Italians invaded; and three weeks later Baldwin announced that an election would be held on 14 November.

This was hardly the ideal start to the election campaign. Lansbury was succeeded by his deputy, Attlee, as a temporary measure pending the return of more senior figures at the election. Attlee had proved a worthy deputy, earning widespread respect within the PLP, but was hardly a nationally known figure at this time.[28] The government, in addition, was able to play the 'national unity in the face of international crisis' card with alacrity. Yet these factors were not the reason for Labour's defeat: no one could claim seriously that had Italy not invaded Abyssinia and Lansbury not been forced to resign Labour would have won the election. In truth, the party could never have hoped to make up such a huge margin, and leading Labourites were predicting privately that the party would win between 200 and 240 seats.[29]

Ultimately, Labour emerged much weaker even than that. True, it exceeded its 1929 poll share, taking 38 per cent of the votes cast. But this improvement over 1931 less than tripled its pre-dissolution strength of 59 MPs, the total rising only to 154. The government took 429 seats, of which the Conservatives claimed 387; the opposition Liberals, with only 161 candidates, could manage only 21. With so few Liberal candidates to split the anti-Labour vote Labour had needed far more than 38 per cent of the votes in order even to restore its 1929 position with regard to seats. Labour had managed to regain a considerable number of the seats lost in 1931, but its performance was very patchy. In no region did it emulate its 1929 performance: even in industrial south Wales it only won 16 seats as opposed to 22 in 1929. In the relatively prosperous Midlands, the party took only 11 seats as opposed to 35 six years earlier. The party's performance in

the south of England outside the London region was truly lamentable. South of the Severn–Wash line there had been two
Labour MPs even in 1918; at the 1929 election, 19 had been returned. Now Labour held only two once again, both in Bristol.
In addition, the cities where Labour had begun to break through
in 1929, like Birmingham and Liverpool, saw little or no progress;
in the former, all 12 seats went to the Conservatives, as in 1931.
Even many depressed areas failed to fall to Labour, no doubt
because not enough people even there could be convinced that
Labour had a better alternative to the 'steady as she goes' policy
of the National government. Labour was not only failing to take
middle-class votes: it was failing even in many areas dominated
by manual occupations. Its performance in agricultural areas, where
it had made some advances in the 1920s, was now all but hope-
less. But at least the PLP was strengthened in quality. Five members
of the 1931 cabinet, including Clynes, Morrison and Alexander,
were returned, along with a number of former junior ministers,
including Dalton and Emanuel Shinwell (who defeated MacDonald
at Seaham).

It had been clearly understood that Attlee was a temporary
leader, and so a leadership election soon followed. The candidates were Attlee, Greenwood and Morrison. In the first ballot,
Attlee emerged with 58 votes to Morrison's 44 and Greenwood's
33; in the second, the supporters of Greenwood seem to have
swung *en bloc* to Attlee, who defeated Morrison by 88 votes to
48. This was rather a negative verdict on all three candidates.
Greenwood was not unpopular, but he seemed to lack steel, and
his freemasonry and heavy drinking aroused suspicion. More significant was the defeat of Morrison. It seems that he suffered
from a number of factors: Dalton's counter-productive campaigning
on his behalf, his absence from parliament between 1931 and
1935, fears that he would seek to become an all-powerful leader
like MacDonald (to whom he had been very close), hostility from
the left and certain union leaders (particularly Bevin, who despised him), and fears that he would be over-concerned with
London. It is also possible that, at a time when issues of pacifism were to the fore, there were those who feared electing someone who had been a conscientious objector during the war.

'Major Attlee', by contrast, was the antithesis of a charismatic
leader in the MacDonald mould; but he was seen as honest, decent
and competent, and had earned the respect of the PLP when

standing in for the ailing Lansbury during the latter's absences. It may well be, too, that Greenwood's supporters backed him because he would prove, at a time when Greenwood's stock might have risen somewhat, easier to remove than Morrison would have been. In this, of course, they were to prove somewhat wide of the mark: Attlee's departure was not to come until 1955, by which time Greenwood was dead. At least Greenwood got the deputy leadership, because Morrison, bitterly disappointed, refused to take what he saw – with some justice – as a meaningless consolation prize.[30]

The party Attlee had been elected to lead would make only limited progress for the remainder of the decade. In parliamentary by-elections, the average swing against the Conservatives between the 1935 election and the outbreak of war in September 1939 was just 3.9 per cent, as opposed to 15.8 per cent between 1931 and 1935. As in 1931–5, Labour lost no seats at by-elections; it gained 13. But it also failed to regain five seats it had won in 1929 but lost subsequently. Municipal elections were also disappointing. In November 1935, Labour made tiny overall gains in the English and Welsh boroughs; a year later it made a small net loss of seats. The next two years saw only minor gains. In Scotland, 1936 saw Labour lose control of five of the 19 burghs it had held up to then; by 1938 the figure had only recovered to 14.[31] In short, Labour had reached what appeared to be an electoral plateau by the later 1930s. It is almost impossible to see how Labour could have avoided a further general election defeat, perhaps almost as severe as that of 1935, had not the Second World War intervened.

Labour's cause was not helped, electorally, by the growing perception of the likelihood of war. Italy had subjugated Abyssinia by May 1936, by which time Hitler had remilitarized the Rhineland and the generals' rebellion against the Spanish republic had resulted in the beginning of a long and bloody civil war, whose ultimate result was victory for General Franco, assisted by the Germans and Italians. In March 1938 Germany annexed Austria. That September Hitler's claims to the German-speaking Sudetenland area of Czechoslovakia seemed likely to lead to war between Britain and Germany; it was only averted when Britain and France, pursuing the policy of appeasement, conceded most of Hitler's claims at the Munich conference. After an apparent lull, the crisis reached a new stage with the German invasion of the

Czech areas of Czechoslovakia in March 1939. Now, Britain and France issued 'guarantees' to a number of states in eastern and central Europe, and somewhat desultory efforts were made to reach an anti-German alliance with the USSR. Ultimately, the Soviet Union tired of this, and sought to secure its own position by making a non-aggression pact with Germany; shortly afterwards, on 1 September, Germany invaded Poland, one of the 'guaranteed' states. Britain and France therefore declared war on Germany.

Such a series of events obviously posed problems for Labour. It was a party of peace, which was essential for the 'ordered progress' to which the party was committed. There was also considerable Labour suspicion of the National government. It was pulling the Empire closer together, through imperial preference and so on, than ever before. Might it not use rearmament and conscription, not to preserve peace and the international rule of law through the League of Nations, but to bolster British imperialism?[32] Other members of the party, however, argued that, since fascism was the main enemy, and one which destroyed what Labourites saw as the guarantors of working-class freedom – free trade unionism and social democratic parties – and was also a cruel, vindictive, reactionary force making 'ordered progress' impossible, its challenge must be met, and defeated, even if this meant accepting rearmament under the National government.[33]

In the early 1930s, pacifist arguments had appeared powerful within the party. However, pacifism was never as strong as it seemed. The pacifist resolution at the 1933 Hastings conference had been passed unanimously, largely for procedural reasons.[34] The period of fascist aggression in Europe had not really started yet. And it was still possible at that stage to have hopes of the world disarmament conference and the Labour and Socialist International as mechanisms to avoid war. Once these factors had ceased to apply, as they had by 1935, the pacifists were easily defeated. However, Labour's policy remained somewhat disingenuous. It supported collective security through the League of Nations, which had itself been strengthened by the USSR's entry in September 1934. But in parliament the PLP continued to vote against rearmament, without which collective security was something of a sham. This position began to be challenged as the danger of war seemed to increase and the League's weakness over the Italian invasion of Abyssinia in 1935 was felt. In July 1936, Alexander and Dalton led a movement within the PLP to abstain on, rather than vote against, the arms estimates; about 20 MPs followed their line. A year later, with the Spanish Civil War in full swing, the PLP voted by 45 to 39 to change the line to one of abstention.[35] Although there remained a small pacifist section around Lansbury, most MPs now pressed for rearmament, though they missed no opportunity to register distrust of the uses to which the National government might put its increased firepower.

The issue of Spain also created dispute and disunity in Labour's ranks.[36] Most Labourites were, in theory, fully behind the Spanish government in its struggle against Franco's 'fascism'. Yet the question of what to do in a practical way was more vexed. For some, Spain was a moral crusade against fascism, and this moral conviction led a number of people, many but not all of them Communists, to volunteer to fight in Spain for the government forces. Such people argued that Labour should do everything in its power to assist the legitimate Spanish government. But in reality it was not that simple. First, there were broad electoral considerations. Most British people had little interest in Spain, and Labour, realizing that it needed to expand its support, not least within the working class, wanted to avoid being dragged into radical causes whose immediate relevance to British work-ers was debatable. More particularly, there was a very real fear of losing the Catholic vote. Franco claimed to be the defender of Catholicism against the 'godless' Spanish Republic. Since the early 1920s, the Catholic vote in Britain had come over substantially to Labour, a factor of great significance in advancing the party's position in many major towns and cities, especially in west Lancashire and on Clydeside. Yet Labour's relationship with the Catholics remained complex. For one thing, Labour had rather a Protestant image: if the party owed more to Methodism than Marxism, as some of its members liked to claim, then this left the Catholics, high-church opponents of nonconformity, in an anomalous position, to say the least. The secession of Wheatley from the Labour front bench in the mid-1920s had merely high-lighted the underrepresentation of Catholics in the party leader-ship. As seen above, the Catholic Church had been alienated by Trevelyan's proposals for its schools, and it seems that Catholic voters deserted Labour in droves during 1930–1. Around the same time there was talk of trying to set up Catholic trade unions on the continental model. Nothing came of this, but the inevitable result was that Labour remained sensitive to the dangers of losing the Catholic vote, not least because Catholics remained underrepresented at all levels of the Labour movement. In short, Labour's leadership was worried that to take too firm a stand on behalf of the Spanish Republic might lead to a haemorrhage of Catholic support. Such a haemorrhage would make a Labour government in Britain less likely than ever, and so in turn reduce the chances of Britain pursuing a more vigorous anti-fascist strategy in general. There were challenges to the leadership's line, but, apart from calling for a lifting of the arms embargo, and pursuing humanitarian efforts, little was done. Some people moved to the more strident Communist party in disgust, but it seems that most Labourites were broadly satisfied with the policy.

The question of Spain raised a wider issue about Labour's line in the 1930s: co-operation with other parties, and with the Communists in particular. From 1933 onwards the CPGB began once again to press for united action. But a proposal for a united front in 1933 was turned down flat by the NEC, and the NJC issued a manifesto, *Democracy versus Dictatorship*, arguing that there was nothing to choose between communism and fascism. The leadership's line was broadly favoured within the party: although some advocated co-operation, the attacks of the 'Class against Class' period had been widely and deeply resented, and trade unionists in particular had been incensed at the CPGB's attempts to form breakaway Communist unions. During 1933–4, the ILP's bitter experience of 'co-operation' with the Communists caused many ILPers to return to Labour, bringing with them tales of the true nature of the Communist definition of 'unity'. However, matters did not rest there. The seventh world congress of the Communist International in the summer of 1935 unfurled the policy of uniting all opponents of fascism in a 'popular front'. The CPGB began to act in a conciliatory manner towards the Labour party; as a sign of good faith, all but two Communist candidates were withdrawn at the 1935 election. However, one of the two, William Gallacher, was elected MP for West Fife, defeating Adamson, which hardly helped matters, and a renewed application for affiliation was turned down by the NEC.

The NEC doubtless hoped that this was an end to the matter, but every crisis in Europe brought renewed calls to reopen the question. By the summer of 1936, some major unions (including the MFGB), around 60 CLPs, and the Socialist League, were all supporting affiliation. That October, the party conference gave the largest vote yet in favour of Communist affiliation, but it was still defeated by a three to one majority. Undeterred, the Communists joined with the ILP and Socialist League in talks for a more limited form of unity. The result was the Unity Campaign, which was launched in January 1937.[37] The NEC's response was to disaffiliate the Socialist League and, shortly afterwards, to declare that membership of the League and of the Labour party were incompatible. That May, League members decided that, rather than face expulsion from the Labour party, they would dissolve their own organization. The Unity Campaign did result in some interparty co-operation at rank-and-file level, but the 1937 party conference voted heavily against the united front once again.[38]

The issue of cross-party links revived in the autumn of 1938, at the time of the Munich Crisis. A Conservative opponent of Munich, Harold Macmillan, approached Dalton proposing a degree of co-operation, and a number of meetings followed. Attlee, Morrison and Cripps were all sympathetic when sounded, but the first two were somewhat cautious, foreseeing problems with the trade unions. In the event, the idea foundered, mainly due to the unwillingness of the former Foreign Secretary, Anthony Eden, to become involved. Eden had a considerable following among Tory MPs and was clearly crucial to Macmillan's idea of a '1931 in reverse'; without him, there was little point in pursuing the idea.[39] 'Unity' with just a handful of malcontents and mavericks like Macmillan and perceived reactionaries like Churchill would have been impossible to sell to the Labour movement as a whole, and of dubious value in any case. There was also, around the same time, a rank-and-file movement towards a popular front. This found expression in two by-elections: at Oxford in October, when an independent candidate opposed to Munich and supported by the local Labour and Liberal parties was defeated narrowly by a Conservative; and at Bridgwater (Somerset) in November, when the journalist and broadcaster, Vernon Bartlett, stood as an Independent Progressive candidate (again with Labour and Liberal support) and overturned a Conservative majority of 10 000.[40] Across parts of Britain, but particularly areas where Labour was weak, like the south-west, calls were heard for some kind of an alliance between Labour and other parties.[41] It was to try to take advantage of this latter movement that Cripps launched his next – and for the time being terminal – venture in January

1939. He proposed a popular front, on the grounds that the international position was now so serious, and Labour's electoral prospects so weak, that some alternative must be sought. Deals should be struck at constituency level, in readiness for the next election, and a national campaign be launched.[42] The NEC, as expected, vetoed the proposals, whereon Cripps circulated them to all constituency Labour parties. Cripps, when asked to withdraw the document, refused and was expelled from the party, along with Trevelyan, the south Wales MP Aneurin Bevan, and other of his supporters. The campaign attracted some Labour support but more condemnation, particularly from the unions. The NEC took the opportunity to pay off old scores, expelling a larger number of more minor figures who had long been a thorn in its side. At that May's party conference Cripps's explanation of his actions was poorly received, and the expulsions were approved by a five to one majority. The proposal for a popular front was even more heavily defeated.[43]

Superficially, Cripps and his supporters had a case, in so far as the international situation was grave and Labour did have little chance of victory at the next election. However, his inability to push Labour on to other courses was utterly predictable. Failure was due, in part, to Cripps himself. His wealth, 'cleverness' and the feeling that he lacked roots in the movement all told heavily against him. Parallels with Mosley, who since the demise of the New party had formed the British Union of Fascists, could be, and were, drawn.[44] But personality was not decisive. To most Labourites there seemed to be little advantage in a popular front: the Communists, though not insignificant, had only 18 000 members and were seen as unreliable, while the Liberal party was apparently in terminal decline. Alliance would only strengthen untrustworthy and ailing parties at the expense of Labour. In practice, even many of the CLPs which were theoretically in favour of a pact would have baulked at not putting up their own candidate when it came to an election. Finally, the conduct of the various unity campaigns, but especially that of 1939, offended deeply against the ethos of the Labour movement. It was disloyal: majority decisions, repeatedly reiterated, were being flouted with no less regularity. This kind of behaviour could only mean disunity in the face of the main enemy – the Conservatives – and perhaps lead ultimately to the break-up of the Labour party. 'Unity', in short, was no short-cut to power, and was a recipe for disunity in Labour's ranks. Labour's leadership realized privately that the party's electoral prospects were dim, but at the same time recognized that these could not be improved, and would probably be damaged, by forming artificial pacts and alliances with other parties.

The fact that the constituency parties were targeted by Cripps shows, if nothing else, the perception that they had become somewhat more important in the 1930s than they had been in the previous decade. Individual membership more than doubled between 1928 and 1937, at a time when union-affiliated membership of the party was fairly static, so that over the same period individual membership rose from 9.4 to 17.7 per cent of the total membership. The Constituency Parties Movement was formed in 1933 to demand a greater amount of say for such members. The NEC's attempts at suppression failed, and at the 1937 conference that year's party chairman, Dalton, steered through reform against some strong union opposition. First, the size of the NEC was increased from 23 to 25 members (plus the party leader and the treasurer), with an increase in the constituency parties' section from five to seven members. Perhaps more significantly, the method of election for the NEC was changed: instead of being elected by the whole conference, the CLP representatives would now be elected by the CLPs alone.[45] The results of this were not, in the short term, particularly significant, but the reform succeeded in taking the wind out of the sails of the constituency parties, much as the adoption of Clause Four in 1918 had deflated the ILP.

A further development of this period was the continuing programmization of the party. In 1936 detailed plans for the nationalization of coal were adopted. In March 1937, *Labour's Immediate Programme* was published, giving details of the measures a majority Labour government would implement in a single five-year term. It promised planning through the national investment board and nationalization of the Bank of England (but not the commercial banks), and of coal, power and transport. There would be state control over the location of industry. Working conditions would be improved through a 40-hour week and the introduction of holidays with pay. The means test would be abolished. The school-leaving age would be raised to 15 and later 16. Health services would be improved.[46] While much of this reiterated earlier programmes, particularly *For Socialism and Peace*, Labour now

had concrete plans for the implementation of most of its policies, whereas earlier programmes had been expressions of wishes
rather than plans of campaign. *Labour's Immediate Programme* was
to form, essentially, the bedrock of the work of the 1945 Attlee
government. At the same time it can be seen as marking an end
to the policy-making process, with little else being done on domestic policy before the war.[47] In that sense, it did serve to a
certain extent to stifle the debate which remained as necessary
as ever to Labour's planning for the future.

The very fact of a detailed programme showing what a Labour
government would do in office, buttressed by existing detailed
plans for its implementation, was in itself a novelty, perhaps
reflecting the greater underlying homogeneity of the Labour party
by this time. The production of a detailed plan of campaign meant
that one of the main criticisms that had been levelled at *Labour
and the Nation* in 1928 had been met. Transported ten years ahead,
the delegates who had applauded that programme would also
have been surprised at specific aspects of Labour policy: in particular, planning, regional policy, and the signs of limited influence from Keynesian ideas. In other senses, though, Labour's
position had not changed all that radically. It remained, and indeed
had become more committed to being, a statist party which con-
ceived of socialism in almost exclusively 'top-down' terms. The
plan would be drawn up in London, and implemented from
London, with perhaps a nod towards the dreaming spires of
Oxford. True, it would take into account regional differences –
hence regional policy – but this would all be defined at the centre,
and implemented through Westminster and Whitehall, with local
government coming in only as an agency of central government.
Industries would be 'nationalized', to be run by boards appointed
by the minister in London, meeting in London. Even the more
diluted forms of worker participation retreated further from view
as the 1930s wore on.

In addition, in so far as Labour was becoming more Keynesian,
it was, paradoxically, allowing the basic premiss of the socialism of MacDonald and Snowden to make a comeback. In his
Politics of Democratic Socialism, written in 1939 although not published until the following year, one of the party's leading young
intellectuals, Evan Durbin, argued that while '[t]he capitalist
economy [was] ossified, restrictionist and unjust', it was 'expanding
and stable', and that it could provide 'a most substantial rate of

expansion'.[48] In other words, capitalism's economic growth would be the basis of the development of a socialist society. Durbin did, of course, see much more clearly than MacDonald and Snowden the need for substantial reforms of the economy within capitalism, but he still predicated his strategy on economic growth under capitalism, and so fell into their trap of failing to work out in any detail what a Labour government would do to advance the cause of socialism if capitalism ran into a crisis. 'Planning' and Keynesianism provided the lubricants which would, supposedly, help avoid such crises, but it remained open to question whether this would in fact prove to be the case. This is not to say, of course, that anyone else in the party, least of all on the left, had any clearer ideas on this point.

By the time Durbin's book was published, however, Britain was at war, and a new phase in the party's history was opening. The 1930s had witnessed a limited revival and consolidation after the disasters of 1929–31. The party's organization had held good, while rising individual membership pointed to a widening appeal in the country. Along with rising trade union affiliation figures from 1935 onwards, this in turn gave the party a sounder financial base. But election results were largely disappointing, reflecting continuing distrust and a failure on the part of Labour to break out of its image as a party primarily of the unemployed and the trade unions. This left it remote from power, but not perhaps as remote as it might have been had it succumbed to the seductive rhetoric of 'co-operation' with other parties. In its foreign policy, Labour emerged from a long period of confusion to become, by late 1938, a staunch opponent of appeasement. At home, the party's policies were better worked out than ever before, but the swing to the left in the early 1930s had produced few lasting results and the party was, if anything, more centralizing and statist than ever before, with few proposals which offered real empowerment to ordinary people in their own lives. By the end of the decade the right was very clearly in the ascendant, partly because, to some extent understandably, the left had spent so much of the decade concentrating on the international situation and advancing various 'fronts'. The Second World War which they had hoped to prevent was, paradoxically, to provide Labour with a massive boost to its fortunes, but also to strengthen the centralizing elements whose attitudes and policies were to cause such problems later on.

5

The Impact of the Second World War, 1939–45

If the First World War hastened Labour's progress in becoming the second party in the state, then the Second World War undoubtedly speeded the party's opportunity of competing with the Conservatives on equal, or even superior, terms. In 1939 Labour looked like losing yet another general election, probably by quite a margin. Six years later it was to win what remains its greatest electoral victory.

The outbreak of the Second World War found Labour less divided on the justice of the conflict and the need for British intervention than had been the case in 1914. Following the German invasion of Poland on 1 September, Labour's leadership remained united, and Greenwood – acting leader for most of 1939 due to Attlee's absence through illness – did his and his party's reputation much good by appearing, in the Commons debates, keener than Chamberlain on an early declaration of war. The great majority of Labour MPs supported the leadership, with only a small group of about 20 MPs, including pacifists and supporters of a negotiated peace, dissenting.[1] But these were marginal figures. Labour refused Chamberlain's offer of a Coalition, but accepted an electoral truce shortly after the war broke out.

The reasons for Labour's greater unity in 1939 than in 1914 are not hard to fathom. The nature of the enemy was much clearer. Germany in 1914 was not a democracy, but it did have a large Social Democratic party, much admired on the British left. It was not clear that the war had been caused by German aggression. By 1939, however, the nature of Hitler's regime was a matter of little debate: it had banned the SPD and imprisoned its leaders, crushed free trade unionism, carried out policies of racial discrimination and persecution which appalled the British left, and, at least since 1936, seemed to pursue an apparently insatiable policy of expansionism. The nature of the expected war was also different: with defence planners expecting massive aerial bombardment of the British mainland to begin as soon as war commenced, this was no time for academic debate, but for action. Finally, the nature of the party itself had changed. In 1914 it had been a much broader church; in the years since then, the party had become more centralized and more disciplined. Dissent had been (more or less) marginalized, while 'disruptive' elements like the ILP had been forced out of the party altogether. Thus Labour's response to the outbreak of war, on the whole, was one of unity in the face of a common – and commonly despised – enemy.

Of course, the expected bombardment of the mainland did not materialize, and a period of 'Phoney War' ensued. For the civilian population this was a confusing and rather demoralizing period. But a number of developments were quite favourable for Labour. Leading members of the front bench were appointed to liaise officially with specific ministers, refreshing the governmental experience of men like Greenwood, Alexander and Dalton.[2] The problem of the leadership, which had brewed during Attlee's absence, was resolved in November when Greenwood, Dalton and Morrison, who had all been nominated against the leader in the annual PLP elections, refused to go forward to election (though rather reluctantly, in Morrison's case).[3] The electoral truce held firm, despite protests from some unions and constituency parties, and Labour candidates at by-elections trounced anti-war candidates. There was renewed thought on policy, with the policy committee deciding in February 1940 that a comprehensive new statement of Labour's aims should be prepared: the result, *Labour's Home Policy* (April 1940) stressed the opportunities presented by the new situation and 'provided the rhetorical framework for later war programmes'.[4] And the readmission of Bevan in late 1939, after some pressure from his union, the MFGB, healed some wounds, although Cripps was not to rejoin the party until 1945.[5]

On the other hand, there were tensions. The electoral truce, and close contacts between the government and opposition front benches, meant that it was sometimes difficult for the PLP to tread the middle line between coalition and outright opposition. The Russo-Finnish War, which began in November 1939 and, because of unexpectedly strong Finnish resistance, lasted until March 1940, also caused problems. After the first flush of enthusiasm for the Five Year Plan, Labour misgivings about the USSR had grown from the mid-1930s onwards. These had intensified massively with the German-Soviet Pact and the consequent Soviet occupation of eastern Poland, and the attack on Finland seemed to many people to be no better than what Hitler was doing: Citrine described it as 'an outburst of savagery' and the NCL carried a strongly worded resolution condemning Soviet actions.[6] A few fellow-travelling Labourites tried to justify the Soviet action, but their leading figure, D. N. Pritt (a member of the NEC) was expelled from the party in March 1940 as a result.[7] The attack on Finland also strengthened the resolve of the NEC to root out supposedly pro-Communist elements within the party. In December 1939 the NEC noted a renewal of Communist activity within the party, and a succession of local parties were disbanded as a result, in the biggest party purge since the later 1920s.[8] Opinion against the USSR remained so strong that, when Laski suggested in April 1940 that Labour should consider ways in which Anglo-Soviet relations could be improved, the NEC (of which he was a member) refused even to discuss the idea.[9]

By the time Laski made his suggestion, the difficulties the party faced were leading some of its leaders to consider whether Labour might fare better as part of a coalition, although not under Chamberlain. However, little came of this until the evacuation of British troops from Norway under ignominious circumstances led the PLP to call for a debate on the Chamberlain government's general direction of the war on 7 and 8 May. Initially, the party leadership was reluctant to call a vote on the issue, fearing it would force Conservative backbenchers to back the government and so shore up its position, but events on 7 May, when a number of Tories spoke against Chamberlain, changed all that. When the vote took place on 8 May the government's majority fell to 81 instead of its usual 200, with some Tories voting against the government and others abstaining. This made a reconstruction of the government inevitable. The NEC, meeting in Bournemouth on the eve of the party conference, refused to serve under Chamberlain, but stated that Labour would be prepared to serve under someone else. At first, Labour's preference was for the Foreign Secretary, Lord Halifax: he was widely respected, and seen as a liberal, consensual figure. The alternative was Churchill, who had returned to the cabinet as First Lord of the Admiralty in September 1939, but who was still widely distrusted in Labour circles as an arch-enemy of socialism and trade unionism. But Churchill's anti-appeasement credentials were impeccable, he was clearly a fighter, and the German attack on France which commenced on 9 May swung opinion towards him. Thus the party conference voted by 2 413 000 votes to 170 000 against a resolution opposing entry into a new Churchill administration. An official opposition was to be maintained for the sake of parliamentary business, but Labour ensured it was led by safe figures nearing the end of their careers: H. B. Lees-Smith (to December 1941), F. W. Pethick-Lawrence (December 1941 to March 1942) and Greenwood (March 1942 onwards). It was to be left to other Labour MPs to offer more stringent criticism.[10]

Labour attained a stronger position in the new government than its parliamentary representation warranted. This was partly because Churchill needed a strong counterbalance against a suspicious Conservative party. In any case, to have offered ministerial posts to Labour in ratio to its number of MPs would have left it a very lopsided coalition, hardly a real coalition at all, in fact. Most substantially, the need for union co-operation in a total war effort meant that the Labour movement's extra-parliamentary strength had also to be taken into account. Labour took two places in the new, five-strong, war cabinet: Attlee became Lord Privy Seal and chair of the Food and Home Policy Committee, while Greenwood, as Minister without Portfolio, was put in charge of the Production and Economic Policy Committee. Attlee was surprisingly effective in office. In 1943 he became Lord President of the Council and *de facto* deputy Prime Minister, co-ordinating the home front during Churchill's frequent absences on war business. Greenwood, on the other hand, had little success in office and was effectively sacked in March 1942.

Ernest Bevin, appointed Minister of Labour and National Service in May 1940, was the Labour minister who, ultimately, made the greatest impact. His appointment was a sign both of his own abilities and of the importance of trade unions in wartime. He became an MP for the first time, being succeeded at the TGWU by his close follower, Arthur Deakin. In October he was promoted to the war cabinet. For a decade or more Bevin had been the most powerful individual in the Labour movement. The Ministry of Labour, meanwhile, had been transformed by war from the Cinderella of government departments into the powerhouse of the war effort, since workers were in short supply, and total war required high levels of production and productivity. During the war, Bevin generally handled manpower problems with an enviable sureness of touch and self-confidence. Although he had draconian powers to coerce labour, he was reluctant to use them, relying instead on persuasion wherever possible.[11] He impressed officials – and Churchill – with his abilities, and further developed his interest in foreign affairs, particularly the German question.[12]

The fourth Labourite to serve in the war cabinet (from November 1942 onwards) was Morrison. After a brief spell as Minister of Supply, he became Home Secretary in October 1940, and retained the position for the duration. An experienced administrator from his time as secretary of the London Labour party, Minister of Transport and leader of the London County Council, he was generally regarded as successful, and remained Attlee's main rival for the leadership.

The other 'Labour' figure to serve at the highest level was Cripps. He had been expelled from the party in 1939, and did not rejoin it until February 1945. However, his left-wing reputation helped persuade Churchill to appoint him Ambassador to the USSR in 1940. He was not notably successful in the post, but his role in forging the Anglo-Soviet Alliance which followed the German invasion of Russia in June 1941 was played up by the press, and he returned to a hero's welcome in January 1942. The following month he joined the war cabinet as Lord Privy Seal. An opinion poll in April 1942 found that if 'anything happened to Mr Churchill', 34 per cent would favour Cripps's succession to the premiership; only Eden, the Foreign Secretary, with 37 per cent, outscored him.[13] During the summer of 1942, with the war going badly, he hoped to succeed Churchill. However, the British victory at El Alamein in October allowed Churchill to pay off old scores, and Cripps was sacked from the war cabinet, although he served as Minister of Aircraft Production for the remainder of the conflict.[14]

Other leading Labour figures also served in office. At ministerial rank outside the war cabinet, Alexander returned to the position of First Lord of the Admiralty that he had held in the 1929 government; Johnston became Secretary of State for Scotland in February 1941 and used his position to push forward a number of valuable reforms, including the development of hydroelectricity in the Highlands;[15] Dalton became Minister for Economic Warfare and then President of the Board of Trade, where he promoted a vigorous regional policy which was of direct assistance to some of Labour's strongest core areas of support;[16] and Sir William Jowitt, who had defected to National Labour in 1931 but rejoined Labour in 1939, held a succession of minor offices. Labour also took more than its fair share of junior posts, with five of those involved – Ellen Wilkinson, George Hall, Tom Williams, James Chuter Ede and Joseph Westwood – later serving in the Attlee cabinet. Finally, a number of Labour's future leaders, like Hugh Gaitskell, Douglas Jay and Harold Wilson, served during the war as temporary civil servants in Whitehall.

Labour derived considerable advantage from this. Its credibility as a governing party, so damaged by the events of 1929–31, was largely restored as its leaders proved their competence and gained, or regained, valuable experience. Policy-making was helped by having both senior and junior figures on the 'inside track' of government. And Labour ministers, although constrained by Coalition politics, were able to push through some important schemes of reform, such as Bevin's Catering Wages Act of 1943 and Dalton's regional policies. However, the generally favourable view of Whitehall gained at this time by the men who were to lead Labour until 1976 was possibly a handicap to them, perhaps at the time and certainly later. It was not a simple process of their being 'nobbled' by 'The Establishment' – that would be far too crass a formulation. Rather, it was a tendency to see things still more than before from the centre. The 'top-down' approach, admittedly well entrenched even before the war, was still further strengthened; and wartime collaboration between state, employers and unions was taken by many as a model of what might be possible in the future, rather than as an exceptional product of exceptional circumstances.

The roots of the PLP's relative docility during the Attlee governments' tenure are also to be found in these years. As seen above, the official leadership of the Labour opposition was in safe hands. This is not to say that the PLP as a whole was supine. A small group of pacifist MPs continued to exist. Bevan and Shinwell were among backbenchers who maintained a consistently critical stance towards the government.[17] And although the 'opposition' only divided the House once after May 1940, it did so on an issue – the Beveridge report – which signalled Labour's distinctive line on welfare, to the party's almost certain benefit at the subsequent election. On the whole, though, the PLP was behind the government and the party leadership, and its political culture was developing in a way which helps to explain its manageability in the latter years of the decade.

The war also had a significant impact on trade unionism and this, of course, had major implications for the party. Union density had fallen from 45.2 per cent in 1920 to 22.6 per cent (lower than in 1913) in 1933. Growing prosperity later in the 1930s had led to revival, but even in 1938 membership and density (4 669 186 and 30.5 per cent) were well below the figures for 1920. The number of trade union members affiliated to the Labour party had fluctuated similarly: standing at 4 317 537 in 1920, it had fallen to 1 857 524 in 1934, followed by a gradual recovery to 2 158 076 in 1938, but then the war led to a massive change. TUC membership soared, rising to a wartime peak of 6 642 317 (40.4 per cent density) in 1943; by 1946 the figure was 7 540 397 (43.0 per cent).[18]

The reasons for this are not difficult to find. As the economy moved on to a full war footing, demand for labour soared. Unemployment, which had stood at 1 471 000 in January 1940, fell to 653 000 a year later, and by December 1941 only 151 000 were out of work, and full employment was maintained for the remainder of the war. Employers' attitudes, naturally, changed. Unions themselves were faced with new challenges which led them to try to recruit more widely: a notable case was the decision of the traditionally all-male Amalgamated Engineering Union to admit women in 1943, not through any great conversion to feminism, but through fears that they might otherwise undercut male earnings or be recruited by general unions, potentially weakening the AEU's hold on the industry. Over 100 000 women joined the union in the first year.[19]

In addition, the unions were taken closer to the centre of government and industry than ever before. The state's powers over the workforce were increased to unprecedented levels. In 1940, Defence Regulation 58A gave the Minister the right to direct labour (something which, as 'industrial conscription', had been bitterly opposed by the Labour movement during the First World War), and Order 1305 banned strikes and lockouts, making all disputes subject to compulsory, binding arbitration. In 1944, Regulation 1AA imposed penalties for agitation and incitement to strike. Dilution of labour and suspension of traditional working practices also took place. However, since Bevin preferred conciliation, and tried to avoid invoking the regulations wherever possible, relatively few workers were 'directed' into specific jobs. Strikes still took place: there were actually more stoppages per year on average than during the First World War, although fewer workers were involved and the disputes were settled more quickly, so that, on average, only a third as many working days were lost per year as in 1914–18. Legal penalties on strikers were used sparingly. The unions' reward was close consultation with government and employers. On the outbreak of war a National Joint Advisory Committee of the Ministry of Labour, with 15 employers and 15 trade unionists, had been established. But Bevin found this ineffective, and appointed a more effective Joint Consultative Committee comprising seven representatives from each side plus himself in the chair. It met twice a month, and monitored events closely.[20] Unions were also represented on regional production committees; and, at factory level, management often consulted closely with shop stewards on how to speed up production. Meanwhile, news censorship of strikes meant the suppression of less favourable images. All this helped the public image of trade unionism. The party's close identification with the unions had handicapped it in the 1930s, but as the unions grew in prestige, became increasingly respectable, and covered wider sections of the population (particularly women), Labour could benefit from the association. High levels of unionization increased the affiliated membership of the party from 2 158 076 in 1938 to 2 510 369 in 1945, and the party's finances were boosted accordingly.[21]

In the retrospective mythology with which some Conservatives rationalized their 1945 defeat, Labour benefited from the war because its organizers were more likely to be in 'reserved' occupations, and hence in their normal place of residence. Even if there was a grain of truth in this, it underestimated the pressures on the civilian population, and on Labour activists in particular, especially in the early part of the war. The electoral truce and confusion about the role of the party (particularly before the Coalition was formed), longer working hours, war duties in the Home Guard, Air Raid Patrols and so on, and the widespread disruption caused by German air raids, all helped to reduce Labour's individual membership. This had stood at just over 400 000 in 1939, but then fell back to only 218 783 in 1942. Thereafter, matters began to improve. People came to terms with their work commitments and were able to negotiate time for party activity, and the end of the major period of German air raids in mid-1941 helped. Then the publication of the Beveridge Report in December 1942, and the PLP's division of the Commons in its favour, gave Labourites a chance to coalesce around a concrete set of issues. The result was that individual party membership rose to 265 763 in 1944 and 487 047 in 1945 (a new record level). The cancellation of local elections for the duration led to a certain withering of CLP activity, but even so Labour remained more active than the Tories in cities like Birmingham and Sheffield, which had hitherto had powerful Conservative party machines.[22]

There were improvements in organization at head office. Middleton, who had succeeded Henderson as party secretary in 1934, was finally prised out in 1944, and replaced by the younger and more able Morgan Phillips. Phillips was replaced as research secretary by the 30-year-old intellectual Michael Young, erstwhile director of the independent think-tank, Political and Economic Planning. The International Department was finally wrested from the dead hand of William Gillies in 1944, and he was succeeded, the following year, by the former Communist and war veteran, Major Denis Healey. Head office was, partly at least, taking on a new, more youthful, more purposeful air.[23]

A further important consequence of war was the refinement of party policy. Even during the 'Phoney War' period the NEC had noted the paucity of specific policy documents in a number of areas. *Labour's Home Policy*, published in April 1940, summed up pre-war policy, but also emphasized the need for planning and controls in order to win the war and stressed that such methods would still be needed in peacetime. As Attlee put it, 'the occasion should be seized to lay the foundations of a planned economic system'.[24] It also highlighted the need for social reform as a means of maintaining morale. In early 1941 the party set up a Central Committee on Problems of Post-War Reconstruction, and from this evolved *The Old World and the New Society*, drafted by Laski and published in February 1942. It repeated the message of *Labour's Home Policy*: planning and controls must remain in place. The post-war world must guarantee full employment, social security, reconstruction, a reform of education, and the establishment of a national health service.[25] Later that year the Beveridge Report on Social Insurance and Allied Services was published, calling for a comprehensive welfare state. It was met with scepticism, to say the least, by the Conservatives, but the Labour members of the war cabinet pressed for a government commitment to the report. Ultimately, a compromise was reached whereby the government would make no commitment for or against legislation on the basis of the report. However, when the matter came up for debate in parliament in February 1943, 97 Labour MPs, led by James Griffiths, voted against the government line, in defiance of the Labour whip. This split actually helped Labour, since it showed clearly which party was more committed to the principles of what was, clearly, an exceptionally popular report.[26] The party supported the Education Act and the introduction of family allowances in 1944. In the same year, the government's White Paper on Employment committed the state to the maintenance of 'a high and stable level of employment'. Unlike Labour's recently published statement, *Full Employment and Financial Policy*, however, it did not commit the government to retaining controls once a full transition to peacetime had been made.[27] The other main development came in December 1944, when, against the advice of the NEC, the party conference voted in favour of a resolution which replaced a vague NEC statement about 'transfer[ring] to the State . . . power to direct the policy of our main industries, services and financial institutions' with a definite pledge to effect 'the transfer to public ownership of the land, large-scale building, heavy industry, and all forms of banking, transport and fuel and power'.[28]

How far did Labour move towards more 'consensual' policies in this period? It has been argued that Labour lost many of the features that had made it distinctive in the 1930s: nationalization was played down, the Beveridge Report and the White Paper on Employment were accepted eagerly as replacements for, or enhancements of, party policy. The party, according to this view, became less interested in physical controls over the economy as a long-term option and moved towards a more 'Keynesian' approach of managing the economy by budgetary and fiscal controls. During the 1940s the Conservatives, for their part, 'were obliged to integrate some of Labour's most important demands into their own philosophy', but they 'were able to do so without too much pain because Labour's demands had largely been cast in a mould of thought provided by the non-socialist intelligentsia between the wars and during World War II'.[29]

This 'consensus' view has come under strong attack in recent years, and is now difficult to sustain.[30] Planning and employment policy, for example, were still debated hotly. Labour had spent much of the 1930s talking about the need for planning, by which it meant a combination of nationalization of basic industries and utilities, physical controls, especially (but not by any means solely) over investment, and a commitment to full employment. The war resulted in the development of controls, and also saw what can be viewed in retrospect as a kind of proto-nationalization in terms of state control of the mines and railways. It also saw the publication of the White Paper on Employment, as stated above. So far, so consensual. But crucial differences remained, even within the war cabinet itself. Labour, for example, saw wartime controls as the start of a permanent process, whereas most Conservatives saw them as something which would not survive the transition to peace. Nationalization was as resolutely opposed by the Tories as it was advocated by Labour. And the phrase about maintaining a 'high and stable level of employment' in the 1944 White Paper was deliberately vague because no one could agree on what level of unemployment would be acceptable: the TUC, Labour and Beveridge plumped for 3 per cent, whereas the Treasury took the view that 8.5 per cent was the desirable level.[31] Yet a figure of 8.5 per cent would have left well over a million out of work. This was hardly acceptable to Labour. It is true that both parties became somewhat less antagonistic towards Keynesian techniques. But at this stage neither was willing to adopt them as any more than a bolt-on addition to their longstanding economic policies. The most that can be said is that there was a blurring of the lines, and perhaps some acceptance of a mixed economy in theory. But this really does not suggest a consensus since the nature of the mixture was still very much open to debate.

There were also sharp divisions in other areas. On health, Labour welcomed wartime advances, and its ministers helped to draft the February 1944 White Paper which promised a national health service free at the point of use. But both sides saw it as a consultation document rather than a definitive plan of campaign. The period between then and the end of the war saw the Conservatives retreating from the White Paper and returning to earlier, less comprehensive proposals, while Labour continued to press for its own distinctive policies, such as a salaried medical profession and provision of health centres.[32] In social insurance, too, Labour continued to press its own policies. It was a different story in education, where there was 'a greater degree of party co-operation than [on] any other aspect of wartime policy'.[33] Labour supported the 1944 Education Act, accepting a number of policies which looked to future generations decidedly compromised, such as the failure to enforce comprehensive schools at secondary level, the continuation of private education, the failure to set specific dates for the raising of the school-leaving age, and the continuation of fees in direct grant schools. However, to focus on these aspects is to overlook what was gained from the Act. It offered an end to the old system of 'elementary' education: for the first time, all children would receive *some* secondary education. Further, fees for secondary schooling were abolished. There was a settlement of the thorny question of religious control of schools, which had stymied Labour's earlier attempts to reform the system and cost it much in electoral terms. It is also important not to be anachronistic. Though there was strong support for 'multilateral' (comprehensive) education, many Labourites continued to see selection and grammar schools as positive, in so far as they allowed the brightest working-class children to gain an education as good as that of their 'social betters'. The 1944 Act, then, was seen as a worthwhile and much-needed reform, one with imperfections, certainly, but ones which could be rectified at a later date. Better that than to saddle a future Labour government with working on the whole question from scratch. The attitude towards education policy, in other words, was more commonsensical than truly consensual.

It seems difficult, then, to sustain the view that there was a thoroughgoing consensus during the war. Labour retained a distinctive outlook, a fact which is further highlighted when the focus is moved to local government. There, disputes over rate levels, post-war planning, a possible extension of the municipal franchise, and the permanence or otherwise of wartime developments like the British Restaurants were commonplace.[34] For their part, the Conservatives, influenced increasingly by the business community from 1944 onwards, were still essentially committed to private enterprise and market forces; that they re-emphasized this during the latter part of the war for fear that a Labour government would nationalize extensively tells its own story.[35] The idea of consensus, then, has been useful for journalists and political commentators, has helped to make academic careers, and has spawned a considerable level of debate in the academic journals. This does not mean that it was a reality.

The approach of the end of the war raised the question of the future of the Coalition. The NEC, in a statement to the December 1944 party conference, declared that there must be an election 'as soon as possible' after the war's end, and that the election must be fought on party lines: there would be no repeat of the 'coupon election' of 1918.[36] This, of course, left the matter of timing open to interpretation; after Germany's surrender in May 1945 there were those who favoured continuing the Coalition until Japan had been defeated. In the event, however, and to general Labour satisfaction, Churchill, himself under some pressure from his party, resigned immediately and was then reappointed as premier of a 'Caretaker' government composed of Conservatives plus a few Liberal Nationals and ostensibly non-party figures. Parliament was dissolved on 5 June, with polling to take place exactly a month later, with the votes being counted on 26 July to allow time for postal votes from members of the armed forces serving overseas to be sent to Britain.

When the results were declared, there was some surprise at the scale, if not entirely at the fact, of the Labour victory. Labour took almost 12 million votes (48.0 per cent of those cast) and emerged with 393 seats, as against the Conservatives and their allies who had only 210. Labour had polled well in all its core areas, but, most strikingly, it ate into what had been, hitherto, more difficult territory. In both the east and west Midlands it smashed through its previous best performance, 1929, to take more than half the seats. It took 84 of the 111 seats in the Greater London area. No fewer than 143 Labour MPs now represented constituencies south of the Severn-Wash line. This all meant a great change in the party's complexion: there was now no region of Great Britain where it did not have at least one MP. Even old Liberal areas like the south-west of England and rural north Wales yielded Labour victories. Labour took unlikely seats like Taunton, Winchester, Wycombe, Great Yarmouth, Dover and Watford. This was truly a national performance: for the first time Labour could really claim, as it had not been able to do even in the aftermath of the 1929 result, that it had a foot in all parts of the country. It truly seemed that Labour had arrived as a party of government.

All sorts of explanation have been advanced for the Labour victory of 1945. Some contemporary Labour explanations suggested that 'gradualness' had been inevitable after all: Labour was simply entering into its inheritance. According to this view, Labour's victory was 'the manifestation not simply of a transitory mood at one general election, but of a genuine and cumulative increase over many years of popular support for Socialist policies', an increase caused by 'the logic of events and the maturing development of circumstance' which had 'shaped the minds of men and women increasingly and inevitably to an understanding of the validity and inevitability of Socialist principles'.[37] Others have argued that 'the People's War' had been important in radicalizing the British people.[38] Yet such arguments rest on dubious assumptions.

A combination of negative and positive factors explained the Labour victory of 1945. The Conservatives suffered at the election from being the party which had taken Britain into a long and difficult war. The National governments of the 1930s were now seen as weak and vacillating, even criminally incompetent, in failing to see the true nature of the German threat and make stronger efforts to resist it: it was widely believed that the results of the war could have been achieved more easily at a much lower cost. In addition, five years of full employment, fostered by government action, suggested that the National governments had been cruelly negligent in allowing mass unemployment to remain a feature of British life in the 1930s. There grew up also the view that Lloyd George's promises of a better post-war world in 1918 had been thwarted by the selfishness of the Conservative MPs who were his main supporters. These were views which Churchill and the other leaders of the Conservative party could do little to counter, not least because many members of the Caretaker government had themselves been staunch critics of the National government in the 1930s, and none more so than Churchill himself. Furthermore, the polls agreed that Churchill had been a fine war leader, but there were misgivings about his future intentions, with fears that he was a warmonger and that he was, as his interwar record had sometimes suggested, somewhat unbalanced at times. Perhaps there was a weariness of 'great men'. All this helped Labour.

At the same time, Labour had had a good war. It no longer seemed as sectional as it had in the 1930s: its leaders were now well-known figures who had served effectively in government for five years. Churchill's attacks on Attlee during the campaign aroused sympathy for the latter and increased his public profile. Labour's policies were more credible and comprehensible than previously, since, as in 1918, the party's main argument was the need to develop and extend the measures which had helped to win the war. In addition, socialism and trade unionism had lost much of the opprobrium that had been attached to them before 1939, given the expansion and apparent statesmanship of the unions, and the fact that 'socialism' was not only clearly anti-fascist but also the doctrine which had helped the USSR to heroic resistance and later victory over Nazi Germany.[39] Furthermore, substantial sections of the population favoured further social reform and believed that Labour was the party most likely to deliver it.

However, as emphasized above, these arguments should not be overstated. There was no mass radicalization. Many voters were undoubtedly cynical as to the motives and potential to fulfil their promises of party politicians generally, and since this seems to have been one of the constant features of British politics since the nineteenth century, it is unlikely to have been absent in 1945.[40] It is possible to surmise, in fact, that three main groups (which to some extent overlapped) were crucial in helping Labour to victory. First, it seems clear that Labour polled a larger proportion of the working-class vote, and over a larger part of the country, than ever before. Here, fear of post-war unemployment was a factor, but there were others, including massively increased levels of unionization and fears about post-war production relations. A distrust of the Conservatives' record on social reform was also important here. Secondly, young voters appear to have swung to Labour. To them, unemployment was associated with the Conservative-dominated National governments, rather than the 1929–31 Labour administration. Housing was also an issue which, while of broad significance, pressed particularly hard on young people, and so Labour's past record in local and national government, and its ongoing commitment to council housing, undoubtedly helped it.[41] More broadly, the idealistic aspects of Labour's rhetoric at the 1945 election might also have helped to swing youthful voters. Thirdly, Labour increased its support among middle-class voters, or more particularly lower middle-class voters.[42] This was probably less significant than the rise in working-class support. But social reform might benefit them too; and some sections of the middle class liked Labour's emphasis on a big state, seeing in it opportunities of employment and status. To a certain extent, it might be argued, the Fabians' aim of a middle-class bureaucracy voting Labour out of self-interest was being achieved.

As with the First World War, it was something of a paradox that Labour, which had always argued that peace was the essential prerequisite of 'progress', should have done so well out of a long and bloody war. Labour was elected to office in 1945 with probably its strongest ever team of leaders, and a programme second to none in its history for coherence, prioritization and applicability to the situation in which the country was placed. It now remained to be seen whether that programme could be implemented, and what the results would be, not just for Britain, but for the Labour party itself.

6

The Attlee Governments, 1945–51

The record of the Labour government elected in 1945 was formidable, and set high standards which subsequent Labour administrations tried in vain to emulate. At home, it introduced significant social reforms, carried out extensive nationalization, and maintained full employment throughout the transition to peace. Abroad, it played a leading role in establishing the system of alliances that dominated the world until the end of the Cold War, and decolonized India and Palestine. At the same time, though, it can be criticized. Left-wing critics have attacked it for the limitations of its nationalization policies, its halting attitude toward redistribution, its failure to remodel power relations in British society radically, its adherence to the United States in foreign policy, and its equivocal position on the Empire.[1] On the other hand, 'new right' critics have launched stinging attacks on what they see as its preference for welfare reform over the need to remodel the industrial base which paid for such changes.[2] Even so, it deserves to be remembered as Labour's most successful period in office.

In the immediate aftermath of victory there were, once again, moves to replace Attlee with Morrison. However, Attlee's public profile had been boosted during the election campaign, not least by Churchill's backfiring attacks; and the latter's decision to resign immediately and advise the King to send for Attlee pre-empted Morrison's efforts, as Attlee accepted the commission and presented Labour MPs with a *fait accompli*. In any case, there was little hope for Morrison, who still aroused animosity among other Labour leaders, especially Bevin. Morrison was appointed Lord President of the Council, to act as *de facto* deputy Prime Minister and co-ordinator of domestic policy as chairman of the Lord President's Committee. After some havering Attlee appointed Dalton as Chancellor of the Exchequer and Bevin as Foreign Secretary.[3] Cripps, the fifth member of the new 'Big Five', who were to dominate the early years of the government, was appointed President of the Board of Trade: he would play the leading role in industrial and production policy.

Of the 'Big Five', only Morrison had served in the previous Labour cabinet under MacDonald, and then only for five months. There were only four other survivors of that cabinet. Greenwood, now well past his best, became Lord Privy Seal; Alexander returned to the Admiralty; Benn (now Lord Stansgate) went to Air; and Addison, also ennobled, went to the Dominions Office. The left was represented in the new cabinet by Ellen Wilkinson (the only woman member) at Education, Aneurin Bevan at Health, and Emanuel Shinwell at Fuel and Power. There were only six trade unionists in the cabinet; other than Bevin and Bevan they were not particularly significant or forceful figures.

The cabinet was altered in piecemeal fashion over the period between 1945 and the 1950 election, but there was never a thoroughgoing reshuffle. The main changes came in the autumn of the government's *annus horrendous* – 1947.[4] Its self-confidence had been severely shaken by the fuel and food crises and later the convertibility crisis (see below). Cripps wanted to replace Attlee with Bevin, but the plot failed because of lack of support from Morrison, Dalton and Bevin himself. Cripps, regardless, told Attlee that he thought the latter should resign. Attlee dismissed the suggestion but did appoint Cripps as Minister of Economic Affairs, and set up a new committee of the Big Five plus Addison – now leader in the Lords – to deal with major issues.[5] Cripps was succeeded at the Board of Trade by the 31-year-old Harold Wilson. Then, in November, Dalton inadvertently leaked budget secrets to a journalist, and, after some hesitation on all sides, resigned (he returned to the cabinet the following year in a more minor post).[6] The Treasury passed to Cripps, who thus combined Economic Affairs with the Exchequer.

This powerful team of leaders received strong support from the PLP throughout its term of office. There were occasional problems, as in 1948 when Alfred Edwards, MP for Middlesbrough East, was expelled from the party after attacking the nationalization of steel and the right to strike. Around the same time John Platts-Mills was expelled after a series of attacks on the government and calls for a pro-Soviet foreign policy. But the general tractability of Labour MPs could be seen in the fact that the PLP's standing orders were suspended throughout the

life of the 1945 and 1950 parliaments. This loyalty had a number
of causes. The suspension of the PLP's standing orders created a
comradely atmosphere, in stark contrast to 1929–31 or to later
governments. As Morrison said, parliament 'would be a dull
assembly if we overdid discipline', and he hoped that there would
be 'a good deal of free speech, even to the extent of disagreeing
with Ministers, so long as it [did]n't upset the apple cart'.[7] The
Liaison Committee between ministers and backbenchers was more
successful than in 1929–31, mainly because the leadership took
it more seriously, and Morrison's appointment of 17 policy committees to liaise with individual ministers generally worked well,
although the foreign policy committee was a notable exception.[8]
In addition, the government did 'produce the goods', going full
speed ahead on its manifesto commitments. Thirdly, two-thirds
of Labour MPs were new to parliament: more than half of these
were middle-class.[9] Thus a large number of MPs were out to
make a career for themselves, and this tended to encourage people
towards loyalty. It might also be that middle-class MPs in a
movement which remained, in spirit, very much working-class,
were feeling their way a little.[10]

A further factor inhibiting fractiousness in the PLP was the
unions' strong support for the government.[11] Labour ministers
in the 1960s and 1970s would look back almost incredulously at
the ease with which union–party relations were handled in the
1940s. Strikes and lockouts remained illegal under wartime Order 1305, which was not formally rescinded until 1951. As in
wartime, disputes did take place, but fewer days were lost through
strikes on average than in the period 1932–8, itself a time of relative
calm. This degree of industrial peace was due less to Order 1305
than to the closeness, both personally and in terms of outlook,
between ministers and union leaders; the union leaders' sense
of involvement in government, both formally and informally; and
general contentment with a government which, in contrast to
1929–31, delivered much of what the unions wanted. The 1927
Trade Disputes Act was repealed in 1946; full employment and
rising working-class living standards were maintained; and social
reform was implemented. The key demands of many individual unions, such as the nationalization of coal mining, were also
fulfilled.

Faced with all this, there were few openings for a cogent left
challenge to the Attlee administration. The parliamentary left was

undoubtedly enervated – as Attlee had intended – by the appointment of Bevan to the cabinet, and Cripps in office was very different from the Cripps of the previous decade. But, in addition, its lack of a coherent and distinctive ideology kept it marginalized. It pushed for further public ownership, and was perhaps decisive in the final determination to go ahead with the nationalization of steel. But it had little else to say, particularly on domestic policy. For example, it did not mount a serious challenge to the public corporation model of nationalization. At first it had more to say on foreign affairs, but, as will be seen below, the onset of the Cold War had helped to drive the left into more or less grudging support of the main outlines of Bevin's foreign policy by 1949.

In part, the perception of the government as successful was based on its ability to handle the economy. In terms of broad economic management, this was the most successful Labour government. The vicissitudes which had followed the First World War were avoided. Unemployment was hardly ever above 500 000, except for the wholly exceptional circumstances of February 1947. Indeed, labour shortages were the main problem. Inflation remained under control, helped by a wage freeze between 1948 to 1950. Taxation remained high, but the standard rate of income tax was reduced from 50 to 45 per cent in 1947.

This was all the more remarkable given that it was achieved in a context of severe and continuing exchange and balance of payments problems. The war had cost Britain about a quarter of its total wealth. Overseas investments had been wound down to pay for the war. Even so, Britain had been heavily reliant on the generous provision of Lend-Lease assistance from the USA. Hopes that this might continue for some time were dashed when the end of the war with Japan in August 1945 was followed by the equally abrupt termination of Lend-Lease. A massive crisis loomed, and a British delegation under Keynes set off for Washington to negotiate a loan. Agreement was finally reached in December 1945 on a loan of $3 750 000 from the USA and $1 250 000 from Canada, but the terms were difficult and included making sterling fully convertible by mid-1947.[12]

The loan gave Britain valuable breathing space, allowing the government to push ahead with reforms safe in the knowledge that domestic living standards could be maintained. Without it, imports would have had to be reduced dramatically, with a concomitant decrease in living standards. But, inevitably, when convertibility was introduced in July 1947, the pound collapsed. The result was a sterling crisis and the suspension of convertibility after just five weeks. Ultimately, as seen above, Cripps replaced Dalton as Chancellor. Judged on its own terms, his tenure at the Treasury was probably the finest period of Cripps's varied career. His ascetic lifestyle fitted well with the nation's need to tighten its belt.[13] Even so, the crucial assistance again came, in 1948, from the United States, in the shape of Marshall Aid, which aimed to revive western Europe and see off the Communist 'threat'. Britain received around $2 700 000 to the end of 1950, by which time the position had improved to such an extent that it could announce that it no longer required assistance.[14]

Before then, however, there had been another sterling crisis. During the spring of 1949 the balance of payments position began to take a turn for the worse, and with Cripps absent, ill, three young ministers, all economists – Gaitskell, Wilson and Jay – were forced to recommend devaluation (although with reluctance in Wilson's case).[15] Cripps and the cabinet agreed, and on 18 September the pound was devalued from $4.03 to $2.80. This was a sensible move: devaluation was not a national disgrace, simply a recognition of changed realities. But the episode had deeper significance, all the same. Unlike in 1931, the government did not panic, and remained united, while the financial establishment, for its part, was willing to see a Labour government devalue. Wilson's reluctance to devalue would prove to be a signpost for his behaviour when, as Prime Minister in the 1960s, he would again be faced with pressure on sterling. Finally, the crisis showed yet again the fragility of Britain's exchange position and, with it, all that Labour was trying to do. That the government was able, nonetheless, to press ahead with its policies for industry and social reform in such a potentially delicate situation makes its achievements in those areas all the more remarkable.

The 1945 manifesto had promised an extensive round of nationalization: the Bank of England, fuel and power, inland transport and iron and steel would all be taken over by the state with 'fair compensation' paid to the owners, and be run 'efficiently in the interests of consumers, coupled with proper status and conditions for the workers employed in them'.[16] The Bank of England and civil aviation were nationalized in 1946; coal, rail, road haulage, and cable and wireless in 1947; and electricity and gas in 1948. Most of these measures were relatively uncontroversial, although there was strong Conservative opposition in the House of Commons over road haulage and gas. Steel, however, was more problematic. The issue divided the cabinet, with Morrison and others favouring an interim measure short of full public ownership and some, like Dalton, favouring postponement. Finally, legislation nationalizing the industry was passed, against strong Conservative opposition, with the proviso that it would not come into effect until after the next general election.[17]

The doubts over steel were due in part to factors like the coolness of the steelworkers' union towards nationalization, and the fact that it was quite efficiently run in private hands. But ministers' hesitancy seems also to have stemmed from growing doubts as to the efficacy of nationalization *per se*. For the nationalization measures passed by the Attlee governments did pose problems. Many of the industries were nationalized because of their erstwhile inefficiency: only the state, it was argued, could sustain vital industries which were unattractive to private investors. This was particularly the case with coal and rail. But this in turn made a rod for these industries' and Labour's backs, since they could be held up, at the time and later, as examples of 'inefficient' 'socialist' industrial policy. Secondly, the form of nationalization, the public corporation, posed problems. The industries were to be run by boards appointed by the minister but free from ministerial interference in day-to-day affairs. But the insistence that each nationalized board should operate its industry on business lines meant a general lack of co-ordination *between* industries. Even worse, the industries varied in the administrative arrangements, some being rather less centralized than others and most adopting different regional coverages.[18] This inevitably led to problems, and, coming from a government supposedly committed to economic planning, was self-defeating. Furthermore, there was no attempt to redistribute the balance of power *within* industries. No attempt was made at workers' control, nor even at trade union representation on the boards, despite the facts that many of the industries were heavily unionized, that, in the case of coal, one union spoke for virtually the entire workforce, and that some people on the left were demanding it.[19] The government does not seem to have taken such proposals seriously, with Cripps speaking witheringly of worker-controlled industry as 'almost impossible' until workers had 'more experience . . . of the managerial side of the industry'.[20] If anything, workers *lost* control since negotiations were now still more likely to take place at the centre, remote from the daily life of the worker. On one level this was understandable. Britain was in a tight spot. It needed efficient industry to help the balance of payments, which was in a precarious position (though at the same time the very existence of the crisis meant that it could not have undertaken an extensive modernization of Britain's industrial base even had it been inclined to do so). On a party political level, Labour wanted to prove it was respectable and responsible, rather than to indulge in untried experiments which might backfire. It has also been argued that traditions of trade-union voluntarism would have meant a reluctance of workers to participate, in any case. Yet there was more to it than that. Joint consultative committees during the war had proved effective, with wholehearted workforce and union participation. Some experiments in workers' control could have been tried at regional or even plant level, with the aim of extending them if they proved successful, or abandoning or modifying them if they did not. Instead, the public corporation model, which carried all before it, led to poor industrial relations and, after a very brief honeymoon period, low levels of worker commitment to the principle of nationalization.

But, of course, experimentation would have flown in the face of the by now almost all-pervasive whig interpretation of Labour history: that is, the view that Labour was moving ever onward and upward. Nowhere was this better demonstrated than in the books published in the run-up to the party's fiftieth birthday, such as Cole's *History of the Labour Party from 1914* (1948), the official three-volume extravaganza *The British Labour Party* (1948) and Francis Williams's *Fifty Years' March* (1949). Labour's rise had been inevitable; it would have come about earlier but for the trickery and shenanigans of the party's opponents, but now, 'Labour was in power with an absolute majority at last'.[21] A second element of this, bearing specifically on nationalization, was the belief that, since 1900, a process of natural selection had been taking place in party policy. Thus guild socialism and its critique of statism was a mutant strain of British socialism which had become extinct through its inherent weaknesses, a historical curio, of about as much immediate relevance as Clarion Cycling Clubs or Labour Churches, and of considerably less salience than Keir Hardie's cap. The few critics of the public corporation who did emerge could make little headway when they were deemed to be sifting through the rubbish heap of history.

Labour's line on nationalization meant that a rigid barrier existed between the public and private sectors. There was no attempt to practise a mixed economy at micro as well as macro level, with government taking a stake in private companies. Indeed, Labour's attitude towards private industry at this time was generally conciliatory and non-interventionist. Wilson noted that 'this problem of the relationship between Government and private industry is almost a vacuum in Socialist thought', and this should come as no surprise.[22] Labour socialism was predicated on the idea of successful capitalist enterprise as the dynamic force which would bring about a socialist society. Since 1931 Labour had switched away from the effective *laissez-faire* approach of MacDonald and Snowden, but the essential reliance on the private sector remained intact. Most Labourites did not want now, any more than their predecessors, to nationalize all industries. The Labour government *was* eager, given its balance of payments problems, to encourage greater production and productivity, especially in the export industries. This, and the legacy of wartime and the pre-war period, meant that it talked a lot about planning, but by 1951 Labour had moved a long way even from this.

During the war, Labour had hoped to secure the co-operation of capitalists in an extensive and enduring system of controls of private industry. At the height of the conflict, some civil servants and industrialists had seemed favourable to the idea, but such enthusiasm as there had been waned in the latter part of the war.[23] This opposition to state intervention posed a problem for Labour once it came to power, since the balance of payments position required the full co-operation of all sides of industry, including industrialists. Accordingly, the decision was taken to avoid confrontation. Labour did attempt, especially later in the period, to push industry towards greater levels of employer–workforce consultation, and to establish development councils for various industries. But these depended on industrialists' good will, and by the later 1940s, with a newly self-confident Conservative party in the wings, there was little pressure on them to conform. Realizing this, Wilson, as President of the Board of Trade, tried to persuade his colleagues of the need for greater coercion, advocating the appointment of government directors on companies' boards, increased controls, and nationalization of persistently recalcitrant companies.[24] However, little was done: policy towards private industry remained one of exhortation and little else, other than a gradually tapering degree of state control over materials and labour power.

Given the reluctance to intervene in private industry, even to have much to do with the day-to-day management of industries taken into the public sector, planning came to grief. Even during the 1930s, some socialists had doubted the efficacy of physical controls and, during the war, many had been impressed with the potential of the budget as a tool of economic management. As it became clear that only coercion could bring private industry fully into planning, the tendency increased to see budgetary methods as a better, more consensual way of proceeding. The unpopularity of controls was also a factor in the move from planning. Rationing and other controls remained long after the war ended; bread rationing was introduced for the first time in 1947. By late 1948 criticism, fuelled by vigorous Conservative propaganda, was reaching fever pitch, and it was in an attempt to ease these attacks that Wilson held his 'Bonfire of Controls' that November. Another problem which was increasingly recognized was that manpower planning, in particular, fell foul of the labourist ethos: direction of labour to particular industries was something the movement had always resisted.[25] Although new efforts were made in 1947, with the establishment of new planning bodies, it was clear by 1950 that physical controls were being replaced by budgetary methods as the chief means of state economic management. The result of this, of course, was a loss of distinctiveness in policy and a growing perception that there was little to choose between Labour and Conservative economic management.

Overall, then, Labour's economic performance was somewhat mixed. The same could be said of its record in social policy. The greatest achievement came in health. The minister responsible, Bevan (at 48 the youngest member of the cabinet in 1945), had a reputation as a rebel, but he also had considerable administrative ability and drive. Although a national health service was already on the political agenda, there was still a great deal of dispute as to its exact nature and scope. In late 1945 the cabinet agreed a draft bill to nationalize hospitals, which would be administered by regional boards, taking them out of the control of local authorities and voluntary bodies. However, there were substantial concessions to the medical profession, including the preservation of capitation fees instead of the introduction of salaries for doctors, and the maintenance of private practice and pay-beds in NHS hospitals. The bill passed its second reading in May 1946, but the doctors remained unhappy, and there followed almost two years of unseemly wrangling with the British Medical Association which only ended in April 1948 when Bevan announced that there was no question of a move towards a salaried medical profession. The service, free at the point of use, now came formally into operation.[26]

Another legacy of wartime was the pressure that had built up to do something about social security. Here, another Welshman, James Griffiths, Minister of National Insurance, piloted the National Insurance Act through parliament in 1946. Under the Act, people in work paid a flat-rate national insurance contribution, in return for which they (and the wives of male contributors) were eligible for flat-rate pensions, sickness benefit, unemployment benefit, and funeral benefit. This was followed in 1948 by the National Assistance Act, which gave financial help to those with no other source of income. To Labourites, this all seemed like a great advance. The universal principle was established, a contrast with the means-testing that had characterized the interwar years (although some means-testing did in fact remain).[27] Yet criticisms were also made. There was inequity in the treatment of men and women. Rates of benefit were not set at a realistic rate of subsistence.[28] In addition, the principle of flat-rate contributions was regressive, taking a larger percentage of one's income the less one earned. However, Labour was under pressure, not least from working-class voters, to ensure that money was not wasted; and the insurance principle was generally accepted as fair.[29] Finally, Labour's continuing concentration on the world of work meant that minds focused most on unemployment benefits, and here the argument was that in a situation of full employment and labour shortages there was no real problem if benefits were pitched rather on the low side: people would not be out of work for long unless they wanted to be, and if they wanted to be then it was not right that they should be supported generously in their idleness.

Labour's record in housing was perceived as less successful. By the end of the war, the situation was grave. Enemy action, lack of repairs during wartime, and the virtual cessation of new building for five years, had all taken their toll. There was a massive

shortage of housing units, while many existing houses had become slums. Many local authorities entered peacetime with high
hopes of rapid progress, but these hopes were soon dashed. In
Hull, for example, it was estimated that there was a shortfall of
32 000 dwellings, and the corporation aimed to build 5000 in the
first post-war year; but due to shortages of materials and labour,
and confusion at the centre, the city was able to build only 1766
permanent and 2457 temporary dwellings by 1950.[30] These failures
were symptomatic of the national position. Early problems of a
large number of starts but few completions were gradually overcome, but the number of houses built remained pretty unimpressive. By the end of 1947 fewer than 200 000 permanent
dwellings had been completed since 1944, and although just over
200 000 were completed in each of the succeeding four years, these
figures did not approach the annual average figure for 1934–8
of 361 000 dwellings.[31] Labour had promised a great deal more
than it delivered, and though it did face severe constraints it
might be argued that the commitment of the minister in charge,
Bevan, to quality over quantity was a mistake. By 1951 there
was a shortfall of over a million housing units.[32] In so far as 79
per cent of the new housing was owned by local authorities,
though, the party was clearly adding further to its clientage up
and down the country.[33]

In education, Labour was not innovative at all. The 1944 Act
had seen to that. Labour was by no means against the principle
of selection at age 11 which most local authorities had adopted,
while an attack on the private sector would have been seen as a
diversion from larger concerns facing the administration and would
also have gone against the non-confrontational image that the
government was trying to portray. The main achievements were
the raising of the school-leaving age to 15 in 1947 and a general
increase in expenditure. By 1951 party policy was moving away
from selection and towards comprehensivization, but as a policy
for a future, rather than the present, Labour government.

Labour's record in social policy, then, was generally sound,
with clear success in the creation of the National Health Service
but with more mixed results elsewhere. But Labour had at least
set out the parameters of a system of state welfare more extensive than anything previously known in Britain. This system,
though it can be criticized, did improve the life-chances of most
of the population. And, had Labour remained in office after 1951,

many of the shortcomings outlined above might have been over-come. However, Labour had created a welfare state without really addressing broader questions about the nature of 'the state'. The war and its aftermath almost doubled the number of civil serv-ants, and the state had taken on new roles in wide areas of the nation's life.[34] Yet Labour in power did not really address any of the constitutional implications of these developments.

The basic premiss of mainstream Labourism was that the existing system of parliamentary government, if not perfect, was quite easily perfectible. Labour, no less than the Conservative party, was committed not just to 'parliamentarism' but to the West-minster model. Accordingly, there were some minor changes. Plural voting was abolished, along with the university seats. There was the first major redistribution of constituencies since 1918, and a boundary commission was set up on a permanent basis to review the situation periodically. The local government franchise, hitherto restricted to ratepayers and their spouses, was now granted to all adults. And in 1949 the delaying powers of the House of Lords were reduced from two years to one.

Otherwise little was done. There was no reform of the elec-toral system (and, it must be admitted, very little demand for it outside the tiny Liberal party). More surprisingly, perhaps, there was no substantial reform of the House of Lords. Apart from the creation of some new Labour peers nothing was done to re-form its composition (life peerages only came in 1958). One reason for this was the innate constitutional conservatism of Labour's leaders, but another was Labour's ability to work with the 'up-per house'. Addison, leader in the Lords from 1940 onwards, formed an effective team of Labour peers and was generally able to pass legislation without difficulty. This merely reinforced the view that to take on the Lords when there was little, if any, popular demand for such a move would appear vindictive, small-minded and doctrinaire, distracting the government from more pressing concerns.

The fate of local government under the Attlee governments was fairly predictable, given the growing statism of Labour over the previous period. Apart from reforming the local government franchise, the governments did little except strip authorities of certain functions. Cole's appeals for a renewed emphasis on lo-cal authorities, and a new regional tier of government, were ig-nored.[35] Councils lost functions, such as their hospitals and, in some cases, the supply of gas and electricity, to nationalized industries or remote regional boards which owed more loyalty to central than to local government. Legislation enacted in 1945, further, made all local authority loan issues subject to Treasury approval. At the time, there was little resistance to all this. Morrison, one of the few members of the cabinet with recent local government experience, did try to resist the nationalization of hospitals, but without success. Yet in the end it was to matter. Ultimately, local government in many parts of the country – not least where Labour was ensconced in power – was to become enfeebled, enervated, and prone to inefficiency and, sometimes, corruption. Turnout in local elections, already falling before the war, fell away further. It would be unfair to blame the Attlee governments alone for this. But they hastened the process. British 'democracy' became more centralized than ever, at just the time when the functions of the state were expanding. The result was a massive concentration of power at the centre and the increasing inability of elected representatives to oversee effectively the actions of the executive. It also meant that, by the 1980s, local government became a soft underbelly via which a government of a very different hue could attack much of what Labour had achieved in the immediate post-war period.

There can be little doubt that the Attlee governments made new departures in domestic policy and set in place a structure which would, more or less, remain in place for many years to come. The same was true in foreign policy. Here, the main theme of the period, in retrospect, was the development of the Cold War. At first, it was hoped that wartime co-operation between Britain, the USA and the USSR could be continued. But during the latter part of 1945 matters began to deteriorate, and by early 1946 Foreign Office officials were beginning to suggest a less conciliatory line should be taken towards the USSR. Meetings of the tripartite Council of Foreign Ministers became increasingly acrimonious. The Labour left blamed Bevin for this, and claimed that he was either virulently anti-Communist or so much in the hands of his officials that he could not see beyond their blind anti-Soviet prejudice. They favoured the creation of a European 'third force' to stand between the two superpowers.[36] But such a course was never realistic, given that the USSR was clearly committed to enforcing its rule over the countries in its sphere. Bevin was his own man and a fierce realist, and the promulgation of the 'Keep Left' manifesto in March 1947 by his Labour critics was a fairly futile exercise, although it caused a stir at the time. Deteriorating relations with the USSR and increased warmth between Britain and the USA meant events were moving away from Keep Left. Suspicion of Soviet aims increased rapidly. In 1948, the Communist coup in Czechoslovakia, the creation of the Communist Information Bureau (seen in the west as a successor to the now defunct Communist International), the Soviet break with Tito in Yugoslavia, and the Soviet blockade of Berlin all suggested that the USSR intended to strengthen its grip on its sphere of influence in eastern and central Europe. Anti-Communist feeling was further strengthened by the Communists' victory in China in 1949 and the announcement that the Soviet Union had developed its own atomic weapons. By 1948 many Labourites who had been criticizing Bevin were admitting that there was now no real prospect of co-operation with the USSR or of wresting eastern Europe from its influence to create a 'third force'.[37]

Meanwhile, relations with the USA improved. At first, there had been very real fears that America would withdraw into isolation, as had happened at the end of the First World War. Relations were not improved by the abrupt termination of Lend-Lease in 1945 and the stringent terms of the American loan agreed in early 1946. It was partly uncertainty about future American intentions that led a small group of cabinet ministers to decide, in January 1947, to develop an independent British nuclear weapons capacity.[38] However, matters soon began to ease with the help of the 'Soviet threat'. When, in February 1947, Bevin told Washington that Britain could no longer aid Greece and Turkey, the Americans agreed to take over those responsibilities. They also accepted the suspension of sterling convertibility that August. Marshall Aid was warmly welcomed in 1948, and Britain's withdrawal from Palestine in the same year removed a source of tension. And in April 1949, the North Atlantic Treaty Organization (NATO) was formed, for the first time binding Britain and the USA together in a formal peacetime alliance. It guaranteed its member states against external aggression, and was to prove, in the event, the basis of British foreign policy to the present day.

By contrast, Labour's attitude towards continental Europe was equivocal. In the interwar period there had been those, particularly in France, who had argued for the development of some kind of unity among European states. This had not gone down very well with such British Labourites as had taken any notice.[39] They argued that such a halfway internationalism would be a negation of true internationalism, though even among people who used this argument there were those who were firmly opposed to any kind of serious engagement with foreign countries at all. After the war, such ideas were revived. In France, especially, many people saw closer European co-operation as the key to avoiding future wars. The result was the development of the agreements and institutions which were to lead, ultimately, to the Treaty of Rome which set up the European Economic Community in 1957. At first, Britain was quite closely involved in these developments. However, the intensification of the process saw gradual British disengagement, so that by 1951 it was reasonably clear that Britain would stand aside.[40] Some people have seen this as a tragic mistake, but such a view is somewhat simplistic. First, there were diplomatic considerations. Up to 1947, Labour still had hopes of 'Big Three' co-operation: in other words, Britain would be a major power in its own right, and so close co-operation in Europe could only be a distraction. The collapse of such hopes led to an increase in British involvement in 1947–8, but then improved relations with the USA provided a further distraction. In addition, there was resistance within the Labour party itself, both from those who wanted a broader internationalism and from those who were essentially nationalist in outlook and wanted no internationalism at all beyond, perhaps, applauding foreign fraternal delegates at Labour party conferences. Finally, there was a third reason – the Empire (or Commonwealth, as it was becoming known).

In Labour mythology, the withdrawal from India in 1947 and Palestine in 1948 were the first manifestations of a general design to wind up the Empire, but no serious historian would now accept this view. Labour ministers were committed to the maintenance of Britain's position as a great power. Though this stance was occasionally questioned, for example by Dalton (eager, as Chancellor, to cut expenditure), it was never successfully challenged.[41] Secondly, as the Cold War developed, Labour's fear of communism made it reluctant to give up areas which might then fall under Soviet influence. Thirdly, there remained questions about whether many of the colonies were 'fit' for self-government or whether, given a British withdrawal, they would collapse into anarchy or white settler tyranny, as seemed to be happening in South Africa with the introduction of apartheid in 1948. Finally, given Britain's straitened economic circumstances, there were hopes that colonial 'development' would provide Britain with increased economic resources. On the other hand, American hostility to the continuation of imperialism of the old kind, the criticism of part of the Labour left which also called for colonial liberation, and the dangers of the Empire becoming an economic burden rather than a boon, all pulled in the opposite direction. In short, there was no 'grand design' for the Empire.

These contradictions fed through into policy. At one extreme were India and Palestine. Labour hoped at first that India would continue gradual political development to become a single entity within the Commonwealth. However, a British mission under Cripps in 1946 made little progress, and it became clear that British rule was breaking down rapidly. In March 1947 the decision was taken to withdraw, in order to prevent disaster, and the process was completed that August. Although withdrawal was presented as a victory for commonsense, it was followed by massive ethnic conflict which claimed up to a million lives and produced millions of refugees. The ultimate result – partition into a largely Hindu India and a mainly Muslim Pakistan – was just the opposite of what the government had wanted.[42] Withdrawal from Palestine the following year was also attended with massive violence. Both withdrawals were prompted more by expediency than by principle, and the British left behind many problems which were only 'solved', ultimately, by bloodshed.

The loss of India did not so much presage the end of the Empire as its reorientation towards Africa. Here, there was very little sense of imminent British withdrawal: far from it. Bevin argued that, if the resources of Britain's African colonies could be fully exploited, she might be able to rival the USA as a superpower.[43] There were, therefore, attempts both to 'develop' the colonies as markets and as sources of raw materials, and to increase their dollar-earning potential in the interests of the home country. The results were, first, a series of attempts to locate and extract mineral resources and to propagate new crops, the most spectacular example of which was the fiasco and public humiliation for the government which attended the attempt to grow groundnuts in Tanganyika; and, secondly, the closer binding together of the sterling area. The latter development was significant especially for the future, since one of Wilson's main arguments against devaluation in the 1960s would be that Britain had a responsibility towards its less developed partners in that community. Overall, the result was that Britain 'actively and blatantly exploited colonial producers': bulk-buying meant producers were getting less than the world price for their goods, while the terms of trade were deliberately turned in Britain's favour.[44]

If there was no grand design for the Empire, there was no masterplan either for one of its legacies: immigration from the 'new Commonwealth', particularly (at this time) from the West Indies. In 1948 a number of Jamaicans arrived to look for work in Britain during the period of labour shortage. Eleven Labour MPs demanded an immediate ban on immigration. More generally, many trade unions saw it as a threat to employment prospects and wage levels, and many union branches refused to accept black workers as members. Although in February 1951 97 Labour MPs signed a Commons motion demanding racial equality throughout the Commonwealth, the government's attitude remained hesitant. No attempt was made to legislate against racial discrimination.[45] Already, in microcosm, Labour's problems with the issue of race were beginning to expose themselves.

By 1949, Labour's reforming impulse had largely atrophied. The early optimism about domestic and foreign policy had been replaced by a more world-weary air as ministers, many of whom had been in office almost continuously since 1940, became stale, and more likely to want to safeguard existing gains than to take risks in trying to make new ones. Increasingly, attention was turned towards the timing of the next general election, and on 11 January 1950 it was announced that this would take place on 23 February.

Labour had reason to be mildly optimistic. Party organization and finance were in good shape, with individual membership continuing to increase from 487 000 in 1945 to 729 000 in 1949, and union-affiliated membership almost doubling to 4 946 000 over the same period.[46] Its record at by-elections had been formidable, with only low swings to the Conservatives and no seats lost. Some progress had continued to be made in local elections, too, although the loss of overall control of Birmingham, Glasgow and Manchester in 1947, and of Bristol, Leicester, Newcastle and Wolverhampton in 1949 served to warn against complacency.

The 1950 general election campaign was not very inspiring. Labour's manifesto was largely a 'stand-pat' affair, with proposals for further nationalization confined to sugar, cement and water supply.[47] By and large, the party leadership was prepared to be judged on its record. The Conservatives, meanwhile, had improved their organization greatly, and had also done enough in the presentation of their policies to suggest that they would not, if elected, start a headlong dismantling of all that Labour had done. The results were not terribly favourable to Labour, since it emerged with an overall majority of just five seats, with 315 to the Conservatives' 298. This was not such a bad performance – only the elections of 1945 and 1966 have left Labour in a stronger parliamentary position – and with 46.1 per cent of the votes cast, the party was some way ahead of the Conservatives' 43.5 per cent. However, the loss of 78 seats compared with 1945 was disappointing, and the fact that there were only nine Liberals and three 'others' meant that Labour's room for parliamentary manoeuvre was very limited.

Three major factors seem to have pulled Labour back from its 1945 heights. First, some middle-class electors who had voted Labour or abstained in 1945 now voted Conservative. The proportion of non-manual workers voting Labour fell from 28 per cent in 1945 to 23 per cent, a much sharper fall than among manual workers.[48] They might well have been alienated by the government's apparent preference for working-class interests and its specific failings, for example in not lifting rationing and controls. It also seems that Labour support among men – where it had had a massive lead over the Conservatives in 1945 – collapsed more than did its support among women (55 to 47 per cent and 46.5 to 43.5 per cent respectively).[49] This suggests, in turn, that explanations which cite militant housewives and resentment from women about rationing as a prime cause of Labour's worse performance are somewhat wide of the mark. Secondly, and linked to this, the Conservatives had greatly improved their image and organization. Finally, the redistribution of seats carried out in 1949 affected Labour adversely by taking seats from its declining heartlands, especially in inner-city areas, and giving them to the suburban areas which had burgeoned since 1918: on the whole, 'Labour's losses were heaviest in the dormitory areas of the big towns, particularly of London'.[50] Of course, Labour still won. But it was a rather hollow victory. Labour had so little left by way of distinctive policies that a further term of office could not fail to be deflating. And, in addition, the Conservatives now had the scent of blood in their nostrils, and felt confident enough to force the Commons through long sittings which weakened Labour morale as its MPs were left with no choice but to attend. Partly as a result of all this, the government began to fall apart.

This was most noticeable at cabinet level. In October 1950 Cripps, terminally ill, was finally forced to resign as Chancellor. The potential successors were Morrison, Bevan and Gaitskell (at this stage, not a member of the cabinet). Morrison's successes were clearly behind him, and in any case Attlee felt a strong antipathy towards him. Bevan had seniority over Gaitskell in both party and cabinet terms, and had a quick mind and might have proved a success. However, it seems that Attlee doubted his stability, feared the effect on American opinion, and was worried that Bevan's appointment would have antagonized Morrison and the right of the party. In the end, therefore, he chose Gaitskell.[51]

In many ways, Gaitskell was well suited to the post. A trained economist and junior minister of proven competence, he had been closely involved with Treasury affairs, virtually deputizing for Cripps at various times. However, it is hard to believe that a mistake was not made. For one thing, the appointment antagonized Bevan, who expressed his 'consternation and astonishment' to Attlee; for another, it upset Wilson, who, though younger and probably not a serious contender himself, had been in cabinet since 1947 and felt threatened by the appointment.[52]

The second result of Gaitskell's appointment was that it hemmed Attlee in when he had to choose a successor to the ailing Bevin in March 1951. For there could now be only one choice: Morrison, whom he could not afford to pass over a second time, given Morrison's continuing popularity on the right and centre of the party. Morrison was to be somewhat unlucky as Foreign Secretary, being faced with crises and spy scandals which were not his fault, but even so he lacked his predecessor's 'feel' for foreign affairs and it is difficult to resist the commonly held view that he was not a success in the office.

Less than seven weeks later, a cabinet crisis erupted. The outbreak of the Korean War in June 1950 meant that Britain had to rearm so that it could take part on the side of the United Nations-backed South against Chinese-backed North Korea. In January 1951 a massive rearmament package of £4.7 billion was announced. Bevan opposed it on the sensible grounds that it was simply too much: such an amount could not be spent (nor was it, in the event).[53] It was also clear that Gaitskell was prepared to sacrifice expenditure in other areas to pay for the programme. In particular, Gaitskell planned to freeze NHS expenditure at £393 million, the figure for 1950–1, by cutting spending on hospitals and saving £20 million by charging for false teeth and spectacles. There followed a period of cabinet wrangling, at the end of which Bevan, Wilson and a junior minister, John Freeman, resigned.

The precise motivations for Bevan's resignation have been much debated. His enemies, then and since, have seen his actions as self-seeking, an attempt to re-establish his credentials as a left-winger, and as the product of frustrated careerism. These factors were certainly not insignificant.[54] But there was more to it than that. For Bevan, there were two main issues. First was the question of the NHS. If a Labour government legitimized charges then the pass would have been sold: the Conservatives, when in office, would be able to cut entitlement to treatment and impose charges while Labour's opposition would be stymied. Secondly, there was the question of the future direction of the Labour party. Bevan was not anti-intellectual: far from it. In the sense of having a questing and open mind, looking for new solutions and being receptive to new ideas, he was more of an intellectual than Gaitskell himself. But he had a strong suspicion of Oxford meritocrats like Gaitskell, whose experience of the Labour movement was, he felt, skin-deep and who, he believed, saw the movement less as a way of empowering the working class than as a means of getting it to do what it was told by its 'betters'.

The majority of the cabinet backed Gaitskell. Loyalty to the leadership was one of the main planks of the Labour movement's ethos: and the leadership was backing the Chancellor very strongly. In retrospect it seems pathetic that some solution could not have been found. The £23 million saving on the NHS was less than half of one per cent of the total rearmament package. In short, Attlee and Morrison both failed a crucial test of leadership; and many of their colleagues put personal distaste for Bevan before political realities. It would be impossible for any but the most unreconstructed Gaitskellite to argue that the government was stronger without Bevan than with him. In the end, two of Labour's greatest post-war figures – Bevan and Wilson – were replaced in the cabinet by the scarcely earth-shattering personalities of Sir Hartley Shawcross and Alfred Robens. More broadly, the degree of backbiting on both sides showed the extent to which the confidence of 1945 had waned.

In policy terms, too, Labour seemed to have lost its way. The nationalization of iron and steel, carried by the previous parliament, was implemented in February 1951. Rationing and controls continued to be abolished, although not so quickly that they took the powerful rallying cry to 'set the people free' from the Conservatives. But other major measures were not forthcoming. Meanwhile, the pay freeze collapsed and industrial relations became more fraught.

It had been accepted from the start of the 1950 parliament that the next general election could not be long delayed. Ultimately, Attlee chose to hold polling on 25 October 1951, having decided against early 1952 because the King would be on a tour of Africa at that time (in fact he would be dead). Labour's manifesto stood largely on the government's record since 1945. It argued that the party was best placed to maintain peace and full employment, to increase production, to reduce the cost of living, and 'to build a just society'. The 'shopping list' of further industries for nationalization, which had characterized the 1950 manifesto, was dropped, and replaced by a vague pledge to take over 'concerns which fail the nation'. Existing policies, such as development councils, would be pushed forward, and there was a promise to 'associate the workers more closely with the administration of public industries and services'. Emphasis continued to be placed on the construction of housing for rent, rather than for sale.[55] But on the whole the manifesto was a defence of the record of the government and an attempt to contrast it with the perceivedly dark days of Conservative domination between the wars.

Labour attracted 13 948 883 votes at the election, 48.8 per cent of those cast. This has proved to be the party's highest ever percentage of the vote, and no party gained a higher number of votes until the Conservatives in 1992. But these votes produced only 295 seats, whereas the Conservatives, with 48.0 per cent, took 321. Labour made a net loss of 20 seats at the election, gaining two from the Liberals (both in rural Wales) but losing 22. The average swing against Labour was only 0.9 per cent, but an above average swing was enough to tip marginal seats in Lancashire, the Home Counties and East Anglia towards the Conservatives.[56] In terms of social class, Labour lost further middle-class support but managed to take a higher share of the working-class vote than ever before. Support among women was almost back to the level of 1945, but male support, though reviving from 1950, was still well below the level achieved in 1945.[57] As in the 1930s, the collapse of the Liberal party (which fielded 109 candidates as against 475 in 1950) worked against the interests of Labour, since those who had voted Liberal in 1950 now split almost two to one in favour of the Conservatives.[58] Still, a national swing of only 1 per cent from the 1951 result would give Labour an over-all majority in parliament at the next election, and a 2 per cent swing would give it a majority of around 30, quite enough to last a full term.[59]

Labour, then, was back in opposition. It had been in office for all but a couple of months of 11 years, almost six of them on its own. During the period since 1945 it had helped to change the face of Britain at home and abroad. It had taken around 20 per cent of the economy into the public sector, created a National Health Service, and made sweeping changes to the social security system, although it had not addressed questions of the nature of the state which were raised by these considerable increases in its functions. It had maintained full employment and, until its last few months in office, kept inflation firmly under control. Abroad, it had, to some extent, muddled through with the Empire, but in deciding to have an independent nuclear weapons capability and playing a leading role in NATO, it had set the parameters for British foreign policy until the end of the Cold War four decades later. There were problems with this legacy, of course. But in the final analysis it would be difficult to argue that this government did not make a significant contribution towards the improvement of the lives of the people who supported it, and indeed of many others. For that alone the Attlee governments deserve most – though not all – the plaudits that Labourites have heaped upon them in the years since 1951. However, the government also left flaws in its legacy which, in retrospect, can be seen to have condemned these achievements to at least a questionable future in the longer term.

7

Searching for a New Direction, 1951–64

In the immediate aftermath of the 1951 election, it was widely believed that Labour would be able to regroup in opposition, and that, for all their talk of having changed, the Conservatives under Churchill would soon reveal their true colours. They would seek to undo the Labour government's achievements and, as a result, face nemesis at the next general election. Of course, things turned out rather differently. The Conservatives were to win elections in 1955 and 1959, each time with a larger majority than before. It would not be until 1964 that Labour would return to office, and even then with an overall majority of only five. However, this period was important for Labour. It saw the 'bedding in' of the Attlee governments' achievements. At the same time, widespread affluence gave fresh underpinning to the revisionists' approach, and this in turn set the parameters for many of the policies which Labour would try to implement during the period after 1964. It was also a time, though, that saw deep and bitter splits within the party, splits which would cast a long shadow over it long after the 1950s were a remote memory.

To some extent, Labour's prospects were impaired by the performance of Churchill's government. Though still firmly committed to private enterprise, the Tories had now accepted that the mixed economy, the welfare state and full employment should not be tampered with too extensively. It must also be said that Labour had fallen victim to its own mythology, for the Conservatives even between the wars had not been so reactionary as Labourites now purported to believe. It was a false view of history to argue, as so many did, that a Tory government meant depression and deprivation. Similarly, the 'whig interpretation of Labour history' once again came into play, to the detriment of the party's true interests. The people who saw history as leading ineluctably towards the socialist millennium argued that Labour's progress had only been put on hold in 1951: had the party not gained more votes than any party ever before? It was simply a question of waiting for the pendulum to swing and the 'forward march' would be resumed. But this was too optimistic. The Conservatives would be able to gain cheap popularity for lifting the remaining controls and rationing, and so present themselves as the party of 'freedom' as opposed to that of 'austerity'. Meanwhile, Labour's splits remained, and were likely to be as deep in opposition as in office. There was, in addition, no sign of the vigorous leadership that would be necessary if Labour was to regroup swiftly and effectively, with Attlee increasingly a liability but showing little sign of wanting to retire.[1] And, finally, there were few signs that the question of the future direction of British socialism had been or was being resolved. In the event, the years from 1951 to 1955 were to be one of the most dismal periods in the history of the Labour party. From a position of potential strength, the party sank deeper and deeper into a mire of squabbling, with poor leadership and a lack of clear policy, in the face of an increasingly self-confident Conservative party.

Despite their small parliamentary majority, the Conservatives were reasonably well set from the beginning. Though Labour led in the polls for much of the period to late 1954, it rarely managed a significant lead after 1952. In by-elections, there was a small swing *towards* the Conservatives in 1953 and 1954. Increasingly it seemed that, if there were no catastrophic errors of timing, the Conservatives would win the next general election. This is not to say that they did not face problems – in particular, Churchill was ailing badly – but many of the difficulties were hidden from public view. The government's handling of the economy, while open to criticism in retrospect, seemed successful at the time, helped by the demands of post-war rebuilding, favourable terms of trade and a temporary lack of foreign competition in export markets. One area of particular success was housing, where the pledge to build 300 000 houses a year was fulfilled, in sharp contrast to Labour's performance. By 1955 the Conservatives could point to prosperity, and contrast it with the perceived austerity of Labour's time in office. It was in some ways an unfair comparison, but it resonated with the voters. In addition, the Tories' continuation of Labour's scepticism about moves towards greater European integration might well have saved it from an electoral backlash.

But events within the Labour party also played a part. As stated above, leadership in this period was often halting and indecisive. Once in opposition, Attlee shrank. Now 68 years old, he clung on to the leadership, but largely to ensure that Morrison, now 63, would be too old to succeed him. Given the alienation of Bevan, there seemed to be few other likely contenders.

This lack of leadership mattered, because this was a time of considerable division and bitterness within the party. At the 1951 election, Bevan had toed the party line as loyally as anyone. However, left-wing discontent with the leadership grew throughout 1952. One major issue was the question of whether or not western Germany should be rearmed in the face of the 'Soviet threat'. In March 1952, 57 MPs (including Bevan) voted against the measure, instead of abstaining as the whips had demanded. This was seen as a left-wing rebellion, and the PLP's standing orders were reimposed, a sure sign that the relatively harmonious times of the immediate post-war period were a thing of the past.[2] At that autumn's party conference, a degree of organization by the left resulted in a coup, whereby six of the seven CLP places on the NEC were taken by 'Bevanites'. Dalton was among those to lose his seat on the executive. Even though the NEC remained firmly under the control of the moderates who dominated the larger trade union section, the left's caucus tactics and success enraged the rest of the party.[3] Late in 1952 the PLP voted to liquidate separate groups, although this had little real effect in reducing tension.[4]

Even so, Bevan was able to secure re-election to the shadow cabinet in 1952, albeit in last place. It was not to be a long stay, however. Early in 1954 it was decided that the party should vote in favour of German rearmament. In April, therefore, Bevan resigned from the shadow cabinet. However, the impact of this move was reduced when Wilson, the runner-up in the previous autumn's election, took Bevan's place, even though he was considered to be a 'Bevanite'. Bevan's standing suffered a further blow that October when he was defeated by a two-to-one majority by Gaitskell for the party treasurership in succession to Greenwood, who had died earlier in the year. Then, in March 1955, Labour accepted that Britain should manufacture the hydrogen bomb. In the Commons vote, Bevan and 62 other Labour MPs abstained, and during the debate many Labour MPs felt that he had insulted Attlee. A few days later, the shadow cabinet voted to withdraw the whip from Bevan, a move confirmed by the PLP by 141 votes to 112. On 30 March, the NEC voted by 15 to 10 to condemn Bevan and warn him as to his future conduct; and, had a general election not been looming, the desire of leading right-wingers like Deakin to have him expelled might have been fulfilled.[5]

The very notion that so eminent a figure as Bevan could be seriously considered for expulsion said a great deal about the deterioration of intra-party relations. The most dramatic manifestation of the deterioration had been seen in the clashes between Bevan and Gaitskell. Bevan, for his part, made little secret of his dislike for his colleague, whom he felt to have no real roots in the movement, who had become Chancellor in 1950 when he, Bevan, had wanted the job, and who had bested him over NHS charges in 1951. When Bevan said in 1954 that it seemed that 'the right kind of leader for the Labour party is a desiccated calculating machine', it was seen as a swipe at Gaitskell.[6] The right, on the other hand, saw Bevan as over-emotional, even mentally unstable, and too much under the influence of his wife, Jennie Lee, and leading colleagues like Michael Foot.[7] Certainly, it is difficult to avoid the view that Bevan took a certain perverse pleasure in putting himself at odds with the party leadership.

All this might not have been so damaging if it had been part of a general rough and tumble from which policy was emerging. But this was not so. There was some debate: 1952, for example, saw the publication of two books which tried to point the future direction of the party. The first was Bevan's *In Place of Fear*. The book sold well, but it was not the great visionary text for which many had hoped. It had some nice autobiographical touches, and was imbued with the author's concern to democratize much of what the last Labour government had achieved: for example, he attacked the boards of nationalized industries as 'a constitutional outrage' because of their lack of accountability, and called for greater industrial democracy.[8] On the whole, however, the book was a disappointment.[9] The second book, *New Fabian Essays*, was edited by Richard Crossman, formerly the leading figure in 'Keep Left'. Among the essayists, the editor and Ian Mikardo represented the left, but most – for example, Anthony Crosland, Denis Healey, and Roy Jenkins – were associated with what was becoming known as the 'revisionist' right. The volume was by no means undistinguished, but it was a starting point for a debate which took time to get off the ground rather than an immediate plan of action. Certainly, it seems to have had little impact on the party's lacklustre new programme, *Challenge to Britain*, adopted in 1953.

There is, then, clear evidence that Labour was in some turmoil between 1951 and 1955. However, this is only part of the story, for Labour remained in a strong position, fundamentally. Trade union membership remained high, and continued to expand slowly, thanks to full employment and relaxed state and employer attitudes: union density remained at around 44 per cent, and membership at around eight million, throughout the period 1951–64.[10] The party's individual membership exceeded a million in 1952 and 1953[11] (though this was almost certainly an inflated figure, and active membership was undoubtedly much lower). Labour was now firmly ensconced in power in local government in many parts of the country. As previously, Labour was being seen as the party which best represented the needs of local authority employees and tenants, and as both these categories expanded this gave it a more and more substantial 'clientage' in local and national elections. This all meant that Labour had a strong base; it did not necessarily mean that it could win elections.

In April 1955, Churchill was finally persuaded to retire, and was succeeded by Eden, who almost immediately dissolved parliament. Having been ahead in the polls since the start of the year, and having engineered a pre-election boom, Eden had few doubts that he would win. Labour can have had few illusions, either: its policies were dull and uninspiring, its leadership cut a superannuated air at the side of the dashing Eden, and it was clearly divided. Labour's manifesto was based largely on consolidation: apart from a commitment to renationalize road haulage and steel, which had been returned to the private sector by the Conservatives, there was little on public ownership; there were vague nods in the direction of greater industrial democracy; and there were new departures in calls for comprehensive secondary education and equal pay for women.[12] But little else made Labour very distinctive. In a sense this was not surprising: Labour's ageing leadership saw the work of the 1945–51 governments as a pinnacle of achievement, for which they would have settled throughout their long, varied and difficult careers. Their memories included Labour as a weak appendage to

Liberalism before 1914, the setbacks and defeats of the interwar years, and the horrors of fascism and war. Like all gerontocracies, the Labour leadership had become somewhat self-satisfied and conservative, and with the left marginalized and rather confused, the unions under little pressure from government and economic circumstances, and younger, more radical right-wingers having little option but to bide their time, there were few more vigorous or coherent critiques on offer.

The election was one which Labour probably could not have won, although a series of strikes led to more public criticism of the unions than at any time since 1940 and hardly helped the party. The election results belied the complacency which had followed the 1951 defeat, as the Conservatives became the first party since the 1867 Reform Act to increase their majority after a substantial period in office, winning 344 seats (with 49.7 per cent of the poll), and more than trebling their majority. Labour emerged with only 277 seats (46.4 per cent). The national swing, as in 1951, was only slight. Labour's support among manual workers fell from 63 to 62 per cent: but this was a very small decrease, the level was still above that of 1945, and the Conservatives also polled less well in this area than in 1951, due largely to the (very muted) Liberal revival. Labour's share of the non-manual vote actually increased slightly.[13] Overall, Labour's support among men increased, but there was a significant fall in its support among women, from 46 to 42.5 per cent.[14] While the result hardly came as a shock, it did signify the need for changes within the party. Leadership, policy and organization would all need attention and, in all probability, alteration.

It was clear that Attlee could not remain for long as leader. He was now 72, and might be 77 by the time of the next election. The shadow cabinet was also ageing. Of the 12 members elected to that body in November 1954, five were over 60, while the deputy leader, Morrison, was 67. Obviously, change was required. When Dalton retired from the front bench he called on his 'fellow veterans' to follow suit.[15] Although Morrison, who still hoped to succeed Attlee, refused to go, most of the others did. That June's shadow cabinet elections saw the election for the first time of younger people like George Brown and Anthony Greenwood, while Bevan returned. On 7 December, Attlee announced his resignation. He remains Labour's longest-serving leader. As leader in opposition, both in the 1930s and 1950s, he had proved to be somewhat ineffectual, with a perceptible tendency towards drift. But in office, surrounded by able colleagues, he had been an effective co-ordinator, successful both in wartime and as post-war premier. His reputation might have stood higher had he retired three or four years earlier.

One of Attlee's main reasons for hanging on so long had been his desire to block Morrison's succession, for personal and political reasons.[16] As late as 1953, Morrison would have been the obvious successor, but since then the anti-Bevanite majority in the PLP and the unions had become divided between him and Gaitskell. This was partly on account of age, but also because Gaitskell had done a lot to push himself into the affections of the Labour right.[17] His McCarthy-style attack on the left in a speech at Stalybridge in 1952, when he had alleged that one-sixth of party conference delegates were 'Communist or Communist-inspired', had earned him the keen attention of the right, and especially of the 'Big Three' union leaders, Deakin (TGWU), Will Lawther (Mineworkers) and Tom Williamson (General and Municipal Workers).[18] Since these three unions made up around 40 per cent of the votes at party conference, this was not a bad alliance to strike. Younger, more appealing electorally (or so it was felt), and less complacent in terms of policy, he began to seem a more attractive proposition than Morrison. Indeed, when Attlee retired some of Morrison's friends tried to persuade him not to stand for the leadership, fearing that he would be humiliated.[19] In the event, he was: Gaitskell won an easy victory on the first ballot with 157 votes to Bevan's 70 and Morrison's 40.

The period between Gaitskell's succession to the leadership in December 1955 and mid-1958 was one of some success and many encouraging signs for Labour. First, the Conservatives were in considerable difficulties for much of the period. Late in 1955 they were forced to introduce a deflationary mini-budget only months after encouraging a pre-election boom. More serious trouble followed the nationalization of the Suez Canal by the Egyptian government in July 1956. That November, British and French forces invaded Suez, but with the USA making clear its opposition, Britain had no alternative but to withdraw. In January 1957 Eden resigned as premier, partly on health grounds but also because of the Suez fiasco.

Secondly, a new spirit of unity emerged at the top of the party. In June 1955 Bevan had been re-elected to the shadow cabinet.

In February 1956 he stood for the deputy leadership, and although he was defeated the fact that he polled 111 votes against the 141 cast for the widely respected and 'safe' James Griffiths was a sign of continuing, and perhaps increasing, popularity. Bevan became shadow Colonial Secretary, and acquitted himself well. That October the party conference elected him party treasurer by a narrow margin over Brown. He co-operated closely with Gaitskell over Suez.[20] In November 1956 Bevan came third in the shadow cabinet elections and was appointed shadow Foreign Secretary; by late 1956 Crossman was writing privately of a 'Gaitskell–Bevan axis'.[21] When, at the 1957 party conference, Bevan launched a fierce attack on unilateral nuclear disarmament as 'an emotional spasm', he dismayed many of his supporters but also drew himself still closer to the leadership.[22]

This transformation from *enfant terrible* into 'statesman' worried many on the left and some on the right. The reasons for it are complex. Both Bevan and Gaitskell seem to have been sobered by the 1955 defeat, which suggested that luxuriation in internecine conflicts had a price. Gaitskell, after all, was now leader of the party, and had a clearer duty and incentive to seek unity than before 1955. His election to the leadership seems to have made him more relaxed and self-confident in dealing with his erstwhile adversary. Bevan, for his part, seems to have realized that continued factionalism was pointless, since the Bevanites had lost every issue they had fought. At the end of the day, too, Bevan disliked Conservatives even more than he disliked the party leader. A Gaitskell government might be pusillanimous and halting, in Bevan's terms, but, on the other hand, it might just make some real gains for working people. It is also likely that, with the Foreign Office in his sights, Bevan was more inclined to compromise. But there was surely an element of calculation in his behaviour. Labour had a new leader whose position was, for the moment, unassailable. Continued sniping at Gaitskell – and that was all it could amount to – could have no positive effect. It would simply allow further measures against the left, and give an excuse to the right if Labour lost the next election; many Labourites had already blamed 'Bevanism' for the defeat of 1955. And so, it seems, Bevan decided that he would show loyalty to Gaitskell. Then, if Labour won the next election, he (and, perhaps, some of his supporters) would be appointed to senior positions in government. If, on the other hand, it lost, no one would be able to say that the left had been to blame. The fault would lie with Gaitskell and his line, and the left would be correspondingly strengthened in a renewed struggle for control of the party.[23]

The new leadership was not the only ostensibly positive development of this period. The party's policy was also becoming better defined. The hints made towards new directions in *New Fabian Essays* were now consolidated, most notably in Crosland's *The Future of Socialism* (1956). Crosland, an Oxford don and Labour MP who had lost his seat in 1955, argued that the tools of Keynesian demand management, rather than the ownership of industry, now enabled governments to control the economy, and to avoid the old cycle of boom and slump. This, plus the growth of joint-stock companies and the running of firms by salaried managers rather than by owners, meant that capitalism in the classical nineteenth-century sense no longer existed, and that in consequence nationalization was largely a policy of the past. Instead, social justice could and should be pursued by the continuation of post-war policies – a mixed economy, demand management, and the welfare state – together with a new radicalism in areas like education to promote greater equality of opportunity. In effect, assured economic growth under capitalism would lead inexorably to the socialist society which Crosland desired. While the party did not swallow Crosland's prescriptions whole, the book was influential and did suggest new directions which chimed in with Gaitskell's thinking. In more concrete terms, Labour issued a number of policy documents, the products of small committees, in the years between 1956 and 1959, which were to lay the basis of party policy into the 1960s.[24]

Attempts were also made to improve party organization in this period. A committee of inquiry appointed to investigate the machine in the aftermath of the 1955 defeat claimed, perhaps with some exaggeration, that it was in poor shape. Wilson, the committee's chairman, said Labour was 'still at the penny-farthing stage in a jet-propelled era'.[25] In particular, he claimed, party headquarters were inefficient, a clear indictment of the secretary, Morgan Phillips, and national agent, Len Williams. In addition, Wilson pointed out that individual membership had begun to fall dramatically, from 1 014 524 in 1952 to 843 356 in 1955. There was also evidence of some constituency, and still more citywide, parties in an advanced state of decrepitude. Glasgow and Liverpool, in particular, were in the hands of right-wing oligarchies which practised 'boss politics' with impunity.[26] At first, it seemed that much would come from the report. An organization sub-committee of the NEC was set up on a permanent basis. A decision was taken in 1957 to weaken the hold of city parties and devolve more power in places like Liverpool to the constituencies.[27] But few of the report's recommendations came to very much. Phillips and Williams remained *in situ*, and Williams went on to succeed Phillips when the latter retired in 1962. Suggestions to concentrate agents in marginal seats foundered. Party membership continued to fall until 1961, when it was just over 750 000. Thereafter, a change in the minimum number of members each CLP had to affiliate to the national party artificially inflated the figures, but the overall downward trend in actual membership continued pretty well unabated, largely unhindered by a party leadership which was coming to see 'television and political advertising [replacing] the need for campaigning foot-soldiers', and freed from financial worries by heavy funding from the unions, whose membership continued to grow to new record levels.[28] In fact, the main result of the Wilson report was that it got its author noticed in CLPs across the country, for in producing it he had made an extensive national tour, meeting activists and officials and generally acquitting himself well.[29] Thus Wilson's career prospects were boosted, but the party's organization did not improve greatly.

Meanwhile, the Conservatives recovered strongly from Suez and its aftermath under their charismatic new leader, Harold Macmillan. There was a recession in the winter of 1958–9, with unemployment rising to a post-1947 peak of 620 000, but by July it had fallen to 395 000. And, more generally, a sense of affluence was engendered by the fact that average real wages rose by 7 per cent between January 1956 and June 1959.[30] On the other hand, increasing strike levels meant more public debate about and criticism of trade unions, whose links with Labour were very prominent. And, within the Labour party itself, there were new divisions opening up, most notably the support given by some prominent left-wingers to the Campaign for Nuclear Disarmament (CND), formed in 1958. All this meant that the electoral tide turned towards the Conservatives. In September 1958, only a year after being 19 points behind, they moved ahead in the opinion polls. Macmillan's approval rating was ahead of Gaitskell's throughout 1959, and did not fall below 50 per cent after June

1958. After 1957, by-election swings against the Conservatives were generally slight. And the borough council elections of May 1959 saw a slump in the Labour vote and a heavy loss of seats.

Thus, although Labour entered the 1959 general election campaign in high spirits, it had little real prospect of forming the next government. With polling set for 8 October, Labour fought a generally effective campaign; in the first TV election, its broadcasts, masterminded by Anthony Wedgwood Benn, were a striking success. The Labour manifesto was based on the policies which had emerged from the three-year policy review (1956–9). The Conservatives were criticized for unemployment and rising prices; the latter had led to a reduction in the real value of benefits, pensions and NHS spending, and Labour pledged to increase these accordingly. Selection in secondary education would be ended, greater protection would be given to consumers, and a Welsh Office would be created. On industry, Labour pledged to encourage modernization of private firms, be more sensitive to the needs of public corporations, and renationalize steel and road haulage. However, the point was emphasized that Labour had 'no other plans for further nationalization' except in the case of industries which were 'failing the nation', although the possibility was held out of the state buying shares in companies.[31]

Despite a 'socialist' peroration, this was very much a revisionist document. Its basic argument was that Labour was better suited to manage welfare capitalism than were the Conservatives. There was no real sense of radicalism. The problem was whether this was distinctive enough to encourage people to risk a change of government which might upset prosperity, especially since the recent recession had shown that that prosperity could be upset. This is not to argue that a more 'radical' programme would have won the election for Labour, but merely to show how difficult the Conservatives were to beat in 1959. Matters were not helped by Gaitskell's performance in a TV interview when he said that Labour's increased spending plans would not mean increased taxes. In a sense this was true, as Gaitskell saw it: the expenditure would be met over time by economic growth. In the short term, though, tax increases might have been necessary, and people were unconvinced by Gaitskell's explanation, which suggested dishonesty.[32] However, it would be farcical to argue that without this gaffe Labour would have fared much better at the election.

Even if the fact of Labour's defeat should not have come as a surprise, the scale of it did. On a national swing of 1.0 per cent, the Conservatives increased their parliamentary representation for the fourth successive election, taking 365 seats with 49.4 per cent of the poll to Labour's 258 (43.8 per cent). Labour lost 28 seats to the Tories, while gaining five in the opposite direction. In some parts of the country it improved its position, but it lost seats heavily, particularly in the west Midlands, where it lost seven of its 27 seats. Conversely, eastern Lancashire, which had swung so heavily against Labour in 1951, now swung towards the party, and there was a swing of 1.4 per cent to Labour in Scotland.[33] Labour's share of the non-manual vote had fallen, from 23 to 21 per cent; similarly, and more noticed at the time, was a fall in its support among manual workers, from 62 to 57 per cent.[34] Support among women had actually increased since 1955, albeit slightly, but among men Labour's share of the poll had fallen from 51 to 47.5 per cent.[35] Age factors were also seen as significant: voters in their twenties, who had split five to four in favour of Labour in 1955, were now almost evenly divided, while it seems that Labour's pensions proposals, plus the ageing of a cohort who were more likely to support Labour, meant a shift in the votes of those aged 65 and over in favour of Labour.[36]

Labour's third successive defeat, each by a wider margin, led to a great deal of fuss among the commentators. In a book entitled *Must Labour Lose?*, Mark Abrams and Richard Rose argued that Labour faced a serious problem, in so far as a large section of the working class no longer saw itself as working class, and that this process of 'embourgoisement' was loosening the ties between Labour and its core support. Increasingly, Labour was being seen as an outdated party representing 'the poor' at a time when 'many workers, regardless of their politics, no longer see themselves as working class'.[37] Some of the evidence presented suggested hostility towards nationalization in particular. Even worse, young people were alienated from Labour in large numbers. It was pointed out that for the party to take office at the next election would require a larger swing than at any previous post-war election.[38] Labour was in trouble.

How accurate was this picture? It is easy to see why it seemed persuasive in the aftermath of yet another electoral defeat for the Labour party. But other surveys, published later, contested it. A 1963–4 study of Luton, a town dominated by the motor industry, found that, despite affluence, there was 'no evidence of any shift in [working-class] political loyalties away from the Labour party'.[39] Where there was a shift, it argued, was in the reason why such voters supported Labour. It was now less of an expression of class solidarity and more of an 'instrumental' position: that is, the workers concerned saw the Labour party and trade unionism as the most likely route to material betterment.[40] This did offer the possibility of future disillusionment, of course, but the idea that Labour was in secular decline was not to be taken too seriously. On the whole, it seems that the picture of Labour in decline due to broad sociological factors was overdone. It is also worth reiterating the underlying strength of Labour's position in the 1950s: the party was polling very well, and losing elections by relatively narrow margins. Part of the problem was that comparisons were being made with the number of votes gained in 1951, when, due to an unusually low number of Liberal candidates, an exceptional proportion of the vote went to the two main parties. The swings of 1955 and 1959 were both very low, yet affluence was expanding significantly. What is surprising, given the general perception of Conservative success in economic management, therefore, is less Labour's failure than its success in retaining so much support. And the Conservatives' share of the manual vote had also been falling from 1951 onwards: from 34 per cent in 1951 to 32 in 1955 and 30 in 1959. While this was partly due to the revival of the Liberals, it hardly suggested that the working class was abandoning Labour in droves for the Conservatives.[41]

In retrospect, it seems clear that the basic cause for Labour's defeat in 1959 was that enough voters continued to believe that the Conservatives were and would remain successful in government. The fact that Labour did worse than in 1955 could probably be attributed to short-term factors, such as the uninspiring nature of Labour's message, doubts about Gaitskell, and perhaps some feeling in the Midlands, in particular, that the Conservatives would be better placed to 'deal with' issues of race and immigration which, following race riots in Notting Hill and Nottingham the previous year, were beginning to achieve a certain electoral saliency. But this was not the message which the leadership took on board, partly because it raised awkward questions about its own performance. It was easier to subscribe instead to the view that radical changes were needed within the

Labour party to enable it to win in the future. The example of the German SPD, which was repudiating Marxism and giving itself a 'softer', less stridently working-class image at this time, culminating in the Bad Godesberg conference of 1959, was seen by some as a good example to follow.[42] The extent of the panic which gripped sections of the party at this time is difficult to credit, in retrospect. But Gaitskell had to find a scapegoat if he was to shore up his position.

This was particularly so since traditional Labour scapegoats were conspicuous by their absence. The unions were so vital to Gaitskell's intra-party position that he could not offend them. Bevan's tactics since 1955 made it difficult to blame the left, and given the fact that the old right-wing dominance among union leaders was beginning to crumble, with, for example, the succession of the left-wing Frank Cousins to lead the TGWU in 1956, the leadership could not afford to be too rude about the left in any case. The media had not been unusually biased. The Soviets had not graced the campaign with correspondence, nor had the bankers deigned to construct a ramp. So the scapegoat found was a small passage in the Labour constitution, drafted in 1918 by Sidney Webb, ritually ignored by every leader since, and virtually unknown to the mass of the population, a passage whose only effective function was to reassure the idealists in the party's ranks that sitting through tedious meetings and tramping around canvassing for often undesirable and egocentric candidates at election times was contributing in some small way to the achievement of a fairer and better society. Gaitskell's failure made him take up Labour theology by challenging Clause Four.

There were some who wanted to go further even than that. The leader's close ally, Jay, wanted to abandon, not just nationalization, but also the unions and even the name 'the Labour party', and to work for a pact with the Liberals.[43] There is no evidence that Gaitskell wanted to go so far, but his close association with people who were expressing such views was hardly likely to endear his proposal to drop Clause Four to the Labour movement at large. After a fierce debate at the 1959 party conference, it was decided that the existing Clause Four would be retained, though supplemented by new statements of principle drawn up by the NEC.[44]

This whole episode throws into question Gaitskell's leadership abilities. Perhaps it was not a bad idea, in the abstract, to get rid of Clause Four. If it had not already been in the constitution, certainly, Labour would not have chosen to insert it in 1959. It had been adopted in 1918 for essentially short-term reasons, and had never formed the touchstone of Labour's policy: the party had never proposed nationalization of 'every pub and garage', as Gaitskell put it.[45] But it was precisely because it was irrelevant that socialists clung to it. It was a question of faith, a matter of almost religious conviction. As Wilson was to show, it would prove possible to lead a modernizing and moderate Labour party with Clause Four still in place. More broadly, Gaitskell's 'smart set' followers who, for example, disliked Wilson because he was 'such a common little man', aroused suspicion, as had Mosley in the 1920s or Cripps in the 1930s.[46] Where, reasoned some Labourites, were their Labour roots, their shopfloor experience? Where would they be in a few years' time? This was unfair, in many ways. But people feared, understandably, that the Labour party would be hijacked in the interests of vocal middle-class groups, people who would ignore the fact that most of Labour's supporters were, like the present author, 'common little men' and women. In a sense, the fears of many Labourites were that they would lose their party, and that it would become not unlike the late nineteenth-century Liberal party which the Labour party had been set up to counter. In that sense, the wheel would have gone full circle. At the same time, though, the left had no particularly coherent alternative to offer. The successful defence of Clause Four was seen as a victory. In the sense that it prevented the right wing of the party from doing something, it was. But the left's outlook remained simply that the party should be moving faster and further. According to this view, there was no need to engage in a meaningful debate about the party's future strategy. It was enough simply to block the right. But this would not necessarily take the party very much further towards the socialist society to which the left aspired.

Bevan had played an essentially conciliatory role in the crisis. He might still have challenged Gaitskell at a later stage, but he died in July 1960. Even so, Gaitskell's position remained under pressure. First, that September's party conference narrowly passed a resolution in favour of unilateral nuclear disarmament. Gaitskell pledged to 'fight and fight and fight again to save the Party we love', which impressed his admirers but raised questions for others – by no means all on the left – about his leadership, particularly his ability to unite the party.[47] This was all the more regrettable in that Gaitskell had done a great deal, between 1955 and 1959, to assuage lingering fears that he was a splitter. It was in this context that he faced a challenge for the party leadership at the start of the new parliamentary session in November 1960. The political position of the challenger, Wilson, was not easy to define. He had attained something of a 'left' reputation for resigning with Bevan in 1951, but had to some extent dissipated this by taking Bevan's place in the shadow cabinet in 1954. However, his performance as shadow Chancellor since 1955 had established his reputation as a formidable parliamentary performer, as he had scourged successive Tory Chancellors. He had little chance of defeating Gaitskell in 1960, but his performance, taking 81 votes to the leader's 166, was far from a humiliation, and suggested that he might be a future contender for the leadership. But, at the time, it aroused great hostility from the leader's supporters, and in the shadow cabinet elections for 1960 he fell from first place to ninth.[48]

All this drama was being played out against the backdrop of continuing success for the Macmillan government, as economic indicators remained favourable, and the Conservatives remained ahead in the polls until late 1961. But things then began to change. Economic growth slowed down. Inflation rose, unemployment edged upwards, and the government's attempts to control public sector wages and salaries through the 'pay pause' of July 1961 suggested continuing Tory antipathy towards the public sector. Slipping behind in the polls, Macmillan sacked a third of his cabinet in the July 1962 'Night of the Long Knives'. This was intended to demonstrate firmness and resolution, but looked more like panic.

Within the Labour party, meanwhile, a *status quo* was reached on the issues which had split the party over the past two years. Gaitskell's victory over Wilson, in this sense, marked something of a watershed. The Clause Four compromise held good, and the issue receded once more. At the 1961 conference, the vote on unilateral nuclear disarmament was reversed after powerful lobbying by Gaitskellites in the Campaign for Democratic Socialism, whose chairman was William Rodgers, secretary of the Fabian Society. When the left-winger, Anthony Greenwood, challenged for the leadership in November 1961, he took only 59 votes to the leader's 171, a significantly worse performance than that of Wilson the previous year. Barbara Castle's attempt to wrest the deputy leadership from George Brown (who had succeeded Bevan) was equally unsuccessful, and Brown was able to defeat a similar challenge from Wilson in 1962. In the latter year, Gaitskell's attack on Macmillan's attempt to take Britain into the European Economic Community (formed in 1957) astonished and appalled many of his usual supporters, but was cheered by the left, which was on the whole strongly opposed to entry.[49] By taking this line, and perhaps even more by so publicly repudiating so many of his leading supporters, Gaitskell greatly strengthened his position within the party as a whole. Some people argued his line was opportunistic, but there was more to it than that. Entry to the six-state EEC could be seen as counter to, rather than a demonstration of, Labour's 'internationalism'. There were also fears that the Commonwealth, of which there were high hopes in the first flush of African decolonization, might have to be sacrificed, and that the hard-won relationship with the USA might also be lost. And there were concerns about further dividing the world into power blocs. This is not to say that straightforward xenophobia did not play its part for many Labourites. But simply to dismiss the arguments against entry in such terms is ludicrous.

By the end of 1962, then, Gaitskell's position was apparently strong, and the party was well ahead in the polls. That year a strong Liberal revival had allowed Labour to gain three seats from the Conservatives at by-elections, and there was little sign that Macmillan could pull his party round. There were real hopes that a Labour government under Gaitskell might follow the next election.

But it was not to be. In January 1963 Gaitskell died of a rare disease at the age of 56. Around him was to develop a mythology not unlike that which was soon to envelop another 'lost leader', US President John F. Kennedy. Gaitskell had many qualities: a good brain for economics, the power to inspire those with whom he was in agreement, and much personal charm. The one general election he fought as Labour leader was probably unwinnable, and by 1962 he did seem to have overcome many problems and secured his leadership. However, he was at times too impatient and too intolerant of honest dissent for his own, or the party's, good. He had led the party, at times, in an over-combative manner. His revisionist view of socialism, finally, meant that he would have had little idea of how to tackle affairs when the economic going became tougher. There is nothing in his record to suggest that a Gaitskell government elected in 1964 would have been any more successful than the Wilson administration that eventually came to power: it must be a moot point whether Gaitskell could even have won in 1964. But Wilson, like Kennedy's successor in the USA, Lyndon Johnson, was to suffer in comparison with a predecessor whose acolytes remained powerful and whose faults were quickly forgotten in an outpouring of grief at an untimely death.

Gaitskell's death threw the party into something of a panic. A general election was due by late 1964, and might come earlier: a new leader would not have long to establish himself. Three men stood for the leadership. Wilson, who could count on the support of the left plus a substantial number of MPs who had been impressed by his parliamentary performances, was the youngest, at 47, but the only one with cabinet experience. The two candidates who were more acceptable to the Gaitskellites were Brown (49), and James Callaghan (51, and a member of the shadow cabinet since 1951). Both had been junior ministers in the last Labour government. In the first ballot, Callaghan took only 41 votes, compared with 88 for Brown and 115 for Wilson, and was eliminated. In the run-off, Wilson beat Brown by 144 votes to 103. Both candidates were seen as having their flaws: Wilson was distrusted by many for his alleged slipperiness and his apparent changes of line during the 1950s, not to mention his opposition to Gaitskell in 1960; Brown was seen by some as too unstable (a condition not helped by heavy drinking), and too combative in internal party affairs. Wilson was seen as more likely to heal rifts, but at the same time the shadow cabinet had voted heavily in favour of his opponent.[50]

In reality, Wilson, the 'man of the left', shared most of the assumptions of the revisionists. He saw a 'fairer' society being funded by the fruits of economic growth. Clause Four was simply there to placate party activists: he had no time for further extensive nationalization. Where he perhaps differed was in his expectation that a greater degree of intervention would be needed to secure higher levels of growth. Frequent visits to the USSR in the 1950s had convinced him of the merits of centralized economic planning and the application of science to industry. To some extent, he was a technocrat and meritocrat, and it was on those grounds that he sought to base his appeal. This was a change of emphasis rather than of content in Labour's message. At the party conference at Scarborough in October 1963, he made a thrilling speech, stressing the need for 'democratic planning' for the new Britain that was going to be 'forged in the white heat' of scientific revolution.[51] Between January and April 1964 Wilson returned to the attack with a series of speeches in which he combined emphasis on socialism being about science and economic growth – an adaptation of the revisionist message – with knockabout rhetoric attacking aristocrats and 'upper-class accents' to appease the inverted snobbery of his followers.[52] This rhetoric, like the other aspects of his reinvented image – pipe-smoking, brown sauce and Huddersfield Town Football Club – marked a sharp and probably conscious contrast to the élitist champagne-sipping image of his predecessor.

All this was taking place alongside continuing difficulties for the government. The economy slowed down, prices and unemployment rose, and there was an increasing perception, much fostered by Wilson, that Britain was falling behind its competitors. The French veto on British entry to the EEC in January 1963, and the Profumo Scandal that summer, severely dented Macmillan's image. Finally, in October 1963, he resigned. His successor was the Earl of Home, who relinquished his title so that he could return to the Commons as Sir Alec Douglas-Home. This conclusion suited Wilson very well: at a time when he was trying to show the Tories as out of date, their new leader was an aristocrat who claimed to use matchsticks to do calculations. Home delayed the election until the last possible moment, allowing the Chancellor, Reginald Maudling, to engineer a long pre-election boom. Labour's poll lead, which had stood at 20 points in June 1963, was pegged back to only 3 points by September 1964.

Labour fought the general election of October 1964 on the basis of revisionism given a significant twist in the direction of Wilsonian state planning and a more *dirigiste* approach to industrial modernization. There were no pledges to extend nationalization beyond the renationalization of iron and steel, although greater co-ordination of the public sector in industry was promised. Efforts would be made to stabilize prices and reform taxation. Social services would be improved. Secondary schools would be comprehensivized, the school-leaving age would be raised, and there would be 'a massive expansion in higher, further and university education'. On immigration, Labour promised to restrict entry but also to introduce legislation outlawing racial discrimination. Foreign aid would be increased. In defence policy, Labour would re-examine Britain's commitments, but despite rhetorical attacks on the government's nuclear weapons policy there were no pledges to disarm. Overall, Labour was, it claimed, 'offering Britain a new way of life that will stir our hearts, rekindle an authentic patriotic faith in our future, and enable our country to re-establish itself as a stable force in the world today for progress, peace, and justice'.[53]

It was clear throughout the campaign that the result would be a close one. Ultimately, Labour emerged with 317 seats to the Conservatives' 304, and a working majority of just five (the Speaker was a Conservative). A national swing of 3.5 per cent left Labour with 44.1 per cent of the poll, as opposed to 43.4 for the Tories and 11.2 for the Liberals. Labour support had risen among both manual and non-manual workers (in the former case, from 57 to 64 per cent).[54] Far from representing further class dealignment, as Abrams and Rose had implied, the 1964 election actually 'marked a peak in relative class voting'.[55] Doubtless this reflected growing disillusionment with the Conservatives' ability to continue increasing working-class living standards on the scale experienced in the 1950s, as well as, perhaps, some response to Wilson's often rather crude working-class rhetoric during the campaign and the months that had preceded it. In terms of gender, a more complex picture emerged, with the proportion of women voting Labour actually falling from 43 to 39.5 per cent.[56] This failure to attract women voters in large enough numbers was increasingly commented on around the time; many saw it as a symptom of the party's continuing reliance on masculine appeal and trade union imagery and ethos.[57] Labour lost five seats; it gained 61, two from the Liberals, the rest from the Conservatives. The gains were spread fairly evenly across the country, but there were regional variations in the swing, with the west Midlands, in particular, providing only a very low swing to Labour (although even here there were gains). This could be attributed to affluence, but also to some white working-class voters switching from Labour because they saw it as a pro-immigrant party: in three of the five seats that Labour lost nationally, '[i]mmigration played some part'.[58] Still, even these sombre facts could not prevent Labour feeling euphoric at its return to office after so long a period in opposition.

In the immediate aftermath of the 1951 election, no Labourite would have predicted that the party would not return to office for 13 years. But assumptions about the Conservatives, based on their perceived performance in government during the interwar period, had proved erroneous. After 1951 the Conservatives had not launched a frontal assault on the achievements of the Attlee governments, but had presided over a period of economic growth and rising living standards. Still worse, once in opposition, Labour had become bitterly divided. In reality, a period of reassessment after 11 years in office had been inevitable, but the bitterness which accompanied it was not, and for that, all concerned must bear a share of the responsibility. Such a long period of opposition should at least have been used to redefine Labour's future strategy and to reorientate its ideology after the first tranche of 'socialism' had been implemented. But despite some advances on policy, Labour's outlook remained largely founded upon the assumption that capitalism would continue to produce the goods. Revisionism was not a new departure but an adaptation of the old belief in inevitable progress clothed in pseudo-Keynesian language. Wilson, it is true, had helped to add a new technocratic, scientific gloss; but in reality all still depended on the ability of the system Labour purported to despise to give it the wherewithal to finance the society it claimed to want. The problem would be that, during the period that was about to open up, British capitalism was to begin to falter.

8

Wilson in Power, 1964–70

The Labour governments elected in 1964 and 1966 have not been remembered with great affection. Even before the defeat of 1970 they had become a by-word for failure and demoralization, broken promises and dashed hopes, not just for Labourites, but for a large section of the wider population. This condemnation is now being questioned by some historians, but popular memory does not accord these governments a high reputation.[1] And it is safe to say that many of the problems faced by Labour in these years were ones which were to continue to cause it difficulty long after the political events of the 1960s had faded from view.

The new government's parliamentary position was, to say the least, difficult, since the election had given it an effective overall majority of just five, and a seat was lost at an early by-election. From then onwards, however, Labour lost no more seats. With the Tory opposition in disarray, Labour had a good year in 1965, implementing many of its policies and promulgating the National Plan that September. Wilson was able to taunt Home's successor, Edward Heath, with threats of an early dissolution. With the economic indicators favourable, and fresh from a resounding victory in a marginal seat in Hull, Wilson called an election for 31 March 1966.

Labour began the campaign eight points ahead in the polls, and that lead was scarcely dented before polling day. The essential appeal was to trust: unlike the Conservatives in recent years, Labour had shown its competence in office. Labour could argue that it would have achieved more had it not been for the difficult parliamentary position and the situation it had inherited from the previous government. Controversial issues which were seen as vote-losers, like the unions, Europe and nationalization, were scarcely mentioned.[2] The results were impressive: Labour took 48.0 per cent of the vote to the Conservatives' 41.4 and the Liberals' 8.6, and won 364 seats to their 253 and 12 respectively. Labour had an overall majority of 97. On a swing of 3.5 per cent, it had made a net gain of 48 seats. The electorate was still

157

highly class-defined in its voting patterns: indeed, Labour had taken its highest ever share, 69 per cent, of the manual workers' vote, while also taking more than a quarter of the non-manual vote for the first time since 1945.[3] Both men and women had increased their support for Labour substantially, which was an encouraging sign.[4] Little was heard now of 'embourgeoisement' and 'affluence', at least as factors damaging Labour's prospects. Freed from the major constraint which had appeared to face it – its small majority – it was hoped that Labour would be able really to press ahead with its policies.

In part, the improvement in Labour's performance in 1966 could be attributed to the able team of leaders that had come to office in 1964. Although only three of the 23-strong cabinet had previous experience at that level, ten others had served as junior ministers under Attlee. The cabinet included 13 graduates (and was, incidentally, the least working-class Labour cabinet yet). Inevitably, it had a strongly 'Gaitskellite' feel, but Wilson strengthened his own position by bringing in people who had not been elected to the shadow cabinet the previous year, like Crossman, Castle and – in an attempt to emulate the success of Bevin in the 1945 government – Frank Cousins of the TGWU. Wilson's main rivals, Callaghan and Brown, were appointed to the Treasury and the new Department of Economic Affairs respectively, which militated against the formation of a Callaghan–Brown axis to threaten his position. Patrick Gordon Walker became Foreign Secretary (despite his having lost his seat at the general election), Healey Defence Secretary, and Griffiths the first Secretary of State for Wales. Promising figures appointed to junior office included Crosland, Benn and Roy Jenkins, while Peter Shore, who had been largely responsible for many of Labour's recent policy statements, became Wilson's parliamentary private secretary.

The changes which took place at the top level over the next five-and-a-half years were made for a variety of reasons. Some were made from choice, with Wilson particularly keen to promote talent and remove time-servers, especially if it enhanced the youthful image of his cabinet. Other alterations were forced on Wilson, but he did retain a penchant for making a virtue of necessity, and there was sufficient talent available for him to make even enforced changes look like beneficial developments.

The first adjustment in the cabinet was forced on Wilson, after Gordon Walker sought to return to parliament by fighting a by-election at Leyton in east London. He was defeated, and now had no alternative but to resign. Michael Stewart replaced him as Foreign Secretary, and was in turn replaced at Education by Crosland. This was something of a humiliation for Labour, but the loss of Gordon Walker was not really a major blow, and it might well be that Wilson was able to work better with Stewart.

A more positive change came in December 1965 when, in readiness for the expected election, Wilson carried out a limited reshuffle which removed some dead wood and brought in talented younger people like Jenkins, who became Home Secretary at the age of 45. Other older figures were removed after the 1966 election. However, alterations continued to be forced on Wilson. Cousins, unhappy as a minister, and opposed to the government's pay policies, resigned in July 1966, although it was not a great loss since Cousins had proved somewhat ineffectual as a minister, and the opportunity was taken to bring in Benn, one of the brightest young prospects in the party and a Wilson loyalist, as Minister of Technology. Wilson was compelled to reshuffle his ministers again when the effective abandonment of the National Plan in the summer of 1966 meant that Brown had to be moved, switching jobs with Stewart at the Foreign Office. Another enforced switch came in November 1967, with the devaluation of sterling, for Callaghan was left with no credibility as Chancellor and switched posts with Jenkins, now very much the government's rising star. Wilson continued to shuffle his team. In March 1968 Brown's frequent threats to resign finally bore fruit, and Stewart returned to the Foreign Office in his place. A major reshuffle followed in April, the most notable move being Castle's promotion from Transport to become First Secretary and head of the Department of Employment and Productivity. After this there were fewer changes, and none affecting the leading figures in the government.

In many cases, these moves reflected the failure of many of Labour's leading figures in office, Jenkins being one of the few leading ministers who had enhanced his reputation by 1970. However, the number of personnel shifts should not mask the fact that there was great political continuity: on the whole, the cabinet was mainly of the right and centre of the party, and even those left-wingers who were included could hardly be described as extremely committed to 'left' causes: on the whole, people like Castle and Crossman were forced to support Wilson for fear of his being succeeded by someone less in sympathy with the left, like Callaghan, Brown or, latterly, Jenkins. The outlook of the cabinet remained essentially revisionist. Wilson, further, was able to shore up his own position by a policy of divide and rule, by being prepared to move ministers between jobs on a fairly regular basis, and through the sheer good fortune that his critics were rarely united, not least on whom they would like to see succeeding Wilson should he be ousted. In short, Wilson's position remained more secure than might be expected given the vicissitudes Labour underwent in this period.

Any account of those vicissitudes must begin with the economy. Labour's 1964 manifesto combined revisionism with the vigorous application of new technology to industry and, in particular, 'Socialist planning'. Only in this way could full employment, faster growth, 'a sensible distribution of industry throughout the country', control of inflation and a cure to Britain's balance of payments problems be achieved.[5] Rather like Crosland, and MacDonald before him, Wilson saw economic growth as the prerequisite of social progress and reform; unlike them, but like the policy-makers of the 1930s, he had faith in planning, based on foreign examples. Once Labour had won the election, administrative changes were made the better to implement such plans. The Department of Economic Affairs (DEA) was set up under Brown, charged with formulating a National Plan to promote faster growth. Cousins was brought in to head the Ministry of Technology ('Mintech'), a new department charged with co-ordinating research and development (R & D) and with increasing the application of new technology in industry generally.[6]

Almost as soon as it began, however, the government faced a major crisis. On taking office, Wilson, Callaghan and Brown were told by civil servants that the trade deficit for 1964 would be £800 million, far worse than the Labour leadership had expected. The three ministers had to choose between devaluation and some form of import controls. Wilson took the lead against devaluation, and a temporary 15 per cent tariff on manufactures and semi-manufactures was imposed. This decision was taken in defiance of the General Agreement on Tariffs and Trade (GATT) and Britain's responsibilities to the European Free Trade Area (EFTA), but it did steady the markets and lead to a marked fall in the level of imports.[7] It seemed that the problem might have been solved.[8]

But a further crisis followed in July 1965, and was met with more austere economic policies. The real difficulty was that, in terms of the respective strength of the British and American economies, the pound *was* overvalued against the dollar. Even so, in the immediate aftermath of the 1966 election, the decision not to devalue was re-endorsed, this time by the whole cabinet. That July a major sterling crisis was sparked by fears about the government's unity and the efficacy of its prices and incomes policies. There were now many supporters of devaluation, including Brown, who saw the issue as a way of ousting Wilson and taking over the premiership. But on 17 July the cabinet voted by 17 to 6 against devaluation, and the following day agreed a severe deflation programme to calm the markets.[9] It worked, at the cost of higher taxes, spending cuts, and a statutory six-month incomes freeze.[10] Once again, though, the benefits proved temporary, and in November 1967 the government was finally forced to devalue from \$2.80 to \$2.40. Another austerity package accompanied this decision, and at length had the desired effect, but at great political cost. Wilson's credibility was dealt a huge blow.

In retrospect, the failure to devalue earlier has become one of the stoutest sticks with which to beat this government and, indeed, Wilson himself. In the end, devaluation 'worked'; in concert with other policies it led to a rectification of the trade balance to such an extent that there was a £700 million trade *surplus* by 1970.[11] Devaluation in 1967 was, according to this view, 'three years and £1500 million of borrowed money too late'.[12] The results for the rest of the government's economic strategy, as will be seen, appeared to have been highly damaging. Hence Wilson becomes the target of abuse: the exchange rate had been allowed to become an obsession, a fetish, a political virility symbol. To read some accounts, one would think that Wilson needed the \$2.80 rate to have any sense of self-worth at all.

Yet this is all too simplistic; at times it degenerates into the worst kind of psychobabble. It is, after all, easy to be wise after the event. Wilson thought that he had good reasons to avoid devaluation. The Treasury feared that devaluation might lead to inflation, and inflation was something Labour was pledged to avoid. There were fears that a British devaluation might lead to a round of competitive devaluations throughout the world, with concomitant worsening of international relations. Past experiences of devaluations had not been politically happy for

Labour: the issue had helped to destroy one Labour government in 1931 and rocked another in 1949. Wilson did not want Labour to be seen as the party that could not maintain the value of sterling. Then there was the old radical belief, with which Wilson's boyhood hero, Philip Snowden, would have concurred, that devaluation would hit hardest those who had managed to save a little and who lived on low incomes; that it was the duty of government to maintain the value of money in the interests, not of financiers, but of the working class. There were also international implications: many poorer countries (particularly, but not exclusively, in the Commonwealth) still held their balances in sterling and would be hard hit by any devaluation. This in turn showed another side of the argument: that devaluation would signal an end to the world role which Wilson still felt it was important for Britain to sustain. And, of course, the choice was not between devaluation and a tight fiscal stance: as Crossman, by that time an avid devaluer, admitted privately during the 1966 crisis, 'the scale of the package [of spending cuts] required to float the pound was not very different from that required to save it'.[13] It must also be noted that Wilson had, perforce, backed himself into a corner. Since 1964 he had had to reassure the markets by stressing that devaluation would not take place: panic would set in the moment he said anything else.[14] The final problem followed from this. Maintaining the parity became identified as Wilson's personal policy. This meant problems for Wilson once the parity was abandoned; but it also made problems for cabinet colleagues who wanted to devalue. For, certainly by 1966, to support devaluation meant to support someone else for the premiership, and that 'someone else' was Brown. And there were not many in the cabinet who, by 1966, wanted Wilson to go if it meant Brown replacing him. In short, there was probably no alternative but to try to the utmost to preserve the parity and, ultimately, be forced into devaluation. But it was a game the government could not win. Only a rapid improvement in Britain's economic performance would have squared the circle.

It seems likely that one of the main reasons why Wilson was reluctant to devalue was that he genuinely believed that his government's policies would strengthen the economy significantly.[15] But there was the catch: long-term stabilization depended on high rates of growth, yet the government's attempts to promote those higher growth rates were stymied by the recurrent exchange crises. Thomas Balogh, who became Wilson's economic adviser, had written in 1963 that Britain could 'create economic dynamism only by a consciously contrived expansion based on the selective encouragement of investment and technological innovation'.[16] It was to this end that the DEA, Mintech and, later, the Industrial Reconstruction Corporation were created. The DEA's National Plan, published in September 1965, aimed at a 25 per cent increase in GDP between 1964 and 1970, which meant an annual growth rate of 3.8 per cent.[17] This was very ambitious: growth even in the generally favourable conditions of 1951 to 1964 had only averaged 2.9 per cent a year, and many of those favourable conditions were now disappearing rapidly.[18] Even before the Plan was published, contractionary measures taken in the light of the 1965 sterling crisis were calling it into question; and it was not given adequate preparation, prioritization or administrative back-up to survive further shocks. In the summer of 1966, as stated above, the Plan was abandoned; the DEA was finally abolished in 1969. The whole affair had been something of a fiasco, though, given the context, it is difficult to see how any Plan so little rooted in realities but simply imposed from the centre could have succeeded.[19] In the event, the average annual growth rate between 1964 and 1970 was 2.2 per cent, exactly that between 1924 and 1937, a period most ministers would have regarded with a shudder as the worst of times.[20]

Part of the National Plan which did survive, however, was the desire to retain full employment while controlling inflation. By later standards, neither rose to massive levels. The period until about 1966 can be seen as a continuation of the full employment trends of the post-war period. However, there was an upward trend from then onwards: in the period 1964–6 the average annual rate was 1.6 per cent, whereas the rate for 1966–70 was 2.5 per cent. In January 1970 unemployment stood at 628 000. While these rates were still relatively low, the increase scarcely added credibility to Labour's claim to be the party of full employment.[21]

But it was the control of inflation that caused more immediate problems for the government. On taking office in 1964 the government took advantage of TUC goodwill to get the latter's agreement to a Joint Statement on Productivity, Prices and Incomes. A National Board for Prices and Incomes was set up in February 1965. However, wages and inflation continued to rise. In April

1965 the TUC agreed to a voluntary incomes policy which set a 'norm' for increases of between 3 and 3.5 per cent, but inflation increased to 4.7 per cent that year.[22] Then, in May 1966, a sea- men's strike blew the agreement apart, and following that July's sterling crisis the government announced a pay freeze to oper- ate until the end of the year, despite TUC opposition. The level of inflation fell in both 1966 and 1967, but the end of the freeze saw further upward pressure on wages. This, combined with the 1967 devaluation and general inflationary trends in all western economies, led to a renewed increase in inflation, which reached 4.7 per cent in 1968 and 5.4 per cent in 1969. It is not surprising that inflation was the most-mentioned issue in Conservative can- didates' election addresses at the 1970 election.[23]

The problem was that wages were the only area where the government felt it could take effective counter-inflationary measures. This in turn implied the need for some action to deal with trade union powers, a 'need' made more urgent, so it seemed, by the rash of 'unofficial' strikes that had followed the increas- ing decentralization of wage bargaining from industry-wide to plant level during the decade.[24] When the government-appointed Donovan Commission on trade unions reported in 1968 it came out broadly in favour of the *status quo*, but Wilson and most of his cabinet colleagues wanted firm action to deal with what was becoming a major issue. Accordingly, Castle's White Paper *In Place of Strife* (January 1969) envisaged sweeping changes in the relationship between unions and the state. Some of these were anathema to the unions: for example, the Secretary of State would have the power to order a 28-day 'conciliation pause' before a strike could commence; strike ballots could be demanded by the Secretary of State; and there would be penal sanctions, culmi- nating in imprisonment, for breaches of these rules. There was a more positive side: employers would be compelled to recognize unions, and the appointment of worker-directors would be en- couraged.[25] However, these concessions did not impress the unions, who remained deeply suspicious of worker participation in man- agement, and did not see mandatory recognition as a burning issue at a time when levels of unionization were still rising steadily. So union attention was concentrated on the penal, restrictive aspects of the proposals.

The result was fairly predictable. Strong opposition, led by Callaghan, emerged within the cabinet itself, and the wider party was very hostile. In March 1969, almost 100 Labour MPs voted against the proposals or abstained, and the NEC declared its opposition. That June, after almost six months of bitter dispute, the White Paper was withdrawn. Instead, the TUC signed a 'solemn and binding undertaking' covering unofficial strikes and inter-union disputes, which amounted, in fact, to little more than a face-saving exercise for the government. The whole episode had been a farce, and had left Wilson, and Castle, severely damaged. Wilson's approval rating in the polls fell to 26 per cent, then the lowest for any Prime Minister since polling began. For the unions, of course, the ultimate results of the rejection of *In Place of Strife* were to be disastrous, but that was not as clear in 1969 as it was to be with hindsight.

These policy failures put severe constraints, in turn, on the government's industrial policy. The mixed economy was maintained in virtually the same balance as had existed before 1964, the only exception being the renationalization of iron and steel in 1967. Some efforts were made to gee up the public sector, and there were productivity gains during the 1960s, although it is hard to see how far these were due to Labour's policies: in any event, the improvement did not last into the 1970s, and much of the gain came from redundancies.[26] In the meantime, little was done to address the problems thrown up by the Morrisonian public corporation. There was no real effort to integrate the nationalized industries more closely. Workforce commitment was not encouraged by the fact that, under the government's various incomes policies, wage increases in nationalized industries were easier to limit than in the private sector. Nothing was done to increase worker participation. It was possible for the government to argue that the unions were not much interested in the idea, but in fact some workers and union leaders were coming round to it.[27] A more open-minded policy from government at this stage might have restored workers' faith in nationalization, and given it a new, more positive image with which to face the last third of the century. As it was, an opportunity was missed or, perhaps more accurately, scarcely seen.

What ministers did see was the need to revamp the private sector and, in particular, manufacturing. To this end, Labour set out to improve government support for the application of science and technology to industry and to use regional policy to redistribute industry more evenly across the whole country. The agent for the execution of the former aspiration was Mintech. The initial idea was that it would shift R & D expenditure from military to civil purposes. In this, it had some success: one estimate suggests that, by 1969, government expenditure on civil R & D was greater than on military R & D for the first time since the war. From 1966, when Benn succeeded Cousins, the scope and profile of Mintech gradually increased, as it absorbed the Ministry of Aviation, much of the DEA, and certain functions of the Board of Trade to become 'one of the first "superministries"'.[28] Mintech oversaw numerous mergers in a decade which saw more company amalgamations than any since the 1920s.[29] However, it was not all success. It was still difficult to get industry to apply R & D developments, as conservatism still ran deep. The expansion of the ministry inevitably meant it lost some of its cutting edge as a pioneer of new technology. It is open to question whether the mergers it encouraged really benefited the economy or consumers.[30] Yet it was a pity that Wilson had raised such high expectations in 1964: judged by that standard, Mintech tended to be seen as something of a failure, but in all probability it did as much as could have been reasonably expected, and deserves to be remembered as one of the government's more successful initiatives, especially given the restrictive nature of macroeconomic policy for much of the period.

The Wilson governments also wanted to use regional policy to end the drift of industry towards the south and build up 'declining economies' elsewhere in Britain.[31] This was motivated by a humanitarian desire to avoid a repetition of the interwar experience of the depressed areas, by a political desire to improve employment prospects in these predominantly Labour areas, and to make macroeconomic management more straightforward. Macmillan had already made a start here, and, in real terms, there was a sixteen-fold increase in regional expenditure between 1962 and 1970. This included new planning machinery; the creation, in 1966, of five development areas (covering almost half of Britain); and subsidies to employers taking on new workers in the development areas. There were significant effects on employment, and the period between 1963 and 1970 has been seen as marking 'the most prolonged, most intensive, and most successful attack ever launched on regional problems in Britain'.[32]

Overall, though, Labour's economic experiences were not particularly positive. Despite some valuable achievements and a slight increase in productivity, the series of austerity packages necessitated by the recurrent sterling crises militated against greater success.[33] Inflation and unemployment proved difficult to control. Given this background, life was always going to be hard for the government in social policy, since it was committed to the revisionist view that a healthy, growing economy was the prerequisite of social reform.

Given the constraints, we should perhaps be more surprised at what the government was able to do, than condemnatory of what it failed to achieve in social policy. In education, Labour's main aims were to comprehensivize secondary schooling, to raise the leaving age from 15 to 16, and to expand further and higher education. There was some success in moving towards these goals. The ongoing elimination of selection was accelerated by Crosland's 1965 circular asking local education authorities to draw up plans for comprehensivization. By 1970, about a third of secondary pupils in England and Wales were in comprehensives, a ten-fold increase over 1964.[34] However, nothing was done about the independent sector, so the degree of 'democratization' was limited. And, as comprehensives came under fierce attack in the 1970s, Labour was to be labelled, unfairly, as the party which favoured 'levelling down' in education. The other areas of significant achievement came in the higher education sector. Here, Labour implemented existing Whitehall plans to set up polytechnics and increase the number of universities. By 1967, 29 polytechnics were being set up.[35] The government's other significant achievement was the establishment of the Open University, using distance-learning methods to offer higher education to those who had missed out earlier in life. As a whole, expenditure on education rose by between six and seven per cent a year under Labour.[36] Problems still remained, nevertheless, and the postponement of the raising of the school-leaving age to 16 in 1968 due to spending cuts was a severe blow.[37]

A still more mixed picture emerged in housing. In numerical terms, there was great achievement: the period from 1965 to 1970 saw just over two million new dwellings built, and a net increase in the housing stock of 1.3 million.[38] In no other five-year period since 1918 have so many new homes been built as in 1965–9.[39] Almost half the new building was council housing for rent, built with financial assistance from central government. But the type of council housing built at this time was often rather cheap and nasty, with much of the high-rise and high-density housing erected proving to be poorly constructed and unpopular with tenants. Social and extended family networks were disrupted by rehousing, a fact which led to increased strain on social services and hence public expenditure as older, informal support networks were ruptured. Labour's achievements were equivocal, and in retrospect many would see its policies as leading to significant social problems.

In other areas of social policy, Labour continued to act as the guardian of the welfare state, but at the same time was forced by economic circumstances into some unpalatable decisions. Spending on health and social services grew, and poorer families in particular benefited from increases in pensions and family allowance and the introduction of rate rebates. On the whole, however, the results of this extra expenditure were not startling.[40] A particular embarrassment was the decision, in 1968, to reintroduce prescription charges, which had been abolished on Labour's return to office in 1964.

Other reforms tended to give the government a more liberal image. The abolition of capital punishment in 1965, the legalization of abortion and male homosexuality (for those over 21) in 1967, and the easing of divorce in 1969 were all creditable achievements: while introduced as private members' bills, the government effectively supported their passage by granting the necessary parliamentary time. However, some Labour voters were unhappy with these changes, and Labour was finding itself caught between the desire to do 'the decent thing' on the one hand, and the beliefs of a substantial section of its supporters on the other. It tended to suggest to many people, among them significant numbers of Labour voters, that the party was 'soft' on crime and irresolute on important matters of personal morality.

If the Attlee governments had left Labour a lot to live up to in the field of domestic policy, the same was true in the field of foreign affairs. At the 1964 election, Labour attacked the Conservatives for having let the country down, but there were few concrete proposals, other than to set up a Ministry of Overseas Development and promote increased Commonwealth trade; and, once elected, Labour found its options to be very limited, and was increasingly constrained by the difficult economic position. Wilson had no doubts about the importance of sustaining Britain's world role, stating on one memorable occasion that Britain's frontiers were on the Himalayas.[41] His Foreign Secretaries, Gordon Walker, Stewart and Brown, were all right-wingers, keen on the EEC; Gordon Walker and Stewart were also pretty lightweight, and even Brown found it hard to assert himself as Foreign Secretary against Wilson. Healey, Defence Secretary throughout the period, had worked closely with Bevin and was very much a NATO man. In personal terms, then, Labour brought expertise into office. In terms of policy, continued adherence to a world role and the Atlantic alliance could be expected, while the issue of Europe was likely to arise at some point. The left, on the other hand, remained marginal to external policy throughout the Wilson years.

Thus Britain remained strongly committed to NATO and the USA. Still, this was a time of increasing left criticism of American conduct, particularly in Vietnam, where US forces were fighting on the side of the South against the Communist North in a bitter civil war. President Johnson wanted Wilson to offer British troops or, at least, arms in order to help the fight. Wilson realized that a public show of support on such a scale would be politically impossible, but in September 1965 he made a secret deal with Johnson promising tacit British support for the American position in Vietnam, and the maintenance of Britain's existing international commitments, in return for American support for the current sterling exchange rate with the dollar.[42] However, the promise to maintain Britain's overseas commitments became increasingly difficult to sustain. The February 1966 Defence White Paper stressed Britain's world role, but pared away at expenditure, which meant that it was increasingly difficult even to pretend that the commitments could be fulfilled.[43] The deflation package of July 1966 forced Britain to give up even this halfway-house, and large spending cuts were made. Following devaluation in 1967, it was decided that British forces would be withdrawn from east of Suez by the end of 1971. This arose not from principle, but from economic necessity. The true colour of government attitudes could be seen in the retention of Britain's nuclear weaponry and its continued loyalty to NATO.

The Commonwealth also posed problems for Labour. The party was pledged to continue decolonization, which had proceeded apace and, compared with other European states, with relative ease since the late 1950s. Unluckily for the Labour government, the easy period soon ended. In Rhodesia (Zimbabwe), a white minority was adamant that there should not be black majority rule on independence, but Labour refused to grant independence without majority rule. The resulting stalemate ended dramatically in November 1965 when the white Rhodesians under Ian Smith unilaterally declared their independence. Inconclusive talks followed, but the problem could not be resolved. Rhodesia's action was illegal, and sanctions were imposed. But the latter proved ineffective. There was considerable criticism of the British government, but it is difficult to see what else could have been done: military intervention would have had no public support in Britain, might have been fruitless, and would almost certainly have spelt political nemesis for Labour. The question was left to drag on for many years to come. Problems in handling the Nigerian civil war later in the decade also posed serious challenges to, and aroused considerable criticism of, the government. In addition, overseas aid was an early casualty of the continuing demands for public expenditure cuts, and the proportion of GDP spent on it actually fell between 1964 and 1970. The Ministry of Overseas Development, set up with high hopes in 1964, was rapidly downgraded. All this aroused left-wing criticism and seems to have turned some vocal young activists against the Labour party, or at least its leadership.[44]

The other contentious area in foreign policy was the question of entry into the EEC. The party was split on the issue, as it had been in 1961. While there were ardent supporters of entry, like Brown and Jenkins, there were many who were sceptical, and on the whole it would seem there were more firm opponents than clear supporters of entry. This was not really a 'left–right' split. It would be true to say that, on the left, few advocates of entry could be found, but there was no corresponding unity in favour in the centre or on the right of the party.[45] Thus people like Jay and Shore, neither of them 'left-wingers', opposed entry. If anything, Wilson was neither pro nor anti, but he did see the issue's destructive potential. The solution was, in the short term, brilliant. In 1967, Britain applied for entry, but knowing that the French President, de Gaulle, was certain to veto it. In this way, the issue was shunted into a siding: pro-Europeans were appeased because the effort had been made, while the antis were relieved that it had come to nothing. But the issue would not go away for ever: even in the medium term there would be a problem when de Gaulle departed the scene and a future Conservative government then reapplied. A classic Wilson fudge, the 1967 application worked only by storing up even greater problems for the future.

At the 1970 election, Labour's manifesto would claim that the government's 'fundamental and historic changes in Britain's defence and foreign policy ha[d] given Britain a more credible and realistic position in world affairs than we ever enjoyed under the last Tory administration'.[46] In fact, the government's foreign policy had not been as purposeful, as skilfully directed, or as successful as that of the 1945–51 administration. Instead, problems had been met with vacillation and procrastination. Great power illusions had served to weaken purpose. And in many areas – Vietnam, Rhodesia, nuclear weapons – the failure to take a stronger line, however understandable, had alienated many, particularly younger, people from Labour altogether, and made many people within the Labour party far more critical of its leadership. Neither in terms of world affairs nor of party management, therefore, was the government's legacy in this area a happy one.

The 1964–70 governments did not, then, live up to the reputation of the Attlee administrations in terms of economic management, social policy or foreign affairs. But this was not all. For Wilson also faced other problems, in issues which had scarcely disturbed the earlier administration. Six areas stood out in particular: the reform of government, Scottish and Welsh nationalism, Northern Ireland, race, gender, and youth.

The question of constitutional reform had hardly bothered the Attlee government. But by the 1960s there was growing interest in the nature and powers of government and, in particular, a growing tendency to see administrative problems as one cause of low economic growth rates. The Wilson government set out to deal with a number of aspects of the question. One answer was the creation of five new ministries in 1964. But these had mixed experiences. The most important, the DEA, was scrapped in 1969, by which time the Ministry of Land and Natural Resources had already been abolished. Overseas Development, though it survived, was downgraded in 1967. Thus, only two of the new ministries, Mintech and the Welsh Office, survived. Other initiatives in this area enjoyed little more success. An attempt to reform the House of Lords foundered in April 1969, a victim of an alliance between the Conservative right, which wanted no change, and the Labour left, which wanted abolition and nothing less. An attempt to reform and modernize the civil service on the basis of the 1968 Fulton Report came to very little. The Redcliffe–Maud committee, set up to look at the functions and boundaries of local authorities, came up with radical proposals, advocating the creation of eight provincial authorities, but this was not adopted by the government; and the sclerosis of local government continued, even despite the plans to redraw boundaries and reallocate functions which resulted, finally, in the 1972 Local Government Act. While Wilson's governments did not substantially reduce the functions of local government, they had no real conception of the need to revitalize it, and in so far as they saw any need for the 'modernization' of local government it was more in the context of the desire to promote faster economic growth than in terms of strengthening democracy and participation.[47] Centralization continued, if only by default.

Increasingly, there was resistance to centralization, and this began to be expressed especially through growing support for Scottish and Welsh nationalism, which emerged during the 1960s as 'new' issues on the British political agenda, and ones with which the Labour party was ill-equipped to deal. Labour had had a paper commitment to Scottish home rule from the 1920s, but in 1958 this had been quietly extinguished, a logical step given the party's commitment to centralization and statism, and the apparent political weakness of nationalism.[48] Labour's commitment to Welsh nationalism had been, if anything, even weaker. Yet the Welsh nationalist party, Plaid Cymru, had made steady progress during the 1950s, taking 3.1 per cent of the vote in Wales in 1955 and 5.2 per cent in 1959. It fell back a little in 1964, but Wilson's creation of the Welsh Office with its own Secretary of State was, in part at least, aimed to reduce this threat in what was one of Labour's strongest areas of support. However, the gesture did little to assuage nationalist discontent; and in Scotland, too, support for nationalism began to grow. At the 1966 election, though electing no MPs, Plaid took 4.3 per cent and the SNP 5.0 per cent of their respective nations' votes. In July 1966, Plaid gained Carmarthen from Labour at a by-election, and subsequently slashed Labour's majorities at West Rhondda and Caerphilly. The nationalists also began to make an impact in Scotland, gaining Hamilton from Labour in November 1967, averaging around 25 per cent in the other three seats they fought during the lifetime of the 1966 parliament, and making gains in local elections.[49] While few Labourites yet saw devolution as necessary, the government did appoint a constitutional commission under Lord Crowther to study the problem, and also tried to alleviate some of the fears of English cultural imperialism in Wales by passing the Welsh Language Act in 1967.[50] However, all this came a little late in the day, and as economic problems mounted, so too did support for the nationalist parties, particularly as unemployment was higher in Wales and Scotland than in most of England. The nationalist backlash in safe Labour areas also represented resentment at virtual one-party rule, with its attendant complacency and, at times, corruption, in many parts of Wales and Scotland.[51] At the 1970 general election both parties polled over 10 per cent of the votes in their respective nations, and it is hard to avoid the conclusion that Labour's rather arrogant centralizing tendencies had sown all kinds of problems which were to cause the party immense difficulty in the following decade.

Problems with Northern Ireland were less of Labour's making. The 1921 settlement had separated Ireland into the Irish Free State (later the Irish Republic) and Northern Ireland, which remained part of the United Kingdom, electing 12 Westminster MPs, but also with its own parliament at Stormont. The Stormont regime was Protestant-dominated, and Catholics had suffered much discrimination. In the 1960s, Catholic civil rights groups became increasingly vocal, and in 1969 there was a Protestant backlash: that summer saw a series of riots and clashes, and in August the Home Secretary, Callaghan, deployed British troops in order to keep the peace. The situation stabilized for a while, and the government, and Callaghan, took credit for what seemed to be a successful operation.[52] However, even before the 1970 election, the situation had begun to deteriorate once more, and in 1972 Heath's government would dissolve Stormont and impose direct rule from London. So far as Labour was concerned, the short-term results were quite favourable: its defence of Catholics against perceivedly oppressive Protestants boosted its image on the left and, possibly, helped to win back some support among Catholics who had been alienated by the legalization of abortion. The imposition of direct rule by the Conservatives in 1972 would lead the Ulster Unionists to cease taking the Conservative whip; had they not broken with Heath at this point, the February 1974 general election would have given the Tories more seats than Labour, although not an overall majority. But in the longer term, the upsurge in violence in Northern Ireland, and its extension to mainland Britain through Irish Republican Army (IRA) bombing campaigns, meant renewed emphasis on an issue – law and order – where the Conservatives were perceived as stronger than Labour by most voters, and would also add to the perceived crisis of governability in the UK which would, ultimately, damage Labour so severely in the 1970s. In the longer term, therefore, the eruption of Ulster was to help the Conservatives to the detriment of the Labour party.[53]

Race and immigration was another issue which broke on to the political agenda in the 1960s, and again it was one with which Labour was ill-equipped to deal. Labour had long been committed to the right of Commonwealth citizens to settle in Britain, and had claimed to be in favour of racial equality. The restrictive immigration legislation of 1962 had faced strong Labour opposition. However, because immigrants settled mostly in working-class areas, there were fears of a backlash among Labour's traditional supporters, and such fears were dramatically confirmed in the 1964 election when Gordon Walker was defeated at Smethwick, a west Midland constituency with a relatively high immigrant population, by an explicitly racist Conservative. The favourable reaction of many working-class people to Enoch Powell's famous anti-immigration speech of April 1968 tended to intensify concerns that Labour was in a difficult position on this issue. Concern about the party's electoral prospects was married to fears of the effects for members of ethnic minorities if there was a strong white backlash, but openly racist attitudes survived in the party and the trade union movement.[54] The Labour leadership deplored such views, wanted to pursue liberal policies as far as it could, and also recognized that it was the most likely beneficiary of ethnic minority votes.[55] Its response, therefore, was to try a balancing act. In 1965, it tightened immigration controls, while passing a Race Relations Act outlawing racial discrimination and establishing a Race Relations Board. There was much less balance about the Commonwealth Immigrants Act, rushed through in 1968 in order to prevent the entry of large numbers of Asians who were being expelled from Kenya and who held British passports. This was a panic measure: it also discriminated on grounds of race, since it gave preference for immigration to those with at least one white grandparent over those with none at all.[56] The issue was not really resolved: to placate white voters, Labour had to some extent upset the ethnic minorities, while at the same time failing to go as far as many white voters wanted. Immigrants began to feel disillusionment with the political system, and the fact that it was not until 1987 that a non-white Labour MP was elected hardly did much to draw in this section of the British population.[57] The real problem, though, was that there were no easy answers for Labour in this area.

The same was true with the issues of gender and youth which attained a higher political profile during the decade. Labour, for all its protestations, had always been essentially a men's party. At times, as in the period immediately before the First World War, it had forged alliances with women's groups, and the 1918 constitution had set up separate women's sections in CLPs, reserved four NEC places for women, and established a separate women's conference. But the conference and the women's sections were largely ignored when it came to decision-making within the party, while the four women on the NEC were elected, not by women, but by the whole Labour party conference. By the 1930s, ambitious women like Barbara Betts (later Castle) were deliberately bypassing the women's organization, realizing its impotence. Between the wars, Labour resisted family allowances on the grounds that they would threaten the principle of the 'family wage', and a Labour government had withdrawn married women's rights to unemployment benefit. During and after the Second World War, Labour ministers had resisted women's demands for equal pay with men. Because, on the whole, the women's movement had been quite weak since the 1920s, these lines had not faced too much opposition. But the 1960s saw the women's movement become more vocal and influential than at any time since the First World War, while Labour found it difficult to change. Although Wilson had some personal commitment to equality, he did not feel he could go too far towards it. True, Castle was promoted higher than any previous woman cabinet minister, and two women sat together in cabinet for the first time in 1968 when Judith Hart joined her as Paymaster-General. In 1970 an Equal Pay Act was passed. But having one or two women in the cabinet was rather a token victory, and the Equal Pay Act, due to come into effect only in 1975, looked like cynical electioneering. Many women who might have come into the Labour party now turned their backs on it in favour of the women's movement or far left groups, while others, who did stay with Labour, became more critical of the leadership. It would not do to overstate this: most women did not suddenly become radical feminists. But Labour's failure to tap a substantial source of radical, politically active and on the whole young women was not an encouraging sign for its future vitality.

The 1960s was also a decade when youth came more clearly on to the political agenda. But here again the party was slow to respond and, when it did, it was often in a discouraging manner. The growth of youth culture, with roots in the 1930s but really blossoming from the 1950s, had left the party cold: there was little attempt even to understand modern movements and feelings among young people. The party's youth movement, Young Socialists, had been disbanded for ultra-leftism in 1965 and reorganized as the Labour Party Young Socialists, with most of its (extremely limited) powers removed. At constituency and ward level, LPYS members were more likely to encounter suspicion and hostility than encouragement, except at election times when, unsurprisingly enough, their commitment to canvassing and committee room work meant a temporary reprieve. In addition to these perennial problems, the youth organization began to crumble as the government struggled, the number of branches halving between 1962 and 1969. Government policies did little to stem the growing alienation of young people from the party. Youth protest movements offended party leaders and many stalwart Labour voters. The reduction of the voting age from 21 to 18 in 1969 was less a principled commitment to young people than a piece of gerrymandering based on the assumption that young people were more likely to vote Labour than Conservative. Here again, then, the political agenda was being amended in ways that did not at all suit the Labour party.

At the same time, many of the old signs of Labour vitality were beginning to fade. Trade union membership was still expanding, but the unions, which had been the crucial underpinning of the party since its early days, were strongest in the very industries that were in decline: the National Union of Mineworkers fell from 586 000 members to 279 000 between 1960 and 1970, while in the same period the NUR shrank from 334 000 to 198 000. Government pay policies and attempts at union reform loosened, perhaps permanently, the commitment of many trade unionists to supporting the Labour party.[58] The Co-operative movement was losing its old vitality, too: greater prosperity, more consumer choice and a rationalization programme all made its shops less central to working-class life than they had been in earlier times, while membership of the Co-operative Women's Guild in 1971 was little more than half what it had been in 1960.[59]

This decline was reflected, to some extent, by a fall in the Labour party's individual membership. The official figure fell from 830 116 in 1964 to 680 191 in 1970, a drop of over 15 per cent in just six years.[60] While the significance of this should not be exaggerated, there was undoubtedly a sharp decrease; and both figures were overstated, reflecting the arcane rules for CLP affiliation to the national party. There were external factors involved, such as the '"privatization" of lifestyles';[61] but many people did seem to be falling out with and from the party, some to join the new far left groups which began to emerge in the period, more to join no party at all. Those who remained were often more rebellious than they had been in earlier periods, and this, allied with growing trade union discontent, meant that the NEC suffered no fewer than 12 defeats on major issues at party conferences in the late 1960s.[62] CLPs were now, on the whole, well to the left of the party leadership, a trend that was to continue into the 1980s.

During the 1966 parliament, electoral trends were generally very unfavourable towards Labour. As late as February 1967 Labour had been 11 points ahead in the polls, but by that December, it trailed by 17 points, and this rose to a peak of 28 in May 1968. In the latter month, Labour fared catastrophically in the local elections; for example, losing control of Sheffield for the first time since 1932. In by-elections, it lost 15 seats between 1966 and 1969. However, although the Conservatives were still 11 points ahead in the polls in December 1969, the worst crises were now past. Jenkins's austerity measures were beginning to bear fruit in improved balance of payments figures, while Wilson's reputation seemed to be recovering remarkably. And there were still widespread doubts about Heath, the Conservative leader, especially as his party seemed to be moving towards a more radical free-market approach. Thus, the early months of 1970 saw some Labour recovery, and Wilson, enjoying a seven-point lead in the polls, dissolved parliament on 29 May 1970. Labour issued a 'safety first' manifesto and asked the voters to trust it. All in all, it seemed, Labour would win the election.

But, on a significantly lower turnout than in 1966, it was defeated. The announcement, two days before polling, of an unexpected balance of payments deficit did not help Labour's cause: it can hardly have been decisive, but it probably helped remind people of the travails of recent years, which was just what Wilson had been trying to avoid. Whatever the reason, enough voters turned to the Conservatives, or abstained, to put Heath in power.[63] Labour made a net loss of 58 seats on a swing of 4.7 per cent, the greatest since 1945: in parts of the Midlands, and in east Lancashire, there were even heavier shifts against Labour. The party performed better in the rest of the north and in Scotland, but in the south outside inner London its performance was weak. Support among men fell more heavily than among women, and while its share of the non-manual vote scarcely declined at all, it suffered a huge loss of manual voters' support, from 69 per cent in 1966 to 58 per cent (only slightly higher than in 1959).[64] This shift is explicable less in terms of 'class dealignment' as such than in terms of policy failure on the part of the government: a significant number of workers, perhaps more 'instrumental' in their voting than previously, felt they had had enough of incomes policies and restrictions, and wanted a change because they felt they could do better economically out of a Conservative government than a Labour one.

Labour, then, was back in opposition. The gap between the leadership, on the one hand, and the unions and party membership, on the other, was wide, and, some thought, unbridgeable. There were worrying signs of a leakage of traditional Labour support. The government's revisionist strategy of seeking a more socialist society through economic growth under capitalism had come to little, because the economy had refused to grow as required, even despite the special efforts that had been expended on it. 'New' issues were posing serious moral and political dilemmas for the party. It was not a happy situation, and in the immediate aftermath of defeat it was unclear how it could be resolved.

9
Drift to Defeat? 1970–9

With the exception of the short-lived experiment of 1924, loss of office had, in the past, been followed by long periods in opposition, and the same was to be true after 1979. By contrast, the party had to wait less than four years after its 1970 setback to resume control of government. Even so, the years between 1970 and 1974 proved a period of intense activity, as economic crisis intensified and the Labour movement sought to reinvigorate itself. Policies were reworked, positions were changed. But the cost of the resulting radicalization of party policy was increasing tension within the party, the sowing of some of the seeds of the split which led to the formation of the Social Democratic party (SDP) in 1981, and a general intensification of doubt both inside and outside the party as to the route it should now take. All these developments were then exacerbated by the five years of Labour government between 1974 and 1979. Shedding party policies left and centre – if not right – and reeling from a concatenation of economic crises and problems with which traditional Labourism found it peculiarly difficult to deal, the party ultimately succumbed to conclusive defeat at the general election of 1979. The roots of many of the problems which were to consign Labour to permanent opposition in the 1980s were to be found in this period.

The Heath government presided over troubled times. Unemployment grew, peaking at 929 000 in January 1972. Inflation rose to an annual average of 8.6 per cent for 1971–3. Keynesians had assumed that there was a trade-off between inflation and unemployment, but now the economy seemed to be in the grip of 'stagflation', where both rose together. External pressures, like the quadrupling of oil prices by Middle Eastern states in 1973, fuelled inflation further. All this led to greater wage militancy on the part of workers, and a further deterioration in industrial relations. Working days lost through strikes averaged just under 4 million per annum between 1965 and 1969; between 1971 and 1973 the figure was almost 15 million, with 24 million days being

179

lost in 1972 alone. When this was linked to the ongoing conflict in Northern Ireland, it seemed to many that the United Kingdom was becoming ungovernable. For the first time since the war it seemed that a crisis of capitalism was at hand.

This crisis was reflected by developments inside the Labour party. Revisionism, already under pressure, lost credibility still further: if socialism was all about an egalitarian distribution of the surplus produced by a growing capitalism, what had it to say or do in a situation in which capitalism was manifestly in trouble? As early as 1962, Crosland had pointed out that a *deus ex machina*, in the form of entry to 'Europe' 'may' well be needed to solve the problem of low growth.[1] By 1970, this 'may' was becoming a 'must' for much of the revisionist right. And it was also combined, increasingly, with strong advocacy of another panacea: 'a prices and incomes policy' to control inflation.[2] The problem with both these solutions, however, was that they aroused the hostility of the bulk of the Labour movement, and particularly of the trade unions. The bankruptcy of revisionism at a time of economic crisis, in short, was leading to the break-up of the historic alliance between the unions and the party's right wing, just as surely as that alliance had cracked under the pressure of economic crisis between 1929 and 1931. Here were the roots of the party's leftward swing in the 1970s and early 1980s, and of the isolation of the right among whose consequences was to be the formation of the SDP.

The other basic element in the beginnings of the swing to the left was the perception that the Wilson governments had failed. Almost every section of the party felt let down, even betrayed. There was a strong feeling that next time it must be different, and so many in the party began to work seriously for new policies and strategies for a future Labour administration.

Given the extent of change in this period, it might be thought surprising that Wilson remained leader. But he was still seen as a great electoral asset, and was canny enough to see off potential threats.[3] Jenkins's election as deputy leader in succession to Brown in 1970 suggested he was the obvious alternative, but there was no attempt to overthrow Wilson in his favour. With Jenkins as shadow Chancellor, Callaghan as shadow Home Secretary and Healey promoted to shadow Foreign Secretary, the leadership was still in centre-right hands. True, Michael Foot, seen as the spiritual heir to Bevan, was elected to the shadow cabinet in 1970, and Benn now emerged as a fervent opponent of entry to the EEC, an advocate of much greater state intervention in industry, and possessor of a new, more populist image. But the right also continued to throw up new stars, such as Shirley Williams, who became one of the most popular figures in the PLP and who served as shadow Home Secretary in 1972–3. Indeed, since it was almost impossible for a CLP to deselect its MP, the PLP remained to a large extent insulated from the leftish pressures in the wider party, and since it alone elected the party leader and shadow cabinet, the party leadership was always likely to remain in cautious hands.[4] The realization of this problem led, in 1973, to the formation of the Campaign for Labour Party Democracy (CLPD), which aimed, *inter alia*, to enfranchise the wider party in the election of the party leader.[5] The NEC, elected annually at party conference, was a different matter altogether; and, after 1970, the left became far more significant. The NEC had always been more prominent when Labour had been in opposition than in office, but now there were conscious efforts to enhance its status at a time when its balance was tilting leftwards. One sign of this was the extensive work done on policy formulation, which culminated in *Labour's Programme for Britain* (1972) and *Labour's Programme 1973*.[6]

To some extent the leftward shift of the NEC reflected a degree of trade union radicalization. This was partly due to disillusionment with the Wilson governments, and anger at *In Place of Strife*, but rising inflation and unemployment also increased militancy. Some of the leading unions, like the TGWU and the Amalgamated Union of Engineering Workers (AUEW), elected more combative leaders, moving matters still further from the days when a bloc of right-wing unions and their leaders had made the party safe for social democracy. The self-marginalization of a section of the party's social democratic right was part cause and part effect of these developments. Thus the party conference, at length, moved still further away from the PLP and its leadership, inflicting regular defeats on the latter and, in 1973, adopting a programme about which Wilson and his colleagues had grave reservations. In addition, strike activity increased. The miners' strikes of 1972 and 1974 both led Heath to declare a state of emergency, and resulted in power cuts. There were overtime bans by train drivers and power workers, among others. Some of these disputes were accompanied by a degree of violence and the use of flying pickets, bussed in from other areas to close down secondary targets. As in other periods, the party leadership felt distinctly uneasy about all this, but could do little to stop it.

But the forces operating on union–party relations were not all divisive in their effects. While the balance was shifting leftwards, many unions remained willing to back the leadership. And Heath himself helped push unions and party back together. Two things in particular antagonized the unions. The first was the 1971 Industrial Relations Act, a massive statute which aimed to provide a comprehensive legal framework for trade unionism. The Act, which included numerous intrusions on unions' powers, backed by penal sanctions, aroused massive union and Labour hostility. Legal actions under the Act, and the imprisonment of the 'Pentonville Five' in July 1972 for breaking an order of the National Industrial Relations Court, led the TUC to demand nothing less than total repeal. Labour accepted this position with alacrity. Secondly, growing government pressure to restrict wage increases, culminating in the enactment of a statutory wages policy in 1972, further antagonized the unions. The result was that, as early as the end of 1971, the TUC and the Labour party were 'in closer alliance than at any time since 1967'.[7]

Union leaders were hostile to pay restraint on the lines implemented by Heath but, nonetheless, many of them, like Jack Jones of the TGWU, did see the need to bring inflation under control. The result was a revival of the concept of the 'social wage': pay restraint would be accepted but only in return for social reforms beneficial to union members. The result of this was the 'Social Contract', adopted as party and TUC policy in 1973. While its details remained vague, it helped to cement still further the renewed bonds between unions and party, and it suggested, if nothing else, that Labour had at least some idea of how to deal with what was rapidly becoming the dominant issue in British politics.

The most radical manifestation of Labour's leftward shift came in the field of economic policy. At one stage almost 50 policy committees were at work under the aegis of the NEC, and the end result of their endeavours was *Labour's Programme 1973*, which was approved by that year's party conference.[8] The programme committed Labour to price controls; to the Social Contract; to increased pensions; to renegotiation of the terms of entry to the

EEC; and to the restoration of free collective bargaining and re-peal of the Industrial Relations Act. Industrial democracy would be extended. A National Enterprise Board (NEB) would buy into individual firms (thus marking the abandonment of the sector-by-sector approach favoured by the party hitherto), and make planning agreements with companies to ensure greater control over their actions. It would also take control of 'twenty-five of our largest manufacturers' at an early stage.[9] The NEC had been split on this last issue, with moderates led by Callaghan, Healey and Williams vocal in their opposition.[10] Wilson had reserved his position, but at the party conference he came out against it, suggesting that it might be ignored in the drafting of the next election manifesto.[11] This aroused considerable left-wing ire.[12] But the programme as a whole was passed, committing Labour to a more radical package of economic proposals than ever before.

The debates on economic policy were bitter, but paled beside the problems posed to the party by the issue of entry to the EEC. The arch-Europhile Heath revived Britain's application and completed negotiations for entry in June 1971. In January 1973 Britain became a member of an enlarged, nine-member EEC. Labour remained split. For some, like Jenkins and Rodgers, it remained axiomatic that Britain must be a member of the EEC on almost any terms. But opposition was hardening. The old considerations against entry (see Chapter 7) still held good for many. They were supplemented by the growing desire of some on the left to see the imposition of import controls – which were incompatible with EEC membership – as a way of bolstering British industry against increasing import penetration.[13] The 1970 party conference almost passed a resolution opposing entry on prin-ciple, but matters eased somewhat once Heath had agreed terms: it could now be argued that the issue of principle was academic, and Labour could, instead, unite very largely in criticism of the terms agreed to by the government.[14] This was the line Wilson took, and it gave him ample ammunition for attacks on the govern-ment, which meant his stock rose with the left. But Jenkins and his followers were infuriated by anything less than wholehearted acceptance, and in the Commons vote on entry in October 1971, 69 Labour MPs (including Jenkins, Williams, Rodgers, David Owen, and Dick Taverne) voted with the government, while a further 20 (including Crosland) abstained.[15] Jenkins, seen as the leader of the revolt, came in for strong criticism, and narrowly beat off

Foot's challenge in that year's deputy leadership election. However, matters did not rest there. Benn, party chairman for 1971–2, had come round to the idea that a referendum should be held on entry. At first the idea had attracted little support, but soon people began to see its value as a way of avoiding a permanent split in the party. Jenkins and his colleagues were staunchly against the idea, ostensibly on constitutional grounds, but probably also fearing that a referendum would result in a vote against membership. In March 1972, Wilson came out in favour of the idea, and the shadow cabinet supported him by a narrow majority. As a result, Jenkins resigned the deputy leadership, and Owen, Harold Lever, and George Thomson resigned from the front bench.[16] But there was no major party split and, all in all, Wilson managed to keep the party more or less together, if not united. In October 1973, Jenkins, his position in the party much diminished, re-entered the shadow cabinet on Wilson's terms. For the time being, the EEC issue was under control. But that control had been bought at the cost, first, of fudging over the splits in the party, and, secondly, of increasing the siege mentality of a section of the party's right wing.

Jenkins rejoined the shadow cabinet just in time, for Heath's government was running into what would turn out to be terminal difficulties. After a series of embarrassing policy U-turns, the Conservatives opted to face down the miners, who were demanding a large pay increase as the price for ending an overtime ban. Emergency fuel-saving measures, such as a reduced speed limit on the roads, and a three-day working week, were introduced from 31 December 1973. When the miners voted overwhelmingly for strike action on 10 February, Heath decided to dissolve parliament and fight an election on what he believed would be the winning slogan of 'Who rules Britain?' His optimism was matched by Labour pessimism, for earlier poll leads had dissipated and the Gallup poll for January 1974 put the Conservatives two points ahead. No seats had been gained from the Conservatives at a by-election since May 1971, while Labour had lost Rochdale to the Liberals in October 1972, Lincoln to the erstwhile Jenkinsite Taverne (now standing as 'Democratic Labour') in March 1973, and a seat in Glasgow to the SNP that November. Since it would be an election in which issues of union power would be central, it was hardly surprising that Labour's expectations were not altogether rosy.[17]

However, the Conservatives were also under pressure: the three-day week was just the latest in a long string of states of emergency, the government had backtracked on a number of its 1970 pledges, and inflation and unemployment were both rising. While Labour's share of the vote fell by almost 6 points to 37.2 per cent, the Conservatives fared even worse, their share plummeting from 46.4 to just 37.9 per cent. The beneficiaries of the collapse of the 'two-party' vote were the minor parties: the Liberals more than doubled their poll share to 19.3 per cent, while the SNP's performance in terms of the Scottish vote was scarcely less spectacular. In terms of seats, though, the electoral system played the trick of 1929 and 1951: it gave the party with the second-highest number of votes the highest number of seats. Labour emerged with 301 MPs, and the Conservatives with 297. Thus, for the first time since 1929, a general election had produced a parliament in which no party had an overall majority: the balance was held by the 37 'others', who included 14 Liberals, 12 Northern Ireland MPs (one of whom was broadly in sympathy with Labour), two independent Labourites, seven Scottish Nationalists and two Plaid Cymru representatives.

It would, therefore, be something of a misnomer to describe the February 1974 election as a Labour victory. The party had made a net gain of 13 seats, but its fall in the share of the popular vote suggested that it was not massively loved by the electorate. The party's main gains came in the west Midlands, where it gained nine more seats than in 1970, and in western Lancashire, where it made a net gain of five seats.

Under the circumstances, Heath tried to stay in office. He appealed to Jeremy Thorpe, the Liberal leader, to form some kind of coalition. However, the Conservatives were clearly discredited, and Thorpe was under pressure from radical elements in his own party to have nothing to do with any such arrangement. To the surprise of no one, the talks soon proved fruitless, and the failure of Heath's attempts to attract Thorpe meant that, on 4 March, Wilson was invited to form his third administration.

Wilson's cabinet was full of experience, and contained few surprises. Healey became Chancellor, Callaghan Foreign Secretary, and, in a clear sign of his diminished standing, Jenkins returned to the Home Office. Other prominent members of the social democratic right included Crosland and Williams (at the newly created Department of Prices and Consumer Protection). But the left was also well represented, and took some crucial posts. Benn went to Industry; Foot became Employment Secretary, a position involving close dealings with the unions, particularly on the Social Contract; and Castle went to Health and Social Security. It would be facile to call this a 'left-wing cabinet', but in no other Labour government have so many important portfolios been handed to the left.

Obviously, a further general election could not be long delayed. For the next six months, there was something of a return to 1964-6, with Wilson and his colleagues manoeuvring to provide themselves with a suitable base from which to launch an appeal for a stronger position. They ended the miners' strike swiftly, reaching a settlement favourable to the miners on 6 March, and repealed the Industrial Relations Act. Value added tax (VAT) was reduced from ten to eight per cent, although income tax was increased. And council house rents, which the Conservatives had aimed to increase considerably, were frozen. Longer-term policies included the start of the renegotiation of British terms of entry to the EEC and a flood of White Papers in the summer on industry, pensions, land and devolution. With Labour slightly ahead in the polls, an election was called for 10 October.

The election campaign was, once again, lacklustre. There was never much doubt that Labour would win, but the polls overpredicted the party's support and, in the event, the result was rather disappointing: Labour took 39.2 per cent of the votes, the Conservatives 35.8 per cent, and the Liberals fell back a little to 18.3 per cent. Plaid Cymru's share of the Welsh vote was static, but the SNP made further advances, to register a 30.4 per cent share of the Scottish vote, more than the Conservatives. All this translated into an overall Labour majority of just three: it took 319 seats, while the Conservatives had 277 and the other parties totalled 39. The seats of Taverne and another Labour rebel, Eddie Milne at Blyth, had been regained, at least. But the parliamentary position was going to be difficult, although Labour had a hefty lead over the Conservatives and the plethora of other groups made it unlikely that all opposition MPs would be able to find an issue around which to unite. Labour had made further gains, especially in the west Midlands, but the lower than average swing in key marginals meant it made fewer gains than it might have expected on a national swing of 2.2 per cent.[18]

A new poll soon followed: the referendum on the EEC. Labour

had started to renegotiate Britain's terms of entry shortly after its return to office. It was clear, however, that the party remained deeply split, and that the division ran right up the party to the cabinet room. Accordingly, it was decided that, following a 1932 precedent, there would be an 'agreement to differ': on this issue alone, ministers would be relieved from the normal obligations of collective responsibility, whereby they were supposed to speak with one voice, although the government's official line would be to support continued membership. To many, this seemed to be a new depth of Wilsonian cynicism, but, if the party was to be kept together, it was hard to see what else could have been done. In March 1975 the negotiations were complete, and a referendum was set for 5 June. The renegotiated terms came in for considerable criticism, with the left in particular feeling that they were 'very far short' of what party policy demanded, and only passed through parliament with opposition support, as a total of 145 Labour MPs, including seven cabinet ministers, voted against.[19] On 26 April, a special party conference rejected the terms by a two-to-one majority.[20] The referendum campaign itself was a strange spectacle, with people like Heath, Jenkins and Thorpe united in the 'Yes' campaign and Foot, Benn and Enoch Powell in the 'No' lobby. Wilson and Callaghan posed as somewhat reluctant supporters of the deal they had negotiated. The result showed a two-to-one majority in favour of continued membership on the new terms. This seemed to settle the matter.[21] Of course, the issue did not go away for long, but in the immediate aftermath Wilson took the opportunity to downgrade the referendum's main advocate, Benn, whose radical policies at Industry had become increasingly embarrassing to the premier. He was switched with the loyalist figure of Eric Varley, erstwhile Energy Secretary. Benn decided against resignation on the grounds that he would have more leverage for the causes in which he believed if he remained within the cabinet.[22]

This whole affair – the 'successful' outcome of the referendum, and the political castration of Benn – was to prove one of Wilson's greatest coups. In fact, with one exception, it was also his last. The final act came, with characteristic theatre, on 16 March 1976 when, to almost universal surprise, he announced that he would resign the leadership as soon as the party had elected a successor.[23] This move gave rise to considerable speculation, but the explanation was prosaic enough. Wilson was 60, and felt stale. He felt a debt to his wife, who had married an Oxford don but then spent three decades in the public spotlight she hated.[24] Finally, and perhaps most of all, there was Wilson's ordinariness, surely his best feature. Civil servants retired at 60. Politicians should do the same, not amble on into their dotage. And so he did. One of the few people to be informed in advance was Callaghan, in order to allow him to prepare for the leadership election: this was a notable sign of the extent to which relations between the two men had improved.[25]

Ultimately, there were six candidates in that election. Callaghan was the centrist figure, sceptical of the enthusiasms of the left and the social democratic right, close to the unions both in style and substance, and with more experience of high office than any of his rivals. Healey, the other centre-right candidate, was handicapped by perceptions that he was over-combative and likely to split the party, and the fact that he was Chancellor, a post in which it is difficult for Labourites to maintain their popularity in the party. The social democratic right provided two candidates, Crosland and Jenkins, both of whom were now rather marginal figures. From the left came Foot, whose ministerial record – especially in dealing with the unions – had impressed many with his leadership potential, and Benn, for whom this was, generally, not the case. The first ballot of the PLP gave Foot 90 votes, Callaghan 84, Jenkins 56, Benn 37, Healey 30 and Crosland a derisory 17. Jenkins, Benn and Crosland withdrew before the second ballot, in which Callaghan took 141 votes against 133 for Foot and 38 for Healey. The final run-off, on 5 April, saw Callaghan pick up Healey's votes to emerge as leader with 176 votes to Foot's 137.[26] Foot's consolation came later in the year, when he defeated Williams for the deputy leadership following Edward Short's resignation.

Callaghan, ironically, was five years older than the man he succeeded, as Wilson was wryly to point out. He had never been a radical. His wide experience of government meant that he was well known and widely respected in Whitehall, his innately cautious instincts chiming in with those of senior civil servants, who called him the 'foxy old peasant'.[27] For all that, Callaghan instilled a new sense of purpose and drive to an administration which, under Wilson, had been drifting. Callaghan made few changes to the cabinet, although he paid off old scores by sacking Castle and did replace some ageing Wilson retainers with younger people. Callaghan's old disciple, Crosland, became Foreign Secretary. Finally, Foot moved from Employment to take a more synoptic role as Lord President of the Council. Callaghan also tried to establish decent relations with Benn, although without offering him a change of post. Clearly, the new premier was trying to pull the team together, and re-establish a sense of common purpose. In this, he was surprisingly successful, and his cabinet was to prove happier than Wilson's.[28] But it would be on his ability to deal with the trade unions that he would be judged: this was supposedly his special area of competence. How well he would fare remained to be seen.

As stated above, one of Callaghan's first acts was to try to improve relations with Benn. In a sense, he was on easy ground, for the radical industrial policy favoured by the latter was by now well off the agenda. Benn's appointment as Industry Secretary had seemed to suggest that the 1973 policy would be carried out, but the private sector and senior civil servants had made little secret of their misgivings, which made Wilson and other leading ministers less keen than ever to give Benn his head. Therefore the August 1974 White Paper dropped or diluted the more coercive elements of the 1973 programme, with planning agreements, in particular, becoming voluntary.[29] Wilson also moved to reassure worried industrialists, giving delegates of the Confederation of British Industries (CBI) 'two draft letters, one to himself and a reply to it', which could be published to demonstrate the government's essential soundness.[30] This looks, and was, pretty shabby. However, simply to condemn Wilson and others who took a similarly sceptical view of the party's radical industrial policy as Treasury-minded obscurantists, while emotionally pleasing, is inadequate. The basic outlook of the leading figures in the party remained based on the premiss that, for 'progress' to occur, there had to be economic growth, and this meant preserving business confidence. A further problem was that the policies were not as well worked out as their advocates would have us believe.[31] All sorts of questions remained unanswered, although, to be fair, more could have been done had the party leadership entered willingly into a real debate instead of simply trying to block. Thirdly, the unions were worried by certain aspects of the proposals, especially on industrial democracy: some on voluntarist grounds, others because they wanted union officials to be most closely involved whereas Benn was keener on 'real' shopfloor militants.[32] Finally, Benn's tactics and approach, stumping the country making radical speeches, enamoured him to the left but aroused considerable distrust both inside and outside the Labour movement.[33]

Thus the tide had already receded a long way by the time the Industry Bill was published in January 1975. The Bill was still further from the 1973 proposals than the White Paper had been, and Varley's succession to Industry was another step in the same direction.[34] In November 1975 the NEB came into existence, but with very limited powers and a 'safe' chairman, Sir Donald Ryder. Essentially it became a device for propping up 'lame ducks'.[35] The only planning agreement ever reached with a private firm was with Chrysler, the car manufacturer, which was bailed out to save jobs; and, in any case, the agreement was breached in 1978 when Chrysler sold its British operation to the French firm, Peugeot.[36] The NEB did have some successes, creating new high-tech companies and revitalizing the ailing Ferranti electronics company, but, overall, industrial intervention remained, as under Heath, 'primarily defensive and reactive, rescuing losers rather than picking winners'.[37]

A number of nationalizations were carried out in these years. In part, these were in key areas of the economy with good long-term prospects, like the creation of the British National Oil Corporation in 1976 and British Aerospace in 1977.[38] But public attention and debate focused much more on the nationalization of the ailing car manufacturer British Leyland (BL) and of the virtually moribund shipbuilding industry, whose collapse would have had disastrous employment implications in a number of already depressed areas like Tyneside and Northern Ireland. There were some productivity gains in the public sector as a whole in the period and, under Callaghan, efforts were made to introduce greater market discipline and appoint more confrontational senior managers.[39] But all this could do little to offset prevailing public perceptions of nationalized industries and of nationalization generally: cash-hungry, inefficient, badly managed and staffed by incompetents at best and idlers at worst, and consumer-unfriendly. Those employed by them, meanwhile, often felt undervalued, and in particular resented the way in which their industries' dependence on government subsidies meant they always tended to bear the brunt of incomes policies. All in all, nationalization was deemed to have failed by the 1970s, and

Labour's failure to implement its 1973 policies meant the party lost its last chance to show public ownership in a more favourable light.

Callaghan thus inherited a fairly 'safe' industrial policy. But the wider economic position remained anything but secure. Inflation, fuelled by internal and external factors, had averaged 9.2 per cent, easily the highest since the war, in 1973. It exceeded 19 per cent by December 1974, and peaked at 26.9 per cent in August 1975. When Wilson resigned it was still 21.1 per cent. One consequence of this was increased wage militancy on the part of trade unions.[40] Labour had tried to anticipate the problem by its adoption of the Social Contract, but although the Wilson government did pass a series of reforms favourable to unions and workers, such as the Employment Protection Act, wage settlements continued to be very high. This in turn meant that inflation soared, while public expenditure and the budget deficit rose. The end results were severe balance of payments difficulties and, eventually, a sterling crisis.[41]

Healey's policy options in the face of this were limited. Import controls, supported by the left, were ruled out by EEC membership; in any case, free trade sentiment within the party remained strong. Healey's solution was deflation. In April 1975 he cut expenditure and increased taxation, in effect abandoning Keynesianism by putting the conquest of inflation before the maintenance of a 'high and stable' level of employment.[42] Meanwhile, there were signs that union leaders were themselves becoming worried by high levels of inflation. Jones, for example, was fearful that, if something were not done to control it, there might be serious political destabilization, possibly culminating in an extreme right-wing *coup d'état*.[43] Finally, in July 1975, after considerable effort by the premier, Healey, Foot, Jones and Hugh Scanlon of the AUEW, it was agreed that there should be a £6 per week ceiling to wage increases, and a freeze for those earning more than £8500 a year. But there was opposition: the TUC general council only approved it narrowly, left-wing MPs voted against it in parliament, and even Scanlon's own union came out against it.[44] When the policy expired in August 1976 it was replaced by a still tighter limit of 5 per cent (subject to a maximum rise of £4 per week).[45] The average level of wage settlements did fall from 26 per cent in 1975 to 15 per cent in 1976 and 10 per cent in 1977, but how far this was due to the incomes policy remains a point of dispute: rising unemployment was perhaps more significant.[46] The annual rate of inflation also fell back from its August 1975 peak of 26.9 per cent to 12.9 per cent in July 1976 (although the rate then edged upwards again to peak at 17.7 per cent the following June). However, sterling remained under severe pressure. Over the summer, loans had to be secured from other central banks to prop it up. Healey was determined initially to avoid an appeal to the International Monetary Fund (IMF), but by September he felt he had no alternative.[47] The cabinet remained to be persuaded.

The cabinet which had to deal with the crisis had just been reshuffled, following Jenkins's resignation to become President of the European Commission. Three new faces (Rodgers, Roy Hattersley and Stanley Orme) had been brought in; overall almost half the members of the cabinet were in new jobs, and thus, to an extent, preoccupied with other things as the crisis broke. On 28 September Callaghan made a stern speech to the party conference in which he told delegates that 'we have been living on borrowed time', failing to face up to realities: governments, he said, could no longer 'spend [their] way out of recession'. Such policies only led to inflation, which 'hit hardest those least able to stand [it]'. The key thing was to reduce labour costs and so make British industry more competitive.[48] It was strikingly similar to the agenda that Snowden had outlined in 1931: the fear of inflation, the belief that higher unemployment would follow inaction on the part of government, the belief that 'progress' could only come through competitive capitalist industry in Britain, and also the warning that the working class was not synonymous with the strongest sections of the trade union movement. Even so, the parallels were limited. Callaghan was a good deal more self-confident than MacDonald had been: the upper echelons of the party now felt thoroughly at home with bankers, civil servants and financial crises. There was also a keen sense that there must be no repetition of the events of 1931.[49] That, at least, was one option which must not be followed.

MacDonald's government had felt itself under great pressure to make a quick decision, but Callaghan was much more relaxed in this respect. The IMF demanded £5000 million of cuts in public expenditure. Wisely, the premier decided not to declare his own position, even though he was clear in his own mind that the loan must be secured.[50] The application for a loan of $3900 million was made on 29 September. Representatives of the IMF arrived in London on 1 November, but Callaghan kept them waiting and talks only opened on 19 November. The premier tried alternative approaches to Germany and the USA, but these failed.[51] Only on 23 November did the cabinet begin to discuss the matter in earnest. While Healey and Edmund Dell (Trade) wanted to secure the loan at all costs, and a group of about nine ministers was prepared simply to follow a Callaghan lead, there was, initially, strong resistance from both the left and the social democratic right around Crosland.[52]

Callaghan allowed ministers to range freely over the issues in cabinet. But neither the social democrats nor the left could convince their colleagues of an alternative, and the two groups themselves began to disintegrate.[53] This all made Healey's position stronger, and eventually it became safe for Callaghan to back the Chancellor. Once he had declared his position, resistance collapsed. On 2 December Crosland told the cabinet that he was 'absolutely unconvinced by the economic arguments', since in theory Britain could afford to run a still bigger budget deficit, but added that it was his duty to support Callaghan.[54] The problem with Crosland's objection, as Healey later pointed out, was that this was a question of confidence, not an academic seminar.[55] At the end of the day, Crosland had done what those who were to claim his mantle a few years later were not willing to do: he had subordinated his views to the Labourist ethos of collective responsibility and loyalty to majority decisions. But in a sense it was a last gasp of such loyalty from the social democratic right, for, as Benn later wrote, 'I think the death of the social democratic wing of the party occurred in that cabinet, when Tony Crosland said at one stage: it is mad but we have no alternative'.[56] At the 2 December cabinet, 18 ministers supported the proposals, and while the six left-wingers were still critical, only Orme seems to have considered resignation.[57] The union leaders were squared, and a cut of £1500 million in the public sector borrowing requirement (PSBR) for 1977–8 was announced, based on the sale of British Petroleum assets plus expenditure cuts of £1000 million in each of the next two years.[58] It was much less than the IMF had originally wanted.[59]

In so far as the crisis was surmounted without a single resignation, and with cuts much lower than the IMF had originally proposed, it is hard to see how Callaghan could have handled it better. But it was also, quite clearly, a watershed for the government. It marked a clear end to the expansive view of public expenditure that had marked its first months in office. It finally drew a line under Keynesian policies and the idea that the conquest of unemployment was government's first responsibility. It also marked a clear end to any lingering hopes that this would be a radical reforming administration. In addition, it held longer-term significance for the development of the Labour party. First, the renunciation of Keynesianism inadvertently legitimized the anti-Keynesian, monetarist critique of the new Conservative leader, Margaret Thatcher. Further, the gap in Labour's economic thinking which had been covered by Keynesianism since the 1940s was embarrassingly re-exposed. The crisis also highlighted further the ideological bankruptcy and self-isolation of the social democratic right within the party. Further, the defeat of the left seemed, even at the time, only to postpone a further round of infighting. Finally, the crisis finally killed the Social Contract. Wage restraint would have to be maintained, given the strategy that the government had adopted, but restrictions on public expenditure would make it difficult to deliver the 'social goods' and, still more significantly, the full employment commitment which had been central to the Contract. Thus 1976 was both a triumph and a disaster for the Labour party.

Ironically, the PSBR estimate provided by the Treasury had been, in the event, 'grossly overestimated', and so in fact the loan had not really been necessary at all.[60] Healey only ever had to draw on half of it, and was able to introduce a reflationary budget in April 1978, and the IMF had received its money back in full by the time Labour left office in 1979.[61] Indeed, economic conditions became calmer after the crisis, helped by recovery from the 1974–6 recession. The incomes policy for 1976–7 held fairly steady, and in August 1977 Stage III, with a 10 per cent maximum limit, was agreed with the unions, to run until July 1978.[62] Inflation had fallen to 7.4 per cent by June 1978, and even unemployment fell back from a peak of 1 522 500 in the third quarter of 1977 to stand at 1 306 300 in the last quarter of 1978. A period of crisis, it seemed, had given way to one which had at least some semblance of tranquillity.

Such economic lurches were hardly conducive to a very effective social policy, however. Growth was supposed to pay for social reform, and, in the main, the government's achievements were confined to continuing with as much expenditure as could be achieved without upsetting the fragile economic situation. While there had been some talk of redistributive taxation, this did not really happen. There were some innovations, like the introduction of the state earnings-related pensions scheme (SERPS), improvements in old-age pensions and child benefits, a freeze on council house rents and subsidies of some foodstuffs; many of these were part of the Social Contract. But real expenditure on personal social services fell dramatically in 1977–8, and towards the end of the government's life there was increasing talk of the need to 'target' benefits, raising the spectre of the means test once again.[63] In some areas, too, Labour faced increasing resistance: thus in education the process of comprehensivization slowed down in the face of resistance, supported by the courts, from recalcitrant local education authorities. The net results of the government's policies were, not surprisingly, minor, and in some cases they merely stored up trouble for the future.

Labour's performance was hindered not only by the economic situation, but also by its parliamentary position. By April 1976 its overall majority had disappeared. That July two MPs defected to form the Scottish Labour party, and further by-election losses meant further problems. However, these were not as great as they might have been. The high number of 'third party' MPs meant that, although it had no overall majority, Labour still had many more MPs than the Conservatives, who were unattractive to the minor parties because of their new, more right-wing line under Thatcher and because, in the case of the SNP and Plaid Cymru, they were the party of the Union. Furthermore, Labour was able to make a number of deals with the minor parties. The ten-strong Ulster Unionists were placated by the promise of a review of Northern Ireland's representation at Westminster (which was ultimately increased from 12 to 17 members), and by Labour's tough anti-terrorist policy, which included the draconian Prevention of Terrorism Act (1974) and a military-based approach to the IRA. The Liberals were attracted in March 1977 with the formation of the Lib–Lab Pact. The new Liberal leader, David Steel, was keen to avoid an election, partly because he was new to the job, and partly because of the scandal surrounding his predecessor, Thorpe, who had been forced to resign when it was revealed that he faced charges of conspiracy to murder a male model with whom he was alleged to have had an affair. The

pact was certainly not a coalition; its main terms were consultation on economic policy, direct elections to the European parliament, and devolution for Scotland and Wales, and Labour 'simply
undert[ook] to do what it had anyway intended to do and de-
sist from what it could not do'.[64] The pact was orchestrated on
the Labour side by Foot, who was emerging as the government's
chief 'fixer'.[65] Liberal criticisms finally forced Steel to abandon it
in August 1978 but, even then, the ongoing Thorpe case and the
Liberals' poor standing in the polls made them reluctant to bring
the government down.[66]

Relations with the Scottish and Welsh Nationalists proved rather
more challenging because both parties were clear on the price of
their co-operation: devolution for Scotland and Wales. In October 1974 the SNP had won 11 seats with 30.4 per cent of the
Scottish poll and Plaid Cymru three seats with 10.8 per cent of
the votes cast in Wales. This meant that Labour, which had been
pre-eminent in both countries since 1945, had to take notice of
nationalist feeling; and its parliamentary position meant that it
had to take direct notice of the nationalist parties. In November
1975 a White Paper offered each country an elected assembly.
The Welsh one would have fewer powers than the Scottish, but
even the latter would not be able to raise revenue or have much
say in economic affairs, and the Secretaries of State would retain wide powers of veto. The Nationalists accepted these proposals as better than nothing, and the Devolution Bill passed its
second reading in December 1976.[67] However, the defeat of a
guillotine motion, essential to speed the passage of the Bill, in
February 1977, spelt its demise. Twenty-two Labour MPs voted
against the motion and 15 abstained.[68] In November 1977, separate bills were introduced for Scotland and Wales, and these became law in July 1978 subject to referenda.[69] However, an
amendment introduced by a Labour backbencher meant that, in
order to be enacted the Acts had to receive the support of at
least 40 per cent of the total electorates in Scotland and Wales.[70]
This made Welsh devolution highly unlikely; the position in
Scotland was cloudier. Still, the passage of the legislation had
kept the nationalist parties close to the government, and their
loyalty was assured at least until the referenda had been held
on 1 March 1979.

While devolution was more prominent in the 1970s than in
the 1960s, the reverse was true of foreign and defence policy.

With the Vietnam War over, debates within the party were somewhat muted: left-wing grumbles about possession of nuclear
weapons and membership of NATO cut little ice with ministers
keen to maintain the Atlantic Alliance and, in particular, retain
American goodwill at a time of economic stress. All three Foreign
Secretaries – Callaghan, Crosland (who died suddenly in February 1977) and the inexperienced David Owen (appointed to keep
the seat warm for Healey)[71] – were from the right of the party.
There were few new initiatives, the main development being the
decision, taken in secret, to press ahead with the modernization
of Britain's nuclear weapons in the Chevaline programme. That
this went against conference votes in 1972 and 1973 in favour of
unilateral nuclear disarmament worried the ministers involved
not a jot.[72]

But then again, by mid-1978 ministers seemed to have less cause
for worry than they had had for some time. The parliamentary
position looked reasonably secure, austerity was giving way to
a degree of reflation, and unemployment and inflation seemed
to be under control. Electorally, the party's record was less impressive, with by-elections still showing swings against Labour,
but even here only one seat was lost in 1978. Similarly there had
been recovery in the opinion polls: from being 20 points behind
the Conservatives in May 1977, Labour recovered so that the
two parties were neck-and-neck that December, and it edged into
a four-point lead in August 1978. In that same month, Stage IV
of the incomes policy specified a 5 per cent limit to pay increases,
with a promise of a return to free collective bargaining – now
being demanded strongly by many trade unionists – in early 1979.[73]
The new limit was clearly nonsensical, given that the TUC refused to back it, and given the fact that pay settlements at that
point were breaking even the 10 per cent limit of Stage III. But
most observers felt that the new pay policy was not intended
seriously; rather, given the apparently favourable electoral signs,
it was seen as a piece of pre-election window-dressing.

But Callaghan and Foot had their doubts about an autumn
election. Party officials believed it would only produce another
minority Labour government, and for Callaghan, who was 'sick
to death' of deals and compromises, this was an unappealing
prospect.[74] An early election would also mean the loss of legislation which was currently going through parliament. Thus
Callaghan and Foot decided to gamble. If they got through the

winter, and broadly enforced the 5 per cent pay policy, they would be able to go to the country the following spring as the party that could work with the unions and control inflation.[75] The announcement that there would be no election was greeted with almost universal surprise. The Labour movement was especially shocked, since it was now clear that Stage IV was not a piece of electoral window-dressing but a policy which the government aimed to implement, a fact which even right-wingers like Dell found scarcely credible.[76]

There was no way that the 5 per cent policy could ever hold the line. In the private sector, the figure was breached with impunity: Ford awarded its workforce 17 per cent, and the government's attempts to impose sanctions against the company for its breach of the policy were defeated in parliament with the help of left-wing Labour MPs. This, in turn, encouraged lorry drivers, who went on strike claiming a 30 per cent rise.[77] The government still had more leverage in the public sector where pay policies had already bitten hard and effected cuts in real wages for many workers.[78] But now, the National Union of Public Employees (NUPE), which represented some of the lowest-paid local authority workers, demanded a 40 per cent increase for its members in January 1979. Various groups of workers struck or started overtime bans. Since groups like dustmen were involved, there was considerable public inconvenience and some threat to public health, much sensationalized by the press.[79] The government was totally wrongfooted. In cabinet, Callaghan became little short of hysterical, suggesting that 'what was happening in this country was a threat to democratic society'.[80] In public, he tried to brazen it out, but this backfired on him when, trying to play the world statesman, he returned from a summit in sunny Guadeloupe on 10 January to be asked what he intended to do about the 'mounting chaos' in which the country found itself. His reply – 'I don't think that other people in the world would share the view that there is mounting chaos' – was rapidly transformed into the screaming tabloid headline 'CRISIS? WHAT CRISIS?'[81] Eventually, a settlement was reached, with immediate pay increases plus the establishment of a Comparability Commission to report by August and suggest 'just' wages. In the end, wage settlements for 1978–9 were higher than they had been in the previous year.[82] The political costs of all this were horrendous. Labour, and Callaghan in particular, had lost their reputation for being able to 'handle' the unions. As late as November 1978 Labour had been five points ahead in the polls: three months later it trailed by 20 points. Callaghan's approval rating collapsed. What became known as the 'Winter of Discontent' could have been largely avoided had Callaghan played safe and called an election in October 1978. But he had gambled; and he had lost.

The denouement was fairly rapid. On 1 March the Scottish and Welsh referenda on devolution were held. In Wales, the result was a conclusive 'No', with only 11.9 per cent of the electorate voting in favour. In Scotland, however, the result was closer. The 'Yes' vote amounted to 32.8 per cent, the 'No' to 30.8 per cent, and 36.4 per cent did not vote. A majority of those voting had supported the measure, but as the figure did not reach 40 per cent of the total electorate, the legislation, like that for Wales, had to be repealed. The nationalist parties were incensed and, seeing their opportunity, the Conservatives put down a motion of no confidence in the government on 28 March. Labour tried to cobble a majority together, but in vain, and the motion was passed by a single vote. Next day an election was called for 3 May.

Labour's campaign got off to an acrimonious start when Callaghan vetoed the inclusion of House of Lords abolition in the manifesto, angering the NEC and many party activists in the process.[83] Labour faced a severe struggle in the campaign. The Conservatives were confident, and boosted by swish advertising. Labour promised to reduce inflation, increase government control of industry, build more houses, and improve pensions. It was not, for all the Conservatives' efforts to portray it as such, a notably radical document: it could hardly be claimed that Labour lost in 1979 because its manifesto was 'too left-wing'.

On a swing of 5.2 per cent – the largest since 1945 – Labour lost 51 seats, all to the Conservatives, while regaining five seats from the minor parties. The party lost particularly heavily in the south-east, the Midlands and the north-west of England. But it maintained or improved its position in most of northern England, in Wales, and in Scotland. Labour particularly lost support among skilled workers, only 42 per cent of whom voted Labour (as opposed to 49 per cent in October 1974 and 55.4 per cent in 1970).[84] But the plain fact was that Labour had lost support in all sectors of the population and in most geographical areas. And the main reason for this seems to have been the party's perceived failure in government: before the winter of 1978/9 enough people might have been willing to give Labour the benefit of the doubt, but the events of that winter put paid to that. The 1979 election was more a negative verdict on Labour's perform- ance in office, not just in the 1970s but since 1964 (or at least 1966), than a positive endorsement of what was to become known as 'Thatcherism'.

The Labour governments of 1974–9 are usually seen as having failed. Conservative propaganda at the time and since has made much use of images of these administrations as reasons for people not to vote Labour. The prosecution case would argue that this was a time of economic mayhem, characterized by high infla- tion, high unemployment, and numerous, and often bitter, strikes. The government's efforts to get the economy moving were, it is argued, counterproductive; and in any case, for most of the time, the administration simply drifted from crisis to crisis, ducking the issues.

From the left, other criticisms would be added, such as the government's failure to carry out the party's radical industrial policy or, more generally, to promote greater equality. Since the later 1960s, the Labour party outside parliament had been shift- ing, quite strongly, towards the left. In many parts of the coun- try, CLPs were now well away from the kind of approach that the government had favoured. They felt let down and angry. In addition, the left now had a programme, based on the autarkic proposals of the 1973 *Programme*, which was, ostensibly at least, more plausible than most of the programmes previously put for- ward by the left. The record of the Wilson and Callaghan govern- ments in the 1960s and 1970s suggested to many party activists that a new departure must be made: never again must there be governments like these.

Certainly, there is something in such criticisms. Yet the record of this government must be seen in a wider context. It faced worse economic problems than any government since the Sec- ond World War, problems which were more the result of world developments – especially the increase in oil prices – and the incompetence of the previous Conservative government than of Labour's own failings. Worse still, the government had had to face those difficulties with either a tiny, or no, parliamentary majority. Serious problems which might have smashed the party to pieces, like the EEC and the IMF crisis, had been overcome without too much short-term damage. The 1976 financial crisis, in particular, had shown Callaghan's political mastery, and at least until the autumn of 1978 he proved a much better premier than most observers had expected. Inflation fell dramatically after 1975. Unemployment fluctuated, and was high by post-war standards, but was not heading out of control as it was to do under the first Thatcher government. Finally, it should be remembered that governments in other industrialized countries were experiencing similar difficulties: Callaghan's colleagues at the Guadeloupe summit, Carter, Giscard d'Estaing and Schmidt, were all out of office, and their parties blamed for the crises of the 1970s, within a relatively short period. It is perhaps worth noting that, after more than a decade of 'hard-headed' (and arguably hard-hearted) policies based on 'conviction politics' and a return to 'market forces' which entailed massive social and economic disruption, Thatcher was to leave office in 1990 with inflation, unemployment, public spending (in real terms), homelessness, dependency and crime rates all higher than they had been when Labour had left office in 'failure' eleven-and-a-half years earlier.[85]

Yet for all that, it would be facile to deny that, in 1979, many people both inside and outside the Labour party were angry with the government's record. The trade unions were antagonized by extended periods of pay restraint which had brought them, ultimately, few of the benefits promised by the Social Contract: many, particularly among skilled workers, responded by voting Conservative in 1979, while their leaders were preparing, in some cases, to take their revenge on Callaghan and Healey. Secondly, the left was angered by its own impotence, and determined that in future a radical plan of campaign like the 1973 *Programme* should not be discarded as soon as Labour returned to office. Thirdly, the social democratic right was increasingly isolated, disillusioned and disaffected with the failure of revisionism, the party's lack of commitment to 'Europe', and the increasing stridency of the unions and the left within the party. Finally, Labour now stood in opposition to a premier whose declared aim was to undo much of what it had achieved in government since 1945. It was very unclear, in the immediate aftermath of the 1979 election, what all this would portend; but no one in the Labour party seriously expected a quiet life in opposition.

10

Disaster and Recovery?
1979–92

The accession of Margaret Thatcher to the premiership on 4 May 1979 was to prove an event of enormous significance for the British Labour party. It did not seem so to everyone at the time: many, Conservatives as well as Labourites, were prepared to write her off as a flash in the pan, and suggest that her government would soon be out of office. However, by 1982 it was reasonably clear that Labour, at least, would not be able to do the ousting, especially since the breakaway of a section of its right wing to form the Social Democratic party in March 1981. At the 1983 general election, Labour was trounced, and, despite vigorous efforts by its new leader, Neil Kinnock, it did little to dent the Conservatives' ascendancy in 1987, either. The Tories had a much rougher ride after 1987, as issues like the European Community and the poll tax led to a crisis of confidence which culminated in Thatcher's downfall in 1990. However, apparently against the odds, her successor, John Major, was able to lead his party to a fourth successive victory at the general election of 1992. By the time of the next election, no one under fifty years of age would have voted in a general election which had given Labour a decent working majority. In retrospect, it seemed that Callaghan's description of the 1979 election as 'a sea-change in politics' was amply justified.[1]

As in the aftermath of 1931, there were various views of the direction Labour should now take. The left argued that defeat, disappointment and economic crisis demanded a more full-blooded policy.[2] As if to symbolize this demand, Benn announced that he would not be standing in the shadow cabinet elections. Meanwhile, the left called for constitutional changes within the party to ensure that there would be no more 'betrayals', insisting, in particular, on mandatory reselection of MPs, election of the party leader by an electoral college comprising all elements of the party, and drafting of the election manifesto by the NEC alone.[3] There was also strong union criticism of Labour's recent record. Pay policies, the failure of the Social Contract, and the Labour leadership's attitude towards the unions in the 'Winter of Discontent' had all stirred up hostility. While many trade unionists at all levels remained loyal to the leadership, the experience of the 1970s governments had moved trade unionism's centre of gravity leftwards.[4] This was not the case with the party leadership, however. Its reaction was not unlike that of Henderson to the débâcle of 1931. They felt, as Callaghan later put it, that '[t]he Labour Government of 1974 to 1979 had no reason to feel ashamed, and much to be proud of'.[5] If Labour continued along its present lines, and waited for more favourable circumstances, it would soon return to office. Others opposed to the left saw this view as too complacent. In particular, Jenkins, in a televised lecture in November 1979, came close to advocating the formation of a new 'centre party'.[6] However, he still had more than a year left in Brussels, and the lecture was more of a marker than a call to arms.[7]

But economic and political circumstances made it difficult for the party leadership to maintain its stand-pat line. Renewed world recession hit Britain late in 1979, and lasted into 1982. Its effects were ferocious: more than 5000 factories were closed between 1979 and 1982.[8] In May 1979, when Conservative election posters had blared out that 'Labour Isn't Working', unemployment had stood at 1 299 000; by October 1981 it had more than doubled. There was negative economic growth in both 1980 and 1981. Inflation more than doubled to peak at 21.9 per cent in May 1980. In such circumstances, the left's hand within the Labour party was strengthened. So deep a recession so soon after the last one suggested that capitalism might well be on the verge of collapse. It was, it seemed, no time to be tinkering with a system that was about to fall apart. And all this was reinforced by the performance of the Thatcher government. Thatcher gloried in the 'free market' and hated 'socialism', which she defined very broadly to include Labour, the trade unions, nationalized industries, the welfare state, high levels of public expenditure, council housing, Labour local authorities, high direct taxation and the redistribution of wealth downwards, and full employment. What unfolded was a fundamental attack on much that Labourites held dear, and on practically all the work of Labour governments since 1945. The results of all this were, first, a feeling that, in the face of a 'reactionary' government, Labour could not afford to prevaricate; and, secondly, many Labourites believed that the government's policies would be so unpopular that electors would be now more willing to listen to arguments in favour of a 'socialist' alternative.

Callaghan clung on to the leadership in order to avoid charges of desertion, to try to secure a Healey succession and to keep the party from moving leftwards, but the party moved leftwards all the same.[9] The 1979 party conference voted in favour of mandatory reselection of MPs, and for a resolution calling on the NEC to submit proposals to the 1980 conference as to how 'the NEC alone' would draw up the final version of the election manifesto. A resolution for an electoral college was defeated in 1979, but passed in 1980, although even then no majority could be found for any concrete form of electoral college, and it was decided that a special conference early in 1981 should settle the matter. However, the NEC's proposals for its having the decisive voice in the drafting of the manifesto were lost by a narrow margin. There was a vote of 5 042 000 votes to 2 097 000 to withdraw from the EC, and a vote in favour of unilateral nuclear disarmament. A motion stating that 'the safety of the British people . . . will be best served by multilateral disarmament in the nuclear and conventional fields' was also passed, and a resolution calling for withdrawal from NATO was heavily defeated.[10]

The defeat of the proposal for the manifesto was clearly a defeat for the left, but the electoral college and mandatory reselection were victories. Why did these changes come about? In part it was due to the general factors mentioned earlier. Groups campaigning for the changes, most notably the CLPD, were also significant. Although CLPD was important in raising consciousness and concentrating party members' minds on a few key issues, its significance should not be exaggerated. It was able to mobilize support on these issues, but it was not able to swing the party to the left by itself. The unions were the key to conference majorities, and some leading union figures were bitterly angered by the record of recent Labour governments, and were looking, at least to a certain extent, to 'pay back' Callaghan and his colleagues. With a general election some years away, they now had the perfect opportunity to do so, as it seemed, without too much long-term damage to the party. But this was more of a tactical manoeuvre, more a fit of pique than a real swing to the left. In addition, many, perhaps even most, trade unionists did not start supporting the left.[11] At the 1980 conference – in many ways the high point of Labour radicalism in this period – the left's margins of victory were very narrow indeed: 50.7 per cent to 49.3 per cent on the electoral college, and 53.2 per cent to 46.8 per cent on reselection. And, of course, the manifesto proposal did not go through at all. In other words, even at this stage, the left was advancing on a knife-edge rather than triumphantly carrying all before it.

Just 12 days after the 1980 conference closed, Callaghan announced his resignation. Since the constitution of the electoral college had still to be decided, his successor would be elected by the PLP only, and the leader's action was attacked bitterly by the left as a pre-emptive strike to install Healey as leader while there was still a chance.[12] This may have been a little unfair, since he was now 68, and keen to retire, but he probably felt some mischievous pleasure in upsetting his left-wing critics.[13] Benn considered standing against Healey, but was dissuaded by his allies, partly on principle and partly because he would clearly not fare well if the PLP was the electorate.[14] Shore and John Silkin came forward, but while both were capable figures with some experience of high office, neither seemed likely to defeat Healey. The only candidate likely to stop the latter, in fact, was Foot, and he was eventually persuaded to stand by left-wing MPs and union leaders. Neil Kinnock, a young Welsh MP, acted as his campaign organizer. On 3 November, the first ballot gave Healey 112 votes, Foot 83, Silkin 38 and Shore 32, and in the run-off Foot took the leadership by 139 votes to 129.[15] Healey became deputy leader.

The result was so close that it is important not to 'over-explain' it – had half-a-dozen MPs switched, Healey would have become leader. Indeed, it seems that a number who had already decided to defect to a new party (discussions were now well under way for its formation) voted for Foot on the grounds that, if he won, the breakaway party could be portrayed as more 'necessary' as a barrier to the 'left'.[16] Even so, Foot had many qualities which appealed to Labour MPs. His left-wing reputation suggested he might be able to get on better with the wider party than the 'Establishment' figure of Healey. He had proved himself an able and loyal minister, and a good conciliator, in the most recent period of Labour government: union leaders, who had worked with him closely, had found him impressive.[17] Healey, meanwhile, had alienated many usually moderate trade union-ists, had not cultivated support, and was seen as a bully.[18] In short, Foot's election did not mark any great swing to the left in the PLP. This was borne out by the subsequent shadow cabinet elections, where all the existing members who stood were re-elected, and Owen (who had refused to stand) and Callaghan were replaced by the right-wing Gerald Kaufman and by Kinnock; Benn failed to gain election.

The special conference on the electoral college took place on 24 January 1981. Six versions were on offer, but in the end it boiled down to a choice between the proposal of David Basnett, leader of the General and Municipal Workers' Union (GMWU) for a college wherein the PLP would have 50 per cent of the votes and the unions and CLPs 25 per cent each, and the left's favoured option, of 40 per cent for the unions and 30 per cent each for the PLP and CLPs. That the latter succeeded was thanks to the extreme right-wing position taken by the AUEW, whose delegation, mandated not to support any proposal giving the PLP less than 51 per cent of the votes, abstained on the final vote. Had it supported Basnett's proposal, the latter would have triumphed: as it was, the 40/30/30 mix went through narrowly. For the first time, Labour was committed to electing its leader on the basis of a party-wide franchise.[19]

On the same day, Jenkins finally returned to Britain. Within 24 hours, he, Owen, Williams and Rodgers – 'the Gang of Four' – issued their 'Limehouse Declaration', stating that the 'calami-tous outcome' of the conference 'demand[ed] a new start in British politics'. It fell short, at this stage, of launching a new party, but it did establish a Council for Social Democracy, 'half in and half out of the Labour Party'.[20] Foot tried to persuade Owen, Williams and Rodgers to remain, but to no avail. On 26 March, the Social Democratic party (SDP) was formally established. News that members could pay their subscriptions by credit card excited deep scorn from Labourites still mired in the 1940s when it came to party organization, but did not put off the thousands who flocked to join in the first week. At first, only 10 MPs followed Owen and Rodgers, but by the time of the dissolution of parlia-ment in 1983 there were to be 30, 27 of whom had been elected as Labour MPs in 1979.[21] Other noteworthy recruits included George Brown.

Why did people defect? Some, like Jenkins, had departed from many of their earlier positions and wanted to strengthen the 'radical centre' – in Jenkins's case, in close alliance with the Liberals. Others, like Owen, were keen on a new radicalism, free from the unions and the block vote. Most felt that Labour was moving too far to the left to be a viable alternative to a government they deplored. Some had their careers in mind: those facing deselection by their CLPs saw the SDP as a life-raft. The issues of the EC and defence were also important, the former for Williams, the latter for Owen. But the formation of the SDP was also a reflection of the deeper trends already traced in previous chapters, namely the apparent bankruptcy of revisionism and the consequent self-isolation of a section of the revisionist right within the party.

However, most of Labour's right wing did *not* join the new party. Jenkins, Owen, Williams and Rodgers went; but Healey, Hattersley, Kaufman and John Smith stayed, even when some on the left would have been delighted to see them go.[22] The defections tended to be heavily localized: eight of those who left were MPs in the London area, four in the north-east, and three in Liverpool, where the local party had swung heavily to the left. By contrast, '[t]he overwhelming view in Scotland's right-wing Labour establishment was in favour of staying and fighting'.[23] So why did so many right-wingers 'stay and fight'? Many calculated that their career prospects would still be better in the Labour party than in the SDP, which might prove to be (as it did) a flash in the pan. But careerism was probably not the main consideration. More important was ethos, an almost tribal loyalty to the Labourism, whereby one did not go home and sulk if one lost a round of the fight, but fought on until victory could be achieved. In addition, MPs with union links were reluctant to break them. Finally, though, there was also a calculation being made about the medium and longer-term direction of the party. For Owen and his colleagues, it was axiomatic that Labour had swung violently to the left and would not swing back. Others made a more sober and, as it proved, sounder judgement. For in retrospect what is most striking about Labour's 'swing to the left' at this time is not its extent but its limitations. For example, neither reselection nor the electoral college gave enormous powers to left-wing 'activists': in most cases, they strengthened the union block vote which, for most of Labour's history, had been close to the party leadership and the PLP in outlook and would be again. The extension of the franchise for electing the leader was hardly revolutionary – the Liberals had done it in the 1970s, after all. And even when the left could get its way in conference – as it could not, significantly enough, on the manifesto issue – it was often by a very narrow majority.

At first, though, the SDP seemed successful. In December 1980 the Gallup poll had given Labour 47 per cent, the Conservatives 35 per cent, and the Liberals 14 per cent. A year later, it suggested the Liberal–SDP Alliance had 50 per cent support against 23 per cent each for Labour and Conservative. At the Warrington by-election, in July 1981, Jenkins, for the SDP, slashed Labour's majority from over 10 000 to 1750. That November, Williams won the 'safe' Conservative seat of Crosby, and Jenkins himself was returned to the Commons when he took Glasgow Hillhead from the Conservatives in March 1982.

Much of this success was gained at the expense of Labour, whose prospects were hardly helped by Benn's decision, in April 1981, to challenge Healey for the deputy leadership. Benn, who had returned to the shadow cabinet when Rodgers had defected to the SDP, believed sincerely that the new machinery of the electoral college should be tested, and so bedded into the party's consciousness. But there was a feeling, shared by some on the left, that Benn's move was opportunistic and selfish.[24] There followed almost six months of campaigning, marred by severe bitterness on both sides and well-publicized episodes of thuggishness as Healey was barracked by left-wingers at some of his meetings. The main significance of the contest came when a number of 'left' Labour MPs, including Kinnock, announced that they would not support Benn, but would vote for Silkin and then abstain should he be eliminated. When the voting took place that September, Silkin was eliminated on the first ballot, and in the run-off Healey defeated Benn by a margin of less than 1 per cent. Benn had trounced Healey among the CLPs, but Healey had taken around two-thirds of the votes in the other two sections. The action of the Silkinite MPs had been enough to tip the balance: had even a proportion of them voted for Benn, the latter would have emerged victorious.[25] The Bennite left was furious, but Kinnock and his colleagues had a stout defence. The party had been plunged into six months of civil war at a time when it faced an unprecedented challenge from the SDP and when the Thatcher government was wreaking havoc with much that Labour held dear, all in the cause of Benn's quest for an essentially meaningless post. The contest was also counter-productive for Benn and the 'hard' left which supported him, for the 1981 conference marked a clear end to the left's advance within the party. Five left-wingers failed to gain re-election to the NEC; the party treasurership was also lost. The left majority on the NEC was thus shattered, and a new alliance of centrist and 'soft left' now began to recover full control of the party. True, Benn and Heffer retained the chairs of the NEC's important Home Policy and Organization committees respectively, but it began to look as though they were living on borrowed time.

Any hopes of a Labour recovery once the deputy leadership imbroglio was over were illusory, however. On 2 April 1982 the military regime in Argentina invaded the British colony of the Falkland Islands. The government dispatched a Task Force to recapture them, a feat finally achieved on 14 June. Thatcher's government undoubtedly gained popularity during the conflict. Foot's line was to support the government, on the grounds that Britain should not allow a quasi-fascist regime the prestige of a victory, especially when that would involve taking the Falkland Islanders, against their will, under the Argentinian flag. Some Labourites were more critical, but to little effect other than to make the party seem split at a time of perceived national crisis.[26] The Falklands issue rallied support to the Conservatives, whose poll rating improved from 31 per cent in April to 46 per cent in July, by which time they had a 19 point lead over Labour. Nevertheless, the 'Falklands factor' probably only gave the Tories a short-term boost: in the longer term the more significant developments were tax cuts in 1982 and the economic upturn which began early in the same year. Labour did not lose the 1983 election because of the Falklands War.[27]

A continuing problem for Labour at this time was its image of factionalism and 'extremism', the most publicized manifestation of which, by early 1982, was Militant Tendency. Militant was an entryist, Trotskyite organization, which sought to radicalize Labour from within and use it as a means for fomenting revolution in Britain. Since it had started with its entryist tactics in the 1960s, it had had some success, and by the early 1980s some members of Militant were securing adoption as Labour parliamentary candidates. With a substantial budget and organization, it was clearly 'a party within a party', and as such was offending against

Labour's constitution. Its membership rose from 1800 in 1979 to 3500 in late 1982. Even so, the overwhelming majority of CLPs were not influenced by Militant, and Militant candidates for the NEC never came anywhere near being elected.[28] Pressure to deal with Militant grew, particularly (but not only) from the right, but was initially resisted. Militant argued that it was no more of a party within a party than right-wing organizations like the Labour Solidarity Campaign (whose members included people like Shore and Hattersley).[29] The Tendency's only function, they argued, was to publish and sell the newspaper, *Militant*. Even if they were dubious as to how far this was really the case, many Labour left-wingers were still reluctant to act, fearing (with a degree of justification, as it turned out) that banning Militant would be the start of a 'witch-hunt' which would end in a general assault on the left.[30] It was a fear that Foot shared, initially at least.[31] The new NEC elected in 1981 set up an inquiry, and on its recommendation the 1982 conference established a register of approved groups.[32] The 1982 NEC elections, meanwhile, gave further gains to the right, and in the aftermath of the conference Benn and Heffer were removed from the chairs of the Home Policy and Organization committees.[33] Militant was proscribed in December 1982, and in February 1983 the NEC voted 19 to 9 to expel the five members of *Militant*'s editorial board from the Labour party.[34] There, for the moment, the matter rested, not least because it was becoming clear that a general election was looming on the horizon.

Electoral trends had been moving in contradictory directions. Labour performed poorly at the May 1982 local elections, held at the height of the Falklands War. And yet, that October a right-wing candidate, John Spellar, gained Birmingham Northfield from the Conservatives against the odds and despite a big and scurrilous Alliance campaign. The Gallup poll for December put Labour only seven points behind the Conservatives and 12 points ahead of the Alliance. However, these buds of promise were soon frozen to death by the chill wind of events in Bermondsey, where in a by-election in 1983 Labour's perceivedly hard-left candidate, Peter Tatchell, was defeated after a bitter campaign in what had been a safe Labour seat. Worse still, Foot's handling of the Tatchell candidature – he had initially disowned him, then retracted – aroused criticism from practically all sides of the party.

There had been various moves against Foot's leadership during

1982, with a number of leading right-wingers and 'soft left' figures making noises behind the scenes.[35] These became much louder when, in February 1983, the Australian Labor party ousted its ageing leader, Bill Hayden, in favour of the more dynamic and telegenic Bob Hawke, and then went on to win the elections.[36] With polls suggesting that Labour would be on equal terms with the Conservatives if Healey were leader, it is not surprising that pressure for a change built up. Foot seems to have considered resignation, but decided ultimately to await the result of the pending by-election in the Labour marginal of Darlington, and this was tacitly accepted by his critics as a litmus test of his leadership.[37] Perhaps Healey could have forced the issue, but he seems to have been reluctant to act 'disloyally', and doubtless realized that to oust an unwilling Foot might reunite the soft left with the Bennites and so give him a truly awful inheritance.[38] But, against all the odds, Labour managed to hold the seat with an increased majority, and any chance of removing Foot had been lost.

Foot's survival cheered the Conservatives. Thatcher dithered over whether to call an early election, but finally did so after favourable local election results on 5 May. The first opinion poll of the campaign showed the Conservatives with 46 per cent support against Labour's 31 and the Alliance's 21. It looked, as Foot later put it, as though Labour 'had a well-nigh insurmountable task ahead'.[39]

Labour's performance at the 1983 general election has become a byword for inefficiency and incompetence. It is difficult to gainsay this conventional wisdom. The manifesto was rushed out before it had been fine-tuned, perhaps with the connivance of right-wingers who wanted to be able to blame a 'left-wing' document for the inevitable defeat.[40] It was not short of policy proposals, including the reduction of unemployment to 'below a million' within five years by a huge increase in public expenditure. There would be a five-year economic plan, the promotion of industrial democracy, and a start to the renationalization of the (few) industries which had been privatized. Social benefits and expenditure on education would be increased. There were also promises to end sexual and racial discrimination. A Labour government would pull Britain out of the EC. On defence, the manifesto was a mess: there had to be a fudge because few of the party's leaders agreed with party policy, which called for unilateral nuclear disarmament. Accordingly, the manifesto came up with the nonsensical formula that 'Unilateralism and multilateralism must go hand in hand if either is to succeed'.[41] The document gave numerous other hostages to fortune. During the campaign Labour speakers spent most of their time trying to explain it away or paper over the cracks, a process not helped by interventions from Callaghan and Wilson attacking the party's defence policy.[42] In addition, organization and propaganda were poor, to say the least, while Foot was a liability, looking uncomfortable on TV, rambling when interviewed, and lacking presence. His tendency to hark back to past battles delighted those in the know, but baffled many, especially the young. At the side of Thatcher he looked amateurish and lacked credibility. Realizing this, Labour strategists tried increasingly to portray an image of a collective leadership, in contrast to Thatcher's autocratic image, but to little effect.

But Labour did not lose in 1983 because of Foot. The party would have been divided, and the economy recovering, whoever had been leader. In reality it was an election that Labour could not have won. If Healey had become leader in 1980, things might have been even worse: for then there would have been a right-wing leader leading a party with a strong and united left, and Healey would have appeared under siege. Under Foot, on the other hand, the left split between 'hard' and 'soft', so forging the soft-left/centrist alliance which was to dominate the party for years to come. Foot's record as party leader was not as bad as the conventional wisdom would have us believe, but there was nothing in his locker to bring about a miracle in 1983.

The results were devastating. No poll published after 5 June gave the Conservatives anything less than a 17-point lead; indeed, five of the last 16 polls published suggested that the Alliance would take more votes than Labour. In the event, Labour emerged with only 209 seats, by far its worst performance since 1935, and 27.6 per cent of the votes, its lowest share since 1918 (when it had put up far fewer candidates). In terms of votes cast per candidate it was the party's worst showing ever. A record 119 deposits were forfeited, and three ex-cabinet ministers, including Benn, were defeated.[43] The Alliance almost pipped Labour into second place in terms of votes, taking 25.4 per cent, but emerged with only 23 MPs, of whom only six were SDPers. Labour had lost particularly heavily in the south-east including London, eastern Lancashire, West Yorkshire and the east Midlands. Outside

Greater London, Labour held only three of the 182 seats south of the Severn-Wash line, as against 31 seats in October 1974 and 42 in 1966. Worse still, in this area in particular, Labour had been beaten into a bad third place behind the Alliance in numerous constituencies. Labour attracted the support of just 38 per cent of skilled workers, only slightly ahead of the Conservatives' 35 per cent, while its share of the non-manual vote fell to 17 per cent, its lowest since the war.[44] While Labour's heartlands remained reasonably solid, the party was obviously a long way from power, and in terms of the popular vote it seemed an open question as to whether Labour could see off the Alliance threat. Clearly, something needed to be done to restore the party's fortunes.

The most obvious, indeed inevitable, change to make was in the leadership. There was no conceivable reason for Foot to stay on. Assured that some big unions, including the TGWU, would support his favoured successor, Kinnock, Foot made it known that he would resign once the electoral college had chosen a new leader at that autumn's party conference.[45] Healey stepped aside, having no desire to emulate Morrison's 1955 humiliation, and it soon emerged that the main choice was between Kinnock and Hattersley. Hattersley had strong support from the right, and was more experienced than Kinnock, who had been an MP for only 13 years and had little front-bench experience. But Kinnock could still get the support of much of the left, certainly in preference to Hattersley; had some appeal to the centre and even the right because of his hostility towards the Benn candidature of 1981; and was younger and appeared more telegenic at a time when memories of Foot meant such things seemed to matter. With Benn out of parliament and thus ineligible to stand, the standard-bearers of the hard left were Eric Heffer for the leadership and Michael Meacher as deputy.

By the time conference convened on 2 October it was widely expected, given what unions, CLPs and MPs were known to have decided, that Kinnock would win the leadership and Hattersley be elected as his deputy, forming the so-called 'dream ticket' balancing left and right. The hard left argued that a real balance would have been Kinnock–Meacher, but Kinnock was keener to work with Hattersley, a message that got across to the broader party.[46] In the event, Kinnock won just over 70 per cent of the votes for the leadership, with Hattersley taking a shade under

20 per cent and Heffer and Shore unable to poll 10 per cent between them. Kinnock had taken three-quarters of the union votes, more than nine-tenths of the CLP votes, and just under half of the MPs' votes. Hattersley went on to win the deputy leadership by a scarcely less impressive margin, taking around 66 per cent of the votes. Interestingly, the CLPs, so often seen at this time as the hotbeds of the hard left, not only voted over-whelmingly in favour of Kinnock rather than Heffer; they also went by a narrow majority in favour of Hattersley over Meacher.[47] This suggested, first, that the party had not been as left-wing in 1979–83 as has often been claimed and that, secondly, the scale of the 1983 defeat had shocked some party members into loos-ening their links with the hard left. The result also meant that Kinnock had a very clear mandate from the party activists, much more so than any previous leader. Paradoxically, this fact would allow him, in the end, to push the party further to the right, in terms of policy and organization, than any leader since Gaitskell. The imprimatur of the electoral college, designed as a guarantor for the left, was ultimately to be a weapon with which to beat it.

When Kinnock took over the leadership there were high hopes for the future. Although the next election would need to pro-duce 117 new seats for Labour on a bigger swing than at any election since 1945, many Labourites believed, in the first flush of enthusiasm for the 'dream ticket', that it might just be possible.

But, of course, it was not. Economic indicators, volatile be-tween 1979 and 1983, were much steadier between 1983 and 1987, helped by favourable world trends. While unemployment con-tinued to rise until 1986, it increased more slowly than in the earlier period, and its heaviest impact tended to be in areas where Labour was already strong. Most of the other economic indica-tors were favourable. GDP grew by 27 per cent between 1981 and 1988, inflation remained relatively low and revenue from North Sea Oil and privatization allowed the government to continue planning cuts in direct taxation.[48] Considerable and, according to many sources, intensifying deprivation remained in much of Britain, but for those in work this was, on the whole, a period of relative prosperity and, in contrast to most of the period since the later 1960s, general optimism. This did not mean that people were suddenly 'converted' to Thatcherite 'values',[49] but it did mean that Labour had a very real problem in attracting new vot-ers, especially as the Alliance was still seen as a viable alternative.

The Conservatives also gained some popularity for their frontal attack on many of the keystones of Labourism. Trade unionism had been a mixed blessing to Labour before the Second World War, a source of strength but also an easy target for Tory attacks. This had changed dramatically in the 1940s, but increasingly adverse comment from the mid-1950s onwards had begun to cause new problems for the party. The failure of Wilson and later Callaghan to 'tame' the unions was merely a prelude to a much more sustained attack under Thatcher, who was able to use rapidly rising unemployment (especially in manufacturing) to weaken the movement. Secondly, there was much employer, and not a little public, support for a legislative attack on union rights. Thatcher's government chose to advance, not by one huge and unworkable statute like Heath's Industrial Relations Act, but by a series of measures over a number of years. The Employment Acts of 1980 and 1982 limited the right to picket, placed strict restrictions on closed shops, and allowed unions to be sued for damages, in effect repealing the 1906 Act. Five further Acts between 1984 and 1990 ate away further at unions' legal immunities, imposed ballots for strikes and political funds, and abolished the pre-entry closed shop. Deregulation – effectively sweeping away the workers' protection that had been built up over the years – was also carried on apace, so that after the 1989 Employment Act had been passed it was legal for women to work in coal mines (although the question was largely academic by then since there were hardly any coal mines left).[50] As a result of all this, union membership fell from an all-time peak of 13 498 000 in 1979 to 11 337 000 in 1983, 10 475 000 in 1987, and 9 585 000 in 1991, by which time union density, at 34.4 per cent, was at its lowest since 1940.[51] This all had a number of effects for the Labour party. First, it held financial implications for the party, although the worst effects were vitiated by increases in affiliation fees. Secondly, it made trade union leaders keener than ever to get rid of the Conservative government under which they were faring so badly, and so they became more responsive to those who claimed that they had a reasonable strategy for achieving this, and increasingly keen to back them. Ultimately, too, it was to make the unions – and hence the party – keener on the EC once it became apparent that the latter might be able to restore some of the rights that workers and unions had lost.

Trade unions were not the only Labour sacred cows to come

under attack, of course. The nationalized industries were largely privatized during the Thatcher regime. Privatization proved in many ways a popular policy: the period from 1983 to 1987 saw the government build on earlier, more limited operations with a whole series of high-profile sell-offs. Because the shares were available in small quantities and also underpriced, large numbers of people could buy them, often to sell on for a short-term windfall profit. It said a lot for the essential failure of the public corporation model that there was so little effective (or ineffective, come to that) resistance from either the workers in, or the customers of, these industries at the time.

Local government also came under sustained attack. Here, Labour had built a very solid base for itself over the years. The Conservatives recognized this and resolved to do something about it. In an attempt to curb local authority expenditure, the government introduced rate-capping (which allowed the minister to set limits to the level of local taxation an authority could raise) and, later, the poll tax (a flat-rate levy), one of whose aims was to ensure that 'wasteful' Labour councils would have to set a high charge to everyone, and so be ousted. Central government also removed functions from local authority control. The first sign of this was the sale of council houses to their tenants at cut prices, which sought to increase owner-occupation. This proved to be a very popular policy; it also seemed to reduce Labour's clientage. Local education authorities lost control over some schools as a result of the 'opting out' procedures introduced in 1988. And local government functions were increasingly delegated to unelected 'quangos' set up by central government bodies.

Thus Kinnock inherited a party which was in difficulties, not least from a self-confident government determined to eat away at Labour's vitals. His strategy was, from the outset, to regain power for Labour. This meant a continuation of the party's shift to the right, which had begun at the 1981 conference. Economic trends further weakened the hard left's case. By the mid-1980s, Labour's leaders could, and did, start to talk again about the need to manage prosperity better. They argued that what was needed was not radical change, but a more egalitarian distribution of the surplus which capitalism was once again producing. Surprisingly rapidly after its apparent demise, revisionism was back on the agenda. At the same time, the hard left was increasingly blamed for the scale, and sometimes for the fact, of the 1983 defeat. In some ways, of course, this was too sweeping. First, many of the most unpopular policies in 1983 had not been the sole preserve of the hard left, but had been based on prejudices shared broadly by Labourites. The case of council house sales is a good example. Labour could have encouraged such sales, and used the receipts to build new council housing. Such a scheme had been considered, in fact, by the last Labour government, but rejected, showing the extent to which paternalism lingered on in the mainstream of the Labour movement.[52] And when people did apply to buy from Labour councils under the Conservatives' legislation after 1979, those councils often treated them as second-class tenants, refusing to carry out any repairs except those they were statutorily obliged to execute, and trying every possible delaying tactic to prevent the sales.[53] As a result, Labour managed to look unsympathetic to one of its core constituencies. Other policies which were more exclusively associated with the left were not necessarily unpopular. Unilateral nuclear disarmament and withdrawal from the EC, for example, fared poorly in opinion polls, but a strong case could have been made for each in the early 1980s, on strategic and economic grounds. The real problem was that the left failed to discipline itself sufficiently to work out the policies and explain them fully, resorting too frequently to the easier option of sloganizing. The Labour left, as so often, proved itself better at criticizing the party leadership than at taking an opportunity to provide a lead itself. Its rigid adherence to the precepts of the 1973 economic programme also showed its failure to accept that there could be change and development in policy without betrayal.[54] The failure of the left to make a credible case, the growing perception of 'left' policies as being unpopular, the scale of the 1983 defeat, the imprimatur of the electoral college, and the easing economic situation all combined to lubricate Kinnock's subsequent efforts to move Labour back to a more centrist position.

Two problems largely overshadowed Kinnock's first two years in the post, however. One was the miner's strike which began in April 1984 and lasted for almost a year.[55] The NUM executive, under its President, Arthur Scargill, refused to hold a strike ballot, and as a result some miners, mainly in Nottinghamshire, refused to come out. Attempts to persuade them to do so by picketing were met by a firm, and at times heavy-handed, police response, and violence ensued. Relations between Scargill and the Labour leadership broke down completely, since the latter was critical of the failure to hold a ballot and felt it could not afford to be associated with violence, a position which led to its failing, on the whole, to argue the economic case against pit closures or even challenge obvious police excesses. Of course, the position was not made easier for Kinnock by the fact that the working miners were overwhelmingly Labour voters. As in 1926, major industrial conflict made it difficult for the Labour leadership to satisfy anyone. The result was that Kinnock only spoke on the dispute once in parliament, and that party headquarters was dissuaded from issuing propaganda on the coal question.[56] But the strike's long duration, and its emotiveness for most Labourites, meant the issue could not just be brushed aside.

In March 1985 the miners were forced back to work; for them, the whole affair had been a catastrophe. Its impact on the Labour party, however, was not so clear-cut. In the short term, it was a disaster. It suggested Labour was split, portrayed its new leader in a poor light, and emphasized issues, like law and order and industrial efficiency, with which the Conservatives were usually perceived as being best able to cope. It also split the NUM with the formation of a breakaway union, the Union of Democratic Mineworkers, in Nottinghamshire. Finally, in so far as it saw the beginning of the virtual cessation of deep mining in Britain, it represented the end of the road for what had been, since 1922 at least, one of the core constituencies of Labour's electoral strength. In the longer term, though, the strike was of great benefit to the Labour leadership. For it was the industrial counterpart to the 1983 election defeat. Like the latter, it could be used by the leadership as an object lesson in the dangers of 'leftism' and the need for moderation and caution.[57]

The other major problem Kinnock faced was Militant. The 1983 party conference confirmed the expulsion of the paper's editorial board by a three-to-one majority. Soon some local parties were following this lead by expelling members, while LPYS's budget was cut drastically.[58] The next two years saw a general hardening of opinion against the hard left in general and Militant in particular. Evidence that the Tendency was a revolutionary party within a party grew. Meanwhile, the conduct of certain Labour local authorities was causing adverse media comment and threatening Labour's chances of portraying itself as a responsible party of government. The most spectacular example came in Liverpool.

In 1985 the Militant-dominated City Council tried to force the government to give the city more money, and its policy of brinkmanship culminated in September 1985 with the council issuing redundancy notices to all its 31 000 employees, as a way of showing what it believed to be the logical conclusion of Conservative policies.[59] But this was a step too far. Union leaders and members were appalled at what they saw as playing with people's livelihoods. Other councils, after all, had managed without such demonstrations despite being in a similar position to Liverpool. Crucially, Militant had offended against a key part of the Labour ethos: security of employment. Kinnock, who had a very keen nose for that ethos, took his chance to strike at Militant at the 1985 party conference. He made a strong attack on Liverpool Council's conduct in his keynote speech, and although there were some shouts of disagreement, there was more applause.[60] Kinnock's approval rating in the polls soared. A group of leading trade unionists who visited Liverpool on behalf of the NEC reported very unfavourably on the performance of the council and on the state of Liverpool Labour party, and a subsequent NEC inquiry found 'very serious and deep-seated problems', including widespread evidence of patronage and intimidation. In February 1986 the district Labour party was suspended. There followed a lengthy process of expulsions, and by 1987 Militant was on the run.[61]

By now the hard left was utterly alienated from Kinnock, but other elements in the party were also having doubts about his leadership qualities. There was a growing feeling, exploited by the media, that he lacked experience and administrative ability. His past could always be trawled by the media for a quotation to show him either as a left-winger or as a hypocrite who would say anything to gain votes. His parliamentary performance continued to be indifferent, and began to be compared unfavourably with that of the shadow spokesman on Trade and Industry, John Smith, a Scottish lawyer who had spent seven months in the cabinet as Trade Secretary in 1978–9, and who gave the Conservatives far more worries over the Westland scandal in early 1986. With the polls showing Labour behind the Alliance, although ahead of the Conservatives, in early 1986, there were grumblings about Kinnock's leadership. No rival emerged to challenge him, however, and this meant that, by the time of the next general election in June 1987, he had been able to push through something of a transformation within the party, in the fields of both party organization and policy.

From 1985 onwards, Kinnock developed the leader's office into an alternative party organization. Charles Clarke (in charge of his private office) and Peter Mandelson (party communications director) were crucial in developing a new emphasis on packaging and presentation, in reaction to the perceived failings of the 1983 campaign.[62] Party representatives were smartened up, Labour became much more media-friendly, and there was a new emphasis on glamour and glitz. From this there followed a downgrading of the party conference. The failures of 1983 and 1984–5 had engendered a feeling of collective guilt among many trade unionists and party activists, and the atmosphere of expulsions was not conducive to resistance to the party leadership. More than that, it was now a question of following the leadership because there seemed to be no viable alternative on offer. The leader's office exploited this: helped by a collaborative shadow cabinet, an increasingly supine NEC and the perceived proximity of the next general election, it ensured that the 1986 party conference was little more than a leadership rally. However, the packaging was not particularly effective. Kinnock's approval rating had slumped again by the end of the year, and did not recover substantially before the election. The private office might have drawn the conclusion (which was to be amply borne out at the 1987 and 1992 elections) that packaging was not very important, and that to see voters merely as 'consumers' was patronizing and counterproductive. Instead, they drew the opposite conclusion: the process must be intensified.

These years also saw changes in party policy. The aim was, essentially, to make policy more 'popular', more credible (there had been widespread disbelief, for example, in Labour's 1983 promise to bring down unemployment below one million), and more congenial to the views of the shadow cabinet. The ensuing shift to the right was buttressed by, even predicated upon, the 'boom' conditions which were clearly prevailing by the end of 1985. At the same time, change was rather piecemeal, so that in 1987 the manifesto would be 'full of compromise and ambiguity'.[63] Abolition of the House of Lords and plans to remove US nuclear bases from Britain were omitted, for example, but the party remained committed to unilateralism. Withdrawal from the EC was dropped, but this simply meant that the party had little to say on Europe at all. 'Social ownership' (some form of national-ization) of gas and British Telecom would be reimposed, but the details were vague. The plan to reduce unemployment was scaled down: now the party only pledged a reduction of a million over two years, but even then it carried little conviction. Large-scale increases in public expenditure, particularly on welfare, were also suggested, but with little real notion of how to pay for them, which allowed plenty of opportunities for the Conservatives to attack them as being 'uncosted'.[64] In short, the policy changes in the run-up to the 1987 general election showed that making policy more 'moderate' did not necessarily make it any more coherent.

There was, nevertheless, great optimism among Labour strat-egists when Thatcher announced on 11 May 1987 that there would be an election in a month's time.[65] But such feelings had more heart than head about them. The European elections of 1984 had seen Labour advance somewhat from its dismal 1979 showing, but still left the Conservatives some way ahead. By-elections had seen the Conservatives lose four of the nine seats they had de-fended, but only one of these had gone to Labour, which had itself lost a seat to the Alliance in February 1987. As late as March 1987 Labour was in third place behind the Alliance in the polls. Thus by the time the election was called, it was less a question of whether Labour could win, but whether it could hold on to second place – in terms of votes, if not seats – in the face of what appeared to be a strong Alliance challenge. Labour did fight a good campaign, which focused particularly on the leader. But it had little to say on some key issues, like the EC, and its poli-cies in other areas (like 'social ownership') were confused or confusing. The party's spending plans were savaged by the Con-servatives as being likely to lead to massive tax increases.

For all its professional campaigning, Labour increased its poll share only by 3.2 points to 30.8 per cent, and managed a net gain of only 20 seats, emerging with 229 MPs. The party's main gains came in the east Midlands, Scotland, Wales and Yorkshire; the image of an electoral 'two nations' scenario was intensified by the fact that it actually lost three seats in the south-east and still held only three seats south of the Severn-Wash line outside London. Had the rules for forfeiture of deposits not been changed since 1983, 94 Labour deposits would have been lost, scarcely fewer than in 1983, and well in excess of the party's previous record (35 in 1929). Labour was still in third place behind the

Alliance in more than 200 seats. It failed to improve its position significantly among non-manual workers, while among skilled workers only 36 per cent supported Labour, whereas 40 per cent voted Conservative.[66] Whatever else Labour had achieved in 1987, it had not built a strong base from which to challenge the Conservative ascendancy next time: to win such an election Labour still needed a swing larger than any achieved by either party at a post-war general election.

In the aftermath of defeat, many commentators expressed the view that Labour was probably finished in its present form. The affluence and embourgeoisement of a section of the working class, particularly skilled workers in the south and Midlands, and the shrinking of the working class overall, had made the party unelectable. This argument was not without its flaws.[67] In particular, it might have been useful to ask why the party was failing to get so many of what might be thought its 'natural' voters – young people, members of ethnic minorities, and the poor – to the polls at all. But the class dealignment argument carried almost all before it in the aftermath of Labour's third successive electoral defeat. The 'logical' corollary was that Labour should move further towards the 'centre ground' of politics. The alternative sometimes touted at the time – that it should form an electoral pact with the Alliance – received little support within the party and, in any case, lost what little force it had once the Alliance began to tear itself apart in the attempt to merge the SDP with the Liberals.

The argument that Labour needed a more 'moderate' image fitted the leadership's agenda perfectly, and between 1987 and 1992 the party shifted further to the right. One side of this was seen in policy. In July 1987 Kinnock announced the establishment of seven 'policy review' groups which would report to the 1989 party conference. The results were broadly as intended. On the economy, Labour moved still further away from nationalization, stressing the need for market disciplines and a government sympathetic to business and willing to create an environment in which it could prosper. This meant, in turn, that Labour ruled out large increases in taxation. Smith, who took over as shadow Chancellor in 1987, embarked on a round of meetings with City and business leaders in which he was at pains to emphasize Labour's 'respectability', while Margaret Beckett, appointed shadow Chief Secretary to the Treasury in 1989, belied her one-time hard left reputation by stressing what became known as 'Beckett's Law': the need to avoid new spending commitments and use the formulation that expenditure would only rise 'as resources allowed'. This was, in short, a return to the notion, generally dominant in the party's history, that socialism (although the word was by now rarely used) would emerge from the redistribution of a growing surplus produced by an increasingly prosperous capitalism. This view, in turn, remained tenable because it did seem, at least until the end of the 1980s, that the economy was still growing significantly; and even after the economy began to move into recession in 1989, the view was still defended, on the grounds that government errors, rather than the inherent nature of capitalism, had been to blame for the end of prosperity. '

In other areas, too, there were changes. Occasionally these were innovative, as with the pledges to introduce a national minimum wage and to create a Ministry for Women.[68] But generally the trend was towards policy becoming more 'moderate'. First, policy on the EC was modified. With withdrawal seeming increasingly a lost cause, and Thatcher's continuing rhetorical opposition to greater integration leaving a fillable gap in the political market, Labour became warmer towards Europe. The process was capped in 1988 when the President of the European Commission, Jacques Delors, impressed delegates at the Trades Union Congress with a speech which emphasized the social policy and workers' protection aspects of the EC. By the time of the next general election Labour would be standing firmly as a pro-'European' party.[69] Secondly, there were changes in industrial relations policy. Previously, Labour had pledged to repeal all the Conservatives' anti-union legislation, but now, even many trade union leaders saw that, paradoxically, the Conservatives' policies had prevented unions from doing things which made them unpopular with the wider public.[70] On welfare, Labour tried to adapt to changing times by moving away from the 'paternalism and bureaucracy' which had so characterized its policies in the past, but the vexed issues of targeted benefits and unification of the tax and benefits systems were left to one side.[71] Finally, the party ditched its commitment to unilateral nuclear disarmament, a step made easier by developments in the outside world, first with the prospect of real progress in disarmament talks between the superpowers, and later with the collapse of the Soviet bloc.

The fact that the policy review took policy out of party politics for two years allowed Kinnock to concentrate on a second area – organization and image. A number of developments took place which aimed to increase the power of the party centre, and, still more, the leader, at the expense of the vestiges of Labour's democratic structures. The party conference became more and more of a rubber-stamping talkshop, where delegates came to applaud rather than to debate. The NEC and shadow cabinet became still more Kinnockite. Potential areas of dissent were marginalized, be they local councillors, women's groups or ethnic minority groups campaigning for Black Sections. Awkward individuals were carted wholesale from the party, often on flimsy or hearsay evidence, in something not far from the witch-hunt that the left had predicted. CLPs' powers were reduced as the NEC took greater powers over candidate selection and, in 1991, instituted a national membership scheme whose results, initially at least, were disastrous.[72] LPYS was effectively disbanded, and replaced by a few short-lived gimmicks, despite the fact that experience showed that even where people might be attracted to Militant and Trotskyism when they first joined, they often developed into loyal and useful members of the party in later life.[73]

All this led, ultimately, to a left-wing reaction. In March 1988 Benn, who since his return to parliament at a by-election in 1984 had been a marginal figure, and Heffer announced their candidatures for the leadership and deputy leadership respectively. A six-month campaign followed, but they had no chance of success. At the 1988 party conference Kinnock easily beat off Benn's challenge, taking almost 89 per cent of the votes. Even Hattersley, who faced a second challenger in the combative figure of shadow cabinet Employment spokesman, John Prescott, took two-thirds of the votes for deputy leader, whereas Prescott took just under 24 per cent and Heffer just under 10. Only 38 MPs voted for Benn; still more depressing for him was that only 119 CLPs did so.[74] This showed the marginalization of the hard left, the extent to which Kinnock had established a firm hold over the party at all levels, and the way in which memories of the 1979–83 period could still be used against the left and to emphasize the need for loyalty to the leadership. The perils of disloyalty were clearly seen when Prescott was punished for standing against Hattersley by being demoted to Transport. But, in truth, there had been an air of futility about the whole affair. The ageing Benn and Heffer seemed in many ways like throwbacks to a bygone era.[75] There was, in any case, little of substance behind their campaign. The parallels with the Cook–Maxton campaign 60 years earlier are striking. Both were left-wing attempts to resist the increasingly accommodationist stance of a moderate leadership which seemed to be carrying all before it; both were, in a sense, profoundly irrelevant to the contemporary situation; and both were doomed to fail, not least because they almost totally failed to excite trade union enthusiasm. Neither made much impact on ordinary party members or MPs who were hoping for victory at the next election and who knew the penalties for crossing an increasingly powerful party leadership. And, of course, both were counter-productive, since they highlighted the weakness of the left and gave the ruling oligarchy ample opportunity to re-emphasize the dangers of division and the value of loyalty. The only concrete result of each was to reinforce the leadership they despised and to ease the path of that leadership towards still more of a swing to the right.

By 1989, then, Kinnock's hegemony within the party was virtually complete. It was buttressed by Labour's improving electoral performance. In March 1989 Labour won the Mid Staffordshire by-election from the Conservatives on a 21 per cent swing.[76] That May there were gains in the local elections, and the following month Labour won 45 seats in the Euro-elections, more than the Conservatives, although on a very low turnout. By April 1990 Labour had a 28-point lead in the polls. However, this was a 'soft' lead, based on the unpopularity of the government and of Thatcher in particular. Rising inflation and interest rates severely dented the Conservatives' claims of economic competence. Thatcher's devotion to the flat-rate poll tax to replace the rates as a way of funding local government weakened her position further. When, in November 1990, the deputy Prime Minister, Sir Geoffrey Howe, resigned in protest at her anti-EC stance, it was the signal for the malcontents to act. Michael Heseltine challenged her for the party leadership, and after she failed to win enough votes to fend off a second ballot, she was persuaded to withdraw, to be succeeded ultimately by the Chancellor of the Exchequer, John Major.

Labour had been looking forward to fighting Thatcher at the next election, believing she could now be portrayed effectively as being out of touch and dictatorial. Major seemed a more conciliatory figure: his first actions were to bring Heseltine back into the cabinet and announce that the poll tax would be abolished. There was some sense of a fresh start, and a feeling widely expressed was that Major should be given a chance. The recession continued, but talk of economic recovery being on the way did not seem wholly ludicrous, and the run-up to the election saw inflation back below 5 per cent, income tax cuts, and a massive stimulus to public expenditure. From December 1991 the Conservatives had a slight edge in the polls, and Labour was still trailing on leadership and economic competence, which would obviously be crucial issues.[77] Still, despite all this, Labour had high hopes of victory in the election which was finally called for 9 April 1992.

Labour's campaign was again highly professional. As in 1987, Kinnock figured largely. However, it did not go quite as well as planned. Labour's 'shadow budget' seemed rather pompous and unnecessary, and allowed the Conservatives to focus on taxation, where Labour was still rather vulnerable. There were disagreements between Kinnock and Smith. The party's celebratory Sheffield rally, held, perversely enough, a week before polling, did the party little good and might even have damaged its prospects.[78] Then, in the last week of the campaign, Kinnock struck a strangely ambivalent note about electoral reform. All in all, it had not been as good a campaign as it should have been, and led to subsequent calls to put the publicity agents and advertisers under closer political control.[79]

On the night of 9 April three exit polls suggested that there would be a hung parliament, but in the event the Conservatives won an overall majority of 21, with 336 seats and 41.9 per cent of the poll, as opposed to Labour's 271 and 34.4 per cent. The overall swing to Labour was only 2.1 per cent, producing a net gain of 42 seats, especially in the west Midlands, the north-west and the London area, and it increased its non-London representation south of the Severn-Wash line from three to ten, although this was still well short of pre-1979 levels.[80] Under the pre-1985 rules, it would still have forfeited 65 deposits, and its share of the total poll was lower than in 1979. It would still take a further 2.3 per cent swing to Labour to make it the largest party, and a 4.1 per cent swing to give it an overall majority.[81] Three elections on from the 1979 defeat, Labour was still not in a particularly strong psephological position from which to launch its next election campaign.

The reasons for the result have been much debated. There was some feeling that an inept campaign had cost Labour victory, but this seems unlikely.[82] In all probability, it was an election that Labour could not have won. The Conservatives had got rid of their two biggest handicaps, Thatcher and the poll tax. They could point with some degree of credibility to the start of economic recovery. At such a time, enough people, having just come through recession and with 'memories' of past Labour governments, were not willing to risk a change, particularly to a party which had changed so rapidly and under a leader who was still not trusted. The 1987 election result had left Labour with a mountain to climb: ultimately it did not have the resources to achieve the feat.

Labour's defeat led to the resignation of Kinnock: he was succeeded, as had been generally expected, by Smith, who trounced his only challenger, Bryan Gould, by a ten-to-one majority in the electoral college. Margaret Beckett beat off challenges from Gould and Prescott to take the deputy leadership, making her the most senior woman in the history of the party to date. Little did anyone expect that within two years she would be acting leader following the death of Smith. He was replaced by Tony Blair, the shadow Home Secretary, with Prescott taking the deputy leadership. After a period of relative calm under Smith, Blair would soon begin pushing the party even further to the right than Kinnock had dared (or perhaps wanted) to go. Blair, far more than Kinnock, stood outside many of the old Labour traditions, after all.

Verdicts on Kinnock's leadership have been mixed. The case for him would state that he pulled the party back from the brink of disaster in 1983 to the brink of office in 1992; that he saw off the challenge of the Alliance; that he got rid of Militant and marginalized the hard left which, the case goes, had done so much damage to the party; and that, part cause and part effect of all this, he made considerable progress in modernizing the party's policy and organization, and so made it possible for future leaders to continue the process and make Labour a party fit to face the challenges of the 1990s and beyond.

There is something in these plaudits. It would be at best churlish and at worst plain wrong to say that Kinnock did not improve the party's electoral prospects over the period, although how far that was despite, rather than because of, Kinnock is a little difficult to say. In particular, there must be questions as to how it was that a leader elected to boost the party's fortunes by running ahead of it in the polls actually managed to trail behind it so often, particularly after 1987. Further, the policies Kinnock was instrumental in pushing through were and remain open to question. In the main, he simply reverted to earlier Labour ideas, especially in the commitment to achieving a 'fairer' society through economic growth; and this maxim had tripped up MacDonald, Crosland, Wilson and others in the past. Little attention was paid to devolving power to the people: to a larger extent than is sometimes recognized, Kinnock's Labour party remained pretty uncritical of the nature of the state and its power, arguing – again, like most previous Labour leaders – that, given the chance, he would use that power to 'do good'. Labour remained remarkably conservative in matters like citizenship or devolution to Scotland and Wales and the English regions, and in retrospect it seems difficult to avoid the view that a Kinnock government would have been just as bureaucratic as, and probably not much less paternalistic than, previous Labour governments. A classic example of this was the party's largely uncritical devotion to 'Europe' from 1988 onwards: because it was believed that this would bring some political advantage and some social policy gains, there was no serious critique, except from marginal figures like Benn, of the EC's bureaucratism and lack of accountability. Finally, Kinnock downgraded the Labour party's own democracy. Admittedly, it was hardly a perfect democracy when he started, but it had kept some power of accountability over the leadership and at least had the potential to militate against some of the worst elements of oligarchical control. Under Kinnock, power was concentrated in the leadership's hands in a way not seen since the days of MacDonald in the later 1920s, and perhaps not even then. The result was a party machine dying on its feet, with useful debate stifled and anyone daring to question the leader's omniscience characterized as 'disloyal'. Loyalty became owed not to the party but to the leader. The path was set for further shifts to the right, and these were to come with a vengeance under Blair's leadership from 1994 onwards.

The period from 1979 onwards was one of massive challenges for the Labour party. The election in that year of a Conservative government determined to undo much of what Labourites had achieved and held dear was a blow whose implications soon became clear. The 1980s were a decade of almost continual defeats. In the face of those defeats, Labour, after briefly and half-heartedly trying a 'leftish' approach, had first edged, and then rushed, rightwards to try to regain its electability. But in spite of all the policy changes, the organizational alterations, and the renewed faith in leaders, the party was unable to regain office, and it remained open to question, first, whether Labour could ever win office again if it so resolutely failed to take up principled positions in opposition to the Conservatives, and secondly whether a future Labour government could avoid the errors, pitfalls and defeats which had characterized so many of its predecessors. The verdict must remain open, but the weight of evidence does not seem to be very heavily in the party leadership's favour.

Conclusion

This book has attempted to trace the broad outlines of the history of the Labour party in a chronological fashion. Such an approach is, to a large extent, dictated by the genre within which this book is situated. No one is more conscious than the author, however, that there are gaps, and areas where more could have been said. It would, indeed, be possible to write a history of the party that concentrated much more on discrete themes. This conclusion aims to look at a few of these, briefly, before going on to say a little about what the future might hold for the party.

LABOUR AND THE ELECTORATE

There was little that was 'inevitable' about the rise of the Labour party. While it seems reasonably clear that some recasting of British politics was taking place before the First World War, there was no clear direction to the process. In all probability, Labour would have expanded over time at the expense of the Liberals, but the speed of the transformation which took place cannot be explained without reference to the events of the First World War. Even then, Labour did not really 'replace' the Liberals: the process was slower, messier and, certainly up to 1945, much less complete than such a formulation would allow.

Up to 1914, the party put up so few candidates that it is difficult to make hard and fast judgements about the scale of the party's support nationally. It is fairly clear, though, that the party tended to be concentrated in northern England, in working-class areas of relatively heavy trade union density. Even so, it fared less well in the larger cities, while its performance in mining areas was problematic. But after 1918, and still more from 1922, it developed a stranglehold on the coalfields, and made significant progress in many – though not all – the big cities of Britain. Indeed, during the interwar period Labour's strongest support remained in mining areas, as the 1931 election results showed. The more working-class areas of the cities were fairly solid for

Labour, helped by the shift of most Catholic voters to Labour from the early 1920s onwards. However, expansion beyond the working class was unimpressive. If the underlying battle in 1920s politics was to take the centre ground – including both work-ing- and middle-class voters – then that battle was lost in the period after 1929, and Labour was unable to break out of a working-class, staple industries-based electoral ghetto before the Second World War.

After 1945 things did change somewhat, Labour becoming rather more effective at appealing to wider sections of the working class and also having somewhat more appeal than previously to middle-class voters. Here the growing fragmentation of the middle class probably helped the party, as did one of its most potent sym-bols, the rise of white-collar trade unionism. There are signs that as early as 1950 the skilled working class was becoming less willing to offer automatic support to Labour, but 1950s predictions of imminent 'embourgeoisement' were premature: 1964 can be seen, indeed, as a peak of class voting. However, after 1966 it is quite clear that working-class voters, particularly skilled workers, be-came more critical of Labour, and the process of defection was especially marked in 1970 and again from 1979 onwards. In the latter period Thatcher's appeal seems to have struck a chord with skilled workers, especially in the south and the Midlands. Mid-dle-class people employed in the public sector did, arguably, begin to loosen their ties to Conservatism, as that sector came under increasing attack from government, but even here the process was not straightforward, particularly given the formation of the SDP and later the Alliance.

What have been Labour's strongest areas? Up to 1914, the answer was undoubtedly industrial northern England. Even this, though, could hardly be called a heartland, and most seats would have been difficult to retain in the face of Liberal opposition. After 1918, Labour rapidly developed heartlands in the mining areas, to the extent that 16 of the 17 seats with the largest proportion of miners in their male working population remained Labour even at the 1931 election. The strongest areas of all in this re-spect were south Wales and the Yorks, Notts and Derby coal-field area around Sheffield. These areas remained the core of Labour's support, with the rest of industrial northern England, the Midlands (the east Midlands being more committed to Labour than the west), Scotland (the west being safer Labour territory than the east), and London all weighing in during the interwar period to a greater or lesser extent. After 1945, these areas generally supported Labour more consistently than they had done before the war. However, the party's performance remained patchy in the west Midlands, particularly from 1959 onwards, and in eastern Scotland; and the east Midlands also became a problem area for Labour from 1979 onwards.

Another area which has proved problematic for Labour has been England south of the Severn-Wash line, outside the London region. Between the wars there were 134 seats in this area, of which Labour won 17 in 1923 and 22 in 1929. These figures were bad enough in themselves, but even more startling is that at no other election before 1945 did the party win as many as five seats in this region. In 1945 Labour won 59 of the 140 seats in the area, but its performances thereafter were less impressive, and although it recovered to win 42 of the 152 seats in 1966 it won only 15 at the next election in 1970. After a rally at the two elections of 1974, it won only 13 seats here in 1979, and its performances in the elections of 1983 and 1987 (three out of 182) and 1992 (10 out of 183), with many Labour candidates being pushed into third place behind the Alliance/Liberal Democrats, were abysmal. Labour's failure here highlights its weakness in rural, farming and middle-class areas, but also its inability to construct large enough groups of loyal working-class voters in these areas.

There has also been a significant gender differential in support for Labour. It seems reasonably safe to say that, with the sole exception of 1987 (when the percentages were equal), a higher proportion of men than of women has voted Labour at every general election since women were first given the vote. Numerous reasons for this can be suggested: women lived longer than men and older people were, generally, more likely to vote Conservative than their younger counterparts; women were less exposed to trade unionism (even at the peak of union membership, 1979, only 38.8 per cent of eligible women were trade union members, as opposed to 65.6 per cent of men); Conservative governments were sometimes more willing to legislate on 'women's issues' than Labour (the 1920s being a case in point); and Conservative rhetoric of domesticity probably had a considerable appeal for much of the period, certainly when set against Labour's hesitant feminism. But the Labour party must also be held responsible, for its close identification with trade unions primarily representing men, and its rather 'macho' image overall, often suggested that it had less to offer women than men.

LABOUR AND TRADE UNIONISM

The basic reason for the formation of the Labour party was defensive. It was not the mark of a working class rising up to take power, but a body established to protect the rights of workers, and of trade unions in particular, at a time when they were coming under renewed threat. This is not to say that it was a 'narrowly' trade union party; for one thing, many trade unionists defined the scope of union concerns very widely indeed, to cover not just industrial relations questions, but also full employment and economic policy, social welfare, and, increasingly, foreign policy. The fact that socialists were often eloquent and ready to work on such matters made them good allies for the unions. There were, of course, tensions, but these can be overstressed, since many trade unionists were also socialists (after a fashion, in some cases), and the generally moderate, 'businesslike' approach of most of the party's leading groups tended to chime in with union attitudes (although there were always tensions between unions and the party leadership when Labour was in government, especially in 1929–31, 1966–70, and 1977–9). However, the link to trade unionism was not beneficial in all ways: in particular, at times when trade unionism was weak and/or unpopular, it allowed Labour to be portrayed as sectarian and/or 'unpatriotic'. At the same time, though, trade unions provided Labour with the wherewithal to set out and establish itself as an independent political party. They also helped to provide a set of values. These included, positively, a sense of community, a coherence of approach, and a mode of political conduct (for example, loyalty to majority decisions). On the other hand, they helped to make the party organizationally obsessed, and distrustful of those who were not from a traditional trade union background.

LABOUR AND SOCIALISM

Although it contained socialists, the Labour party was not, for the most part, seriously concerned with the question of how to produce a socialist society in anything but a utopian and remote future. But this is not to argue that socialism was unimportant. The very vagueness of 'socialism' as a concept meant it could act as a unifying myth when all else failed. It inspired party activists to the humdrum tasks of canvassing, committee work and so on, connecting all such activities into a grander design. At the same time, it acted as a magnet to the left, which, along with the adversarial tendency of British politics fostered by the electoral system, helped to keep the party together and prevent breakaways (it was for this reason, partly, that Clause Four was adopted in 1918). However, while socialism had a valuable unifying effect, it also enabled Labour to be portrayed by its opponents as extremist and doctrinaire.

This was a little ironic, to say the least. While there were always those prepared to speak in the radical terms of the class warrior, the leadership's outlook remained essentially revisionist for most of the party's history. This approach was predicated on the potential of capitalism to prosper in such a way as to deliver social 'goods' through increased revenues for government. This allowed it to be consensual, avoiding issues such as widespread redistribution of existing wealth, and chimed in with the essentially defensive nature of the trade unions' input. However, it also meant that Labour tended to fare worst in periods of economic recession, partly because it left the party with little to say that was convincing, and partly because at such times the left, always the weaker end of the party, was likely to become strong enough to split the party but hardly ever strong enough to take it over. Indeed, the ascendancy of generally unquestioning revisionism within the party for so much of its history is as much the fault of the weaknesses and shortcomings of the left as of the right. At only one point in the history of the Labour party, the early 1970s, did the left really sit down and think hard about policy, the result being the 1973 programme. But even this was a mixed blessing: first, because the left failed spectacularly to convert the existing party leadership to its views or, failing that, to change the leadership; secondly, because the programme was not as coherent or robust as was usually claimed; thirdly, because the left failed to explain its message to the electorate, relying increasingly on sloganizing; and finally because, once adopted, the policy became a touchstone of faith rather than a live programme evolving with changing circumstances.

But then, the left almost always found the going difficult because of Labour's penchant for discipline and managerialism in party affairs. This, while to some extent necessary, was frequently overdone, and crushed out dissent which was not really 'disloyal', and which might have answered some of the problems that Labour faced. This preference for discipline over debate was particularly important in allowing the development of a largely unthinking statism as the fundamental basis of Labour's approach, yet it was this statism which was to cause the party such problems in the period from the 1960s onwards in particular.

LABOUR IN GOVERNMENT

At national level, Labour has had only five spells in office since its formation, totalling just under 20 years. These governments had very mixed fortunes. That of 1924 was intended mainly to show that Labour could govern; it was not really expected to, and did not, deliver a great deal in terms of concrete changes. Labour was, later, unfortunate enough to win the 1929 general election: and its second government, ill-prepared for reasonably stable times, let alone the economic blizzard which it did ultimately face, lurched along until it was finally crushed by financial crisis and its own ineptitude in the summer of 1931. The third period in office, after the Second World War, was much more successful, in many ways, fulfilling a large part of the party's programme and setting the agenda for British government for a generation. The fourth period in office, between 1964 and 1970, has excited considerable debate: the condemnatory views of years past are now giving way to a much more balanced, perhaps even over-sympathetic orthodoxy which stresses the extreme difficulties the government faced and the fact that, even if the government did not always have the answers, it at least asked the 'right' questions about society, the economy and the state of Britain. At the time of writing, the last period of Labour government was 1974 to 1979. This government has attracted less work of a 'revisionist' kind, and is still held in the popular memory as, according to taste, simply incompetent or a betrayal of all that Labour stood for. In fact, it might well be that historians will eventually suggest a rather softer verdict on the government: given the economic circumstances in which it operated, it is difficult to see how it could have achieved more than it did, and it did, at least after Callaghan's succession to the premiership in 1976, have some purpose and success according to its own fairly limited aspirations.

Labour governments have contributed virtually nothing to constitutional reform in twentieth-century Britain. Between the wars, some people wanted to give greater powers to local government, but nothing was done. The Attlee governments were centralizing in their effects, but did little to reform the state machine which was taking on so many new functions. The governments of the 1960s did at least begin to look at reform, with investigations of the House of Lords, devolution, and the civil service, but little came of any of these, and the devolution legislation of the 1970s owed more to political expediency than conviction (and did not come into effect in any case). Although there was a revival of talk of constitutional reform in the 1980s, much of this was due to the fact that it seemed that only by changing the goalposts could Thatcher be stopped, and it remains to be seen whether all the fine talk of change has really altered the outlook of what has been a surprisingly conservative party where the constitution has been concerned. Labour's view of the state has tended to be that it is like a car: it will go anywhere the driver wants, and the main thing is to ensure that Labour is driving it. What the party has failed to address is the point made by many on the left that the car can only be driven with the handbrake on.

Labour governments have been much more concerned with economic management, not surprisingly since they have seen a prosperous economy as the key to reform in other areas. Here their record has been mixed, although it has to be added that in retrospect Labour won some elections which it might have been better to have lost, such as 1929 and those of 1974. The 1929–31 government has to go down as the least successful: although it was undoubtedly faced with a hard situation, it did nothing to even begin to make matters better, and arguably made them worse than they needed to be. Otherwise, though, Labour governments have not performed too badly. That of 1924 proved that the economy would not collapse under Labour. Attlee and his colleagues managed a sensible and effective transition from a wartime to a peacetime economy. The 1970s administration, what-ever its failings in other areas, did at least bring inflation under some degree of control. As for the 1964–70 administration, it could be argued that it would not have been so heavily criticized for its economic failings had the critics known of the worse times that were to follow and had the government not pitched its aims in this area so high.

Labour liked to see itself as the party that would make the economy grow faster, and hence enable government to spend more on social projects, but here its success has been muted, to say the least. Labour governments were not helped by coming into office in difficult economic times, but even allowing for this little progress was made. The party was too apt to seize upon panaceas – rationalization in the 1920s, planning and national-ization in the 1940s, the 'white heat' of technology in the 1960s – and did too little to work out, when in opposition, what these things actually involved in practice. In particular, the legacy of nationalization was hardly one of which the party could be proud, other than in terms of keeping people in employment in the in-dustries concerned. The result was that policy was often ineffec-tive in promoting higher growth rates.

Even allowing for the fact that the economy generally remained sluggish, Labour governments did achieve much of value in social policy. Pride of place here must go to the National Health Serv-ice, although at the time of writing it is a moot point as to how far the extended service established in the 1940s will survive into the next millennium. In housing, too, Labour governments could point to a reasonable record, although not an entirely unmixed one (significantly, this was the one area of domestic policy where both the first and second Labour governments ac-quitted themselves well). Less was done in education, at least until the 1960s, but, even here, there were achievements. Over-all, Labour could claim both that it was the creator of the post-war Welfare State and that, even when out of office, its presence in opposition, at least until the 1980s, was a strong brake on Conservative impulses to make significant cuts in provision.

Labour's achievements in foreign affairs should not go unno-ticed, either. This was the area where the first two governments seemed to achieve most, even if those achievements were to be, sadly, ephemeral. The Attlee government, for its part, established the parameters for British foreign policy for the Cold War; and

while the fact of that 'conflict' can be regretted, if it is once accepted that there was a problem for Britain in the late 1940s,
then that government solved it by ensuring the continuing commitment of the USA to European security through NATO. Labour
suffered over the EEC issue, of course, but there were hard choices
to be made, and the advantages were never all on one side or
the other of the debate. It has to be said, in addition, that this is
an issue where the Conservative party has also experienced horrendous difficulties.

When it comes to the Empire/Commonwealth, Labour has
combined a lot of high-sounding talk with quite a bit of low-
looking action. The party was never, at least until the
decolonization process was well under way, consistently anti-
imperialist. Labour governments in 1929–31 and again after 1945
passed colonial development legislation whose purpose, notwith-
standing its noble title, was the better to exploit Britain's colonial possessions. The Attlee governments can only be seen as
starting the wind-up of the Empire in retrospect: it was not really
what was intended at the time. And in increasingly difficult times
after 1964, and with the bait of Europe increasingly taking cen-
tre-stage, Labour's commitment to Britain's Commonwealth partners has been neither strong nor consistent.

The picture of Labour in government at national level, then, is
a very mixed one, with real successes countered by significant
failures. Meanwhile, it must also be remembered that the national
picture is not the sum total of Labour's achievements in government. Even before the formation of the LRC, 'Labour' members
were being elected to local councils, school boards, and so on.
After 1918 there was a surge of Labour representation, particularly in the larger towns and cities. Many areas of the country,
such as south Wales, or Sheffield, have been under almost constant Labour control ever since the 1920s or 1930s. Further advances were made after 1945. As local government gradually lost
functions to Whitehall, so the scope for local initiative was reduced (a process added to, it should be remembered, by Labour
governments, particularly that of 1945–51). And yet it is clear
that Labour local authorities have often made a significant contribution towards improving the lives of their citizens, be it in
housing, sanitation, education, or (a particular favourite of many
interwar Labour authorities) work with the blind. The picture
has not been wholly rosy, of course. Labour authorities were

sometimes inefficient; occasionally they were corrupt. It has perhaps not been altogether healthy that, at local level, so many parts of the country have been under virtual one-party rule for so long (although until recently the same point could have been made about the vast swathes of Britain which never elected anything other than a Conservative or an 'Independent' council).

Having said all that, it must be doubted whether there would have been so much 'progress' in twentieth-century Britain without the existence of the Labour party. Even in opposition, its presence was – certainly until the 1980s – a warning to its opponents not to go too far in the other direction.

UNITIES AND DISUNITIES

Any political party is something of a coalition: even that archetypally 'monolithic' party, the Soviet Communist party, in the days of Stalin, contained divergent views on many issues. At the same time, there needs to be an underlying core of agreement on certain matters, otherwise a party will become fissile and will eventually collapse, the case of the British Liberal party in the interwar period being a good example.

What were the 'unities' within the Labour party? Among other things, the following can be adduced. Labour was committed to liberal parliamentary democracy, not even giving up on this in the early 1930s. The party was committed to the British state, although this commitment could coexist, for many, with devolution for Scotland and Wales, and sometimes for the English regions, or with a greater degree of European integration, or with a commitment to internationalism. Although not pacifist, it was a party of peace, believing that war was a catastrophe which would hit no one harder than the working classes, and seeing peace as the first prerequisite of the 'ordered progress' to which the party was committed (somewhat ironically, given the importance of the two World Wars in boosting Labour's fortunes). The party was committed in policy terms to reducing the uncertainties and arbitrariness which seemed to be inherent in the unregulated market system. It advocated greater security for people, especially in the jobs market: Labour was the party of full employment or, failing that, was committed to the idea that unemployment was a moral wrong whose evils the state should seek to alleviate through a system of benefits payments. This desire for security and fairness also meant that Labour was committed to social reform on a considerable scale and, rhetorically at least (after 1918), to 'socialism', although this had perhaps more value as a unifying myth than as a guide to immediate action. The party was also, of course, committed to trade unionism, although there was debate about the exact role of the unions in the party under capitalism and in the socialist state which, it was hoped, would one day succeed it.

Here, then, was a solid basis for unity, which essentially held the party together even at times of pressure. Without understanding these forces for unity one cannot begin to comprehend why it was that, apparently despite the odds, Labour survived the First World War virtually intact (with only a few defections to Coalition Labour in 1918); why it could manage, almost uniquely among moderate left parties in Europe, to avoid a major split resulting in the formation of a strong Communist party; why it was able to shrug off the formation of no fewer than three new parties in a little over a year in 1931–2; and why the SDP did not draw off more Labourites than the (relatively) few it did attract. Even after a decade of moves to the right, the left-wing rebellion which resulted in the formation of Scargill's Socialist Labour party in 1996 aroused more condemnation than support from the Labour left.

Yet at the same time, the party was split in a number of ways, and although many of these divisions, particularly after the early years, were often hidden from view, they did not, on the whole, disappear. There were splits between nationalists and internationalists, further complicated, after the Second World War, by a third group who saw the best expression of Labour's internationalism as entry into 'Europe'. There were arguments over the role of the state: by mid-century, Labour had become a largely statist party, but this should not mask the fact that many remained committed to a greater role for local government, industrial democracy, and so on. There were divergent views of the working class: should it be accepted as it was, or pushed towards more 'wholesome' habits; was it the role of the party to give 'the people' what they wanted, or to educate them into wanting something 'better'? In economic policy, there were differences between those who advocated full public control and those who felt that the market had a role to play, and much of the party's history in this area is one of an uneasy compromise. There was also the question of gender. The Labour party has liked to claim that it has been the 'women's party', yet it has remained deeply divided on the issue, and for some periods the claim was patently absurd. In fact, for all the hopes of feminists within it, Labour was always, to a greater or lesser extent, a party that put men first, and one which has been uneasy with 'women's issues'.

Having said all that, these splits can be seen, not as a weakness (although at times they did little to help the party's fortunes) but as a source of strength. The fact that the party often faced in more than one direction, but had a strong core of unity underlying it, meant that it was able to draw support quite widely. As a 'broad church' (Wilson's phrase) it was not brittle; it was very robust. It might be that any attempts to move the Labour party still further to the 'centre ground' of British politics might introduce a brittleness which has not, so far, been a major problem.

THE FUTURE?

It is not the job of the historian to predict the future. There is, after all, enough of the past to work at to mean that he or she does not really need to 'moonlight' as a fortune-teller. However, two points remain to be made. The first is that Labour, so long as it remains essentially revisionist in outlook (and it seems unlikely that it will cease to do so), will fare better when the economy is in reasonable shape. This is not to say that prosperous times mean a Labour government: the 1950s alone give the lie to such a formulation. But during more prosperous times, Labour does at least have something coherent to say: namely, that the fruits of that prosperity should be used in order to create a fairer society. At the same time, voters are more relaxed, as a whole, about public expenditure, and more willing to listen to alternative proposals as to how such expenditure should be made. The problem, throughout Labour's history, is what to do when the economy moves into difficulties: that was the lesson of the late 1920s and early 1930s, and of the 1970s and early 1980s. For the foreseeable future there is no sign that future Labour governments will be any better equipped to deal with difficult times than were those of MacDonald or Wilson.

The second point is more speculative. Labour has been a political party, based very much on the Westminster model of politics. Neither of these forms, however, looks to have an altogether bright future. It is at least arguable that, as the significance of the European Union grows, so will the role of the European parliament, and so will arguments for the devolution of some powers downwards from Westminster to Scotland and Wales and, perhaps, to the English regions. That alone poses a challenge to the future of all our political parties which they have yet to address seriously. And there might be questions over the future of political parties *per se*, at least in the way that Britain has known them since the late nineteenth century, with the continuing development of issues which divide the parties internally, the growth of extra-party political action, and the changing nature of the post-Communist world. It might well be that, a hundred years from now, historians will be asking, not how it was that the Labour party was so divided, but how it was that such a coalition of interests, passions, obsessions and fads could ever have held together for as long as it did.

Appendix 1 Seats Won at General Elections, 1900–92

Year	Labour	Conservative & Allies	Liberal	Other	Total
1900	2	402	183	83	670
1906	29	156	399	86	670
1910 (Jan)	40	272	274	84	670
1910 (Dec)	42	272	272	84	670
1918	57	473	36	141	707
1922	142	344	115	14	615
1923	191	258	158	8	615
1924	151	412	40	12	615
1929	287	260	59	9	615
1931	46	554	(a)	15	615
1935	154	429	21	11	615
1945	393	210	12	25	640
1950	315	298	9	3	625
1951	295	321	6	3	625
1955	277	345	6	2	630
1959	258	365	6	1	630
1964	317	304	9	–	630
1966	364	253	12	1	630
1970	288	330	6	6	630
1974 (Feb)	301	297	14	23	635
1974 (Oct)	319	277	13	26	635
1979	269	339	11	16	635
1983	209	397	23 (b)	21	650
1987	229	376	22 (b)	23	650
1992	271	336	20 (c)	24	651

NOTES
(a) A total of 72 Liberals were elected in various guises, namely 35 Liberal Nationals, who remained part of the National government and eventually joined the Conservatives; 33 official Liberals, who later withdrew support from the National government; and 4 others, led by Lloyd George, who opposed the government throughout.
(b) Liberal/SDP Alliance
(c) Liberal Democrats

Appendix 2   Labour Party Leaders

Chairman of the Parliamentary Labour Party, 1906–22
1906–8   Keir Hardie
1908–10   Arthur Henderson
1910–11   George Barnes
1911–14   Ramsay MacDonald
1914–17   Arthur Henderson
1917–21   William Adamson
1921–2   John Clynes

Leader of the Labour Party
1922–31   Ramsay MacDonald
1931–2   Arthur Henderson
1932–5   George Lansbury
1935–55   Clement Attlee
1955–63   Hugh Gaitskell
1963–76   Harold Wilson
1976–80   James Callaghan
1980–3   Michael Foot
1983–92   Neil Kinnock
1992–4   John Smith
1994–   Tony Blair

Appendix 3 Labour Cabinets

MacDonald's Cabinet, Jan. to Nov. 1924

Prime Minister and Foreign Secretary	J. R. MacDonald
Lord Chancellor	Viscount Haldane
Lord President	Lord Parmoor
Lord Privy Seal	J. R. Clynes
Chancellor of the Exchequer	P. Snowden
Home Secretary	A. Henderson
Colonial Secretary	J. H. Thomas
War Secretary	S. Walsh
Indian Secretary	Lord Olivier
Scottish Secretary	W. Adamson
Air Secretary	Lord Thomson
First Lord of Admiralty	Viscount Chelmsford
Chancellor, Duchy of Lancaster	J. Wedgwood
President, Board of Trade	S. Webb
Minister of Agriculture	N. Buxton
President, Board of Education	C. P. Trevelyan
Postmaster General	V. Hartshorn
First Commissioner of Works	F. W. Jowett
Minister of Labour	T. Shaw
Minister of Health	J. Wheatley

MacDonald's Cabinet, June 1929 to Aug. 1931

Prime Minister	J. R. MacDonald
Lord Chancellor	Lord Sankey
Lord President	Lord Parmoor
Lord Privy Seal	J. H. Thomas (to June 1930)
	V. Hartshorn (June 1930 to Mar. 1931)
	T. Johnston (from Mar. 1931)
Chancellor of the Exchequer	P. Snowden
Home Secretary	J. R. Clynes
Foreign Secretary	A. Henderson
Colonial Secretary	Lord Passfield
Dominions Secretary	Lord Passfield (to June 1930)
	J. H. Thomas (from June 1930)
War Secretary	T. Shaw
Indian Secretary	W. Wedgwood Benn

Scottish Secretary	W. Adamson
Air Secretary	Lord Thomson (to Oct. 1930)
	Lord Amulree (from Oct. 1930)
First Lord of Admiralty	A. V. Alexander
President, Board of Trade	W. Graham
Minister of Agriculture	N. Buxton (to June 1930)
	C. Addison (from June 1930)
President, Board of Education	Sir C. P. Trevelyan (to Mar. 1931)
	H. B. Lees-Smith (from Mar. 1931)
First Commissioner of Works	G. Lansbury
Minister of Labour	M. Bondfield
Minister of Health	Arthur Greenwood
Minister of Transport	H. Morrison (in cabinet from Mar. 1931)

Attlee's Cabinet, July 1945 to Oct. 1951

Prime Minister	C. R. Attlee
Lord Chancellor	Lord Jowitt
Lord President	H. Morrison (to Mar. 1951)
	Lord Addison (from Mar. 1951)
Lord Privy Seal	Arthur Greenwood (to Apr. 1947)
	Lord Inman (Apr. to Oct. 1947)
	Lord Addison (Oct. 1947 to Mar. 1951)
	E. Bevin (Mar. to Apr. 1951)
	R. Stokes (from Apr. 1951)
Chancellor of the Exchequer	H. Dalton (to Nov. 1947)
	Sir S. Cripps (Nov. 1947 to Oct. 1950)
	H. Gaitskell (from Oct. 1950)
Minister of Economic Affairs	Sir S. Cripps (Sep. to Nov. 1947)
Home Secretary	C. Ede
Foreign Secretary	E. Bevin (to Mar. 1951)
	H. Morrison (from Mar. 1951)
Colonial Secretary	G. Hall (to Oct. 1946)
	A. Creech Jones (Oct. 1946 to Feb. 1950)
	J. Griffiths (from Feb. 1950)
Dominions Secretary (Commonwealth Relations from July 1947)	Lord Addison (to Oct. 1947)
	P. Noel-Baker (Oct. 1947 to Feb. 1950)
	P. Gordon Walker (from Feb. 1950)
Defence Secretary	C. R. Attlee (to Dec. 1946)
	A. V. Alexander (Dec. 1946 to Feb. 1950)

	E. Shinwell (from Feb. 1950)
War Secretary	J. Lawson (to Oct. 1946)
Indian Secretary	Lord Pethick-Lawrence (to Apr. 1947)
	Earl of Listowel (Apr. to Aug 1947)
Scottish Secretary	J. Westwood (to Oct. 1947)
	A. Woodburn (Oct. 1947 to Feb. 1950)
	H. McNeil (from Feb. 1950)
Air Secretary	Viscount Stansgate (to Oct. 1946)
Minister of Civil Aviation	Lord Pakenham (May 1948 to Feb. 1950)
First Lord of Admiralty	A. V. Alexander (to Oct. 1946)
Chancellor, Duchy of Lancaster	H. Dalton (May 1948 to Feb. 1950)
	Viscount Alexander (from Feb. 1950)
President, Board of Trade	Sir S. Cripps (to Sep. 1947)
	H. Wilson (Sep. 1947 to Apr. 1951)
	Sir H. Shawcross (from Apr. 1951)
Minister of Agriculture	T. Williams
Minister of Education	E. Wilkinson (to Feb. 1947)
	G. Tomlinson (from Feb. 1947)
Minister of Labour and National Service	G. Isaacs (to Jan. 1951)
	A. Bevan (Jan. to Apr. 1951)
	A. Robens (from Apr. 1951)
Minister of Health	A. Bevan (to Jan. 1951)
Minister, Town & Country Planning	H. Dalton (from Feb. 1950)
Paymaster-General	Arthur Greenwood (July 1946 to Mar. 1947)
	Viscount Addison (July 1948 to Apr. 1949)
Minister of Fuel and Power	E. Shinwell (to Oct. 1947)
Minister without Portfolio	A. V. Alexander (Oct. to Dec. 1946)
	Arthur Greenwood (Apr. to Sep. 1947)

Wilson's Cabinet, Oct. 1964 to June 1970

Prime Minister	H. Wilson
First Secretary of State	G. Brown (to Aug. 1966)
	M. Stewart (Aug. 1966 to Mar. 1968)
	B. Castle (from Apr. 1968)
Lord Chancellor	Lord Gardiner
Lord President	H. Bowden (to Aug. 1966)

	R. Crossman (Aug. 1966 to Oct. 1968)
	F. Peart (from Oct. 1968)
Lord Privy Seal	Earl of Longford (to Dec. 1965)
	Sir F. Soskice (Dec. 1965 to Apr. 1966)
	Earl of Longford (Apr. 1966 to Jan. 1968)
	Lord Shackleton (Jan. to Apr. 1968)
	F. Peart (Apr. to Oct. 1968)
	Lord Shackleton (from Oct. 1968)
Chancellor of the Exchequer	J. Callaghan (to Nov. 1967)
	R. Jenkins (from Nov. 1967)
Chief Secretary to Treasury	J. Diamond (from Nov. 1968)
Economic Affairs Secretary	G. Brown (to Aug. 1966)
	M. Stewart (Aug. 1966 to Aug. 1967)
	P. Shore (Aug. 1967 to Oct. 1969)
Home Secretary	Sir F. Soskice (to Dec. 1965)
	R. Jenkins (Dec. 1965 to Nov. 1967)
	J. Callaghan (from Nov. 1967)
Foreign Secretary	P. Gordon Walker (to Jan 1965)
	M. Stewart (Jan. 1965 to Aug. 1966)
	G. Brown (Aug. 1966 to Mar. 1968)
	M. Stewart (from Mar. 1968)
Commonwealth Secretary	A. Bottomley (to Aug. 1966)
	H. Bowden (Aug. 1966 to Aug. 1967)
	G. Thomson (Aug. 1967 to Oct. 1968)
Scottish Secretary	W. Ross
Welsh Secretary	J. Griffiths (to Apr. 1966)
	C. Hughes (Apr. 1966 to Apr. 1968)
	G. Thomas (from Apr. 1968)
Chancellor, Duchy of Lancaster	D. Houghton (to Apr. 1966)
	G. Thomson (from Oct. 1969)
President, Board of Trade	D. Jay (to Aug. 1967)
	A. Crosland (Aug. 1967 to Oct. 1969)
	R. Mason (from Oct. 1969)
Minister of Technology	F. Cousins (to July 1966)
	A. Benn (from July 1966)
Minister of Agriculture	F. Peart (to Apr. 1968)
	C. Hughes (from Apr. 1968)

Education Secretary	M. Stewart (to Jan. 1965)
	A. Crosland (Jan. 1965 to Aug. 1967)
	P. Gordon Walker (Aug. 1967 to Apr. 1968)
	E. Short (from Apr. 1968)
Minister of Labour	R. Gunter (to Apr. 1968)
Employment Secretary	B. Castle (from Apr. 1968)
Minister, Housing & Local Govt.	R. Crossman (to Aug. 1966)
	Anthony Greenwood (Aug. 1966 to Oct. 1969)
Minister, Local Govt. & Planning	A. Crosland (from Oct. 1969)
Health and Social Security Secretary	R. Crossman (from Nov. 1968)
Paymaster-General	Lord Shackleton (Apr. to Nov. 1968)
	J. Hart (Nov. 1948 to Oct. 1969)
	H. Lever (from Oct. 1969)
Minister of Power	F. Lee (to Apr. 1966)
	R. Marsh (Apr. 1966 to Apr. 1968)
	R. Gunter (Apr. to July 1968)
	R. Mason (July 1968 to Oct. 1969)
Minister of Transport	T. Fraser (to Dec. 1965)
	B. Castle (Dec. 1965 to Apr. 1968)
	R. Marsh (Apr. 1968 to Oct. 1969)
Minister without Portfolio	D. Houghton (Apr. 1966 to Jan. 1967)
	P. Gordon Walker (Jan. to Aug. 1967)
	G. Thomson (Oct. 1968 to Oct. 1969)
	P. Shore (from Oct. 1969)

Wilson's and Callaghan's Cabinets, Mar. 1974 to May 1979

Prime Minister	H. Wilson (to Apr. 1976)
	J. Callaghan (from Apr. 1976)
Lord Chancellor	Lord Elwyn-Jones
Lord President	E. Short (to Apr. 1976)
	M. Foot (from Apr. 1976)
Lord Privy Seal	Lord Shepherd (to Sep. 1976)
	Lord Peart (from Sep. 1976)
Chancellor of the Exchequer	D. Healey
Parl. Sec. to Treasury	R. Mellish (July 1974 to Apr. 1976)
Chief Sec. to Treasury	J. Barnett (from Feb. 1977)

Home Secretary	R. Jenkins (to Sep. 1976)
	M. Rees (from Sep. 1976)
Foreign Secretary	J. Callaghan (to Apr. 1976)
	A. Crosland (Apr. 1976 to Feb. 1977)
	D. Owen (from Feb. 1977)
Minister of Overseas Development	R. Prentice (June 1975 to Dec. 1976)
Defence Secretary	R. Mason (to Sep. 1976)
	F. Mulley (from Sep. 1976)
Scottish Secretary	W. Ross (to Apr. 1976)
	B. Millan (from Apr. 1976)
Welsh Secretary	J. Morris
Northern Ireland Secretary	M. Rees (to Sep. 1976)
	R. Mason (from Sep. 1976)
Chancellor, Duchy of Lancaster	H. Lever
Trade Secretary	P. Shore (to Apr. 1976)
	E. Dell (Apr. 1976 to Nov. 1978)
	J. Smith (from Nov. 1978)
Industry Secretary	A. Benn (to June 1975)
	E. Varley (from June 1975)
Minister of Agriculture	F. Peart (to Sep. 1976)
	J. Silkin (from Sep. 1976)
Education Secretary	R. Prentice (to June 1975)
	F. Mulley (June 1975 to Sep. 1976)
	S. Williams (from Sep. 1976)
Employment Secretary	M. Foot (to Apr. 1976)
	A. Booth (from Apr. 1976)
Environment Secretary	A. Crosland (to Apr. 1976)
	P. Shore (from Apr. 1976)
Minister, Planning & Local Govt.	J. Silkin (Oct. 1974 to Sep. 1976)
Health and Social Security Sec.	B. Castle (to Apr. 1976)
	D. Ennals (from Apr. 1976)
Minister of Social Security	S. Orme (from Sep. 1976)
Minister, Prices & Consumer Protection	S. Williams (to Sep. 1976)
	R. Hattersley (from Sep. 1976)
Energy Secretary	E. Varley (to June 1975)
	A. Benn (from June 1975)
Minister of Transport	W. Rodgers (from Sep. 1976)

Notes

(Place of publication is London unless otherwise stated.)

Introduction

1. Labour party, *Annual Report, 1929* (1929), pp. 150–3; A. Howard, '"We Are the Masters Now"', in M. Sissons and P. French (eds.), *Age of Austerity 1945–1951* (1963), p. 16; H. Wilson, *A Prime Minister on Prime Ministers* (1977), p. 211.
2. R. Miliband, *Parliamentary Socialism: A Study in the Politics of Labour* (1961), esp. p. 13.
3. D. Coates, *The Labour Party and the Struggle for Socialism* (Cambridge, 1975), p. 230; see also D. Howell, *British Social Democracy: A Study in Development and Decay* (1976).

1 Creation and Early Years 1900–14

1. Labour Party, *Labour Party Foundation Conference and Annual reports, 1900–1905* (1967), pp. 18, 23, 16.
2. H. Pelling, *A History of British Trade Unionism* (4th edn., 1987), p. 73.
3. D. Tanner, *Political Change and the Labour Party, 1900–1918* (Cambridge, 1990), p. 102.
4. D. Hamer, *Liberal Politics in the Age of Gladstone and Rosebery: A Study in Leadership and Policy* (Oxford, 1972), pp. 307–8.
5. W. Lancaster, *Radicalism, Co-operation and Socialism: Leicester Working-Class Politics 1860–1906* (Leicester, 1987), p. 109.
6. A. J. Reid, 'The Division of Labour and Politics in Britain, 1880–1920', in W. J. Mommsen and H. G. Husung (eds.), *The Development of Trade Unionism in Great Britain and Germany, 1880–1914* (1985), p. 150.
7. J. Benson, *The Working Class in England, 1875–1914* (1985), p. 68.
8. J. Zeitlin, 'Industrial Structure, Employer Strategy and the Diffusion of Job Control in Britain, 1880–1920', in Mommsen and Husung, *Development of Trade Unionism*, p. 325.
9. D. Blaazer, *The Popular Front and the Progressive Tradition: Socialists, Liberals and the Quest for Unity, 1884–1939* (Cambridge, 1992), p. 47.
10. R. Price and G. S. Bain, 'The Labour Force', in A. H. Halsey (ed.), *British Social Trends since 1900: A Guide to the Changing Social Structure of Britain* (1988), p. 186.
11. See N. Thompson, *The Market and Its Critics: Socialist Political Economy in Nineteenth-Century Britain* (1988), esp. pp. 281–6.

251

12. See e.g. A. J. Reid, 'Old Unionism Reconsidered: The Radicalism of Robert Knight, 1870–1900', in E. F. Biagini and A. J. Reid (eds.), *Currents of Radicalism: Popular Radicalism, Organised Labour and Party Politics in Britain, 1850–1914* (Cambridge, 1991), pp. 214–43.
13. Labour Party, *Labour Party Foundation Conference*, p. 17.
14. Ibid., p. 20.
15. H. Pelling, *The Origins of the Labour Party, 1880–1900* (2nd edn., Oxford, 1965), p. 230.
16. D. Marquand, *Ramsay MacDonald* (1977), p. 51.
17. D. Howell, *British Workers and the Independent Labour Party 1888–1906* (Manchester, 1983), p. 22.
18. Labour Party, *Labour Party Foundation Conference*, p. 87.
19. Ibid., pp. 210, 202.
20. F. Bealey and H. Pelling, *Labour and Politics 1900–1906: A History of the Labour Representation Committee* (1958), p. 132.
21. E. F. Biagini, 'Popular Liberals, Gladstonian Finance and the Debate on Taxation, 1860–1874', in Biagini and Reid, *Currents of Radicalism*, pp. 135–6.
22. D. Tanner, 'Ideological Debate in Edwardian Labour Politics: Radicalism, Revisionism and Socialism', in Biagini and Reid, *Currents of Radicalism*, p. 292.
23. Tanner, *Political Change*, pp. 22–3.
24. See e.g. F. Williams, *Fifty Years' March: The Rise of the Labour Party* (1948), pp. 148–58.
25. D. E. Martin, 'Ideology and Composition', in K. D. Brown (ed.), *The First Labour Party, 1906–1914* (1985), pp. 17–37.
26. C. J. Wrigley, *Arthur Henderson* (Cardiff, 1990), p. 63.
27. J. Harris, *Unemployment and Politics: A Study in English Social Policy, 1886–1914* (Oxford, 1972), pp. 242–4.
28. J. Schneer, *Ben Tillett: Portrait of a Labour Leader* (1982), pp. 133–6.
29. Author's calculations based on figures in H. Pelling, *A Short History of the Labour Party* (8th edn., 1985), p. 193.
30. J. Shepherd, 'Labour and Parliament: The Lib–Labs as the First Working-Class MPs, 1885–1906', in Biagini and Reid, *Currents of Radicalism*, pp. 187–213.
31. Howell, *British Workers*, pp. 50–1; C. Baylies, *The History of the Yorkshire Miners, 1881–1918* (1993), pp. 261, 264.
32. R. Gregory, *The Miners in British Politics, 1906–1914* (Oxford, 1968), p. 29.
33. Ibid., pp. 29, 32, 188.
34. R. I. McKibbin, *The Evolution of the Labour Party, 1910–1924* (Oxford, 1974), p. 1.
35. Ibid., pp. 1–2.
36. M. G. Sheppard and J. L. Halstead, 'Labour's Municipal Election Performance in Provincial England and Wales, 1901–13', *Bulletin of the Society for the Study of Labour History*, 39 (1979), pp. 39–62.
37. McKibbin, *Evolution*, p. 72.
38. Tanner, *Political Change*, p. 321.
39. Pelling, *British Trade Unionism*, pp. 297–8, and Pelling, *Short History*,

p. 193, for these and the other figures in this and the next paragraph.

40. S. Boston, *Women Workers and the Trade Union Movement* (1980), pp. 73–8.
41. See e.g. H. Mitchell, *The Hard Way Up* (1977); C. Collette, *For Labour and For Women: The Women's Labour League, 1906–1918* (Manchester, 1989); P. Thane, 'The Women of the British Labour Party and Feminism, 1906–1945', in H. L. Smith (ed.), *British Feminism in the Twentieth Century* (Aldershot, 1990), pp. 124–43.
42. M. Pugh, 'Labour and Women's Suffrage', in K. D. Brown (ed.), *The First Labour Party, 1906–1914* (1985), pp. 233–53.
43. R. Challinor, *The Origins of British Bolshevism* (1977), p. 121; W. Kendall, *The Revolutionary Movement in Britain, 1900–1921: The Origins of British Communism* (1969), esp. pp. 28–31, 45, 63–76; M. Crick, *The History of the Social Democratic Federation* (Keele, 1994), pp. 222–60.
44. J. White, 'Syndicalism in a Mature Industrial Setting: The Case of Britain', in M. van der Linden and W. Thorpe (eds.), *Revolutionary Syndicalism: An International Perspective* (Aldershot, 1990), pp. 101–18.
45. See G. D. H. Cole, *The World of Labour* (1913); A. Wright, *G. D. H. Cole and Socialist Democracy* (Oxford, 1979).
46. C. Howard, 'MacDonald, Henderson, and the Outbreak of War, 1914', *Historical Journal*, 20 (1977), p. 872; McKibbin, *Evolution*, p. 76.
47. Tanner, *Political Change*, pp. 317–37.

2 The Surge to Second-Party Status, 1914–22

1. Howard, 'MacDonald, Henderson, and the Outbreak of War'; J. N. Horne, *Labour at War: France and Britain, 1914–1918* (Oxford, 1991), pp. 42–5.
2. R. Harrison, 'The War Emergency Workers' National Committee, 1914–1920', in A. Briggs and J. Saville, *Essays in Labour History, 1886–1923* (1971), pp. 212–15.
3. J. Turner, *British Politics and the Great War: Coalition and Conflict, 1915–1918* (1992), pp. 70, 78–90.
4. Wrigley, *Henderson*, p. 107.
5. Turner, *British Politics*, pp. 205–9.
6. Marquand, *MacDonald*, p. 179.
7. Harrison, 'War Emergency Workers' National Committee', pp. 217–24.
8. B. Waites, *A Class Society at War: England, 1914–1918* (Leamington Spa, 1987), pp. 190, 231–5.
9. J. M. McEwen, 'Lloyd George's Liberal Supporters in December 1916: A Note', *Bulletin of the Institute of Historical Research*, 53 (1980), pp. 265–72.
10. Tanner, *Political Change*, p. 427.
11. Ibid., p. 382.
12. M. Pinto-Duschinsky, *British Political Finance, 1830–1980* (Washington, DC, 1981), p. 84.

13. H. C. G. Matthew, R. I. McKibbin and J. Kay, 'The Franchise Factor in the Rise of the Labour Party', *English Historical Review*, 91 (1976), pp. 723–52.
14. D. Tanner, 'The Parliamentary Electoral System, the "Fourth" Reform Act and the Rise of Labour in England and Wales', *Bulletin of the Institute of Historical Research*, 56 (1983), pp. 205–19.
15. Pelling, *History of British Trade Unionism*, p. 298.
16. Pelling, *Short History*, p. 193.
17. R. Price, *Labour in British Society: An Interpretative History* (1986), pp. 158–9.
18. For the alternative view, see J. Hinton, *The First Shop Stewards' Movement* (1973), esp. pp. 254, 330–7.
19. S. and B. Webb, *The Consumers' Co-operative Movement* (1921), pp. 17–18.
20. A. Bonner, *British Co-operation: The History, Principles and Organisation of the British Co-operative Movement* (rev. edn., Manchester, 1970), pp. 132–3; T. F. Carbery, *Consumers in Politics: A History and General Review of the Co-operative Party* (Manchester, 1969), pp. 3, 17; S. Pollard, 'The Foundation of the Co-operative Party', in Briggs and Saville, *Essays in Labour History, 1886–1923*, pp. 185–210; T. Adams, 'The Formation of the Co-operative Party Reconsidered', *International Review of Social History*, 32 (1987), pp. 48–68.
21. J. Melling, 'Work, Culture and Politics on "Red Clydeside": the ILP during the First World War', in A. McKinlay and R. J. Morris (eds.), *The ILP on Clydeside, 1893–1932: From Foundation to Disintegration* (Manchester, 1991), pp. 106–14.
22. P. E. Dewey, 'Nutrition and Living Standards in Wartime Britain', in R. Wall and J. M. Winter, *The Upheaval of War: Family, Work and Welfare in Europe, 1914–1918* (Cambridge, 1988), pp. 201–2.
23. See e.g. L. C. Money, *The Triumph of Nationalization* (1920), esp. pp. vii–viii.
24. A. J. A. Morris, *Radicalism Against War: The Advocacy of Peace and Retrenchment* (1972), pp. 28, 204–5.
25. C. A. Cline, *Recruits to Labour: The British Labour Party 1914–1931* (Syracuse, 1963), pp. 8–23.
26. Horne, *Labour at War*, p. 221.
27. J. M. Winter, 'Arthur Henderson, the Russian Revolution, and the Reconstruction of the Labour Party', *Historical Journal*, 15 (1972), p. 755.
28. Cline, *Recruits to Labour*, pp. 20–2; M. Swartz, *The Union of Democratic Control in British Politics during the First World War* (Oxford, 1971), pp. 168–9.
29. Ibid., p. 199.
30. McKibbin, *Evolution*, pp. 90–1.
31. G. D. H. Cole, *A History of the Labour Party from 1914* (1948), pp. 47–8.
32. McKibbin, *Evolution*, p. 100.
33. Wright, *G. D. H. Cole*, pp. 43–7, 280; L. P. Carpenter, *G. D. H. Cole: An Intellectual Biography* (Cambridge, 1973), pp. 71–111.

34. Cole, *History of the Labour Party*, p. 55.
35. Turner, *British Politics*, p. 318.
36. Ibid., p. 404.
37. See e.g. M. Kinnear, *The Fall of Lloyd George: The Political Crisis of 1922* (1973), p. 32.
38. J. E. Cronin, *Labour and Society in Britain, 1918–1979* (1983), pp. 241–3; C. J. Wrigley, *Lloyd George and the Challenge of Labour: The Post-War Coalition, 1918–1922* (Hemel Hempstead, 1990), pp. 249–50.
39. Quoted in Cole, *History*, p. 105.
40. Quoted in R. I. McKibbin, 'Arthur Henderson as Labour Leader', *International Review of Social History*, 23 (1978), p. 93.
41. Wrigley, *Lloyd George and the Challenge of Labour*, p. 271; K. O. Morgan, *Consensus and Disunity: The Lloyd George Coalition Government, 1918–1922* (Oxford, 1979), p. 221.
42. D. H. Aldcroft, *The British Economy, Volume 1: Years of Turmoil, 1920–1951* (Brighton, 1986), pp. 5–6.
43. P. S. Bagwell, 'The Triple Industrial Alliance, 1913–1922', in Briggs and Saville, *Essays in Labour History, 1886–1923*, pp. 117–18.
44. McKibbin, *Evolution*, pp. 124–5, 137–9, 141, 143, 213.
45. C. J. Howard, 'Expectations Born to Death: Local Labour Party Expansion in the 1920s', in J. M. Winter (ed.), *The Working Class in Modern British History: Essays in Honour of Henry Pelling* (Cambridge, 1983), pp. 77–8.
46. Ibid., p. 71; McKibbin, *Evolution*, p. 147.
47. McKibbin, *Evolution*, pp. 221–34; S. Koss, *The Rise and Fall of the Political Press in Britain* (paperback edn., 1990), pp. 920–1.
48. McKibbin, *Evolution*, pp. 157–8.

3 Progress and Collapse, 1922–31

1. Calculations by the author based on the 1931 *Census*.
2. P. Williamson, 'The Doctrinal Politics of Stanley Baldwin', in M. Bentley (ed.), *Public and Private Doctrine: Essays in British History Presented to Maurice Cowling* (Cambridge, 1993), pp. 194–5.
3. C. Cook, *The Age of Alignment: Electoral Politics in Britain, 1922–1929* (1975), p. 149.
4. L. Radice, *Beatrice and Sidney Webb: Fabian Socialists* (1984), p. 239.
5. Marquand, *MacDonald*, p. 299; M. I. Cole (ed.), *Beatrice Webb's Diaries, 1924–1932* (1956), pp. 1–2, entry for 18 Jan. 1924.
6. R. W. Lyman, *The First Labour Government, 1924* (1958), p. 102; Marquand, *MacDonald*, pp. 301–3.
7. Cook, *Age of Alignment*, pp. 201–2, 216, 221–2, 265.
8. R. E. Dowse, *Left in the Centre: The Independent Labour Party, 1893–1940* (1966), pp. 102–3; Marquand, *MacDonald*, p. 297.
9. For 'economic internationalism', see R. W. D. Boyce, *British Capitalism at the Crossroads, 1919–1932: A Study in Politics, Economics and International Relations* (Cambridge, 1987), pp. 13–18.
10. Lyman, *First Labour Government*, pp. 230–47; Cook, *Age of Alignment*, p. 201; Marquand, *MacDonald*, pp. 357–61, 364–78.

11. There are solid grounds for believing the Letter was genuine. See C. Andrew, *Secret Service: The Making of the British Intelligence Community* (1985), pp. 301–16.
12. Cook, *Age of Alignment*, pp. 199–201.
13. A. Thorpe, 'The Industrial Meaning of "Gradualism": The Labour Party and Industry, 1918–1931', *Journal of British Studies*, 35 (1996), pp. 84–113.
14. A. Bullock, *The Life and Times of Ernest Bevin, Volume 1: Trade Union Leader, 1881–1940* (1960), pp. 258–60.
15. C. Cross, *Philip Snowden* (1966), p. 214; Marquand, *MacDonald*, pp. 391–2.
16. A. Morgan, *J. Ramsay MacDonald* (Manchester, 1987), p. 132.
17. H. A. Clegg, *A History of British Trade Unions since 1889, Volume 2: 1911–1933* (Oxford, 1985), p. 381.
18. Ibid., pp. 422–3; P. Renshaw, 'The Depression Years', in B. Pimlott and C. Cook (eds.), *Trade Unions in British Politics: The First 250 Years* (1991), p. 100.
19. See esp. C. Howard, 'Expectations Born to Death: Local Labour Party Expansion in the 1920s', in J. M. Winter (ed.), *The Working Class in Modern British History: Essays in Honour of Henry Pelling* (Cambridge, 1983), pp. 65–81.
20. H. Dewar, *Communist Politics in Britain: The CPGB From its Origins to the Second World War* (1976), p. 38.
21. R. W. Garner, 'Ideology and Electoral Politics in Labour's Rise to Major Party Status, 1918–1931', unpublished Ph.D. thesis, University of Manchester, 1988, pp. 220–1.
22. P. Graves, *Labour Women: Women in British Working-Class Politics, 1918–1939* (Cambridge, 1994), p. 223.
23. J. E. Cronin, *The Politics of State Expansion: War, State and Society in Twentieth-Century Britain* (1991), p. 117.
24. Labour party, *Annual Report, 1928* (1928), p. 212.
25. R. H. Tawney, 'The Choice Before the Labour Party', *Political Quarterly*, 1932, reprinted in W. A. Robson (ed.), *The Political Quarterly in the Thirties* (1971), p. 98.
26. See e.g. B. Pimlott (ed.), *The Political Diary of Hugh Dalton, 1918–1940, 1945–1960* (1986), p. 47.
27. K. Laybourn, *Philip Snowden: A Biography* (Aldershot, 1988), pp. 110–12.
28. E. Wertheimer, *Portrait of the Labour Party* (1929), p. 177.
29. Dowse, *Left in the Centre*, pp. 130–46.
30. A. Thorpe, *The British General Election of 1931* (Oxford, 1991), pp. 8–10.
31. Marquand, *MacDonald*, pp. 489–91.
32. See Thorpe, *1931*, pp. 49–56; P. Williamson, *National Crisis and National Government: British Politics, the Economy and Empire, 1926–1932* (Cambridge, 1992), pp. 204–5, 207–12.
33. D. Carlton, *MacDonald versus Henderson: The Foreign Policy of the Second Labour Government* (1970), pp. 48, 124–7, 98–9; C. Wrigley, *Arthur Henderson* (Cardiff, 1990), p. 168.

34. Thorpe, 'Industrial Meaning of "Gradualism"', pp. 109–10.
35. Ibid., p. 104.
36. R. Skidelsky, *Politicians and the Slump: The Labour Government of 1929–1931* (1967), pp. 171–82; R. Skidelsky, *Oswald Mosley* (1975), pp. 199–201.
37. Ibid., pp. 201–45.
38. Skidelsky, *Politicians and the Slump*, pp. 389–92.
39. Thorpe, *1931*, pp. 61–2.
40. For fuller discussion of these issues, see A. Thorpe, *Britain in the 1930s* (Oxford, 1992), pp. 77–83.
41. Marquand, *MacDonald*, pp. 554–64.
42. Thorpe, *1931*, pp. 23–4.
43. F. Owen, *Tempestuous Journey: Lloyd George, His Life and Times* (1954), p. 717; Marquand, *MacDonald*, pp. 602–3; Williamson, *National Crisis*, pp. 234–42.
44. R. Shackleton, 'Trade Unions and the Slump', in Pimlott and Cook, *Trade Unions*, pp. 110–12; Thorpe, *1931*, pp. 14–19.
45. For more detail on the remainder of this chapter, see ibid., pp. 63–93, 127–53, 219–71.
46. See P. Williamson, 'A "Bankers' Ramp"'? Financiers and the British Political Crisis of August 1931', *English Historical Review*, 99 (1984), pp. 770–806.
47. F. W. S. Craig, *British Electoral Facts, 1832–1980* (Chichester, 1981), p. 162.

4 Remaking the Party? 1931–9

1. Thorpe, *1931*, pp. 270–1.
2. Shackleton, 'Trade Unions and the Slump', p. 112.
3. W. Knox, *James Maxton* (Manchester, 1987), p. 98.
4. Dowse, *Left in the Centre*, p. 184.
5. Ibid., p. 185; J. Jupp, *The Radical Left in Britain, 1931–1941* (1982), p. 35.
6. Ibid., p. 69.
7. B. Pimlott, *Labour and the Left in the 1930s* (Cambridge, 1977), p. 49.
8. Labour party, NEC minutes, 10 Nov. 1931, 'Report on the General Election by the Secretary' [Henderson].
9. Labour party, *Annual Report, 1932* (1932), pp. 204–5.
10. Wrigley, *Henderson*, p. 180; Pimlott, *Labour and the Left*, p. 22.
11. Bullock, *Bevin, Volume 1*, pp. 511–12.
12. G. D. H. Cole, *The Next Ten Years: In British Social and Economic Policy* (1929), pp. 37–8, 134.
13. Pimlott, *Labour and the Left*, pp. 36–40; E. Durbin, *New Jerusalems: The Labour Party and the Economics of Democratic Socialism* (1985), pp. 73–83.
14. S. Cripps, 'Can Socialism Come by Constitutional Methods?', in C. Addison et al., *Problems of a Socialist Government* (1933), pp. 35–66.
15. R. Miliband, *Parliamentary Socialism: A Study in the Politics of Labour* (2nd edn., 1972), pp. 229–30.
16. Pimlott, *Labour and the Left*, pp. 38, 54; Durbin, *New Jerusalems*, pp.

87–90; A. Booth and M. Pack, *Employment, Capital and Economic Policy: Great Britain, 1918–1939* (Oxford, 1985), pp. 125–33.

17. Pimlott, *Labour and the Left*, p. 49.
18. See e.g. S. and B. Webb, *A Constitution for the Socialist Commonwealth of Great Britain* (1920), pp. 213–15.
19. See e.g. R. H. Tawney, *The Acquisitive Society* (1921), p. 48; H. Laski, *A Grammar of Politics* (5th edn., 1967; 1st published 1925), p. 88; Cole, *Next Ten Years*, pp. 163–8.
20. Cole, *History of the Labour Party*, p. 452.
21. C. R. Attlee, *The Labour Party in Perspective* (1937), pp. 31–3, 141; Durbin, *New Jerusalems*, pp. 156–7; G. Walker, *Thomas Johnston* (Manchester, 1988), p. 170.
22. Tawney, 'Choice Before the Labour Party', pp. 103–4.
23. Cronin, *Labour and Society*, pp. 241–2.
24. Pimlott, *Labour and the Left*, p. 201.
25. Williamson, *National Crisis*, pp. 514–15.
26. G. Peele, 'Revolt over India', in G. Peele and C. Cook, *The Politics of Reappraisal* (1975), pp. 114–45; F. Miller, 'The British Unemployment Assistance Crisis of 1935', *Journal of Contemporary History*, 14 (1979), pp. 329–52.
27. E. Estorick, *Stafford Cripps: A Biography* (1949), p. 141.
28. K. Harris, *Attlee* (1982), pp. 111–18.
29. Pimlott, *Political Diary of Hugh Dalton*, p. 191.
30. See Pimlott, *Labour and the Left*, pp. 73–5; H. Dalton, *The Fateful Years: Memoirs, 1931–1945* (1957), pp. 79–82; Harris, *Attlee*, pp. 121–2; B. Donoughue and G. W. Jones, *Herbert Morrison: Portrait of a Politician* (1973), p. 239.
31. Cole, *History of the Labour Party*, pp. 458–9.
32. See e.g. C. Cooke, *The Life of Richard Stafford Cripps* (1957), p. 173.
33. Bullock, *Bevin, Volume 1*, pp. 528, 593–4; Pimlott, *Dalton*, pp. 241–2.
34. Dalton, *Fateful Years*, p. 44.
35. Ibid., pp. 132–3; Pimlott, *Dalton*, pp. 241–2.
36. This paragraph draws heavily on T. Buchanan, *The Spanish Civil War and the British Labour Movement* (Cambridge, 1991).
37. Pimlott, *Labour and the Left*, pp. 95–7.
38. Ibid., p. 106.
39. Dalton, *Fateful Years*, p. 202.
40. I. McLean, 'Oxford and Bridgwater', in C. Cook and J. Ramsden (eds.), *By-Elections in British Politics* (1973), pp. 140–64.
41. G. Tregidga, 'The Liberal Party in Cornwall, 1918–1939', unpublished M. Phil. thesis, University of Exeter, 1991, pp. 234–42.
42. Pimlott, *Labour and the Left*, p. 171.
43. Ibid., p. 180.
44. K. Martin, *Harold Laski (1893–1950): A Biographical Memoir* (1953), p. 110.
45. Pimlott, *Labour and the Left*, pp. 134–40.
46. Durbin, *New Jerusalems*, pp. 243–8.
47. S. Brooke, *Labour's War: The Labour Party During the Second World War* (Oxford, 1992), p. 32.

48. E. F. M. Durbin, *The Politics of Democratic Socialism* (1940), pp. 146–7.

5 The Impact of the Second World War, 1939–45

1. Brooke, *Labour's War*, pp. 34–5, 75.
2. Ibid., p. 37.
3. Ibid., pp. 40–1.
4. Ibid., p. 43.
5. J. Campbell, *Nye Bevan and the Mirage of British Socialism* (1987), p. 84; Estorick, *Cripps*, p. 326.
6. W. Citrine, *My Finnish Diary* (Harmondsworth, 1940), p. 5.
7. Labour party, national executive committee minutes, 20 Mar. 1940.
8. Labour party, *Annual Report, 1941* (1941), p. 20.
9. Labour party, national executive committee minutes, 17 Apr. 1940.
10. Brooke, *Labour's War*, pp. 46–54; K. Jefferys, *The Churchill Coalition and Wartime Politics, 1940–1945* (Manchester, 1991), pp. 21–7; Pimlott, *Dalton*, pp. 271–6.
11. A. Bullock, *The Life and Times of Ernest Bevin, Volume 2: Minister of Labour, 1940–1945* (1967), pp. 14–15.
12. T. D. Burridge, *British Labour and Hitler's War* (1976), pp. 16, 123–4.
13. P. Addison, *The Road to 1945: British Politics and the Second World War* (1975), p. 200.
14. Ibid., pp. 206–10.
15. Walker, *Johnston*, pp. 151–62; C. Harvie, 'Labour in Scotland during the Second World War', *Historical Journal*, 26 (1983), pp. 929–31, 944.
16. Pimlott, *Dalton*, pp. 400–7.
17. Campbell, *Bevan*, pp. 91–145; P. Slowe, *Manny Shinwell: An Authorized Biography* (1993), pp. 188–202.
18. Cronin, *Labour in British Society*, pp. 241–2; Pelling, *Short History*, pp. 193–4.
19. P. Summerfield, *Women Workers in the Second World War: Production and Patriarchy in Conflict* (1984), p. 157.
20. Bullock, *Bevin, Volume 2*, p. 22.
21. Membership figures in this and the next paragraph are from Pelling, *Short History*, p. 194.
22. R. P. Hastings, 'The Birmingham Labour Movement, 1918–1945', *Midland History*, 5 (1980), p. 88; A. Thorpe, 'The Consolidation of a Labour Stronghold, 1926–1951', in C. Binfield et al. (eds.), *The History of the City of Sheffield, Volume 1: Politics* (Sheffield, 1993), p. 110.
23. B. Pimlott (ed.), *The Second World War Diary of Hugh Dalton, 1940–1945* (1986), pp. 657–9, 725–6, 858, 823–4; D. Healey, *The Time of My Life* (1989), pp. 69–71.
24. Brooke, *Labour's War*, p. 43.
25. Ibid., pp. 108–9.
26. Jefferys, *Churchill Coalition*, pp. 117–22.
27. Brooke, *Labour's War*, pp. 260–1.
28. Quoted in Addison, *Road to 1945*, p. 256.
29. Ibid., p. 278.
30. See especially Brooke, *Labour's War*; Jefferys, *Churchill Coalition*.

31.   W. Beveridge, *Full Employment in a Free Society* (1944), p. 128; Jefferys, *Churchill Coalition*, p. 171.
32.   H. Jones, *Health and Society in Twentieth-Century Britain* (1994), pp. 108–12.
33.   K. Jefferys, 'British Politics and Social Policy during the Second World War', *Historical Journal*, 30 (1987), p. 140.
34.   See e.g. Thorpe, 'Consolidation of a Labour Stronghold', pp. 148–9.
35.   L. Johnman, 'The Labour Party and Industrial Policy, 1940–1945', in N. Tiratsoo (ed.), *The Attlee Years* (1991), pp. 42, 47.
36.   Quoted in Cole, *History of the Labour Party*, p. 411.
37.   Williams, *Fifty Years' March*, p. 358.
38.   See e.g. A. Marwick, *Britain in the Century of Total War: War, Peace and Social Change, 1900–1967* (1968), p. 328.
39.   H. Pelling, 'The Impact of the War on the Labour Party', in H. L. Smith (ed.), *War and Social Change: British Society in the Second World War* (Manchester, 1986), pp. 142–3.
40.   For more on this, see e.g. J. Lawrence, 'Popular politics and the Limitations of Party: Wolverhampton, 1867–1900', in Biagini and Reid, *Currents of Radicalism*, pp. 67, 84; S. Fielding, 'What did "The People" Want? The Meaning of the 1945 General Election', *Historical Journal*, 35 (1992), pp. 623–39.
41.   S. Fielding, P. Thompson and N. Tiratsoo, *'England Arise!' The Labour Party and Popular Politics in 1940s Britain* (Manchester, 1995), pp. 58, 68; Hastings, 'Birmingham Labour Movement', p. 87.
42.   Fielding et al., *'England Arise!'*, p. 64.

6 The Attlee Governments, 1945–51

1.   See e.g. D. Rubinstein, 'Socialism and the Labour Party: The Labour Left and Domestic Policy, 1945–1950', in D. E. Martin and D. Rubinstein (eds.), *Ideology and the Labour Movement: Essays Presented to John Saville* (1979), pp. 226–57.
2.   C. Barnett, *The Audit of War: The Illusion and Reality of Britain as a Great Nation* (1986).
3.   K. O. Morgan, *Labour in Power, 1945–1951* (Oxford, 1984), pp. 49–50.
4.   The phrase was Dalton's: see H. Dalton, *High Tide and After: Memoirs, 1945–1960* (1962), p. 187.
5.   Morgan, *Labour in Power*, pp. 350–8; Harris, *Attlee*, pp. 347–50.
6.   Ibid., pp. 353–4; Pimlott, *Dalton*, pp. 524–48.
7.   Donoughue and Jones, *Morrison*, p. 369.
8.   Morgan, *Labour in Power*, p. 60.
9.   M. Jones, *Michael Foot* (1994), p. 135.
10.   Morgan, *Labour in Power*, pp. 59–69.
11.   J. Schneer, *Labour's Conscience: The Labour Left, 1945–1951* (1988), pp. 155–6.
12.   D. E. Moggridge, *Maynard Keynes: An Economist's Biography* (1992), pp. 796–820.

13. K. O. Morgan, *Labour People: Leaders and Lieutenants from Hardie to Kinnock* (Oxford, 1987), pp. 162–3.
14. H. Pelling, *Britain and the Marshall Plan* (1988), p. 113.
15. B. Pimlott, *Harold Wilson* (1992), pp. 134–43.
16. F. W. S. Craig (ed.), *British General Election Manifestos, 1900–1974* (1975), p. 127.
17. Morgan, *Labour in Power*, pp. 110–21.
18. J. Dunkerley and P. Hare, 'Nationalized Industries', in N. F. R. Crafts and N. Woodward (eds.), *The British Economy since 1945* (Oxford, 1991), p. 388.
19. H. A. Clegg, *A History of British Trade Unions since 1889, Volume 3: 1934–1951* (Oxford, 1994), pp. 342–5; Schneer, *Labour's Conscience*, pp. 144–51.
20. Ibid., p. 147.
21. Williams, *Fifty Years' March*, p. 358.
22. Quoted in H. Mercer, 'The Labour Governments of 1945–51 and Private Industry', in Tiratsoo, *The Attlee Years*, p. 71.
23. L. Johnman, 'Labour and Industrial Policy, 1940–1945', in Tiratsoo, *The Attlee Years*, pp. 47–8.
24. Pimlott, *Wilson*, pp. 129–30.
25. J. Tomlinson, 'Planning: Debate and Policy in the 1940s', *Twentieth Century British History*, 3 (1992), pp. 154–74, but cf. S. Brooke, 'Problems of "Socialist Planning": Evan Durbin and the Labour Government of 1945', *Historical Journal*, 34 (1991), pp. 687–702.
26. Campbell, *Bevan*, pp. 165–85.
27. Morgan, *Labour in Power*, p. 172.
28. G. C. Peden, *British Economic and Social Policy: Lloyd George to Margaret Thatcher* (2nd edn., London, 1991), p. 146.
29. J. Harris, 'Did British Workers want the Welfare State? G. D. H. Cole's Survey of 1942', in Winter, *Working Class in Modern British History*, pp. 213–14.
30. N. Tiratsoo, 'Labour and the Reconstruction of Hull, 1945–51', in Tiratsoo, *The Attlee Years*, pp. 128, 135.
31. Morgan, *Labour in Power*, pp. 167, 170.
32. A. M. Carr–Saunders, D. Caradog Jones and C. A. Moser, *A Survey of Social Conditions in England and Wales* (Oxford, 1958), p. 40.
33. Peden, *British Economic and Social Policy*, p. 149.
34. J. Harris, 'War and Social History: Britain and the Home Front during the Second World War', *Contemporary European History*, 1 (1992), p. 25.
35. G. D. H. Cole, *Regional and Local Government* (1947), p. 47.
36. Schneer, *Labour's Conscience*, pp. 52–78.
37. Ibid., p. 75.
38. M. Gowing, 'Britain, America and the Bomb', in M. Dockrill and J. W. Young (eds.), *British Foreign Policy, 1945–1956* (1989), pp. 31–46.
39. Boyce, *British Capitalism at the Crossroads*, pp. 241–50.
40. J. W. Young, *Britain, France and the Unity of Europe, 1945–1951* (Leicester, 1984), pp. 185–6, 191.

41. A. Bullock, *Ernest Bevin, Foreign Secretary, 1945–1951* (Oxford, 1983), p. 348.
42. J. Gallacher, *The Decline, Revival and Fall of the British Empire* (Cambridge, 1982), pp. 144–5.
43. Ibid., p. 146.
44. J. Tomlinson, 'The Attlee Government and the Balance of Payments, 1945–1951', *Twentieth Century British History*, 2 (1991), pp. 63–4.
45. P. S. Gupta, 'Imperialism and the Labour Government of 1945–51', in Winter, *Working Class in Modern British History*, pp. 120–3.
46. Pelling, *Short History*, p. 194.
47. Craig, *British General Election Manifestos*, pp. 152–61.
48. A. Heath, R. Jowell and J. Curtice, *How Britain Votes* (Oxford, 1985), p. 30.
49. J. Hinton, 'Women and the Labour Vote, 1945–1950', *Labour History Review*, 57 (1992), pp. 59–66; N. Hart, 'Gender and the Rise and Fall of Class Politics', *New Left Review*, 175 (1989), p. 22.
50. H. G. Nicholas, *The British General Election of 1950* (1951), pp. 296.
51. Harris, *Attlee*, p. 460.
52. Ibid., p. 460; Pimlott, *Wilson*, pp. 156–7; P. Ziegler, *Wilson: The Authorized Life of Lord Wilson of Rievaulx* (London, 1993), pp. 80–2.
53. Campbell, *Bevan*, p. 246.
54. Ibid., pp. 245–50.
55. Craig (ed.), *British General Election Manifestos*, pp. 173–4.
56. C. Cook, 'Labour's Electoral Base', in C. Cook and I. Taylor (eds.), *The Labour Party: An Introduction to its History, Structure and Politics* (1980), p. 99.
57. Hart, 'Gender', p. 22.
58. D. E. Butler, *The British General Election of 1951* (1952), pp. 27, 271.
59. Ibid., p. 277.

7 Searching for a New Direction, 1951–64

1. Harris, *Attlee*, p. 495.
2. Campbell, *Bevan*, pp. 262–3.
3. P. M. Williams, *Hugh Gaitskell: A Political Biography* (1979), pp. 302–4.
4. S. Haseler, *The Gaitskellites: Revisionism in the British Labour Party, 1951–1964* (1969), p. 23.
5. Campbell, *Bevan*, pp. 296–300; Williams, *Gaitskell*, pp. 339–47.
6. Ibid., pp. 332–2.
7. Ibid., p. 319.
8. A. Bevan, *In Place of Fear* (1952), pp. 98, 103–5.
9. Campbell, *Bevan*, p. 264.
10. Price and Bain, 'The Labour Force', pp. 187–8, 191–2.
11. Pelling, *Short History*, p. 194.
12. Craig, *British General Election Manifestos*, pp. 202–8.
13. Heath et al., *How Britain Votes*, p. 30.
14. Hart, 'Gender', p. 22.
15. Pimlott, *Dalton*, p. 622.
16. Harris, *Attlee*, p. 499; Williams, *Gaitskell*, p. 300.

17. Ibid., pp. 361–7.
18. Ibid., p. 304.
19. Donoughue and Jones, *Morrison*, pp. 538–9.
20. Campbell, *Bevan*, p. 320.
21. J. Morgan (ed.), *The Backbench Diaries of Richard Crossman* (1981), p. 556.
22. Campbell, *Bevan*, p. 337; Jones, *Foot*, pp. 222–5; B. Castle, *Fighting all the Way* (1993), p. 256; I. Mikardo, *Back–Bencher* (1988), pp. 158–60.
23. For a rather different discussion of Bevan's motives, see Campbell, *Bevan*, pp. 339–40.
24. M. Donnelly, 'Labour Politics and the Affluent Society, 1951–1964', unpublished Ph.D. thesis, University of Surrey, 1995, pp. 92–125.
25. Pimlott, *Wilson*, p. 194.
26. T. Gallagher, *Glasgow, The Uneasy Peace: Religious Tension in Modern Scotland* (Manchester, 1987), pp. 271–2; E. Shaw, *Discipline and Discord in the Labour Party: The Politics of Managerial Control in the Labour Party, 1951–1987* (Manchester, 1988), pp. 78–83.
27. Shaw, *Discipline*, p. 81.
28. P. Seyd and P. Whiteley, *Labour's Grass Roots: The Politics of Party Membership* (Oxford, 1992), p. 18.
29. Pimlott, *Wilson*, pp. 195–6.
30. D. E. Butler and R. Rose, *The British General Election of 1959* (1960), p. 38.
31. Craig, *British General Election Manifestos*, pp. 223–32.
32. Williams, *Gaitskell*, pp. 525–9.
33. Butler and Rose, *1959*, pp. 211, 206, 216.
34. Heath et al., *How Britain Votes*, p. 30.
35. Hart, 'Gender', p. 22.
36. Butler and Rose, *1959*, p. 193.
37. M. Abrams and R. Rose, *Must Labour Lose?* (Harmondsworth, 1960), p. 23.
38. Ibid., p. 63.
39. J. H. Goldthorpe et al., *The Affluent Worker: Political Attitudes and Behaviour* (1968), p. 73.
40. Ibid., p. 76.
41. Heath et al., *How Britain Votes*, p. 30.
42. S. Berger and D. Broughton (eds.), *The Force of Labour: The Western European Labour Movement and the Working Class in the Twentieth Century* (Oxford, 1995), pp. 86–8, 253–4.
43. Pimlott, *Political Diary of Hugh Dalton*, p. 695.
44. Williams, *Gaitskell*, pp. 537–73; Haseler, *Gaitskellites*, pp. 158–77.
45. Williams, *Gaitskell*, p. 553.
46. Pimlott, *Wilson*, p. 213.
47. Williams, *Gaitskell*, pp. 612–13.
48. Pimlott, *Wilson*, pp. 237–45.
49. Haseler, *Gaitskellites*, pp. 227–36.
50. Pimlott, *Wilson*, pp. 252–64.
51. Ziegler, *Wilson*, pp. 143–4.

264 *Notes to pp. 154–163*

52. See e.g. H. Wilson, *The New Britain: Labour's Plan* (Harmondsworth, 1964), pp. 14–15.
53. Craig, *British General Election Manifestos*, pp. 255–72.
54. Heath et al., *How Britain Votes*, p. 30.
55. Ibid., p. 34.
56. Hart, 'Gender', p. 22.
57. P. Anderson, 'Problems of Socialist Strategy', in P. Anderson and R. Blackburn (eds.), *Towards Socialism* (1965), pp. 276–8.
58. D. E. Butler and A. King, *The British General Election of 1964* (1966), pp. 291, 311.

8 Wilson in Power, 1964–70

1. Condemnatory views include P. Foot, *The Politics of Harold Wilson* (Harmondsworth, 1968); C. Ponting, *Breach of Promise: Labour in Power, 1964–1970* (1989); and A. Morgan, *Harold Wilson* (1992). Among more sympathetic accounts, see especially Pimlott, *Wilson* and Ziegler, *Wilson*.
2. Ibid., p. 245.
3. Heath et al., *How Britain Votes*, p. 30.
4. Hart, 'Gender', p. 22.
5. Craig, *British General Election Manifestos*, p. 259.
6. R. Coopey, 'Industrial Policy in the White Heat of the Scientific Revolution', in R. Coopey, S. Fielding and N. Tiratsoo (eds.), *The Wilson Governments, 1964–1970* (1993), p. 103.
7. Pimlott, *Wilson*, p. 351.
8. J. Foreman-Peck, 'Trade and the Balance of Payments', in Crafts and Woodward, *British Economy since 1945*, p. 161.
9. Pimlott, *Wilson*, p. 424.
10. Foreman-Peck, 'Trade and the Balance of Payments', p. 168.
11. J. Tomlinson, *Public Policy and the Economy* (Oxford, 1990), p. 242.
12. S. Newton and D. Porter, *Modernization Frustrated: The Politics of Industrial Decline in Britain since 1900* (1985), p. 155.
13. R. Crossman, *The Diaries of a Cabinet Minister, Volume I: Minister of Housing, 1964–1966* (1975), p. 575.
14. Pimlott, *Wilson*, p. 353.
15. N. Woodward, 'Labour's Economic Performance, 1964–1970', in Coopey et al., *Wilson Governments*, p. 99.
16. T. Balogh, 'The Drift Towards Planning', in Anderson and Blackburn, *Towards Socialism*, p. 76.
17. D. Walker, 'The First Wilson Governments, 1964–1970', in P. Hennessy and A. Seldon (eds.), *Ruling Performance: British Governments from Attlee to Thatcher* (Oxford, 1987), p. 203.
18. S. Pollard, *The Development of the British Economy, 1914–1980* (1983), p. 345.
19. M. W. Kirby, 'Supply-Side Management', in Crafts and Woodward, *British Economy since 1945*, p. 246.
20. Walker, 'First Wilson Governments', p. 203; Pollard, *Development*, p. 345.

21. S. N. Broadberry, 'Unemployment', in Crafts and Woodward, *British Economy since 1945*, p. 212.
22. P. Browning, *The Treasury and Economic Policy, 1964–1985* (1986), pp. 17, 358.
23. N. W. C. Woodward, 'Inflation', in Crafts and Woodward, *British Economy since 1945*, pp. 197–8; D. E. Butler and M. Pinto-Duschinsky, *The British General Election of 1970* (1971), p. 439.
24. Woodward, 'Inflation', p. 199.
25. R. Richardson, 'Trade Unions and Industrial Policy', in Crafts and Woodward, *British Economy since 1945*, pp. 426–9.
26. J. Dunkerley and P. Hare, 'Nationalized Industries', in Crafts and Woodward, *British Economy since 1945*, p. 404; Tomlinson, *Public Policy*, p. 268.
27. See e.g. Jack Jones in *Tribune*, 11 Feb. 1966, reprinted in K. Coates and A. Topham, *Industrial Democracy in Great Britain: A Book of Readings and Witnesses for Workers' Control* (1968), pp. 372–3.
28. Coopey, 'Industrial Policy', p. 114.
29. N. K. Buxton, 'Introduction', in N. K. Buxton and D. H. Aldcroft (eds.), *British Industry Between the Wars: Instability and Development, 1919–1939* (1979), p. 19.
30. J. G. Watkins, 'Industrial Organization and Competition Policy', in Crafts and Woodward, *British Economy since 1945*, p. 379; Coopey, 'Industrial Policy', pp. 102–22.
31. Craig, *British General Election Manifestos*, p. 261.
32. H. W. Armstrong, 'Regional Problems and Policies', in Crafts and Woodward, *British Economy since 1945*, p. 315.
33. N. F. R. Crafts, 'Economic Growth', in Crafts and Woodward, *British Economy since 1945*, p. 261.
34. H. Perkin, *The Rise of Professional Society: England since 1880* (1989), p. 449.
35. Ponting, *Breach of Promise*, p. 133.
36. Ibid, p. 130.
37. G. Brown, *In My Way: The Political Memoirs of Lord George-Brown* (Pelican edn., Harmondsworth, 1972), p. 168.
38. Ponting, *Breach of Promise*, p. 122.
39. J. Parker and C. Mirrlees, 'Housing', in A. H. Halsey (ed.), *British Social Trends*, p. 384.
40. Ponting, *Breach of Promise*, p. 392.
41. Ibid., pp. 98–9.
42. Ibid., pp. 40–60.
43. Ibid., p. 101.
44. Foot, *Politics of Harold Wilson*, passim.
45. R. Crossman, *The Diaries of a Cabinet Minister, Volume 2: Lord President of the Council and Leader of the House of Commons, 1966–1968* (1976), p. 84.
46. Craig, *British General Election Manifestos*, p. 363.
47. B. Jones and M. Keating, *Labour and the British State* (Oxford, 1985), p. 105.
48. Ibid., p. 104; M. Keating and D. Bleiman, *Labour and Scottish Nationalism* (1979), p. 147.

49. Gallagher, *Glasgow*, pp. 276–7, 326.
50. A. B. Philip, *The Welsh Question: Nationalism in Welsh Politics, 1945–1970* (Cardiff, 1975), p. 233.
51. K. O. Morgan, *Rebirth of a Nation: Wales 1880–1980* (Oxford, 1981), p. 411; C. Harvie, *No Gods and Precious Few Heroes: Scotland, 1914–1980* (1981), pp. 154–5.
52. Ponting, *Breach of Promise*, p. 341.
53. See e.g. T. Nairn, *The Break-Up of Britain: Crisis and Neo-Nationalism* (1977), esp. p. 253.
54. Ponting, *Breach of Promise*, p. 331; M. Dresser, 'The Colour Bar in Bristol, 1963', in R. Samuel (ed.), *Patriotism: The Making and Unmaking of British National Identity, Volume I: History and Politics* (1989), pp. 284–5, 301.
55. P. Ratcliffe, *Racism and Reaction: A Profile of Handsworth* (1981), pp. 279–81.
56. Ponting, *Breach of Promise*, p. 333.
57. C. Holmes, *John Bull's Island: Immigration and British Society, 1871–1971* (1988), p. 292.
58. Cronin, *Politics of State Expansion*, p. 235.
59. Bonner, *British Co-operation*, p. 274; J. Gaffin and D. Thoms, *Caring and Sharing: The Centenary History of the Co-operative Women's Guild* (Manchester, 1983), p. 268.
60. Pelling, *Short History*, p. 194.
61. T. Forrester, *The Labour Party and the Working Class* (1976), p. 80.
62. D. Howell, *British Social Democracy: A Study in Development and Decay* (1976), p. 246.
63. D. E. Butler, *British General Elections since 1945* (Oxford, 1989), pp. 26–7.
64. Hart, 'Gender', p. 22; Heath et al., *How Britain Votes*, p. 30.

9 Drift to Defeat? 1970–9

1. C. A. R. Crosland, *The Conservative Enemy: A Programme of Radical Reform for the 1960s* (1962), p. 25.
2. C. A. R. Crosland, *A Social Democratic Britain* (1971), p. 8.
3. Pimlott, *Wilson*, p. 571.
4. P. Seyd, *The Rise and Fall of the Labour Left* (1987), p. 54.
5. D. Kogan and M. Kogan, *The Battle for the Labour Party* (Glasgow, 1982), pp. 23–35.
6. L. Minkin, *The Labour Party Conference: A Study in the Politics of Intra-Party Democracy* (1978), pp. 336–7.
7. K. Middlemas, *Power, Competition and the State, Volume II: Threats to the Post-War Settlement, 1961–1974* (1990), p. 321; L. Minkin, *The Contentious Alliance: Trade Unions and the Labour Party* (Edinburgh, 1991), p. 118.
8. Mikardo, *Back-Bencher*, p. 183; Minkin, *Labour Party Conference*, pp. 336–7.
9. S. Holland, *The Socialist Challenge* (1975), p. 255 and *passim*; J. Tomlinson, *The Unequal Struggle? British Socialism and the Capitalist*

Enterprise (1982), pp. 99–122; G. Foote, *The Labour Party's Political Thought: A History* (2nd edn., 1986), pp. 316–23.

10. M. Hatfield, *The House the Left Built: Inside Labour Policy-Making, 1970–1975* (1978), p. 189.
11. Labour Party, *Annual Report, 1973* (1973), p. 167.
12. Mikardo, *Back-Bencher*, p. 187; Kogan and Kogan, *Battle for the Labour Party*, p. 23.
13. Seyd, *Rise and Fall of the Labour Left*, p. 29.
14. Pimlott, *Wilson*, pp. 580–1.
15. Shaw, *Discipline*, pp. 167, 179; J. Callaghan, *Time and Chance* (1987), p. 298; D. Owen, *Time to Declare* (1991), pp. 185–6.
16. Callaghan, *Time and Chance*, p. 299.
17. Pimlott, *Wilson*, p. 608; Callaghan, *Time and Chance*, p. 293; R. Jenkins, *A Life at the Centre* (1991), p. 365; Healey, *Time of My Life*, p. 370.
18. Cook, 'Labour's Electoral Base', pp. 104–5.
19. D. Coates, *Labour in Power? A Study of the Labour Government, 1974–1979* (1980), p. 231.
20. H. Wilson, *Final Term: The Labour Government, 1974–1976* (1979), p. 107.
21. Ibid., p. 109.
22. T. Benn, *Against the Tide: Diaries 1973–1976* (1990), pp. 389–95; J. Adams, *Tony Benn* (1992), pp. 371–6; for a more caustic view, see B. Donoughue, *Prime Minister: The Conduct of Policy under Harold Wilson and James Callaghan* (1987), pp. 55–6.
23. See e.g. Benn, *Against the Tide*, p. 535; B. Castle, *The Castle Diaries, 1974–1976* (1980), p. 689.
24. Ziegler, *Wilson*, p. 484.
25. Callaghan, *Time and Chance*, pp. 386, 390.
26. Pimlott, *Wilson*, p. 678; Callaghan, *Time and Chance*, pp. 392–4; Jones, *Foot*, pp. 394–5; Healey, *Time of My Life*, pp. 446–7; Jenkins, *Life at the Centre*, pp. 434–6; Adams, *Benn*, pp. 379–80; S. Crosland, *Tony Crosland* (1982), pp. 311–21.
27. P. Whitehead, 'The Labour Governments, 1974–1979', in Hennessy and Seldon, *Ruling Performance*, p. 258.
28. Callaghan, *Time and Chance*, p. 444; Adams, *Benn*, p. 380.
29. M. Sawyer, 'Industrial Policy', in M. Artis and D. Cobham (eds.), *Labour's Economic Policies, 1974–1979* (Manchester, 1991), p. 160.
30. P. Whitehead, *The Writing on the Wall: Britain in the Seventies* (1985), p. 131.
31. Sawyer, 'Industrial Policy', pp. 171–2; E. Dell, *A Hard Pounding: Politics and Economic Crisis, 1974–1976* (Oxford, 1991), pp. 89–90.
32. Wilson, *Final Term*, p. 141; Healey, *Time of My Life*, p. 459.
33. Adams, *Benn*, p. 353.
34. Sawyer, 'Industrial Policy', p. 160.
35. Tomlinson, *Public Policy*, p. 294.
36. E. Dell, 'The Chrysler UK Rescue', *Contemporary Record*, 6 (1992), pp. 1–44; M. C. Fleming, 'Industrial Policy', in W. P. J. Maunder (ed.), *The British Economy in the 1970s* (1980), p. 151; T. Forrester, 'Neutralising the Industrial Strategy', in K. Coates (ed.), *What Went*

Wrong: Explaining the Fall of the Labour Government (Nottingham, 1979), p. 87.
37. Tomlinson, *Public Policy*, pp. 294–5.
38. T. G. Weyman-Jones, 'The Nationalised Industries: Changing Attitudes and Changing Roles', in Maunder, *British Economy in the 1970s*, pp. 195–6.
39. Dunkerley and Hare, 'Nationalized Industries', pp. 404–7, 415–16; K. Middlemas, *Power, Competition and the State, Volume III: The End of the Post-War Era, Britain since 1974* (1991).
40. P. Ormerod, 'Incomes Policy', in Artis and Cobham, *Labour's Economic Policies*, p. 58.
41. Tomlinson, *Public Policy*, p. 301; T. J. Hatton and K. A. Chrystal, 'The Budget and Fiscal Policy', in Crafts and Woodward, *British Economy since 1945*, p. 80.
42. Dell, *Hard Pounding*, p. 137.
43. Whitehead, *Writing on the Wall*, pp. 148–9; Minkin, *Contentious Alliance*, p. 168.
44. Middlemas, *Power, Competition and the State, Volume III*, pp. 94–6.
45. Ormerod, 'Incomes Policy', p. 57.
46. Ibid., pp. 60–4.
47. Healey, *Time of My Life*, p. 428.
48. Callaghan, *Time and Chance*, pp. 425–7.
49. Ibid., pp. 438–9.
50. Ibid., p. 434.
51. Dell, *Hard Pounding*, pp. 237, 247–8, 254–6.
52. Ibid., p. 258; Healey, *Time of My Life*, pp. 429–30; Crosland, *Crosland*, p. 377; Adams, *Benn*, pp. 383–4.
53. Dell, *Hard Pounding*, p. 267.
54. Crosland, *Crosland*, pp. 381–2.
55. Whitehead, *Writing on the Wall*, pp. 196–7.
56. Ibid., p. 199.
57. Benn, *Against the Tide*, pp. 670–9, 682.
58. Whitehead, *Writing on the Wall*, pp. 198–9.
59. Callaghan, *Time and Chance*, pp. 439–41.
60. Healey, *Time of My Life*, p. 432.
61. Ibid., p. 433; T. Westaway, 'Stabilisation Policy and Fiscal Reform', in Maunder, *British Economy in the 1970s*, p. 24.
62. Ormerod, 'Incomes Policy', p. 57.
63. R. Lowe, *The Welfare State in Britain since 1945* (1993), pp. 316, 314.
64. Whitehead, *Writing on the Wall*, p. 259.
65. Jones, *Foot*, p. 414.
66. Whitehead, *Writing on the Wall*, p. 277.
67. K. O. Morgan, *The People's Peace: British History, 1945–1989* (Oxford, 1990), pp. 369–70.
68. Jones, *Foot*, p. 413.
69. W. L. Miller, *The End of British Politics? Scots and English Political Behaviour in the Seventies* (Oxford, 1981), p. 240.
70. Morgan, *People's Peace*, p. 410.
71. Callaghan, *Time and Chance*, p. 448; Healey, *Time of My Life*, p. 458.

72. Minkin, *Contentious Alliance*, p. 176.
73. Ormerod, 'Incomes Policy', p. 57; Middlemas, *Power, Competition and the State, Volume III*, p. 161.
74. Callaghan, *Time and Chance*, pp. 514–16; Healey, *Time of My Life*, p. 462.
75. Jones, *Foot*, pp. 423–4; Callaghan, *Time and Chance*, p. 516.
76. Dell, *Hard Pounding*, p. 285.
77. Healey, *Time of My Life*, p. 463.
78. Ormerod, 'Incomes Policy', pp. 70–1; Kirby, 'Supply-Side Management', p. 257.
79. Healey, *Time of My Life*, p. 463.
80. T. Benn, *Conflicts of Interest: Diaries, 1976–1980* (1990), p. 449.
81. Whitehead, *Writing on the Wall*, pp. 281–2.
82. Middlemas, *Power, Competition and the State, Volume III*, pp. 163–4.
83. Benn, *Conflicts of Interest*, pp. 485–8; E. Heffer, *Never a Yes Man: The Life and Politics of an Adopted Liverpudlian* (1991), pp. 172–3.
84. D. E. Butler and D. Kavanagh, *The British General Election of October 1974* (1975), p. 278; D. E. Butler and D. Kavanagh, *The British General Election of 1979* (1980), p. 343; Butler and Pinto–Duschinsky, *1970*, p. 342.
85. P. Riddell, *The Thatcher Era and its Legacy* (Oxford, 1991), pp. 233–4.

10 Disaster and Recovery? 1979–92

1. Whitehead, *Writing on the Wall*, p. 366.
2. K. Coates, 'What Went Wrong', in Coates, *What Went Wrong*, pp. 7–33; N. Bosanquet, 'Labour and Public Expenditure: An Overall View', in N. Bosanquet and P. Townsend (eds.), *Labour and Equality: A Fabian Study of Labour in Power, 1974–1979* (1980), p. 43.
3. Kogan and Kogan, *Battle for the Labour Party*, pp. 54–67; Shaw, *Discipline*, pp. 199–200.
4. B. Pimlott, 'Trade Unions and the Second Coming of CND', in Pimlott and Cook, *Trade Unions in British Politics*, p. 217; Minkin, *Contentious Alliance*, pp. 204–5 warns against taking too 'left' a view of the unions at this time, however.
5. Callaghan, *Time and Chance*, p. 564.
6. R. Jenkins, 'Home Thoughts from Abroad: The 1979 Dimbleby Lecture', in W. Kennet (ed.), *The Rebirth of Britain* (1982), pp. 9–29.
7. Jenkins, *Life at the Centre*, pp. 520–1.
8. Crafts, 'Economic Growth', in Crafts and Woodward, *British Economy since 1945*, p. 285.
9. Callaghan, *Time and Chance*, p. 565; Jones, *Foot*, p. 442; Healey, *Time of My Life*, p. 466.
10. Labour party, *Annual Report, 1980* (1980), pp. 157, 159.
11. Minkin, *Contentious Alliance*, pp. 204–5.
12. Kogan and Kogan, *Battle for the Labour Party*, p. 90.
13. Callaghan, *Time and Chance*, p. 565; Healey, *Time of My Life*, p. 476; Mikardo, *Back-Bencher*, p. 201.
14. Kogan and Kogan, *Battle for the Labour Party*, p. 91; T. Benn, *The*

End of an Era: Diaries 1980–1990 (1992), pp. 37–8.
15. Jones, *Foot*, pp. 452–3.
16. Jenkins, *Life at the Centre*, pp. 522–3, 530.
17. Minkin, *Contentious Alliance*, pp. 123, 131, 214.
18. Healey, *Time of My Life*, p. 478; Owen, *Time to Declare*, p. 458; Jenkins, *Life at the Centre*, p. 531; Mikardo, *Back-Bencher*, pp. 202–3.
19. Kogan and Kogan, *Battle for the Labour Party*, pp. 94–7; Jones, *Foot*, pp. 458–9.
20. Jenkins, *Life at the Centre*, pp. 534–6.
21. Minkin, *Contentious Alliance*, pp. 234–5.
22. Jones, *Foot*, p. 468.
23. A. McSmith, *John Smith: Playing the Long Game* (1993), p. 83.
24. Jones, *Foot*, p. 467; Adams, *Benn*, p. 410; see also the milder misgivings of Heffer, *Never a Yes Man*, pp. 177–8.
25. Benn, *End of an Era*, pp. 154–5.
26. Adams, *Benn*, p. 423.
27. See esp. D. Sanders, H. Ward and D. Marsh, 'Government Popularity and the Falklands War: A Reassessment', *British Journal of Political Science*, 17 (1987), pp. 281–313.
28. M. Crick, *Militant* (1984), pp. 132, 213–14.
29. R. Heffernan and M. Marqusee, *Defeat from the Jaws of Victory: Inside Kinnock's Labour Party* (1992), p. 127.
30. Ibid., pp. 261–300.
31. Jones, *Foot*, p. 492.
32. Shaw, *Discipline*, pp. 225–6, 230, 235.
33. Ibid., pp. 235–6.
34. Ibid., p. 243.
35. Jones, *Foot*, p. 499; M. Foot, *Another Heart and Other Pulses: The Alternative to the Thatcher Society* (1984), pp. 20, 41.
36. R. McMullin, *The Light on the Hill: The Australian Labor Party, 1891–1991* (Oxford, 1991), pp. 407–9; D. E. Butler and D. Kavanagh, *The British General Election of 1983* (1984), pp. 59–60.
37. A. Mitchell, *Four Years in the Death of the Labour Party* (1983), pp. 101–2; Jones, *Foot*, pp. 505–6.
38. Healey, *Time of My Life*, pp. 499–500.
39. Foot, *Another Heart*, p. 29.
40. Butler and Kavanagh, *1983*, p. 85.
41. Labour Party, *The New Hope for Britain: Labour's Manifesto, 1983* (1983), esp. p. 8.
42. Jones, *Foot*, pp. 513–14.
43. Butler and Kavanagh, *1983*, p. 119.
44. P. Dunleavy and C. T. Husbands, *British Democracy at the Crossroads: Voting and Party Competition in the 1980s* (1985), p. 123; Heath et al., *How Britain Votes*, p. 30.
45. Jones, *Foot*, p. 517.
46. Heffernan and Marqusee, *Defeat from the Jaws of Victory*, pp. 40–1.
47. Labour party, *Annual Report, 1983* (1983), p. 29 and enclosure after p. 366.
48. Riddell, *Thatcher Era*, p. 233.

49. I. Crewe, 'Values: The Crusade that Failed', in D. Kavanagh and A. Seldon, *The Thatcher Effect: A Decade of Change* (Oxford, 1989), pp. 239–50.
50. R. Taylor, *The Trade Union Question in British Politics: Government and Trade Unions since 1945* (Oxford, 1993), pp. 321–5.
51. Ibid., p. 382; Price and Bain, 'Labour Force', p. 188.
52. J. Haines, *The Politics of Power* (1977), pp. 94–111.
53. This was certainly the case in Sheffield, where the author was a Housing Repairs Clerk in 1983–4.
54. N. Ellison, *Egalitarian Thought and Labour Politics: Retreating Visions* (1994), pp. 175–8.
55. G. Goodman, *The Miners' Strike* (1985), for much of what follows.
56. Heffernan and Marqusee, *Defeat from the Jaws of Victory*, p. 53.
57. Ibid., p. 61.
58. Shaw, *Discipline*, pp. 256–7.
59. Minkin, *Contentious Alliance*, p. 421.
60. Labour party, *Annual Report, 1985* (1985), p. 128.
61. Shaw, *Discipline*, pp. 262–3.
62. C. Hughes and P. Wintour, *Labour Rebuilt: The New Model Party* (1990), p. 13; Heffernan and Marqusee, *Defeat from the Jaws of Victory*, pp. 111–13; M. Scammell, 'The Phenomenon of Political Marketing: The Thatcher Contribution', *Contemporary Record*, 8 (1994), pp. 23–43.
63. M. J. Smith, 'The Labour Party in Opposition', in M. J. Smith and J. Spear (eds.), *The Changing Labour Party* (1992), p. 10.
64. D. E. Butler and D. Kavanagh, *The British General Election of 1987* (1988), pp. 70–1.
65. Heffernan and Marqusee, *Defeat from the Jaws of Victory*, pp. 85–6.
66. Butler, *British General Elections since 1945*, p. 64.
67. H. Kitschelt, 'Class Structure and Social Democratic Party Strategy', *British Journal of Political Science*, 23 (1993), pp. 299–337.
68. V. Atkinson and J. Spear, 'The Labour Party and Women', in Smith and Spear, *Changing Labour Party*, pp. 165–7.
69. S. George and B. Rosamond, 'The European Community', in Smith and Spear, *Changing Labour Party*, p. 173.
70. B. Rosamond, 'The Labour Party, Trade Unions and Industrial Relations', ibid., p. 92; Taylor, *Trade Union Question*, p. 370.
71. P. Alcock, 'The Labour Party and the Welfare State', ibid., p. 141.
72. Heffernan and Marqusee, *Defeat from the Jaws of Victory*, pp. 325–35.
73. Ibid., pp. 172–4.
74. Labour party, *Annual Report, 1988* (1988), pp. 11, 211–21.
75. Adams, *Benn*, p. 454.
76. D. E. Butler and D. Kavanagh, *The British General Election of 1992* (1992), p. 15.
77. Butler and Kavanagh, *1992*, p. 65.
78. McSmith, *Smith*, pp. 200, 242; Heffernan and Marqusee, *Defeat from the Jaws of Victory*, p. 319.

79. McSmith, *Smith*, p. 242.
80. Butler and Kavanagh, *1992*, pp. 146, 282.
81. Ibid., p. 351.
82. P. Clifford and A. Heath, 'The Election Campaign', in A. Heath, R. Jowell and J. Curtice (eds.), *Labour's Last Chance? The 1992 Election and Beyond* (Aldershot, 1994), p. 20.

Bibliography

(*Place of publication is London unless otherwise stated.*)

General

The standard short account has long been H. Pelling, *A Short History of the Labour Party* (1st edn. 1961, 11th edn. 1996). Alternative general books are C. F. Brand, *The British Labour Party: A Short History* (Stanford, 1965), D. Howell, *British Social Democracy: A Study in Development and Decay* (1976), R. Miliband, *Parliamentary Socialism: A Study in the Politics of Labour* (2nd edn., 1972), D. Coates, *The Labour Party and the Struggle for Socialism* (Cambridge, 1975), J. Hinton, *Labour and Socialism: A History of the British Labour Movement, 1867–1974* (Brighton, 1983), J. E. Cronin, *Labour and Society in Britain, 1918–1979* (1983) and K. Laybourn, *The Rise of Labour: The British Labour Party, 1890–1979* (1988). G. D. H. Cole, *History of the Labour Party from 1914* (1948) remains valuable for the interwar years. K. Jefferys, *The Labour Party since 1945* (1992) is a good straightforward account of post-war developments. C. Cook & I. Taylor (eds.), *The Labour Party: An Introduction to its History, Structure and Politics* (1980) is a useful collection of essays. M. Pinto-Duschinsky, *British Political Finance, 1830–1980* (Washington, DC, 1981) is indispensable.

Among books operating at a rather more profound level, see especially H. M. Drucker, *Doctrine and Ethos in the Labour Party* (1979), D. Marquand, *The Progressive Dilemma* (1991), R. I. McKibbin, *The Ideologies of Class* (Oxford, 1990), B. Jones and M. Keating, *Labour and the British State* (Oxford, 1985), and R. Price, *Labour in British Society: An Interpretative History* (1986).

For biographical details, see two extremely useful collections: J. Bellamy and J. Saville (eds.), *Dictionary of Labour Biography* (9 vols., 1972–93) and K. O. Morgan, *Labour People: Leaders and Lieutenants from Hardie to Kinnock* (Oxford, 1987).

On the trade unions, see especially H. Pelling, *A History of British Trade Unionism* (4th edn., Harmondsworth, 1987), R. Martin, *TUC: The Growth of a Pressure Group, 1868–1976* (Oxford, 1980), S. Boston, *Women Workers and the Trade Union Movement* (1980), and the stimulating collection of essays edited by B. Pimlott and C. Cook, *Trade Unions in British Politics: The First 250 Years* (2nd edn., 1991).

On socialism, see especially J. Callaghan, *Socialism in Britain since 1884* (Oxford, 1990), G. Foote, *The Labour Party's Political Thought: A History* (2nd edn., 1986), and W. H. Greenleaf, *The British Political Tradition, Volume 2: The Ideological Heritage* (1983). There are two very useful collections of documents: A. Wright (ed.), *British Socialism: Socialist Thought from the 1880s to the 1960s* (1983) and F. Bealey (ed.), *The Social and Political Thought of the British Labour Party* (1970).

273

Increasingly the debates surrounding the development of Labour politics have been enlivened by local and regional studies. On Scotland see I. McLean, *The Legend of Red Clydeside* (Edinburgh, 1980), T. Gallacher, *Glasgow, The Uneasy Peace: Religious Tension in Modern Scotland* (Manchester, 1987), A. McKinlay and R. J. Morris (eds.), *The ILP on Clydeside, 1893–1932: From Foundation to Disintegration* (Manchester, 1990), J. Melling, 'Whatever Happened to Red Clydeside', *International Review of Social History*, 35 (1990), I. C. G. Hutchison, *A Political History of Scotland, 1832–1924: Parties. Elections and Issues* (Edinburgh, 1986), C. Harvie, 'Labour in Scotland during the Second World War', *Historical Journal*, 26 (1983), and G. Walker, *Thomas Johnston* (Manchester, 1988). For Wales, see K. O. Morgan, *Wales in British Politics, 1868–1922* (3rd edn., Oxford, 1980) and *Rebirth of a Nation: Wales, 1880–1980* (Oxford, 1981). Among a large number of studies of northern England, see especially the seminal work of M. Savage, *The Dynamics of Working-Class Politics: The Labour Movement in Preston, 1880–1940* (Cambridge, 1987). Also of value are P. J. Waller, *Democracy and Sectarianism: A Political and Social History of Liverpool, 1868–1939* (Liverpool, 1981), J. Smith, 'The Labour Tradition in Glasgow and Liverpool', *History Workshop Journal*, 17 (1984), K. Laybourn and J. Reynolds, *Liberalism and the Rise of Labour, 1880–1914* (1985), J. Reynolds and K. Laybourn, *Labour Heartland: The History of the Labour Party in West Yorkshire during the Inter-War Years, 1918–1939* (Bradford, 1987), S. Pollard, *A History of Labour in Sheffield* (Liverpool, 1959), C. Binfield et al. (eds.), *The History of the City of Sheffield, 1843–1993, Volume 1: Politics* (Sheffield, 1993), and M. Callcott, 'The Nature and Extent of Political Change in the Inter-War Years: The Example of Co. Durham', *Northern History*, 16 (1980). The Midlands have also excited considerable interest: see among other works P. Wyncoll, *The Nottingham Labour Movement, 1880–1939* (1985), R. J. Waller, *The Dukeries Transformed: The Social and Political Development of a Twentieth-Century Coalfield* (Oxford, 1983), A. Thorpe, 'J. H. Thomas and the Rise of Labour in Derby, 1880–1940', *Midland History*, 15 (1990), B. Lancaster, *Radicalism, Co-operation and Socialism: Leicester Working-Class Politics, 1860–1906* (1988), R. P. Hastings, 'The Birmingham Labour Movement, 1918–45', *Midland History*, 5 (1979–80), D. Rolf, 'Birmingham Labour and the Background to the 1945 General Election', in A. Wright and R. M. Y. Shackleton (eds.), *Worlds of Labour: Essays in Birmingham Labour History* (Birmingham, 1981), B. Lancaster and T. Mason (eds.), *Life and Labour in a Twentieth-Century City: The Experience of Coventry* (Coventry, 1986), N. Tiratsoo, *Reconstruction, Affluence and Labour Politics: Coventry 1945–60* (1990), and R. C. Whiting, *The View From Cowley: The Impact of Industrialization upon Oxford, 1918–1939* (Oxford, 1983). Work on southern England is less extensive and, where it exists, is mostly about London: see P. Thompson, *Socialists, Liberals and Labour: The Struggle for London, 1885–1914* (1967), J. Marriott, *The Culture of Labourism: The East End between the Wars* (Edinburgh, 1991), and S. Goss, *Local Labour and Local Government: A Study of Changing Interests, Politics and Policy in Southwark from 1919 to 1982* (1988).

1 Creation and Early Years, 1900–14

The best general introduction to the 'Socialist Revival' is H. Pelling, *The Origins of the Labour Party, 1880–1900* (Oxford, 1965). The collection of essays in E. F. Biagini and A. J. Reid (eds.), *Currents of Radicalism: Popular Radicalism, Organized Labour and Party Politics in Britain, 1850–1914* (Cambridge, 1991) suggests that there was considerable continuity on the British left in the late nineteenth and early twentieth centuries. J. Lawrence, 'Popular Radicalism and the Socialist Revival in Britain', *Journal of British Studies*, 31 (1992), is also important.

On particular parties, D. Howell, *British Workers and the Independent Labour Party 1888–1906* (Manchester, 1983) is comprehensive. On the SDF, see especially M. Crick, *The History of the Social Democratic Federation* (Keele, 1994). For the Fabians, see A. M. McBriar, *Fabian Socialism and English Politics, 1884–1918* (Cambridge, 1962), and E. J. Hobsbawm, 'The Fabians reconsidered' in his *Labouring Men: Studies in the History of Labour* (1964). C. Waters, *British Socialists and the Politics of Popular Culture, 1884–1914* (Manchester, 1990) looks at broader cultural aspects.

The standard work on the Labour party in the period between its formation and the First World War is D. Tanner, *Political Change and the Labour Party, 1900–18* (Cambridge, 1990). A number of older works, however, remain important. F. Bealey and H. Pelling, *Labour and Politics 1900–1906: A History of the Labour Representation Committee* (1958), and P. Poirier, *The Advent of the Labour Party* (1958) cover much the same ground, while K. D. Brown (ed.), *The First Labour Party, 1906–1914* (1985) takes the story from then up to 1914. J. Harris, *Unemployment and Politics: A Study in English Social Policy, 1886–1914* (Oxford, 1972) has interesting things to say about Labour's approach in that area. The Labour movement as a whole is covered by G. Phillips, 'The British Labour Movement before 1914', in R. Geary (ed.), *Labour and Socialist Movements in Europe Before 1914* (Oxford, 1989). See also D. Powell, 'New Liberalism and the Rise of Labour, 1886–1906' *Historical Journal*, 29 (1986), and A. W. Purdue, 'Arthur Henderson and Liberal, Liberal–Labour and Labour Politics in the North-East of England, 1892–1903', *Northern History*, 11 (1975).

On international aspects, see D. J. Newton, *British Labour, European Socialism and the Struggle for Peace 1889–1914* (Oxford, 1985) and A. J. A. Morris, *Radicalism Against War: The Advocacy of Peace and Retrenchment* (1972).

On the unions, the best place to start is H. A. Clegg, A. Fox and A. F. Thompson, *A History of British Trade Unions since 1889, Volume 1: 1889–1910* (Oxford, 1964). There are some useful essays in W. J. Mommsen and H. G. Husung (eds.), *The Development of Trade Unionism in Great Britain and Germany, 1880–1914* (1985). Specific union histories of value include C. Baylies, *The History of the Yorkshire Miners 1881–1918* (1993), K. Coates and T. Topham, *The History of the Transport and General Workers' Union, Volume 1: 1870–1922* (Oxford, 1991), P. S. Bagwell, *The Railwaymen: A History of the National Union of Railwaymen* (1963), R. Gregory, *The Miners and British Politics, 1906–14* (1963), and R. Church, 'Edwardian

Labour Unrest and Coalfield Militancy, 1890–1914', *Historical Journal*, 30 (1987). The legal problems faced by the unions in these years are dealt with by J. Saville, 'Trade Unions and Free Labour: The Background to the Taff Vale Decision', in A. Briggs and J. Saville (eds.), *Essays in Labour History: In Memory of G. D. H. Cole* (rev. edn., 1967) and by H. Pelling, 'The Politics of the Osborne Judgment', *Historical Journal*, 25 (1982). J. White, '1910–14 reconsidered', in J. E. Cronin and J. Schneer (eds.), *Social Conflict and the Political Order in Modern Britain* (1982) is a useful digest of the literature. For radical movements in the unions, see especially in B. Holton, *British Syndicalism, 1900–14: Myths and Realities* (1976), and J. White, 'Syndicalism in a Mature Industrial Setting: The Case of Britain', in M. van der Linden and W. Thorpe (eds.), *Revolutionary Syndicalism: An International Perspective* (Aldershot, 1990).

Relations between the party and the women's suffrage campaign can be followed in S. S. Holton, *Feminism and Democracy: Women's Suffrage and Reform Politics in Britain, 1900–18* (Cambridge, 1986), J. Liddington and J. Norris, *One Hand Tied Behind Us: The Rise of the Women's Suffrage Movement* (1978) and C. Collette, *For Labour and For Women: The Women's Labour League, 1906–1918* (Manchester, 1989). More broadly, see P. Thane, 'The Women of the British Labour Party and Feminism, 1906–45', in H. L. Smith (ed.), *British Feminism in the Twentieth Century* (Aldershot, 1990). Also of interest here is J. Liddington, *The Life and Times of a Respectable Rebel: Selina Cooper (1864–1946)* (1984).

L. Smith, *Religion and the Rise of Labour: Nonconformity and the Independent Labour Movement in Lancashire and the West Riding, 1880–1914* (Keele, 1993) looks at that aspect.

For the 'rise of Labour/decline of Liberals' debate, see especially K. Laybourn, 'The Rise of Labour and the Decline of Liberalism: The State of the Debate', *History*, 80 (1995), P. F. Clarke, *Lancashire and the New Liberalism* (1971) and 'The Electoral Position of the Liberal and Labour Parties, 1910–14' *English Historical Review*, 90 (1975), H. C. G. Matthew, R. I. McKibbin and J. Kay, 'The Franchise Factor in the Rise of the Labour Party', *English Historical Review*, 91 (1976), D. Tanner, 'The Parliamentary Electoral System, the "Fourth" Reform Act and the Rise of Labour', *Institute of Historical Research Bulletin*, 56 (1983), and M. Bentley, *The Climax of Liberal Politics: British Liberalism in Theory and Practice, 1868–1918* (1987).

For the leading figure in the early Labour party, see K. O. Morgan, *Keir Hardie: Radical and Socialist* (1975).

2 The Surge to Second-Party Status, 1914–22

R. I. McKibbin, *The Evolution of the Labour Party, 1910–24* (Oxford, 1974) is the best book on the organization of the Labour party during this period. On the role of ideas, see J. M. Winter, *Socialism and the Challenge of War: Ideas and Politics in Britain, 1912–1928* (1974) and 'Arthur Henderson, the Russian Revolution and the Reconstruction of the Labour Party', *Historical Journal*, 15 (1972). J. Turner, *British Politics and the Great War: Coalition and Conflict, 1915–1918* (1992) has a lot to say about Labour.

Other important works include C. Howard, 'MacDonald, Henderson and the Outbreak of War, 1914', *Historical Journal*, 20 (1977), and R. Harrison, 'The War Emergency Workers' National Committee, 1914–20', in A. Briggs and J. Saville (eds.), *Essays in Labour History, 1886–1923* (1971). J. N. Horne, *Labour at War: France and Britain 1914–1918* (Oxford, 1991) is a good comparative study, as is S. Berger, *The British Labour Party and the German Social Democrats, 1900–1931* (Oxford, 1994).

Among works on trade unionism, special notice should be paid to C. J. Wrigley, *David Lloyd George and the British Labour Movement: Peace and War* (Brighton, 1976), J. Hinton, *The First Shop Stewards' Movement* (1973), P. S. Bagwell, 'The Triple Industrial Alliance 1913–1922' in A. Briggs and J. Saville (eds.), *Essays in Labour History, 1886–1923* (1971) and, for guild socialism, A. Wright, *G. D. H. Cole and Socialist Democracy* (Oxford, 1979).

For the Co-operative movement, see T. F. Carbery, *Consumers in Politics: A History and General Review of the Co-operative Party* (Manchester, 1969), S. Pollard, 'The Foundation of the Co-operative Party', in A. Briggs and J. Saville (eds.), *Essays in Labour History, 1882–1923* (1971), and T. Adams, 'The Formation of the Co-operative Party Reconsidered', *International Review of Social History*, 32 (1987).

On the UDC and related matters, see M. Swartz, *The Union of Democratic Control in British Politics during the First World War* (Oxford, 1971) and C. A. Cline, *Recruits to Labour: The British Labour Party, 1914–1931* (Syracuse, 1963).

For the period after 1918, Labour's electoral and political strategy is discussed in K. D. Wald, 'Advance by Retreat? The Formulation of Labour's Electoral Strategy', *Journal of British Studies*, 27 (1988) and A. Thorpe, 'Labour and the Frustration of the Extreme Left' in A. Thorpe (ed.), *The Failure of Political Extremism in Inter-War Britain* (Exeter, 1988). For the immediate post-war position, see C. J. Wrigley, *Lloyd George and the Challenge of Labour: The Post-War Coalition, 1918–22* (Hemel Hempstead, 1990), K. O. Morgan, *Consensus and Disunity: The Lloyd George Coalition Government 1918–22* (Oxford, 1979) and M. Cowling, *The Impact of Labour 1920–1924: The Beginning of Modern British Politics* (Cambridge, 1971).

On women, see especially G. Braybon, *Women Workers in the First World War: The British Experience* (1981), P. Graves, *Labour Women: Women in British Working-Class Politics, 1918–39* (Cambridge, 1994), J. Alberti, *Beyond Suffrage: Women in War and Peace, 1914–28* (1989), M. Pugh, *Women and the Women's Movement in Britain 1914–59* (1992), and S. K. Kent, 'The Politics of Sexual Difference: World War I and the Demise of British Feminism', *Journal of British Studies*, 27 (1988).

3 Progress and Collapse, 1922–31

There is no single volume devoted to the party's history over the whole of this period. For the 1924 government, the standard work remains R. W. Lyman, *The First Labour Government, 1924* (1958). The second administration is discussed in stimulating fashion in R. Skidelsky, *Politicians and the Slump: The Labour Government of 1929–31* (1967), but some of the reasons why it needs to be approached with caution can be seen in R. I. McKibbin, 'The Economic Policy of the Second Labour Government', *Past and Present*, 78 (1975). See also P. Williamson, *National Crisis and National Government: British Politics, the Economy and Empire, 1926–32* (Cambridge, 1992). The foreign policy of that government, and the personal bitterness it engendered, can be seen in D. Carlton, *MacDonald versus Henderson: The Foreign Policy of the Second Labour Government* (1970). A contemporary work, E. Wertheimer, *Portrait of the Labour Party* (1929) remains valuable. The inside, official view, betraying the smugness of the 'inevitability of gradualism' approach can be seen in H. Tracey (ed.), *The Book of the Labour Party: Its History, Growth, Policy and Leaders* (3 vols., 1925). C. Howard, 'Expectations Born to Death: Local Labour Party Expansion in the 1920s', in J. M. Winter (ed.), *The Working Class in Modern British History: Essays in Honour of Henry Pelling* (Cambridge, 1983) goes a long way towards explaining why Labour's triumph over the Liberals was only partial in this period. Religious aspects are dealt with in P. Catterall, 'Morality and Politics: The Free Churches and the Labour Party between the Wars', *Historical Journal*, 36 (1993), and J. Keating, 'The Making of the Catholic Labour Activist: The Catholic Social Guild and Catholic Workers' College, 1909–1939', *Labour History Review*, 59 (1994).

The 1931 crisis is the subject of A. Thorpe, *The British General Election of 1931* (Oxford, 1991) and D. H. Close, 'The Realignment of the British Electorate in 1931', *History*, 67 (1982). See also P. Williamson, 'A "Bankers' Ramp"? Financiers and the British Political Crisis of August 1931', *English Historical Review*, 99 (1984), A. Thorpe, 'Arthur Henderson and the British Political Crisis of 1931', *Historical Journal*, 31 (1988), and '"I am in the Cabinet": J. H. Thomas's Decision to join the National Government in 1931', *Historical Research*, 64 (1991).

For the ILP, see especially R. E. Dowse, *Left in the Centre: The Independent Labour Party, 1893–1940* (1966) and R. K. Middlemas, *The Clydesiders: A Left-Wing Struggle for Parliamentary Power* (1965).

Among notable biographies of the leaders in this period, see especially D. Marquand, *Ramsay MacDonald* (1977), K. Laybourn, *Philip Snowden: A Biography* (Aldershot, 1988), C. J. Wrigley, *Arthur Henderson* (Cardiff, 1990), and R. Skidelsky, *Oswald Mosley* (1975). Philip, Viscount Snowden, *An Autobiography* (2 vols., 1934) stands out among a plethora of often mediocre memoirs; see also H. Dalton, *Call Back Yesterday: Memoirs, 1887–1931* (1953) and M. I. Cole (ed.), *Beatrice Webb's Diaries, 1912–24* (1952) and *1924–32* (1956).

On trade unionism, K. Laybourn, *The General Strike of 1926* (Manchester, 1993) is a decent up-to-date account of its subject. The broader context is ably portrayed in H. A. Clegg, *A History of British Trade Unions, Volume 2: 1911–1933* (Oxford, 1985). Lord Citrine, *Men and Work: An Autobiography* (1964) and A. Bullock, *The Life and Times of Ernest Bevin, Volume 1: Trade Union Leader, 1881–1940* (1960) are indispensable.

4 Remaking the Party? 1931–9

The best book on the party in this period is B. Pimlott, *Labour and the Left in the 1930s* (Cambridge, 1977), but T. Buchanan, *The Spanish Civil War and the British Labour Movement* (Cambridge, 1992) is also important, and much broader than its title would suggest. Specifically on reactions to 1931, see R. Eatwell and A. Wright, 'Labour and the Lessons of 1931', *History*, 63 (1978). Two useful contemporary accounts are D. E. McHenry, *The Labour Party in Transition, 1931–1938* (1938) and C. R. Attlee, *The Labour Party in Perspective* (1937).

On the development of economic policy, see E. Durbin, *New Jerusalems: The Labour Party and the Economics of Democratic Socialism* (1985), and A. Booth and M. Pack, *Employment, Capital and Economic Policy: Great Britain, 1918–1939* (Oxford, 1985). B. C. Malament, 'British Labour and Roosevelt's New Deal', *Journal of British Studies*, 17 (1977–8), and S. Brooke, 'Atlantic Crossing? American Views of Capitalism and British Socialist Thought, 1932–1962', *Twentieth Century British History*, 2 (1991) also repay attention.

P. Seyd, 'Factionalism within the Labour Party: The Socialist League, 1932–1937', in A. Briggs and J. Saville (eds.), *Essays in Labour History, 1918–1939* (1977) covers that aspect, while J. Jupp, *The Radical Left in Britain, 1931–41* (1982) is useful for the rump ILP and the various efforts at 'unity'. See also R. Dare, 'Instinct and Organisation: Intellectuals and British Labour after 1931', *Historical Journal*, 26 (1983).

For the unions, see H. A. Clegg, *A History of British Trade Unions since 1889, Volume 3: 1934–51* (Oxford, 1994), K. Middlemas, *Politics in Industrial Society: The Experience of the British System since 1911* (1979) and L. P. Carpenter, 'Corporatism in Britain, 1930–45', *Journal of Contemporary History*, 11 (1976).

The memoirs of Hugh Dalton for this period, *The Fateful Years: Memoirs, 1931–1945* (1957) are revealing, as are B. Pimlott (ed.), *The Political Diary of Hugh Dalton, 1918–1940, 1945–1960* (1986) and B. Pimlott, *Hugh Dalton* (1985). Other notable biographies of leading figures include K. Harris, *Attlee* (1982), B. Donoughue and G. W. Jones, *Herbert Morrison: Portrait of a Politician* (1973), E. Estorick, *Stafford Cripps: A Biography* (1949), and I. Kramnick and B. Sheerman, *Harold Laski: A Life on the Left* (1993).

5 The Impact of the Second World War, 1939–45

This period has begun to attract much more attention in recent years, and there is now a good comprehensive account: S. Brooke, *Labour's War: The Labour Party during the Second World War* (Oxford, 1992). H. Pelling, 'The impact of the war on the Labour party', in H. L. Smith (ed.), *War and Social Change: British Society in the Second World War* (Manchester, 1986) is crisp and to the point. On the Coalition, see P. Addison, *The Road to 1945: British Politics and the Second World War* (1975), which argues for the emergence of a consensus in wartime, and K. Jefferys, *The Churchill Coalition and Wartime Politics, 1940–1945* (Manchester, 1991), which largely rejects this view. A. Bullock, *The Life and Times of Ernest Bevin, Volume 2: Minister of Labour, 1940–1945* (1967) covers developments within the movement in these years in great depth. See also the important articles by S. Fielding, 'The Second World War and Popular Radicalism: The Significance of the "Movement away from Party"', *History*, 80 (1995), and 'Labourism in the 1940s', *Twentieth Century British History*, 3 (1992). I. Taylor, 'Labour and the impact of war 1939–45' and T. Mason and P. Thompson, '"Reflections on a Revolution"? The Political Mood in Wartime Britain', both in N. Tiratsoo (ed.), *The Attlee Years* (1991), are also important. Specifically on the 1945 election, see R. B. McCallum and A. Readman, *The British General Election of 1945* (Oxford, 1947) and S. Fielding, 'What did "The People" Want? The Meaning of the 1945 General Election', *Historical Journal*, 35 (1992).

Foreign policy aspects are covered in T. D. Burridge, *British Labour and Hitler's War* (1976).

On economic policy, see S. Brooke, 'Revisionists and Fundamentalists: The Labour Party and Economic Policy during the Second World War', *Historical Journal*, 32 (1989), J. Tomlinson, 'Planning: Debate and Policy in the 1940s', *Twentieth Century British History*, 3 (1992) and L. Johnman, 'The Labour Party and Industrial Policy, 1940–45' in N. Tiratsoo (ed.), *The Attlee Years* (1991).

For social policy, see J. Harris, 'War and Social History: Britain and the Home Front during the Second World War', *Contemporary European History*, 1 (1992), and 'Did British Workers Want the Welfare State? G. D. H. Cole's Survey of 1942', in J. M. Winter (ed.), *The Working Class in Modern British History: Essays in Honour of Henry Pelling* (Cambridge, 1983).

On women, see especially P. Summerfield, *Women Workers in the Second World War: Production and Patriarchy in Conflict* (1984), and H. L. Smith, 'The Problem of Equal Pay for Equal Work in Great Britain during World War II', *Journal of Modern History*, 53 (1981).

Two excellent primary sources are B. Pimlott (ed.), *The Second World War Diary of Hugh Dalton, 1940–1945* (1985), and K. Jefferys (ed.), *Labour and the Wartime Coalition: From the Diary of James Chuter Ede, 1941–1945* (1987).

6 The Attlee Governments, 1945–51

The last fifteen years have seen a boom in work on this period. The best general history remains K. O. Morgan, *Labour in Power, 1945–1951* (Oxford, 1984), but H. Pelling, *The Labour Governments, 1945–51* (1984) and P. Hennessy, *Never Again: Britain, 1945–51* (1992) are good alternatives. N. Tiratsoo (ed.), *The Attlee Years* (1991) is a stimulating collection of essays.

For the left, see D. Rubinstein, 'Socialism and the Labour Party: The Labour Left and Domestic Policy, 1945–50', in D. E. Martin and D. Rubinstein (eds.), *Ideology and the Labour Movement: Essays in Honour of John Saville* (1979), J. Schneer, *Labour's Conscience: The Labour Left, 1945–1951* (1988), and A. Howard, *Crossman: The Pursuit of Power* (1990).

On the unions see, as well as the works cited earlier, R. Taylor, *The*

Trade Union Question in British Politics: Government and Unions since 1945 (Oxford, 1993), M. Harrison, *Trade Unions and the Labour Party since 1945* (1960), and K. Middlemas, *Power, Competition and the State, Volume 1: Britain in Search of Balance, 1940–1961* (1987).

On women, see especially J. Hinton, 'Women and the Labour Vote, 1945–1950', *Labour History Review*, 57 (1992) and 'Militant housewives: the British Housewives' League and the Attlee government', *History Workshop Journal*, 38 (1994). For this and subsequent chapters, see N. Hart, 'Gender and the Rise and Fall of Class Politics', *New Left Review*, 175 (1989).

Electoral trends can be followed in H. G. Nicholas, *The British General Election of 1950* (1951) and D. E. Butler, *The British General Election of 1951* (1952).

On the economic side, see A. Cairncross, *Years of Recovery: British Economic Policy, 1945–1951* (1985), J. Fyrth (ed.), *Labour's High Noon: The Government and the Economy, 1945–51* (1993), J. Tomlinson, 'The Iron Quadrilateral: Political Obstacles to Economic Reform under the Attlee Government', *Journal of British Studies*, 34 (1995), S. Brooke, 'Problems of Socialist Planning: Evan Durbin and the Labour Government of 1945', *Historical Journal*, 34 (1991), and J. Tomlinson, 'The Attlee Government and the Balance of Payments, 1945–51', *Twentieth Century British History*, 2 (1991). For this and subsequent chapters, the essays in N. F. R. Crafts and N. Woodward (eds.), *The British Economy since 1945* (Oxford, 1991), are of considerable value.

Specifically on foreign policy, see A. Bullock, *Ernest Bevin, Foreign Secretary, 1945–1951* (Oxford, 1983), R. J. Ovendale (ed.) *The Foreign Policy of the British Labour Governments, 1945–1951* (1984), and J. Schneer, 'Hope Deferred and Shattered: The British Labour Left and the Third Force Movement, 1945–9', *Journal of Modern History*, 56 (1984). See also P. Weiler, *British Labour and the Cold War* (Stanford, 1988). M. Gowing, 'Britain, America and the Bomb' in M. Dockrill and J. W. Young (eds.), *British Foreign Policy, 1945–56* (1989) is also important.

P. S. Gupta, *Imperialism and the British Labour Movement* (1975) and S. Howe, *Anti-Colonialism in British Politics: The Left and the End of Empire, 1918–64* (Oxford, 1993) look at that aspect. P. S. Gupta, 'Imperialism and the Labour Government of 1945–51' in J. M. Winter (ed.), *The Working Class in Modern British History: Essays in Honour of Henry Pelling* (Cambridge, 1983), R. Hyam, 'Africa and the Labour Government, 1945–51', *Journal of Imperial and Commonwealth History*, 16 (1988), K. Paul, '"British Subjects" and "British Stock": Labour's Postwar Imperialism', *Journal of British Studies*, 34 (1995), and J. Kent, 'Bevin's Imperialism and the Idea of Euro-Africa', in M. Dockrill and J. W. Young (eds.), *British Foreign Policy, 1945–56* (1989) are also useful.

7 Searching for a New Direction, 1951–64

Published work on this period remains relatively thin on the ground. The standard books on the two 'wings' of the party are M. Jenkins, *Bevanism: Labour's High Tide* (Nottingham, 1979), and S. Haseler, *The*

Gaitskellites: Revisionism in the British Labour Party, 1951–1964 (1969). E. Shaw, *Discipline and Discord in the Labour Party 1951–87: The Politics of Managerial Control in the Labour Party, 1951–1987* (Manchester, 1988) is an excellent work with both great detail and a compelling thesis, and is valuable for this and all the remaining chapters in the book. On the conference from 1956 onwards see L. Minkin, *The Labour Party Conference: A Study in the Politics of Intra-Party Democracy* (1978). A journalistic view is L. Hunter, *The Road to Brighton Pier* (1959).

The most important works of socialist theory in this period were A. Bevan, *In Place of Fear* (1952), R. H. S. Crossman (ed.), *New Fabian Essays* (1952) and C. A. R. Crosland, *The Future of Socialism* (1956).

On elections, see D. E. Butler, *The British General Election of 1955* (1955), D. E. Butler and R. Rose, *The British General Election of 1959* (1960) and D. E. Butler and A. King, *The British General Election of 1964* (1966). Also of great importance here are M. Abrams and R. Rose, *Must Labour Lose?* (Harmondsworth, 1960) and J. H. Goldthorpe et al., *The Affluent Worker: Political Attitudes and Behaviour* (1968).

Biographies help to flesh out the picture. See especially, among works already cited, K. Harris, *Attlee*, B. Donoughue and G. W. Jones, *Herbert Morrison*, and B. Pimlott, *Hugh Dalton*. M. Foot, *Aneurin Bevan: A Biography, Volume 2: 1945–1960* (1973) must be read in conjunction with the more dispassionate J. Campbell, *Nye Bevan and the Mirage of British Socialism* (1987). On Gaitskell, see P. Williams, *Hugh Gaitskell: A Political Biography* (1979). See also S. Crosland, *Tony Crosland* (1982) and B. Pimlott, *Harold Wilson* (1992).

Three diary sources are also of particular interest: Pimlott's edition of the Dalton diaries (cited above), P. Williams (ed.), *The Diary of Hugh Gaitskell, 1945–56* (1983), and J. Morgan (ed.), *The Backbench Diaries of Richard Crossman* (1981).

8   Wilson in Power, 1964–70

The standard account is now C. Ponting, *Breach of Promise: Labour in Power, 1964–1970* (1989), a very thorough and incisive analysis. B. Lapping, *The Labour Government 1964–70* (Harmondsworth, 1970) gives a general contemporary account. R. Coopey, S. Fielding and N. Tiratsoo (eds.), *The Wilson Governments, 1964–1970* (1993) is an excellent collection of essays. D. Walker, 'The First Wilson Governments, 1964–1970' in P. Hennessy and A. Seldon (eds.), *Ruling Performance: British Governments from Attlee to Thatcher* (Oxford, 1987) is a good introduction. Minkin, *The Labour Party Conference* and Shaw, *Discipline and Discord in the Labour Party* are vital sources for Labour's internal dynamics.

The *In Place of Strife* episode is covered, rather facetiously, by P. Jenkins in *The Battle of Downing Street* (1970). K. Middlemas, *Power, Competition and the State, Volume 2: Threats to the Post-War Settlement* (1990) and L. Panitch, *Social Democracy and Industrial Militancy: The Labour Party, the Trade Unions and Incomes Policy, 1945–1974* (Cambridge, 1976) are weightier.

On the economy, see in particular the essays in Crafts and Woodward,

The British Economy since 1945 and Coopey et al., *The Wilson Governments*, as well as P. Browning, *The Treasury and Economic Policy, 1964–1985* (1986) and J. Tomlinson, *Public Policy and the Economy since 1900* (Oxford, 1990).

On nationalism, see T. Nairn, *The Break-Up of Britain: Crisis and Neo-Nationalism* (1977), V. Bogdanor, *Devolution* (Oxford, 1979), M. Keating and D. Bleiman, *Labour and Scottish Nationalism* (1979), K. O. Morgan, *Rebirth of a Nation: Wales, 1880–1980* (Oxford, 1981), and A. Butt Philip, *The Welsh Question: Nationalism in Welsh Politics, 1945–1970* (Cardiff, 1975). On race, see especially C. Holmes, *John Bull's Island: Immigration and British Society, 1871–1971* (1988).

Wilson is the subject of three recent lives: B. Pimlott, *Harold Wilson* (1992), P. Ziegler, *Wilson: The Authorized Life of Lord Wilson of Rievaulx* (1993), and A. Morgan, *Harold Wilson: A Life* (1991). P. Foot, *The Politics of Harold Wilson* (1968) is a contemporary attack on Wilson and Labourism from a far left perspective.

On the elections of the period, see D. E. Butler and A. King, *The British General Election of 1966* (1966) and D. E. Butler and M. Pinto-Duschinsky, *The British General Election of 1970* (1971).

Memoirs and published diaries are very rich for this period. Among the former, see especially H. Wilson, *The Labour Government 1964–70: A Personal Record* (1971), G. Brown, *In My Way: The Political Memoirs of Lord George-Brown* (1971), J. Callaghan, *Time and Chance* (1987), R. Jenkins, *A Life in the Centre* (1991), D. Healey, *The Time of My Life* (1989), B. Castle, *Fighting All the Way* (1993), and M. Stewart, *Life and Labour: An Autobiography* (1980). Among the latter, see R. Crossman, *The Diaries of a Cabinet Minister* (3 vols., 1975–1977), B. Castle, *The Castle Diaries, 1964–1970* (1984) and T. Benn, *Out of the Wilderness: Diaries, 1963–1967* (1987) and *Office Without Power: Diaries, 1968–1972* (1988).

9   Drift to Defeat? 1970–9

The best introduction to the period, written by someone who was a Labour MP at the time, is P. Whitehead, *The Writing on the Wall: Britain in the Seventies* (1985). The period up to 1974 can be followed, to an extent, in M. Hatfield, *The House the Left Built: Inside Labour Policy-Making 1970–1975* (1978). The 1974–9 period is covered in D. Coates, *Labour in Power? A Study of the Labour Government, 1974–1979* (1980), K. Coates (ed.), *What Went Wrong: Explaining the Fall of the Labour Government* (Nottingham, 1979), M. Holmes, *The Labour Government 1974–79: Political Aims and Economic Reality* (1985) and P. Whitehead, 'The Labour Governments, 1974–1979', in P. Hennessy and A. Seldon (eds.), *Ruling Performance: British Governments from Attlee to Thatcher* (Oxford, 1987).

On developments within the party, see B. Hindess, *The Decline of Working-Class Politics* (1971), T. Forester, *The Labour Party and the Working Class* (1976), Minkin, *The Labour Party Conference*, Shaw, *Discipline and Discord in the Labour Party*, and P. Seyd, *The Rise and Fall of the Labour Left* (1987). The left's policy views can be seen in S. Holland, *The Socialist Challenge* (1975).

For general elections, see the Nuffield studies by D. E. Butler and D. Kavanagh, *The British General Election of February 1974* (1974), *October 1974* (1975), and *1979* (1980).

Specifically on economic policy, see M. Artis and D. Cobham (eds.), *Labour's Economic Policies, 1974–1979* (Manchester, 1991) and W. P. J. Maunder (ed.), *The British Economy in the 1970s* (1980). The essays in Crafts and Woodward, *The British Economy since 1945*, are also important here. For social policy, see N. Bosanquet and P. Townsend, *Labour and Equality: A Fabian Study of Labour in Power, 1974–1979* (1980) and R. Lowe, *The Welfare State in Britain since 1945* (1993).

See also the biographies of Wilson cited earlier, as well as H. Wilson, *Final Term: The Labour Government, 1974–1976* (1979), Callaghan, *Time and Chance*, Healey, *The Time of My Life*, J. Adams, *Tony Benn* (1992), B. Castle, *The Castle Diaries, 1974–1976* (1980), E. Dell, *A Hard Pounding: Politics and Economic Crisis, 1974–1976* (Oxford, 1991), I. Mikardo, *Back-Bencher* (1988), J. Haines, *The Politics of Power* (1977), and T. Benn, *Against the Tide: Diaries, 1973–1976* (1989) and *Conflicts of Interest: Diaries, 1977–1980* (1990).

On the unions, see the books cited in previous sections, as well as K. Middlemas, *Power, Competition and the State, Volume III: The End of the Post-War Era, Britain since 1974* (1991) and P. Ferris, *The New Militants: Crisis in the Trade Unions* (1972).

10   Disaster and Recovery? 1979–92

The best book on the period since 1979 is now E. Shaw, *The Labour Party since 1979: Crisis and Transformation* (1994). See also D. and M. Kogan, *The Battle for the Labour Party* (1982), P. Whiteley, *The Labour Party in Crisis* (1983), L. Minkin, *The Contentious Alliance: Trade Unions and the Labour Party* (1992) and E. Shaw, *Discipline and Discord in the Labour Party*. M. Crick, *Militant* (1984) is important and was so at the time. See also J. Bloomfield, 'Labour's Long Haul', in S. Hall and M. Jacques (eds.), *The Politics of Thatcherism* (1983) and D. Kavanagh, *Thatcherism and British Politics: The End of Consensus?* (2nd edn., Oxford, 1990).

The SDP episode can be followed in R. Jenkins, *A Life at the Centre*, W. Kennet, *The Rebirth of Britain* and P. Zentner, *Social Democracy in Britain: Must Labour Lose?* (both 1982), in I. Bradley, *Breaking the Mould? The Birth and Prospects of the Social Democratic Party* (1981), and in the works of the 'Gang of Three': S. Williams, *Politics is for People* (1981), W. Rodgers, *The Politics of Change* and D. Owen, *Face the Future*.

On Kinnock's attempts to revamp the party, see the quasi-official view, C. Hughes and P. Wintour, *Labour Rebuilt: The New Model Party* (1990), M. J. Smith and J. Spear (eds.), *The Changing Labour Party* (1992) and the left perspective of R. Heffernan and M. Marqusee, *Defeat from the Jaws of Victory* (1992). The changing membership is analysed in P. Seyd and P. Whiteley, *Labour's Grass Roots: The Politics of Party Membership* (Oxford, 1992).

On trade unionism, see G. Goodman, *The Miners' Strike* (1985), T. Lane,

'The Tories and the Trade Unions' in S. Hall and M. Jacques (eds.), *Politics of Thatcherism* (1983), J. McIlroy, 'Trade Unions and the Law' in B. Jones (ed.), *Political Issues in Britain Today* (Manchester, 1985), and D. Deaton, 'The Labour Market and Industrial Relations Policy of the Thatcher Government', in D. S. Bell (ed.), *The Conservative Government 1979–84: An Interim Report* (1985).

The relevant Nuffield election studies are all by D. E. Butler and D. Kavanagh: *The British General Election of 1983* (1984), *1987* (1988) and *1992* (1992). On the debate over whether sociological trends made Labour unelectable, see B. Sarlvik and I. Crewe, *Decade of Dealignment: The Conservative Victory of 1979 and Electoral Trends in the 1970s* (Cambridge, 1983), I. McAllister and R. Rose, *The Nationwide Competition for Votes: the 1983 British Election* (1984), P. Dunleavy and C. T. Husbands, *British Democracy at the Crossroads: Voting and Party Competition in the 1980s* (Oxford, 1985), M. N. Franklin, *The Decline of Class Voting in Britain: Changes in the Basis of Electoral Choice, 1964–1983* (Oxford, 1985), H. T. Himmelweit et al., *How Voters Decide: A Longitudinal Study of Political Attitudes and Voting Extending over 15 Years* (1981), I. Budge and D. J. Fairlie, *Explaining and Predicting Elections: Issue Effects and Party Strategies in 23 Democracies* (1983), R. J. Johnston, *The Geography of English Politics: The 1983 General Election* (1985), A. Heath, R. Jowell and J. Curtice, *How Britain Votes* (Oxford, 1985) and (as eds.), *Labour's Last Chance? The 1992 Election and Beyond* (Aldershot, 1994), and H. Kitschelt, 'Class Structure and Social Democratic Party Strategy', *British Journal of Political Studies*, 23 (1993).

Once again, biographies and memoirs flesh out the picture. As well as books already cited, see M. Foot, *Another Heart and Other Pulses: The Alternative to the Thatcher Society* (1984), T. Benn, *The End of an Era: Diaries, 1980–1990* (1992), R. Harris, *The Making of Neil Kinnock* (1984), A. McSmith, *John Smith: Playing the Long Game* (1993), and E. Heffer, *Never a Yes Man: The Life and Politics of an Adopted Liverpudlian* (1991).

Index